Four by

SONDHEIM

WHEELER, LAPINE, SHEVELOVE and GELBART

THE APPLAUSE MUSICAL LIBRARY

A CHORUS LINE: The Book of the Musical
Michael Bennett, James Kirkwood, Nicholas Dante and Edward Kleban

CITY OF ANGELS
Larry Gelbart, Cy Coleman and David Zippel

THE FANTASTICKS
Harvey Schmidt and Tom Jones

A FUNNY THING HAPPENED ON THE WAY TO THE FORUM
Music and Lyrics by Stephen Sondheim
Book by Burt Shevelove and Larry Gelbart

THE GREAT MOVIE MUSICAL TRIVIA BOOK
Jeff Kurtti

A LITTLE NIGHT MUSIC
Music and Lyrics by Stephen Sondheim • Book by Hugh Wheeler

THE LONGEST LINE
Broadway's Most Singular Sensation: A Chorus Line
Gary Stevens and Alan George

THE MUSICAL: A Look at the American Musical Theater
Richard Kislan

THE NEW YORK MUSICALS OF COMDEN & GREEN
On the Town • Wonderful Town • Bells are Ringing

SUNDAY IN THE PARK WITH GEORGE
Music and Lyrics by Stephen Sondheim • Book by James Lapine

SWEENEY TODD, The Demon Barber of Fleet Street
Music and Lyrics by Stephen Sondheim • Book by Hugh Wheeler

TITANIC: The Complete Book of the Musical
Story and book by Peter Stone • Lyrics by Maury Yeston

Four by
SONDHEIM

WHEELER, LAPINE,
SHEVELOVE and GELBART

A Funny Thing Happened on the Way to the Forum
A Little Night Music
Sweeney Todd, the Demon Barber of Fleet Street
Sunday in the Park with George

APPLAUSE
NEW YORK • LONDON

Four by Sondheim, Wheeler, Lapine, Shevelove and Gelbart

An anthology of musicals als published in individual volumes by Applause.

Copyright © 2000 by Applause Theatre & Cinema Books

Grateful acknowledgement is made to the following for permission to include their photographs and scene and costume designs: Van Williams, Zoë Dominic Photography, MGM/UA Communications Co., Center Theater Group of the Music Center of Los Angeles, Tony Walton, Concorde-New Horizons Corp./Wein Film Gmbh/Polygram Pictures, Martha Swope Associates/Carol Rosegg, Boris Aronson, Florence Klotz, Michael Anania, Lindsay W. Davis, Eugene Lee, Frannie Lee, Tony Straiges, Patricia Zipprodt and Ann Hould-Ward.

Drawings by Hirschfeld Copyright © 1962, 1971, 1973, 1979, 1984, 1989 by Al Hirschfeld and reproduced by special arrangement with Hirschfeld's exclusive representative, the Margo Feiden Galleries Ltd., New York.

Library of Congress Cataloging-in-Publication Data

Library of Congress Card Number: 00-100279

British Cataloging-in-Publication Data

A catalogue copy of this book is available from the British Library.

APPLAUSE BOOKS

1841 Broadway
Suite 1100
New York, NY 10023
Phone (212) 765-7880
FAX (212) 765-7875

Combined Book Services
Units I/K Paddock Wood Dist. Ctr.
Paddock Wood,
Tonbridge Kent TN12 6UU
Phone 0189 283-7171
Fax 0189 283-7272

 **PRINTED IN CANADA**

CONTENTS

A FVNNY THING HAPPENED ON THE WAY TO THE FORVM

BASED ON THE PLAYS OF PLAUTUS

BOOK BY
BURT SHEVELOVE AND LARRY GELBART

MUSIC AND LYRICS BY
STEPHEN SONDHEIM

INTRODUCTION BY LARRY GELBART

Zero Mostel, Jack Gilford and David Burns in the original Broadway production of *A Funny Thing Happened on the Way to the Forum*

Larry Blyden and Phil Silvers in the revival of *A Funny Thing Happened on the Way to the Forum*

To and From
T. M. P.

INTRODUCTION

As a rule, authors suspect the quality of any work that is written quickly and rather painlessly. *A Funny Thing Happened on the Way to the Forum* was never an object of that sort of suspicion. The only aspect of the project that ever came fast and free of any pain was the dialogue. Even when we lost our way in terms of plotting, and I cannot tell you how many man-hours (women- and children-hours, as well) we spent in a wilderness of our own creation, we were never at a loss for words, funny words, mostly-funny words, or words that led up to the funny words, or funny words that paved the way for even funnier words. (Lovers of modesty will find little to their liking in this foreword, since I have absolutely none to offer when it comes to *Forum.* Nearly thirty years after its first performance, and having, in the intervening period, written enough words to circle the globe and the Old Globe dozens of times, it remains for me the best piece of work I've been lucky enough to see my name on.)

Irwin Shaw once advised all writers, in order to withstand criticism from without and compromise from within, to be vain about their work. Until *A Funny Thing Happened on the Way to the Forum,* I confess there was little I had done that warranted any sort of vanity.

The initial idea to do the show was the late Burt Shevelove's. Burt had done an embryonic version of a Roman comedy in his university days and had long felt that a professional, full-blown Broadway production would have every chance of success.

Although Burt and I had worked together on many television shows during the 1950s, we had never functioned before as a writing team. Burt produced and directed several comedy/variety shows that I had written in that period; working in separate capacities, we learned that we laughed at the same things and, happily, always at the same time.

Our goal was to construct a musical comedy based on the style and spirit of the twenty-six surviving plays of Titus Maccius Plautus, the third-century Roman playwright, who invented all the devices of theatrical comedy, teaching amphitheater audiences up and down Caesar's Circuit to laugh for the first time at character and situation instead of that old staple they found so amusing, bloodshed.

Certainly, there was comedy in everyday life before Plautus set quill to parchment, but it was he who created comic conventions and made use of humorous wordplay within the discipline of well-made plays.

With Stephen Sondheim as the third member of the team (it was to be the first Broadway show for which he created words and music; before *Forum* Steve had *merely* supplied the lyrics for *West Side Story* and *Gypsy*), we began the task of reading and dissecting the writings of and about Plautus, extracting from his works a character here, a relationship there, and then went about creating a considerable amount of new material, both dramatic and musical, as connective tissue to bond our work to his.

What a treat he was to research! How incredibly Plautus's aged, ageless writings based on man's gift for silliness, for pomposity and hypocrisy, have survived; how well it all stood up, the comedy that would serve as fodder not only for the theater, but for future stand-up comedians as well. Digging about as archaeologists might have, what unbelievable treasure we found in his plays, a catacomb filled with nothing but funnybones. It was as though Titus (I feel he would forgive the name-dropping) had written some great and generous last will and testament, a comic estate, and that Burt, Steve, and I had been appointed his heirs.

There they were, in the pages of Plautus, appearing for our pleasure for the first time anywhere: the brash Prologus, working very much in the manner of a modern-day master of ceremonies, addressing his remarks directly to the audience, hitting them with one-liners, warning them to sit up and pay attention and not to go to sleep during the play that was to follow. There were the sly servants, those wily slaves, scheming and plotting and outwitting everyone in sight, constantly getting the upper hand on the upper class, which was largely composed of senile skirt-chasers and henpecked husbands, very often one and the same; domineering matrons, Gorgon-like women, past their prime in every aspect of life but possessiveness; lovesick young men, so much in love they were sickening; and, of course, comely courtesans with hair and hearts of gold that you couldn't bring home without fear of possibly offending your mother—and the certainty of arousing your father; page after page of disguise and mistaken identity, scene after scene of double takes and double meanings.

We were, of course, not Plautus's only benefactors. From the sublime Shakespeare to the somewhat less-so sitcoms, those writers who, through the ages, have presented audiences with surrogate fools acting out their own foibles (each member of the crowd, secure in the belief that he or she is above ridicule, that it is the person in the *next* seat who is being so portrayed), we are all indebted to Titus Maccius Plautus, high priest of low comedy, inventor of the genre, builder of the machine on which all theater humor has run for over two millennia.

I believe it is safe to say that there is not a joke form, comic character, or farcical situation that exists today that does not find its origin in Plautus's work. *Forum* contains at least one taste of his original flavor. When Miles Gloriosus, the impossibly pompous, braggart warrior, gets a huge laugh (and he always does) by stating "I am a parade!" the audience is responding to a line that is over two thousand years old.

Our goal was not to modernize the master. That is an ongoing process we preferred to leave to others. What we hoped to prove was that Plautus's characters (always one-dimensional) and his style of plotting (which could be as complicated as a Rubik's cube) were timeless. If the three of us occasionally resembled croquet wickets during our labors, it's because we spent so much time bending over backward to avoid using anachronisms (one such line which we rejected, and which we related to the writers of the *Forum* screenplay, found its way into a scene in the movie in which Pseudolus, the leading character, wanting to know about the quality of the wine he's being served, asks, "Was 1 a good year?").

We were after more than purity, however. We were not simply out to prove some esoteric point that would have had an appreciative audience of three. We wanted a commercial as well as an artistic success. We were confident we could have both. Cocky would be more accurate. More than simply confidence is required to get a musical comedy on the boards. Vanity all on its own is not that much help either.

We knew that we were grounding our show in an element that had been long missing from the theater scene. Over the years, Broadway, in its development of the musical comedy had improved the quality of the former at the expense of a good deal of the latter. Musicals had come to be populated by performers who could sell a melody and a set of lyrics but who couldn't deliver a punchline in a handbasket. It was a talent they had no need for, since punchlines had all but disappeared. The Rodgerses and Harts and Hammersteins, the Lerners and Loewes, brilliant men of music and artists of great refinement, had created a vulgarity vacuum, a space we were happy, even anxious to fill.

Our Roman comedy opened in New York on May 8, 1962, complete with leggy showgirls being chased from house to house by cunning slaves, who, in drag a few scenes later, found *themselves* being chased by their own lecherous masters, unsuspecting dupes high on love potions prepared by these very same slaves, using recipes that called for such exotic ingredients as mare's sweat.

The show that *Time* magazine called "good clean, dirty fun" has been running somewhere everywhere in the world for the last twenty-seven years. There was a time when the three of us thought it was going to take at least that long to finish writing it.

Steve has said that "the book of *Forum* plays like such a romp it seems it might have been dashed off in a weekend, and yet it took four years to write." I disagree with him only slightly. While it does, or at least should, play like a romp, I remember it taking us closer to five years to dash it off. That's approximately two hundred and sixty weekends— and most of the weekdays in between—which was all well and good for Plautus, who was that most helpful of collaborators, a dead one (even more helpful, so were his agents and lawyers), but for those of us among the living it was a big chunk of time.

A Roman Comedy was its working title. We were far too busy trying to get the piece right to take any time out to think about what some lucky marquee would one day read if we ever actually completed a final draft. There were to be ten drafts in all before we arrived at the last, merciful version of the book and score that represented the most successful execution of our vision. It's not that we kept getting it wrong all the time. It was more a matter of never getting it right all at the same time.

In the process, we rewrote and rewrote endlessly. Rewrote it, rethought it, restructured it. You name it, we redid it. It seemed a lifetime before we permitted ourselves to write that sweetest of all words in the vocabulary of the theater: "Curtain."

Only then did we dare christen it, if one can use that verb

in connection with a pagan comedy. Why the particular title we hit on? Since we wanted to suggest that the play was a comedy without actually using that word, we picked the phrase "A funny thing happened on the way to" because that's the beginning of a stock opening line which comics have used for ages. "Forum" was chosen to complete the title because we wanted the audience to think immediately of Rome.

But it took us hundreds and hundreds of pages before our comedy was ready for its naming day. And probably just as many measures of music, and reams of rhymes. Steve has said that he threw more songs out of the score for *Forum* than he's ever had to on any other show he's done since. Whole numbers—not fragments or starts with no finishes—written, polished, perfected, and then cut from the show.

For those of you who keep score of scores:

"I Do Like You." A duet between Pseudolus and Hysterium, in which the first slave shamelessly butters up the second, who is reluctant to join in on some servant/master scam. Cut.

"There's Something About a War." A hymn to mayhem and massacre, sung by the vainglorious Miles Gloriosus. Cut.

"Echo Song." A solo for a courtesan from the house of Lycus named Philia. A virgin, she sings the song to the boy next door, Hero, her co-virgin. Replaced by "That'll Show Him," but restored in a revival.

"Love Is in the Air." Originally, the show's opening song, performed as a soft-shoe dance and sung by Prologus, who was played by the same actor who portrayed Senex. When "Comedy Tonight" replaced this number, Pseudolus became the Prologus and the only trace of "Love Is in the Air" that remains in the show is as instrumental background to the opening of Act Two. Much has been written about what a lifesaver "Comedy Tonight" proved to be in getting the show off the ground in the proper manner and style. It also provided us with a happy landing when, reprised at the final curtain, it served as a witty, musical wrap-up, one that had eluded us from the show's inception.

"Invocation." The first of three tries at an opening number.

"The House of Marcus Lycus." Reduced to one verse during the New Haven tryout.

"Your Eyes Are Blue." Cut in New Haven.

"The Gaggle of Geese." Written for Erronius. Cut before rehearsals began.

"Farewell." Added for the Los Angeles revival in 1971.

"What Do You Do with a Woman?" A song for the innocent Hero in which he asks for advice on the subject of amour from his far more experienced friend and next-door neighbor, Vino.

Vino? Those of you who know the play know there is no one named Vino in it. Those of you unfamiliar with it can read the pages which follow for as many years as we took to write them and not find anyone anywhere named Vino, not even a mention of him, for Vino was to suffer the fate that befalls many a dramatic character who does not survive the embryonic stage—he died in playbirth. Having survived through two or three drafts, Vino developed a severe case of anemia of purpose and never made it to the fourth.

We planned the action of *Forum* to take place before the entrances to three houses on a street in ancient Rome. In the center, the house of Senex, a patrician, and his family. To one side of Senex, the house of Marcus Lycus, a dealer of courtesans, a trader of tarts; on the other, the house of another patrician, Erronius, who has been abroad for some time.

From day one, that original geography remained intact. Early on, however, we had installed Vino in the house of Erronius, as the son the old man leaves behind to be looked after by his household slave, Hysterium. Vino was a dissolute

7

youth, much given to wine, women, and, hopefully, a song that wouldn't be cut. His constant companions were twin courtesans, purchased from Lycus, who were forever entwining themselves around various of Vino's limbs, a pair of torrid tourniquets.

All of this kept Hysterium in a perpetual state of hysteria. He lived in fear of the flogging or worse he'd receive when Erronius returned for allowing his son to pursue such a decadent and expensive life.

Vino's best friend was Hero, the son of Senex, whose own slave was Pseudolus, a name we borrowed from the title of a play by Plautus. The idea of twins comes from yet another, entitled *The Menachmae*. It was Pseudolus in whom Hysterium confided, looked to for advice on how to deal with the excesses of his young charge.

Pseudolus, too, had his hands full with *his* master, Hero, the only son of Senex and his wife of too many years, Domina. (Plautus was, naturally, the inventor of jokes on marital strife. In one of his works, two Roman citizens meet on the street. The first citizen asks the second, "How's your wife?" The second citizen replies with a sigh, "Immortal.")

Hero, too, is smitten with a young woman from the wrong side of the stage, having fallen in love with the most recent addition to Lycus's inventory, the adorable, totally vapid Philia (about whom one might have asked, "Was 1 a good IQ?") Pseudolus's task was to keep Hero's parents from finding out that their son coveted a common courtesan.

You will, of course, have immediately spotted the duplication of situations in the houses of Senex and Erronius, the common problem shared by Pseudolus and Hysterium. Not being as bright as you, it took us a couple of years to become aware of these redundancies. Once we did, we decided that Vino had to go. It was quite painless: over a number of pages we got the character drunk and then arranged for him to have a head-on collision with an eraser.

He never saw it coming. We then moved Hysterium into the house of Senex, giving him the position of head slave, which created one more obstacle for Pseudolus to contend with in handling his problems with Hero. Best of all, the changes served to make the center house the center of the audience's attention.

These revisions and others like them necessitated countless further alterations. If one could take *Forum* apart, unscrew the back of it, so to speak, it would be not unlike looking at the works of a computer or the jumble of different-colored wires telephone repairmen deal in. The play is that dense, that tangled. Add or subtract one character and his or her absence or altered presence affects the behavior of every other character in the piece.

"Simplify it," George Abbott told the authors. "Stop writing all that 'wrong-note' music," Leonard Bernstein told the composer. But we had no choice other than to write the show our way, which required the exhausting exercise of finding out what that way was.

In preparing this foreword, I'm indebted to Steve Sondheim for helping me recall a number of details I'd long forgotten. Thank God for his memory. My own, its warranty having run out some time ago, I forget exactly when, is such that more and more I find myself spraying my hair with room freshener.

I know I speak for both of us when I express our gratitude to Burt Shevelove, who died in April of 1982. Presenting us with the challenge of writing our Plautine comedy, Burt initiated an experience that was as entertaining as it was educational, one that has been a source of pride and pleasure for over a quarter of a century.

I hope that none of what I've written here—how difficult it all was, how long the writing took—has in any way sounded like a complaint. If I have one at all it is that we finally *did* finish it, did at last put together all our self-created puzzles, did make our way out of the maddening mazes in which we seemed endlessly to entrap ourselves, that the day ultimately came when we had no choice but to say goodbye to all of the terribly hard work that had become such a source of joy.

Odd, that I should have that same feeling as I write this; once more reluctant to let go of the play, to give it up, to let it belong to the audience. But in the theater that passes for my mind, I hear the orchestra tuning up, I see the comics in the wings rehearsing their leers, the courtesans practicing their pouts.

Anyone for a comedy tonight?

Larry Gelbart

17 September 1990

CAST OF CHARACTERS

PROLOGUS, *an actor*

THE PROTEANS

SENEX, *an old man*

DOMINA, *his wife*

HERO, *his son, in love with Philia*

HYSTERIUM, *slave to Senex and Domina*

PSEUDOLUS, *slave to Hero*

LYCUS, *a buyer and seller of courtesans*

TINTINABULA, *a courtesan*

PANACEA, *a courtesan*

THE GEMINAE, *courtesans*

VIBRATA, *a courtesan*

GYMNASIA, *a courtesan*

PHILIA, *a virgin*

ERRONIUS, *an old man*

MILES GLORIOSUS, *a warrior*

AUTHORS' NOTE

This is a scenario for vaudevillians. There are many details omitted from the script. They are part of any comedian's bag of tricks: the double take, the mad walk, the sighs, the smirks, the stammerings. All these and more are intended to be supplied by the actor and you, the reader.

MUSICAL NUMBERS

ACT I

"Comedy Tonight"	PROLOGUS, PROTEANS, COMPANY
"Love, I Hear"	HERO
"Free"	PSEUDOLUS, HERO
"The House of Marcus Lycus"	LYCUS, PSEUDOLUS, COURTESANS
"Lovely"	HERO, PHILIA
"Pretty Little Picture"	PSEUDOLUS, HERO, PHILIA
"Everybody Ought to Have a Maid"	SENEX, PSEUDOLUS, HYSTERIUM, LYCUS
"I'm Calm"	HYSTERIUM
"Impossible"	SENEX, HERO
"Bring Me My Bride"	MILES, PSEUDOLUS, COURTESANS, PROTEANS

ACT II

"That Dirty Old Man"	DOMINA
"That'll Show Him"	PHILIA
"Lovely"	PSEUDOLUS, HYSTERIUM
Funeral Sequence and Dance	PSEUDOLUS, MILES, COURTESANS, PROTEANS
"Comedy Tonight"	COMPANY

12

ACT I

PROLOGUS *enters through traveler, salutes audience, addresses them.*

PROLOGUS: Playgoers, I bid you welcome. The theatre is a temple, and we are here to worship the gods of comedy and tragedy. Tonight, I am pleased to announce a comedy. We shall employ every device we know in our desire to divert you.

> (*During this scene, there are musical interludes during which* PROLOGUS *and the* PROTEANS *do various bits of pantomime and general clowning, using a prop leg.* PRO-LOGUS *gestures to orchestra, sings*)

Something familiar,
Something peculiar,
Something for everyone — a comedy tonight!
Something appealing,
Something appalling,
Something for everyone — a comedy tonight!
Nothing with kings,
Nothing with crowns,
Bring on the lovers, liars and clowns!
Old situations,
New complications,
Nothing portentous or polite:
Tragedy tomorrow,
Comedy tonight!

13

(During the following, he brings on the three PROTEANS)
Something familiar,
Something peculiar,
Something for everyone — a comedy tonight!
Something appealing,
Something appalling,
Something for everyone — a comedy tonight!

PROTEANS:
Tragedy tomorrow —

PROLOGUS:
Comedy tonight!
Something convulsive,
Something repulsive,
Something for everyone —

ALL:
A comedy tonight!

PROLOGUS:
Something esthetic,

PROTEANS:
Something frenetic,

PROLOGUS:
Something for everyone —

ALL:
A comedy tonight!

PROTEANS:
Nothing with gods,
Nothing with fate.

PROLOGUS:
Weighty affairs will just have to wait.

PROTEANS:
Nothing that's formal,

14

PROLOGUS:
  Nothing that's normal,

ALL:
  No recitations to recite!
  Open up the curtain —
    (*The traveler parts halfway, then closes as if by accident,
    causing confusion. After a moment, it reopens completely,
    revealing a street in Rome. Stage center stands the house of
    SENEX; on either side, the houses of LYCUS and ERRONIUS.
    SENEX's house is hidden behind another curtain*)

PROLOGUS:
  Comedy tonight!
                    (*Speaks*)
  It all takes place on a street in Rome, around and about
  these three houses.
                 (*Indicates ERRONIUS's house*)
  First, the house of Erronius, a befuddled old man abroad
  now in search of his children, stolen in infancy by pirates.
                        (*Sings*)
  Something for everyone — a comedy tonight!
    (*The PROTEANS appear in the upper window of the house
    and pantomime*)
  Something erratic,
  Something dramatic,
  Something for everyone — a comedy tonight!
  Frenzy and frolic,
  Strictly symbolic,
  Something for everyone — a comedy tonight!
              (*Speaks, indicating LYCUS's house*)
  Second, the house of Lycus, a buyer and seller of the
  flesh of beautiful women. That's for those of you who
  have absolutely no interest in pirates.
                        (*Sings*)
  Something for everyone — a comedy tonight!

15

(PROTEANS *dance in front of the house; one of them disappears
into the floor.* PROLOGUS *reacts, then continues, speaking*)

Raise the curtain!

(*Inner curtain drops into floor*)

And finally, the house of Senex, who lives here with his
wife and son. Also in this house lives Pseudolus, slave to
the son. Pseudolus is probably my favorite character in
the piece. A role of enormous variety and nuance, and
played by an actor of such . . . let me put it this way . . .
I play the part.

(*Sings*)

Anything you ask for — comedy tonight!

(PROTEANS *re-enter*)

And these are the Proteans, only three, yet they do the
work of thirty. They are difficult to recognize in the
many parts they play. Watch them closely.

(PROTEANS *appear in and out of* SENEX's *house in assort-
ed costumes as* PROLOGUS *comments*)

A proud Roman. A patrician Roman. A pretty Roman.
A Roman slave. A Roman soldier.

(PROTEAN *appears with crude wooden ladder*)

A Roman ladder.

(PROTEAN *enters, juggling*)

Tremendous skill!

(*He juggles badly.* PROTEAN *enters*)

Incredible versatility!

(*He fumbles in changing wigs.* PROTEAN *enters with
gong*)

And, above all, dignity!

(*He strikes gong, his skirt falls*)

And now, the entire company!

(*The company enters from* SENEX's *house and forms a line*)

ALL (*Sing*):
Something familiar,

16

Something peculiar,
Something for everybody — comedy tonight!

STAGE RIGHT:
Something that's gaudy,

STAGE LEFT:
Something that's bawdy,

PROLOGUS:
Something for everybawdy —

ALL:
Comedy tonight!

MILES:
Nothing that's grim,

DOMINA:
Nothing that's Greek!

PROLOGUS (*Leading* GYMNASIA *center*):
She plays Medea later this week.

ALL:
Stunning surprises,
Cunning disguises,
Hundreds of actors out of sight!

ERRONIUS:
Pantaloons and tunics!

SENEX:
Courtesans and eunuchs!

DOMINA:
Funerals and chases!

LYCUS:
Baritones and basses!

PHILIA:
Panderers!

HERO:
    Philanderers!

HYSTERIUM:
    Cupidity!

MILES:
    Timidity!

LYCUS:
    Mistakes!

ERRONIUS:
    Fakes!

PHILIA:
    Rhymes!

DOMINA:
    Mimes!

PROLOGUS:
    Tumblers!
    Grumblers!
    Fumblers!
    Bumblers!

ALL:
    No royal curse,
    No Trojan horse,
    And a happy ending, of course!
    Goodness and badness,
    Man in his madness,
    This time it all turns out all right!
    Tragedy tomorrow!
    Comedy tonight!
    One — two — three!
                    (*All exit, except* PROLOGUS)

PROLOGUS (*Addresses the heavens*): Oh, Thespis, we place ourselves in your hands.
                (*To audience*)
The play begins.
                (*Exits*)

(*Music up.* PHILIA *appears at window of* LYCUS*'s house
and* HERO *appears on balcony of* SENEX*'s house.* SENEX
enters from his house)

SENEX (*Calls*): Slaves!
        (PHILIA *exits, as* PROTEANS *enter from* SENEX*'s house,
        dressed as* SLAVES, *assume slavish attitudes*)
We are about to start our journey. My robe!
                (PROTEANS *place robe on him*)
My wreath.
                (PROTEANS *place wreath on his head*)

DOMINA (*Appearing in doorway of* SENEX*'s house*): Senex!

SENEX (*Frowns*): My wife.

DOMINA: Slaves! Stop cringing and fetch the baggage!

PROTEANS (*Exiting into* SENEX*'s house*): Yes, yes, yes.

DOMINA: Senex, you are master of the house and no help at
all. Where is Pseudolus? Where is Hysterium? Summon
them!
        (SENEX *is about to speak,* DOMINA *calls out*)
Pseudolus! Hysterium!
        (HYSTERIUM *enters from* SENEX*'s house. During the follow-
        ing,* SENEX *drifts toward* LYCUS*'s house*)

HYSTERIUM: Ah, madam, you called?

DOMINA: Yes, Hysterium.

HYSTERIUM: And I answered. Ever your humble.
                (*Kisses hem of her cape*)

DOMINA: Have you prepared my potions?

HYSTERIUM (*Holds up small bag*): Yes, madam. In addition to your usual potions, I have included one for tantrums and one for queasiness.

DOMINA: Thank you, Hysterium, slave of slaves.

HYSTERIUM: I live to grovel.
(*Kisses her hem.* DOMINA *calls to* HERO *on balcony of* SENEX*'s house*)

DOMINA: Hero, come kiss your mother goodbye.

HERO: Yes, mother.
(*Exits into* SENEX*'s house.* SLAVES *re-enter, carrying baggage*)

DOMINA: Slaves, take that baggage and go before us, you clumsies!

PROTEANS (*As they scurry off*): Yes, yes, clumsies, yes.

DOMINA: Senex! Come away from that house of shame!

SENEX (*Crossing to her*): I was just standing there saying, "Shame, shame, shame!"

DOMINA: Hysterium!

HYSTERIUM: Yes, madam?

DOMINA: Where is Pseudolus?

HYSTERIUM: Where is he indeed! I have not seen him since he dressed Hero this morning.

DOMINA: Tell him that while we are gone, he is to watch over Hero. He is to keep him cheerful, well-fed, and far from the opposite sex.

SENEX: My dear, the boy has to learn sometime.

DOMINA: And when that time comes, *you* shall tell him . . .

SENEX: Yes, dear.

DOMINA: . . . what little you know. Now, go and fetch the gift we bring my mother.

SENEX: Yes, dear.
(*Exits into his house, as* HERO *enters from it*)

HERO: Good morning, father.

DOMINA: Ah, Hero. Your father and I are off to visit my mother in the country. What a joy it would be were you to accompany us. But, alas, the sight of anyone in good health fills my mother with rage.
(SENEX *re-enters carrying a bust of* DOMINA)
Ah, there I am. Do you think it will please my mother?

HYSTERIUM: Oh, yes, madam. The craftsmanship is superb.

DOMINA: And the resemblance?

HYSTERIUM: Frightening.

DOMINA: The time of farewell is at hand. Hysterium, slave-in-chief, here are my husband's final instructions.
(SENEX *opens his mouth to speak, she continues*)
In his absence, his entire household is in your spotless care. Your word shall be absolute, your authority unquestioned.

SENEX: And furthermore —

DOMINA: We are on our way!

SENEX (*Mutters*): We are on our way.

DOMINA: Farewell, beloved son. Farewell, thoughtful Hysterium. Senex, come along! And carry my bust with pride.
(*Exits. A beat, and then her voice is heard*)
Senex!

SENEX: Yes, dear.
> (*To audience*)

A lesson for you all. Never fall in love during a total eclipse!
> (*Exits*)

HYSTERIUM (*To audience*): Well, to work, to work! Now that I am completely in charge, I am going to be a very busy slave.
> (*Sees* HERO, *who has drifted toward* LYCUS*'s house*)

Here! Come away from there. You must never know what goes on in that house.

HERO: But I do know.

HYSTERIUM: You do?
> (HERO *nods*)

Isn't it amazing? Well, I can't stand here talking.
> (*Goes to* SENEX*'s house, picks something from a column, stamps it out, grimaces, enters house, calling*)

Pseudolus!
> (HERO *watches him go, then turns to audience*)

HERO (*Sings*):
Now that we're alone,
May I tell you
I've been feeling very strange?
Either something's in the air
Or else a change
Is happening in me.
I think I know the cause,
I hope I know the cause.
From everything I've heard,
There's only one cause it can be . . .

Love, I hear,
Makes you sigh a lot.
Also, love, I hear,
Leaves you weak.

22

Love, I hear,
Makes you blush
And turns you ashen.
You try to speak with passion
And squeak,
I hear.

Love, they say,
Makes you pine away,
But you pine away
With an idiotic grin.
I pine, I blush,
I squeak, I squawk.
Today I woke
Too weak to walk.
What's love, I hear,
I feel ... I fear ...
I'm in.

                              (*Sighs*)
See what I mean?
Da-da-da-da-da-da-da ...
(I hum a lot, too.)
I'm dazed, I'm pale,
I'm sick, I'm sore;
I've never felt so well before!
What's love, I hear,
I feel ... I fear ...
I know I am ...
I'm sure ... I mean ...
I think ... I trust ...
I pray ... I must ...
Be in!

Forgive me if I shout ...
Forgive me if I crow ...
I've only just found out

And, well . . .
I thought you ought to know.
> (PROTEANS *enter dressed as* CITIZENS, *holding* PSEUDOLUS *by the arms. They utter obviously fake chatter*)

HERO: Pseudolus!

FIRST CITIZEN (*Salutes*): Citizen! This is your slave? He was parading as a citizen.

PSEUDOLUS: Believe me, master, I was not parading. This is parading.
> (*Demonstrates*)

I was walking.
> (*Starts to walk off.* CITIZEN *stops him*)

SECOND CITIZEN: Come back here!

THIRD CITIZEN (*To* HERO): He invited us to game with him, and, in a matter of moments, he had taken all our money.

FIRST CITIZEN: He was using weighted dice!

HERO (*To* PSEUDOLUS): Return the money.

SECOND CITIZEN: He took nine minae.

PSEUDOLUS: Nine?! I took seven!

HERO: Give them nine.

PSEUDOLUS (*Handing coins to* CITIZEN): One, two, three, four . . . I am being cheated out of the money I won fairly.

HERO: Pseudolus!

PSEUDOLUS (*Giving* CITIZENS *coins*): Seven, eight.

FIRST CITIZEN: What happened to five and six?
> (HERO *glares at* PSEUDOLUS)

PSEUDOLUS: I'm coming to them. Nine, five, six!
> (*Hands them three more coins*)

SECOND CITIZEN: Come, fellow citizens!
(CITIZENS *exit, chattering*)

PSEUDOLUS (*Sheepishly*): I should be whipped . . . gently. But I only did it for money. I thought if I could raise enough you'd let me buy my freedom from you.

HERO: Oh, Pseudolus, not again!

PSEUDOLUS: It's all I think about. I hate being a slave.

HERO: Better a slave than a slave to love.

PSEUDOLUS: That's easy for you to . . . Love? You? Tell me, master, who is she? Anyone I know?

HERO: Sometimes you can see her through that window.
(*Points to* LYCUS*'s house*)

PSEUDOLUS: Through that win —
(*Horrified*)
A courtesan in the house of Lycus? Your parents would be outraged if they could hear you.

HERO: I don't care!

PSEUDOLUS: Do you know how many minae a girl like that would cost?

HERO: And worth every drachma! Oh, Pseudolus, I would give anything for her.

PSEUDOLUS: You would? You really love this girl?
(HERO *sighs*)
I like the way you said that. Now, you cannot afford to buy this girl, but in spite of that, suppose someone, some- one with tremendous cunning and guile, could arrange for her to be yours.

HERO: Yes?

PSEUDOLUS: If that someone could arrange it, what would you give me?

25

HERO: Everything!

PSEUDOLUS: Everything? What do you own? Twenty minae, a collection of sea shells and me.

HERO: Right.

PSEUDOLUS: You don't have to give me the twenty minae, or the sea shells. If I get you that girl, just give me me.

HERO: Give you you?

PSEUDOLUS: My freedom.

HERO: Pseudolus! People do not go about freeing slaves.

PSEUDOLUS: Be the first! Start a fashion!

HERO (*A pause, then*): Get me that girl!

PSEUDOLUS: And if I can?

HERO: You are free!

PSEUDOLUS: I am what?

HERO: Free!

PSEUDOLUS: Free!

(*Sings*)

Oh, what a word!
Oh, what a word!

(*Speaks*)

Say it again!

HERO: Free!

PSEUDOLUS (*Sings*):
I've often thought,
I've often dreamed
How it would be ...
And yet I never thought I'd be ...
(*Speaks*)

26

Once more.

HERO: Free!

PSEUDOLUS (*Sings*):
But when you come to think of such things ...
A man should have the rights that all others ...
Can you imagine
What it will be like when I am ...
Can you see me?

Can you see me as a Roman with my head unbowed?
(Sing it good and loud ...)

HERO:
Free!

PSEUDOLUS:
Like a Roman, having rights
And like a Roman, proud!
Can you see me?

HERO:
I can see you!

PSEUDOLUS:
Can you see me as a voter fighting graft and vice?
(Sing it soft and nice ...)

HERO:
Free.

PSEUDOLUS:
Why, I'll be so conscientious that I may vote twice!
Can you see me?
Can you see me?

When I'm free to be whatever I want to be,
Think what wonders I'll accomplish then!
When the master that I serve is me and just me,

Can you see me being equal with my countrymen?
Can you see me being Pseudolus the Citizen?
Can you see me being . . . ?
Give it to me once again!

HERO:

Free!

PSEUDOLUS:

That's it!

HERO:

Free!

PSEUDOLUS:

Yes!

HERO:

Fr . . .

PSEUDOLUS (*Claps his hand over* HERO*'s mouth*):

Now, not so fast!
I didn't think . . .
The way I am,
I have a roof,
Three meals a day,
And I don't have to pay a thing . . .
I'm just a slave and everything's free.
If I were free,
Then nothing would be free,
And if I'm beaten now and then,
What does it matter?

HERO (*Softly, seductively*):

Free.

PSEUDOLUS (*Brightening*):

Can you see me?

Can you see me as a poet writing poetry?
All my verse will be . . .

HERO:

Free!

PSEUDOLUS:

A museum will have me pickled for posterity!
Can you see me?

HERO (*With a grimace*):

I can see you!

PSEUDOLUS:

Can you see me as a lover, one of great renown,
Women falling down?

HERO:

Free?

PSEUDOLUS: No,

But I'll buy the house of Lycus for my house in town.
Can you see me?
Can't you see me?

Be you anything from king to baker of cakes,
You're a vegetable unless you're free!
It's a little word, but oh, the difference it makes:
It's the necessary essence of democracy,
It's the thing that every slave should have the right to be,
And I soon will have the right to buy a slave for me!
Can you see him?
Well, I'll free him!

When a Pseudolus can move, the universe shakes,
But I'll never move until I'm free!
Such a little word, but oh, the difference it makes:
I'll be Pseudolus the founder of a family,
I'll be Pseudolus the pillar of society,
I'll be Pseudolus the man, if I can only be . . .

HERO:

Free!

PSEUDOLUS:
  Sing it!

HERO:
  Free!

PSEUDOLUS:
  Spell it!

HERO:
  F-r-double . . .

PSEUDOLUS:
  No, the long way . . .

HERO:
  F-R-E-E —

BOTH:
  FREE!!!
          (LYCUS *enters from his house, calls into it*)

LYCUS: What a day! What a day! Come out here!
          (PROTEAN, *dressed as* EUNUCH, *enters from house, holding*
          fan)
What do you think you are doing, eunuch? I have told you
a thousand times not to fan the girls while they're still wet!
You'll never learn. You'll be a eunuch all your life!
          (EUNUCH *exits into house.* LYCUS *turns to audience*)
What a day! I have to go to the Senate this morning. I'm
blackmailing one of the Senators.
          (*Starts off, as* PSEUDOLUS *whispers to* HERO)

PSEUDOLUS: Quick! Your money bag!
                    (HERO *hands him money bag*)
Good morning, Lycus.
          (*Jingles money bag behind* LYCUS*'s back.* LYCUS *stops*)

LYCUS: I know that sound, and I love it.
                    (*Turns to* PSEUDOLUS)

30

Is that money?

PSEUDOLUS: What do you think?

LYCUS: How did you come to all this?

PSEUDOLUS: An unexpected legacy. My uncle Simo, the noted Carthaginian elephant breeder, came to an untimely end. He was crushed to death on the last day of the mating season. This morning I bought my freedom.

LYCUS: Congratulations!

PSEUDOLUS: With this much left over for one gross indulgence.

LYCUS: Good.

PSEUDOLUS: Lycus, I am now in the market for a lifetime companion. Tell me, have you anything lying about in there, anything to satisfy an Olympian appetite?

LYCUS: Pseudolus, friend and *citizen*, I have traveled the world in search of beauty, and I can say with modesty that I have the finest assortment in Rome.

PSEUDOLUS: Show me.

(LYCUS *claps his hands*)

LYCUS: Eunuchs! A buyer!

(EUNUCHS *enter from* LYCUS*'s house, drape banner over door.* PSEUDOLUS *sits on stool.* LYCUS *sings*)

There is merchandise for every need
At the house of Marcus Lycus.
All the merchandise is guaranteed
At the house of Marcus Lycus.
For a sense of sensuality
Or an opulence thereof,
Patronize the house of Marcus Lycus,
Merchant of love.

For your most assured approval and your more than possible purchase, here are the fruits of my search. Behold
. . . Tintinabula.

(TINTINABULA *enters from behind banner, poses*)

Out of the East, with the face of an idol . . . the arms of a willow tree . . . and the pelvis of a camel.

(*She dances.* PSEUDOLUS *looks at* HERO, *who shakes his head no*)

PSEUDOLUS (*To* LYCUS): Don't you have anyone in there a bit less . . . noisy?

LYCUS: I have. May I present Panacea.

(PANACEA *enters*)

To make her available to you, I outbid the King of Nubia. Panacea, with a face that holds a thousand promises, and a body that stands behind each promise.

(PANACEA *dances.* HERO *shakes his head no.* PSEUDOLUS *looks* PANACEA *over, yawns*)

You are disturbed?

PSEUDOLUS: The proportions. Don't misunderstand me.

(*Spreading his hands before her bosom*)

I love the breadth. It's the length. She may be the right length, but is it right for me? You see what I mean.

(*Stands with her, back-to-back*)

Isn't she a bit too short?

LYCUS: Definitely not.

PSEUDOLUS (*Wiggles, then*): Too tall?

LYCUS: No. Like that you look perfect together.

PSEUDOLUS: Yes, but how often will we find ourselves in this position?

(*Turns to face her*)

Perhaps if we . . .

LYCUS: No need to compromise. Consider the Geminae.

(GEMINAE *enter*)

A matched pair.

(*They dance*)

Either one a divinely assembled woman, together an infinite number of mathematical possibilities. They are flawless.

(HERO *shakes his head no*)

PSEUDOLUS: I quite agree. But I am a man of limited means and I don't suppose you'd break up a set.

LYCUS: I couldn't. You understand.

PSEUDOLUS: Completely.

LYCUS: Fortunately, we still have ... Vibrata.

(VIBRATA enters)

Exotic as a desert bloom ... wondrous as a flamingo ... lithe as a tigress ... for the man whose interest is wild life ...

(VIBRATA *sings, dances.* HERO *shakes his head no.* PSEUDOLUS *goes to* VIBRATA)

PSEUDOLUS: Lycus, all that I can see is a sight to behold, but I keep feeling there is something wrong. Perhaps a cleft palate, a hammer toe ...

LYCUS: Wait. I know exactly what you want. May I present ... Gymnasia.

(GYMNASIA *enters, does bump.* PSEUDOLUS *falls off stool.* HERO *shakes his head no, but* PSEUDOLUS *is completely captivated*)

Gymnasia, a giant stage on which a thousand dramas can be played.

(PSEUDOLUS *circles her, stops behind her, gestures to* LYCUS)

PSEUDOLUS: Lycus, could I see you back here a moment?

33

(LYCUS *disappears behind* GYMNASIA. *He and* PSEUDOLUS *gesture.* PSEUDOLUS *steps into the clear*)
Two hundred minae?! For what?!

LYCUS: Figure it out for yourself.

PSEUDOLUS: Yes, it is a fair price by the pound. But what disturbs me, frankly, is the upkeep. Perhaps you would have more success selling her to some fraternal organization. A group dedicated to good works. But on the other hand . . .
(*Puts his head on her bosom*)

HERO: Pseudolus!

PSEUDOLUS: Yes, darling?

HERO (*Pulls him aside*): Do you want your freedom?

PSEUDOLUS (*Looks back at* GYMNASIA): More than ever.
(*To* LYCUS)
May I see the next girl?

LYCUS: That is the entire lot. Surely there is one among these to satisfy you.

PSEUDOLUS: As yet I have not seen exactly what I had in mind.

LYCUS (*Claps hands*): Courtesans! Out of the sun and into the house. I shall return in time to lead you in midday prayers.
(COURTESANS *and* EUNUCHS *exit.* PHILIA *'s head appears in upper window of* LYCUS *'s house*)

HERO (*Whispers to* PSEUDOLUS): Pseudolus, there she is!

PSEUDOLUS (*To* LYCUS): Oh, you fox! "That is the entire lot." Did I not just spy a golden head and a pair of sky blue eyes? A body clad in flowing white?

LYCUS: Oh, that one. A recent arrival from Crete. A virgin.

34

PSEUDOLUS (*Nudging* HERO): A virgin.

HERO: A virgin!

PSEUDOLUS (*To* LYCUS): Well??

LYCUS: Only yesterday she was sold.

HERO: Sold!
> (*Draws his dagger melodramatically.* PSEUDOLUS *wrests it from him*)

PSEUDOLUS: Behave yourself!
> (*Begins casually cleaning his nails with dagger*)

She was sold?

LYCUS: To the great captain, **Miles Gloriosus**, who comes this day to claim her. She cost five hundred minae.

PSEUDOLUS (*Amazed*): Five hundred!

LYCUS: A great sum, to be sure. But being a man of conquest, his heart was set on a virgin.

PSEUDOLUS: You say she just arrived from Crete?

LYCUS: Yes.

PSEUDOLUS: Mmm. I hope the great captain is kind to her. She deserves a bit of affection before . . .
> (*Sighs, then to* HERO)

Tragic, is it not?
> (HERO *moans*)

LYCUS: What is tragic?

PSEUDOLUS: The news from Crete.

LYCUS: What news?

PSEUDOLUS: Why should I darken your day? Farewell, Lycus.

LYCUS (*Grabs him*): What is the news?

PSEUDOLUS: What news?

LYCUS: The news from Crete.

PSEUDOLUS: I heard it. Tragic.

LYCUS: Pseudolus!

(*Shakes him*)

PSEUDOLUS: You force me to tell you! Crete is ravaged by a great plague. People are dying by the thousands.

LYCUS: But this girl is healthy. She goes smiling through the day.

PSEUDOLUS: She doesn't! I thought you knew. When they start to smile, the end is near.

LYCUS: No!

PSEUDOLUS: Yes. I am told it is lovely now in Crete. Everyone lying there, smiling.

LYCUS: Is it contagious?

PSEUDOLUS: Did you ever see a plague that wasn't?

LYCUS: My other girls!

PSEUDOLUS: You had best get her out of there.

HERO: Yes!

LYCUS: And then?

PSEUDOLUS: I could look after her until the captain comes.

HERO: He could!

LYCUS: But would *you* not be . . . ?

PSEUDOLUS: I have already had the plague. I would tell you about it but . . .

(*Pantomimes disgust*)

LYCUS: I do hope she lives until the captain gets here.
(*Exits into his house*)

HERO (*Elated*): Pseudolus, I am to be with her!

PSEUDOLUS: Until the captain arrives.

HERO (*Sadly*): Yes.

PSEUDOLUS: Wait!
(*Thinks a moment*)

HERO: Yes?

PSEUDOLUS: A brilliant idea!

HERO: Yes?

PSEUDOLUS: That's what we have to find. A brilliant idea.

HERO: You must find one.

LYCUS (*Speaking into his house as he backs out of it*): Come, come, my dear. This way. Don't touch that pillar. Here is someone I want you to meet.
(PHILIA *enters from house, carrying a bag*)
Philia, this is Pseudolus. You are to stay with him until the captain comes. It will not be long.
(*Aside to* PSEUDOLUS)
Pseudolus! Thank you, Pseudolus. If none in the house were to your liking, there will soon be new arrivals. You shall have first choice, because, Pseudolus, you are a friend.
(*Bows*)

PSEUDOLUS (*Returning the bow*): And you, Lycus, are a gentleman and a procurer.
(LYCUS *exits.* HERO *and* PHILIA *stand staring at each other.* PSEUDOLUS *looks at them, then turns to audience*)
There they are. Together. And I must keep them that way, together, if I am to be free. What to do? What to do?
(*To himself*)

I need help. I'll go to the harbor. There I may find a way out! I am off! The captain!
(HERO *and* PHILIA *turn to him, alarmed*)
Watch for him. He may arrive this way ...
(PHILIA *turns from* HERO, *looks off*)
... or he may arrive this way.
(HERO *turns, looks off*)
No, no. You watch this way.
(*Turns* PHILIA *around*)
And you watch that way.
(*Turns* HERO *around.* HERO *and* PHILIA *now face each other*)
Much better.
(*Starts to exit, stops, addresses audience*)
Don't worry. Nothing will happen. He's a virgin, too.
(*Runs off*)

PHILIA: My name is Philia.

HERO: Yes.

PHILIA: I do not know your name, but you have beautiful legs.

HERO: My name is Hero and ... uh ... you have beautiful legs ... I imagine.

PHILIA: I would show them to you, but they are sold.

HERO: I know.

PHILIA: Along with the rest of me. I cost five hundred minae. Is that a lot of money?

HERO: Oh, yes.

PHILIA: More than three hundred?

HERO: Nearly twice as much.

PHILIA: Those are the two numbers that mix me up, three

and five. I hope that captain doesn't expect me to do a lot of adding.

HERO: You can't add?

PHILIA: We are taught beauty and grace, and no more. I cannot add, or spell, or anything. I have but one talent.
(*Sings*)
I'm lovely,
All I am is lovely,
Lovely is the one thing I can do.
Winsome,
What I am is winsome,
Radiant as in some
Dream come true.
Oh,
Isn't it a shame?
I can neither sew
Nor cook nor read nor write my name.
But I'm happy
Merely being lovely,
For it's one thing I can give to you.

HERO: Philia . . .

PHILIA: Yes?

HERO: Say my name.

PHILIA: Just say your name?

HERO: Yes.

PHILIA: Very well.
(*A blank look*)
I have forgotten it.

HERO (*Disappointed*): It's Hero.

PHILIA: Forgive me, Hero. I have no memory for names.

HERO: You don't need one. You don't need anything.
(*Sings*)
You're lovely,
Absolutely lovely,
Who'd believe the loveliness of you?
Winsome,
Sweet and warm and winsome,
Radiant as in some
Dream come true.

PHILIA:
True!

HERO:
Now
Venus would seem tame,
Helen and her thou-
Sand ships would have to die of shame.

BOTH:
And I'm happy,
Happy that you're (I'm) lovely,
For there's one thing loveliness can do:
It's a gift for me to share with you!
(*They kiss*)

HERO: Do you know? I've never been kissed before.

PHILIA: That's the very first thing they teach us.

HERO: Philia ... I love you.

PHILIA: And I love you.
(*They embrace, as* HYSTERIUM *enters from* SENEX'*s house, muttering*)

HYSTERIUM: Pseudolus! Where is that — ?
(*Sees* HERO *and* PHILIA)
Oh, no! No, no, no, no!

HERO (*Frightened*): Hysterium — this is Philia.

HYSTERIUM: Never mind who she is, who is she? Where is she from?

HERO (*Haltingly*): She is from the house of Lycus.

HYSTERIUM: A courtesan!

PHILIA: I am a virgin.

HYSTERIUM (*Disbelievingly, with a fake smile*): Of course. Hero, this will never do. Never, never. Bid farewell to this young lady so that she can go about her ... uh ... business.

HERO: But Pseudolus said ...

HYSTERIUM: Pseudolus! I might have known!
(PSEUDOLUS *runs on*)

PSEUDOLUS (*Spots* HYSTERIUM, *then to* HERO): Hero! Master!

HYSTERIUM: Pseudolus!
(PSEUDOLUS *reacts, polishes pillar of house*)
Pseudolus!

PSEUDOLUS: Yes, Hysterium?

HYSTERIUM: Pseudolus!

PSEUDOLUS: Pronounced perfectly! You know, a lot of people say *P*seudolus, and I hate it.
(*Aside to* HERO)
Show the girl our garden.
(HERO *and* PHILIA *exit behind* SENEX*'s house*)

HYSTERIUM: How dare you! Arranging an assignation between an innocent boy and a you-know-what!

PSEUDOLUS (*Stopping him*): Hysterium, there is something you should know about that you-know-what.

HYSTERIUM: What?

PSEUDOLUS: That girl, about whom you think the worst, is my daughter.

HYSTERIUM: Your what?

PSEUDOLUS: My daughter. You've heard me speak of her.

HYSTERIUM: Never!

PSEUDOLUS: Well, I don't like to talk about her.
(*Polishes pillar*)

HYSTERIUM: That girl is not your daughter.

PSEUDOLUS: My sister?

HYSTERIUM: I shall go tell his parents.

PSEUDOLUS: Wait! Hysterium, the truth. She has been sold to a captain who comes any moment now to claim her.

HYSTERIUM: Oh. I go tell his parents!

PSEUDOLUS: I go with you!

HYSTERIUM: You don't want to be there when I tell them about you!

PSEUDOLUS: No, I want *you* to be there when I tell them about *you*!

HYSTERIUM: Tell them *what* about me? I have nothing to fear. I am a pillar of virtue. I go.
(*Starts to leave,* PSEUDOLUS *stops him*)

PSEUDOLUS: I think it might be of interest to the family that their slave-in-chief, their pillar of virtue, has secreted within the confines of his cubicle Rome's most extensive and diversified collection of erotic pottery.
(HYSTERIUM *freezes in horror*)

HYSTERIUM: Pseudolus!
(*Calls out*)
Hero!

PSEUDOLUS: Tell me, where did you ever get that fruit bowl with the frieze of . . . ?

(Indicates an erotic pose or two)

HYSTERIUM: Pseudolus!

(HERO *and* PHILIA *enter*)

Hero, as you know, your mother and father placed me in charge of your innocence. However, I have decided to allow you to remain with the girl until the arrival of her captain.

HERO: Oh, Philia!

(Embraces her)

HYSTERIUM: Here! Stop doing that!

(Separates them)

You could hurt each other!

(Exiting into SENEX*'s house)*

Ohhhhh!

PSEUDOLUS: Master, I said we needed a brilliant idea.

HERO: Yes?

PSEUDOLUS: I have been to the harbor, and I have found one. Come along!

PHILIA: Are we going somewhere?

PSEUDOLUS: *You* are. You have your belongings.

(To HERO*)*

Let us fetch yours.

HERO: Where are we to go?

PSEUDOLUS: Away.

HERO: *Where* away?

PSEUDOLUS: *Far* away!

HERO: But my family . . .

PHILIA: My captain . . .

PSEUDOLUS: There is only room for two of you.

HERO: Where?

PSEUDOLUS (*Sings*):
In the Tiber there sits a boat,
Gently dipping its bow,
Trim and tidy and built to float.
Pretty little picture?
Now . . .
Put a boy on the starboard side,
Leaning out at the rail.
Next to him put a blushing bride,
Slim and slender and starry-eyed.
Down below put a tiny bed.
The sun gets pale,
The sea gets red,
And off they sail
On the first high tide,
The boat and the bed and the boy and the bride!

It's a pretty little picture, oh, my!
Pretty little picture, how true!
Pretty little picture which I,
Pseudolittlelus, give to you!

Feel the roll of the playful waves!
See the sails as they swell!
Hear the whips on the galley slaves!
Pretty little picture?
Well . . .
Let it carry your cares away,
Out of sight, out of mind,
Past the buoy and through the bay —
Soon there's nothing but sea and spray.
Night descends and the moon's aglow.
Your arms entwined,
You steal below,

44

And far behind
At the edge of day,
The bong of the bell of the buoy in the bay,
And the boat and the boy and the bride are away!

It's a pretty little picture to share
As the little boat sails to sea.
Take a little trip free as air,
Have a little freedom on me!

HERO *and* PHILIA:

No worries,
No bothers,
No captains,
No fathers!

PSEUDOLUS:

In the ocean an island waits,
Smooth and sandy and pink,
Filled with lemons and nuts and dates.
Pretty little picture?
Think:
In a cottage of cypress trees,
Sea-shells dotting the door,
Boy and bride live a life of ease,
Doing nothing but what they please.
And every night when the stars appear,
There's nothing more
To see or hear,
There's just the shore
Where the lovers lie,
The sand and the sea and the stars and the sky,
And the sound of a soft little satisfied sigh ...
(HERO *and* PHILIA *sigh*)

ALL:

All your petty little problems will cease,
And your little blessings will flow,

And your little family increase.
Pretty little picture?

PSEUDOLUS:
No, no!
Pretty little masterpiece!

ALL:
Pretty little picture!

PSEUDOLUS: Come! We go!

HERO: Yes!

PHILIA: Wait! I cannot go.

PSEUDOLUS: Why can you not?!

PHILIA: As long as the captain has a contract I must go with him. That is the way of a courtesan.

HERO: Oh, Venus, why did you bring us together, only to part us?

PHILIA: Be brave, Hero.

HERO: For us there will never be happiness.

PHILIA: We will have to learn to be happy without it.

PSEUDOLUS (*To audience*): Have you been listening? Do you believe this? And not a word about me or my freedom.
(*Firmly*)
She *must* go with him!

PHILIA: This waiting out here is torture. Why doesn't he come and take me?

PSEUDOLUS: In good time you will be taken. But not on the street. Inside.

PHILIA: You will tell me when he comes?

PSEUDOLUS: I shall have him knock. On the door. Three times.

PHILIA: That's two and one more?

PSEUDOLUS: Correct. Three times. Now, in, in, in.
>   (PHILIA *exits into* SENEX*'s house*)

HERO (*Despondently*): Pseudolus, what is going to happen?

PSEUDOLUS (*Confidently*): She will go with you.
>   (HYSTERIUM *enters from* SENEX*'s house*)

HYSTERIUM: Hero, I am off to market. While you are alone
with the girl, remember who you are.
>   (HERO *exits into* SENEX*'s house*)
I have yet to begin my daily chores.

PSEUDOLUS: Hysterium, before you go. Just one more favor.

HYSTERIUM: What is it?

PSEUDOLUS: May I borrow your book of potions?

HYSTERIUM: Oh, no, no, no! That stays right here . . .
>   (*Pats his back pocket*)
Where it belongs.
>   (*Calls off*)
You there, bird seller! What do you have in the way of a
plump peahen?
>   (*As he exits,* PSEUDOLUS *deftly lifts potion book from* HYS-
>   TERIUM*'s back pocket, addresses audience*)

PSEUDOLUS: His book of potions! And my pass to freedom!
What I need is his sleeping potion. With a drop or two of
that, the breath stops short, the eyes slam shut, the body
hangs limp. I shall mix a few drops in a beaker of wine
and give it to the girl to drink. I show Lycus that she has
died of the plague and tell Hero to dispose of the body.
Then they to the boat, I to the hills . . .
>   (*Points to audience*)
and you to your homes.
>   (*Looks through pages, then to audience*)

I just remembered something frightening. I cannot read!
(*Calls*)
Hero! Come out here.
(HERO *enters from* SENEX *'s house*)
Call these pages off to me.

HERO: Not now?!

PSEUDOLUS: Yes, now! Read!

HERO (*Reading as he turns pages*): "Fever Potion" . . . "Headache Potion" . . . "Passion Potion" . . . "Sleeping Potion" . . .

PSEUDOLUS: That's it! The formula. What do we need? The ingredients?

HERO: "The eye of an eel."

PSEUDOLUS: That we have.

HERO: "The heart of a snail."

PSEUDOLUS: That we have.

HERO: "A cup of mare's sweat."

PSEUDOLUS: Mare's sweat? That we have not.

HERO: Why are you preparing this?

PSEUDOLUS: I intend to give it to the girl. Asleep, she will go with you.

HERO: She will?

PSEUDOLUS (*Worried*): Mare's sweat . . .

HERO: Where will you find it?

PSEUDOLUS: Leave that to me. *You* go to the harbor! Give the boatman your twenty minae and tell him that you sail with him this day! *I* shall prepare the potion!

HERO: This is exciting!

PSEUDOLUS: Isn't it! Go!

(HERO *exits*)

Mare's sweat! Where am I going to find mare's sweat on a balmy day like this?

(PSEUDOLUS *exits, as* SENEX *enters with* DOMINA*'s bust, calling*)

SENEX: Pseudolus! Pseudolus! . . . He could have taken this to the stonecutter for me.

(*To audience*)

I dropped it, and now the nose has to be re-sharpened. Hysterium will take it for me.

(*Goes to his house, kicks door three times. A pause, then* PHILIA *enters from house, arms outstretched*)

PHILIA: Take me!

(SENEX *looks around*)

Take me!

SENEX: What did you say?

PHILIA: Take me!

SENEX: One moment.

(*Puts statue on stoop, starts for* PHILIA, *returns to statue, and turns its face away from* PHILIA)

PHILIA: Here on the street if you like! My body is yours. Say it. Say it!

SENEX(*Looks around, then quickly*): Your body is mine.

PHILIA: Then take me!

(*Throws herself at him*)

Is this not what you want?

SENEX: It does cross my mind now and then.

PHILIA: You must know one thing.

SENEX: What is that?

49

PHILIA: Though you have my body, you shall never have my heart.

SENEX: Well, you can't have everything.
(*Looks heavenward*)
A thousand thanks, whichever one of you did this.
(*She seizes him. They hold their embrace as* PSEUDOLUS *enters, carrying a vial. Not seeing* SENEX *and* PHILIA, *he addresses audience*)

PSEUDOLUS: Would you believe it? There was a mare sweating not two streets from here.
(*Holds up vial, turns, sees embrace.* SENEX*'s face is hidden from him.* PSEUDOLUS *turns to audience*)
Gets to look more like his father every day!

PHILIA (*Still in* SENEX*'s arms*): Pseudolus, he is here.

PSEUDOLUS: No!
(SENEX *looks from* PHILIA *to* PSEUDOLUS, *then back to* PHILIA)

SENEX: Remember where we stopped.
(*Slips out from under her, goes to* PSEUDOLUS)

PSEUDOLUS: Sir, you're back.

SENEX (*Holding his spine*): She almost broke it.

PSEUDOLUS: You've returned!

SENEX: Yes!

PSEUDOLUS: Unexpectedly!

SENEX: Apparently! Who is she?

PHILIA: I shall wait your bidding.

SENEX: Yes, dear.

PHILIA: Ever your servant.
(*Bows, exits into* SENEX*'s house*)

SENEX (*Sighs*): Ever my servant.

PSEUDOLUS (*Quickly*): Yes, sir. Your servant. Your new maid. We needed someone to help.

SENEX: A new maid. She seems very loyal.

PSEUDOLUS: And very efficient and very courteous and very thoughtful.

SENEX: Maids like me. I'm neat. I like maids. *They're* neat. Something no household should be without.
    (*Sings,* PSEUDOLUS *all the while encouraging him*)
Everybody ought to have a maid.
Everybody ought to have a working girl,
Everybody ought to have a lurking girl
To putter around the house.

Everybody ought to have a maid.
Everybody ought to have a menial,
Consistently congenial
And quieter than a mouse.

Oh! Oh! Wouldn't she be delicious,
Tidying up the dishes,
Neat as a pin?
Oh! Oh! Wouldn't she be delightful,
Sweeping out, sleeping in?

Everybody ought to have a maid!
Someone whom you hire when you're short of help
To offer you the sort of help
You never get from a spouse!
Fluttering up the stairway,
Shuttering up the windows,
Cluttering up the bedroom,
Buttering up the master,
Puttering all around
The house!

(PSEUDOLUS *pantomimes a maid*)
Oh! Oh! Wouldn't she be delicious,
Tidying up the dishes,
Neat as a pin?
Oh! Oh! Wouldn't she be delightful,
Sweeping out, sleeping in?

Everybody ought to have a maid!
Someone who, when fetching you your slipper, will
Be winsome as a whippoorwill
And graceful as a grouse!
Skittering down the hallway,
Flittering through the parlor,
Tittering in the pantry,
Littering up the bedroom,
Twittering all around
The house!
(HYSTERIUM *enters, reacts at the sight of* SENEX. PSEUDO-
LUS *whispers to him*)

HYSTERIUM: A maid?

PSEUDOLUS: A maid.

SENEX: A maid.

ALL: A maid!
Everybody ought to have a maid.
Everybody ought to have a serving girl,
A loyal and unswerving girl
Who's quieter than a mouse.

Oh! Oh!
Think of her at the dustbin,
'Specially when she's just been
Traipsing about.
Oh! Oh!
Wouldn't she be delightful?

HYSTERIUM:
   Living in ...

SENEX:
   Giving out!

ALL:
   Everybody ought to have a maid,
   Daintily collecting bits of paper 'n' strings,
   Appealing in her apron strings,
   Beguiling in her blouse!

HYSTERIUM:
   Pattering through the attic,

SENEX:
   Chattering in the cellar,

PSEUDOLUS:
   Clattering in the kitchen,

SENEX:
   Flattering in the bedroom,

ALL:
   Puttering all around the house,
   The house,
   The house!
            (LYCUS *enters.* HYSTERIUM *whispers to him*)

LYCUS: A maid?

HYSTERIUM: A maid.

PSEUDOLUS: A maid.

SENEX: A maid!

ALL:
   Everybody ought to have a maid,
   Someone who's efficient and reliable,

Obedient and pliable
And quieter than a mouse.

Oh! Oh! Wouldn't she be so nimble,
Fiddling with her thimble,
Mending a gown?
Oh! Oh! Wouldn't she be delightful?

LYCUS:
Cleaning up . . .

SENEX:
Leaning down!

ALL:
Everybody ought to have a maid!
Someone who'll be busy as a bumblebee
And, even if you grumble, be
As graceful as a grouse!

LYCUS:
Wriggling in the anteroom,

HYSTERIUM:
Jiggling in the living-room,

PSEUDOLUS:
Giggling in the dining-room,

SENEX:
Wiggling in the other rooms,

ALL:
Puttering all around
The house!
The house!
The house!
(LYCUS *exits into his house*)

SENEX: I know how busy both of you are. Therefore, it is for *me* to instruct her in the niceties of housework.
(*Starting for his house*)

54

We shall start in my room.

HYSTERIUM: Sir!

PSEUDOLUS: Sir, your son is in there!

SENEX: Oh!

(Thinks a moment, then:)

Before my friend and neighbor, Erronius, went abroad in search of his children stolen in infancy by pirates, he asked me to look into his house from time to time.

(Goes to ERRONIUS's house, takes key from ledge and opens door)

This seems as good a time as any. I shall have a chat with the girl in here. Send her to me.

PSEUDOLUS: Sir.

SENEX: Yes?

PSEUDOLUS: Only my great devotion to you allows me to speak so frankly.

(Unseen by SENEX, PSEUDOLUS sprinkles contents of vial on him)

You trudged along the road quite some way, and I fear that the great physical exertion . . .

(Sniffs)

SENEX *(Sniffing)*: Is that me?!

PSEUDOLUS: Yes, sir.

SENEX: My heavens, I smell like an overheated horse! I shall have to bathe.

PSEUDOLUS: At least!

(SENEX exits into ERRONIUS's house)

HYSTERIUM: Why did I ever let her in the house? I should never have listened to you!

PSEUDOLUS: Everything is going to be fine, pussycat.

(Hands him potion book)

HYSTERIUM: Oh, you! You just see that she gets out of that house.

PSEUDOLUS (*Picking up statue*): And you just see that he *stays* in *that* house. Keep calm!

(*Exits into* SENEX*'s house*)

HYSTERIUM: Calm? Calm? Mustn't be excited. Calm. Calm.

(*Sings excitedly*)

I'm calm, I'm calm,
I'm perfectly calm,
I'm utterly under control.
I haven't a worry —
Where others would hurry,
I stroll.

(*He runs frantically around the stage*)

I'm calm, I'm cool,
A gibbering fool
Is something I never become!
When thunder is rumbling
And others are crumbling,
I hum.

(*He tries to hum; it becomes a stifled scream*)

I must think calm, comforting things:
Butterfly wings,
Emerald rings.
Or a murmuring brook,
Murmuring, murmuring, murmuring . . .
Look:

(*Steadying his hands, seemingly calm*)

I'm calm, I'm calm,
I haven't a qualm,
I'm utterly under control.
Let nothing confuse me
Or faze me —

(*Yawns*)

Excuse me —

I'm calm,
Oh, so calm,
Oh, so . . .

SENEX (*Calls from inside* ERRONIUS*'s house*): Hysterium!
   (HYSTERIUM *runs into* SENEX*'s house*. PROTEANS, *dressed as* SAILORS, *enter with bags, drop them, as* ERRONIUS *enters behind them*)

ERRONIUS: Bring up the baggage. Fetch the rest from the harbor.

                    (SAILORS *exit*)
Ah, home at last! After years of searching for my long lost children.
   (HYSTERIUM *enters from* SENEX*'s house, carrying plucked chicken, reacts in horror*)
How good it is to see this street once more. These tired old eyes fill with tears at the sight of the little they see.
                 (*Bumps into* HYSTERIUM)
Pardon me, young woman, I was just . . . that is . . . I mean to say . . . Ah, lovely baby.
                    (*Pats chicken*)
About the age of my children when they were stolen by pirates.
                 (*Going to his house*)
Well, at least I have the comfort of my lonely house.
     (HYSTERIUM *rushes to door of* ERRONIUS*'s house*)

HYSTERIUM: Sir!

ERRONIUS: And who are you?

HYSTERIUM: Hysterium, sir, servant to Senex.

ERRONIUS (*To pillar*): Yes, of course. I should have known you anywhere.
   (SENEX *is heard singing from inside house a bit of "Everybody Ought to Have a Maid"*)

What was that?

HYSTERIUM: I didn't hear anything.
(SENEX *sings a bit more*)
I didn't hear that either.

ERRONIUS: You did not hear that eerie sound?

HYSTERIUM: Eerie?

ERRONIUS: Eerie, as if haunted.

HYSTERIUM (*To himself*): Eerie, as if haunted?
(*To* ERRONIUS)
Sir, what I am about to tell you is eerie ... Your house is
... is haunted.

ERRONIUS: Haunted?

HYSTERIUM: As haunted as the day is long!
(PSEUDOLUS *enters, stirring the potion, listens*)

ERRONIUS: Impossible! My house haunted, you say? Strange.

HYSTERIUM: But true. Perhaps you ought to stay with relatives ... distant relatives.

ERRONIUS: Yes! No! Fetch me a soothsayer.

HYSTERIUM: A soothsayer?

ERRONIUS: Yes, I must have him search my house immediately.
(PSEUDOLUS *puts cloth over his head, runs to* ERRONIUS,
chants ghoulishly)

PSEUDOLUS: You are in need of a soothsayer?

ERRONIUS: How did you know?

PSEUDOLUS: I'd be a fine soothsayer if I didn't!

ERRONIUS: There is a spirit in my ...

PSEUDOLUS: Silence! I am about to say the sooth! Wait!
(*Chants incoherently*)

I see it. I see everything.
(HYSTERIUM *steps behind* ERRONIUS, *pantomimes distance*)
You have been abroad.

ERRONIUS: Yes, yes.

PSEUDOLUS: For . . .
(*Looks at* HYSTERIUM, *who flashes his ten fingers twice*)
. . . twenty years!
(ERRONIUS *nods vigorously.* HYSTERIUM *shades his eyes with one hand*)
You have been searching . . . for . . .
(HYSTERIUM *cradles his arms, rocks them*)
A child!
(HYSTERIUM *holds up two fingers*)
Two children!

ERRONIUS: Yes, yes!
(HYSTERIUM *flexes his muscles*)

PSEUDOLUS: A fine, big boy.

ERRONIUS: Yes.

PSEUDOLUS: And . . .
(HYSTERIUM *places hand on his hip, pantomimes a girl*)
A strange, little boy.
(HYSTERIUM *shakes his head no*)
A girl! A girl! A boy and a girl!

ERRONIUS: Yes! Can you find them for me?

PSEUDOLUS: Certainly. I can find them for you.

ERRONIUS (*Takes ring from his finger, gives it to* PSEUDOLUS):
Each wears a ring on which is engraven a gaggle of geese.

PSEUDOLUS: A gaggle of what?

ERRONIUS: A gaggle of geese. Look!
(*Points to ring*)

There are only two others like it in the world. And my children wear them.

PSEUDOLUS: How many geese in a gaggle?

ERRONIUS: At least seven.

PSEUDOLUS: Seven? Then before I say the sooth again you must walk seven times around the seven hills of Rome.

ERRONIUS: Seven times?

HYSTERIUM: Slowly.

ERRONIUS: Seven times around the seven hills?
>   (SAILORS *enter with more baggage*)
Take it all back to the harbor!
>   (*Proudly*)
My house is haunted.
>   (SAILORS *exit with baggage.* SENEX *is heard singing again.* PSEUDOLUS *joins in, eerily*)
And the spirit?

PSEUDOLUS: It shall be gone by the time you have done my bidding.

ERRONIUS: Thank you.

PSEUDOLUS: To the hills!

ERRONIUS: To the hills!
>   (*Starts for the footlights,* PSEUDOLUS *and* HYSTERIUM *stop him, head him toward the wings*)

HYSTERIUM: This is the way, sir!

ERRONIUS: Thank you, young woman!
>   (*Exits*)

PSEUDOLUS (*Calls*): Sir, you forgot your gaggle!
>   (*Puts ring on his own finger.* SENEX *enters from* ERRONIUS*'s house*)

SENEX: Hysterium!

HYSTERIUM (*Jumping*): Sir!

SENEX: Prepare my bath!

HYSTERIUM: Yes, sir!
(*Runs into* ERRONIUS's *house*)

SENEX: Ah, Pseudolus, that little maid. Do you know what her first words were to me? She said "Take me."

PSEUDOLUS (*Picking up potion bowl*): And you shall, sir.

SENEX: . . . I'll try.

PSEUDOLUS (*Exiting into* SENEX's *house*): Yes, sir.

SENEX (*Starting into* ERRONIUS's *house*): Remember, Hysterium. Not too hot and not too cold.
(HERO *runs on, calling*)

HERO: Philia! Philia!

SENEX (*Stops in doorway, turns*): Son!

HERO: Father! Where's mother?

SENEX (*Frightened, turns*): Where?!
(*Realizes*)
Oh. I — I have returned without her. Pressing business.
(PHILIA *appears on balcony of* SENEX's *house. Aside to* HERO)
Lovely new maid.

HERO: New maid?

SENEX: Pseudolus told me about it.

HERO: Oh.

SENEX (*To* PHILIA): Presently, my dear.
(PHILIA *exits into house, waving.* SENEX *turns to audience, sings*)

Why did he look at her that way?

HERO (*Sings, to audience*):
Why did he look at her that way?

BOTH:
Must be my imagination ...

SENEX:
She's a lovely blooming flower,
He's just a sprout — impossible!

HERO:
She's a lovely blooming flower,
He's all worn out — impossible!

SENEX:
Just a fledgling in the nest ...

HERO:
Just a man who needs a rest ...

SENEX:
He's a beamish boy at best ...

HERO:
Poor old fellow ...

SENEX:
He's a child and love's a test
He's too young to pass — impassable!

HERO:
He has asthma, gout, a wife,
Lumbago and gas — irascible!

SENEX:
Romping in the nursery ...

HERO:
He looks tired ...

SENEX (*To* HERO, *warmly*):
Son, sit on your father's knee.

HERO (*To* SENEX, *warmly*):
Father, you can lean on me.

BOTH (*To audience*):
Him?
Impossible!

HERO:
But why did she wave at him that way?

SENEX:
Why did she wave at him that way?

BOTH:
Could there be an explanation?

HERO:
Women often want a father,
She may want mine — it's possible!

SENEX:
He's a handsome lad of twenty,
I'm thirty-nine — it's possible!

HERO:
Older men know so much more ...

SENEX:
In a way, I'm forty-four ...

HERO:
Next to him, I'll seem a bore ...

SENEX:
All right, fifty!

HERO:
Then again, he *is* my father,

I ought to trust — impossible!

SENEX:

Then again, with love at my age,
Sometimes it's just — impossible!

HERO:

With a girl, I'm ill-at-ease . . .

SENEX:

I don't feel well . . .

HERO (*To* SENEX, *helplessly*):
Sir, about those birds and bees . . .

SENEX (*To* HERO, *helplessly*):
Son, a glass of water, please . . .

BOTH (*To audience*):
The situation's fraught,
Fraughter than I thought,
With horrible,
Impossible
Possibilities!

SENEX (*Calling to his house*): Pseudolus!
(*To* HERO)
Son, it grieves me to see a boy your age moping about the
house.
(PSEUDOLUS *enters, stirring potion*)
Pseudolus, I want you to take Hero to the baths.

HERO: Sir!

PSEUDOLUS: Very good, sir. Allow me to finish a brew master
Hero asked me to prepare.
(*To* HERO)
Master, I shall meet you in front of the baths of Aqua
Salina. You know where it is? Next to the harbor. And I
shall have a surprise for you.

HERO: Oh, yes. Yes, of course. Farewell, father. Farewell, Pseudolus.

(*Exits*)

SENEX: Well, he to his bath and I to mine.

(HYSTERIUM *enters from* ERRONIUS's *house, wiping hands on tunic*)

HYSTERIUM: Just the way you like it, sir.

SENEX: One thing more, Hysterium.

HYSTERIUM: Yes, sir?

SENEX: I shall need a complete change of garb. Let me see . . . my tunic with the tassels!

HYSTERIUM: Sir, it needs taking in.

SENEX: Well, take it in and bring it out!

(*Exits into* ERRONIUS's *house.* HYSTERIUM *exits into* SENEX's *house singing a bit of "I'm Calm."* LYCUS *enters from his house*)

LYCUS: Pseudolus! The girl! I want to know the worst. How is she?

PSEUDOLUS: She is very low.

LYCUS: Still smiling?

PSEUDOLUS: Laughing!

(LYCUS *reacts in horror*)

There is one hope! I have prepared a plague potion. If it is not too late, we may yet save her life.

LYCUS: Give it to her!

PSEUDOLUS: Yes!

(PSEUDOLUS *starts for* SENEX's *house as fanfare is heard and* PROTEAN, *dressed as* SOLDIER, *enters, carrying spear*)

SOLDIER: Ho, there!

(*They turn, stare at him with horror*)

65

I seek the house of Marcus Lycus.

LYCUS (*Stammering superbly*): Who heeks the souse of Mycus Leecus?

PSEUDOLUS (*A hand on* LYCUS's *shoulder*): Hold, sir.

LYCUS: But he . . . who . . .

PSEUDOLUS: You're not holding.
(*To* SOLDIER, *enunciating grotesquely*)
Who is he who seeks the house of Marcus Lycus?

SOLDIER: A foot soldier of Captain Miles Gloriosus!
(*Executes an elaborate salute. Fanfare*)

PSEUDOLUS: Smartly done!

SOLDIER: My captain has dispatched me to inform you that he is but half a league away. Prepare to greet him!
(*Salutes, exits. Fanfare*)

PSEUDOLUS: Half a league!

LYCUS: We have only moments!

PSEUDOLUS: I'll give her the potion!

LYCUS: Yes!

PSEUDOLUS: Yes!
(*Starts for* SENEX's *house*)

LYCUS: Wait!

PSEUDOLUS (*Returns to* LYCUS): What?

LYCUS: Don't leave me!

PSEUDOLUS: Why not?

LYCUS: He's coming!

PSEUDOLUS: I know he's coming!

LYCUS (*Takes bowl from him*): You speak to him. *I'll* give her the potion!

PSEUDOLUS: Wait! You can't give her the potion!

LYCUS: Why not?

PSEUDOLUS: You'll catch the plague!

LYCUS (*Hands him bowl quickly*): Oh, I don't want the plague!

PSEUDOLUS: I've got to give her the potion!

LYCUS: Yes!

PSEUDOLUS: Yes!

> (*Starts for* SENEX*'s house*)

LYCUS: Wait!

PSEUDOLUS: What?

> (*Returns to* LYCUS)

LYCUS: She is in the house of Senex!

PSEUDOLUS: What will we do? . . . Does he know which house is your house?

LYCUS: No!

PSEUDOLUS (*Points to* SENEX*'s house*): *This* is your house!

LYCUS: Will he believe it?

PSEUDOLUS: Get the girls!

LYCUS: Good!

PSEUDOLUS: I'll give her the potion!

LYCUS: And I'll get the girls!

PSEUDOLUS: Good!

LYCUS: Yes!

PSEUDOLUS: Yes!

> (*Starts for* SENEX*'s house*)

LYCUS: Wait!

PSEUDOLUS (*Returns to* LYCUS): *What is it??!!*

LYCUS: I forgot.

PSEUDOLUS: Lycus, we must not lose our heads!

LYCUS: Yes! No!

PSEUDOLUS (*Screams*): We must remain serene!

> (*Fanfare is heard*)

LYCUS: Pseudolus, *you* must speak to the captain! I have no talent for bravery.

PSEUDOLUS: You grant me permission to represent you?

LYCUS: Complete!

PSEUDOLUS: All right. Collect the courtesans and bring them out. Then you are to wait in your house.

LYCUS: Pseudolus, I am eternally grateful. I am your friend until death!

PSEUDOLUS: Go!

LYCUS: Yes!

PSEUDOLUS: Yes!

> (*Starts for* SENEX*'s house*)

LYCUS: Wait!

PSEUDOLUS (*Stops, yells*): No!

> (*A fanfare, and two* PROTEANS, *dressed as* SOLDIERS, *enter, come to a smart halt.* LYCUS *ducks into his house.* PSEUDOLUS *puts down potion bowl*)

SECOND SOLDIER: Ho, there!

THIRD SOLDIER: We seek the house of Marcus Lycus!

PSEUDOLUS: Who seeks the mouse of Larkus Heekus?

THIRD SOLDIER: Foot soldiers of Captain Miles Gloriosus.

SECOND SOLDIER: He is but a quarter of a league away and bids you honor this.
(*Hands* PSEUDOLUS *parchment*)

PSEUDOLUS (*Studies parchment*): Oh, yes, of course.

SECOND SOLDIER: You know what this is?

PSEUDOLUS: Of course I know what this is. This is writing.

THIRD SOLDIER: It is your contract with the captain.

PSEUDOLUS: And a pretty piece of work. What is this word here?
(*Points to spot on parchment*)

THIRD SOLDIER: That is "Lycus."

PSEUDOLUS: Oh, yes. Then you realize whom you are speaking to.

SECOND SOLDIER: Yes, sir.

THIRD SOLDIER: And do you see what it says there?
(*Points to another spot*)

PSEUDOLUS: It says . . . words. And I intend to stand behind those words, or my name is not Marcus Lycus!
(HYSTERIUM *enters*)

HYSTERIUM: Pseudolus!

PSEUDOLUS (*Without missing a beat*): Or my name is not Pseudolus Marcus Lycus! A moment. I must have a word with my eunuch.
(*Taking* HYSTERIUM *aside*)
Come here, eunuch!

HYSTERIUM: How dare you call me that?

PSEUDOLUS: You know it's not true, and I know it's not true, so what do we care what they think?

HYSTERIUM: Those soldiers, have they come for the girl? I'll go right in and get her.

PSEUDOLUS: They have not come for the girl. They have come for me.

HYSTERIUM: What?

PSEUDOLUS: Hysterium, I have never told you this, but years ago I deserted from the army.

HYSTERIUM: No!

PSEUDOLUS: Sh! I was very young. I wanted to be an archer. Instead, they made me a slinger. Then, one day, at the height of battle, I lost my head. I arched when I should have slung. I had to flee.

HYSTERIUM: And now they have found you. Oh, Pseudolus!

PSEUDOLUS: Sh! They are looking for Pseudolus. I told them I am Lycus.

HYSTERIUM: And Lycus you are! Rely on me!

PSEUDOLUS: I must.
　　　　　　　　(Picks up potion bowl)
Hysterium, more bad news!

HYSTERIUM: I hope it's good.

PSEUDOLUS: It's terrible! The girl refuses to go with her captain. That is why I have prepared your sleeping potion. You are to give her a drop or two in a beaker of wine, and upon hearing me say "Present the bride," carry her out in your arms!

HYSTERIUM: Trust me, Pseu—
　　　　　　　　(Catches himself, then loudly)

Trust me, Lycus!

(*Takes bowl from* PSEUDOLUS, *speaking for* SOLDIERS' *benefit*)

I go, Lycus. Farewell, Lycus!

(*Exits into* SENEX*'s house*)

PSEUDOLUS (*To* SOLDIERS): Bid your captain come! His bride awaits him!

(SOLDIERS *execute fancy salute, run off.* PSEUDOLUS *calls out*)

Lycus! The girls! Quickly!

LYCUS (*Opening his door*): Yes!

(*Calls into house*)

Eunuchs! The girls! Quickly!

(*To* PSEUDOLUS)

We shall pose them informally!

PSEUDOLUS: Give the place a friendly look.

(EUNUCHS *herd* COURTESANS *out of house*)

EUNUCH: Hurry, there! Hurry! Hurry!

GYMNASIA: Don't you lower your voice to me!

LYCUS: You are to do exactly as Pseudolus bids. He will represent me.

PSEUDOLUS (*Points to* SENEX*'s house*): All you girls over here! Now, you eunuchs . . .

(*Indicates manly pose he wants them to assume.* EUNUCHS *squeal with delight*)

Lycus, do we really need these eunuchs?

LYCUS (*To* EUNUCHS): Into the house.

EUNUCHS (*Chirping*): Into the house! Into the house!

(EUNUCHS *exit into* LYCUS*'s house.* PSEUDOLUS *arranges* COURTESANS)

PSEUDOLUS (*To* PANACEA): You there.
> (*To* TINTINABULA *and* VIBRATA)

You there.
> (*To* GEMINAE)

You there.
> (*To* GYMNASIA)

You there ... Oh, there's so much of you there!
> (*Leans on her bosom, as* ERRONIUS *enters*)

ERRONIUS (*To audience*): First time around!
> (*All watch as he crosses stage, exits*)

PSEUDOLUS (*To* COURTESANS): Now, may I have your attention? You are about to meet a great captain. Remember who you are and what you stand for. Now, will you all please strike ... vocational attitudes?
> (COURTESANS *strike poses*)

Perfect! I would like a mosaic of this scene. An entire wall made up of ...
> (*Fanfare is heard*)

LYCUS: The captain! Pseudolus, again my heartfelt ...

PSEUDOLUS: In! In!
> (LYCUS *exits into his house. A second fanfare is heard*)

MILES (*Offstage*): Stand aside, everyone! I take large steps!
> (*Enters with* SOLDIERS, *counting off, music under*)

SOLDIERS:
  One, two, one, two ...

MILES:
  We not only fought but we won, too!

SOLDIERS:
  One, two, one, two ...
  Left, right, left, right ...

MILES:

There's none of the enemy left, right?

SOLDIERS:

Right! Left! . . . uh . . . Ri — uh — left!

(*Utter confusion*)

MILES: Halt!

PSEUDOLUS (*Saluting*): Hail, Miles Gloriosus.

MILES: You are?

PSEUDOLUS: Marcus Lycus, sir. I am dazzled by your presence.

MILES: Everyone is.

PSEUDOLUS (*Indicating* SENEX*'s house*): Welcome to my house, great captain. Your bride awaits you.

MILES: My bride!

(*Sings*)

My bride! My bride!
I've come to claim my bride,
Come tenderly to crush her against my side!
Let haste be made,
I cannot be delayed!
There are lands to conquer,
Cities to loot,
And peoples to degrade!

SOLDIERS:

Look at those arms!
Look at that chest!
Look at them!

MILES:

Not to mention the rest!
Even I am impressed.

My bride! My bride!
Come bring to me my bride!
My lust for her no longer can be denied!
Convey the news,
I have no time to lose!
There are towns to plunder,
Temples to burn
And women to abuse!

SOLDIERS:

Look at that foot!
Look at that heel!
Mark the magnificent muscles of steel!

MILES:

I am my ideal!

I, Miles Gloriosus,
I, slaughterer of thousands,
I, oppressor of the meek,
Subduer of the weak,
Degrader of the Greek,
Destroyer of the Turk,
Must hurry back to work!

MILES:	COURTESANS:	SOLDIERS:
I, Miles Gloriosus,	Him, Miles Gloriosus,	A man among men!
I, paragon of virtues,	Him, paragon of virtues,	With sword and with pen!

MILES:	ALL:
I, in war the most admired,	Himmm!
In wit the most inspired,	Himmm!
In love the most desired,	Himmm!
In dress the best displayed,	
I am a parade!	

SOLDIERS:

Look at those eyes,
Cunning and keen!
Look at the size of those thighs,
Like a mighty machine!

PSEUDOLUS:

Those are the mightiest thighs that I ever have theen!
I mean . . .

MILES:

My bride! My bride!
Inform my lucky bride:
The fabled arms of Miles are open wide!
Make haste! Make haste!
I have no time to waste!
There are shrines I should be sacking,
Ribs I should be cracking,
Eyes to gouge and booty to divide!
Bring me my bride!

SOLDIERS:

Bring him his bride!

ALL:

Bring him his bride!
> (PSEUDOLUS *goes to* SENEX *'s house*)

PSEUDOLUS: Present the bride!
> (*Fanfare*)

Pay homage all! Here, in one being is Juno, Diana and
Venus.
> (*All kneel*)

Present the bride!
> (*Fanfare.* PSEUDOLUS *bows.* HYSTERIUM *enters. To* MILES)

A short delay, sir!
> (*Pulls* HYSTERIUM *aside*)

What happened?

HYSTERIUM: I'll tell you what happened! Nothing! She won't drink!

PSEUDOLUS: What?

HYSTERIUM: She says on Crete her religion forbids it.

PSEUDOLUS: He had to fall in love with a religious Cretan! *I'll* get her to drink! Captain, forgive the girl. She primps and preens. She wants to be worthy of so great a warrior.
    (*Exits into* SENEX *'s house with* HYSTERIUM)

MILES: Understandable. I *am* a legend in my own time.
    (*Laughs.* SOLDIERS *join in*)
Men! Close ranks! Stand tall!
    (PSEUDOLUS *enters from* SENEX *'s house*)
Lycus!
    (LYCUS *peeks out of upper window of his house, listens*)
Where is my bride?

PSEUDOLUS: Did she not come through this door?

MILES: No! What are you saying, man?

PSEUDOLUS: The virgin has escaped!

MILES: Oh, no! The beautiful bride I bargained for!

PSEUDOLUS: Vanished!

MILES: This is monstrous!

PSEUDOLUS: It certainly is. But look at it this way. Since I cannot deliver her to you, you do not have to pay me the five hundred minae.

MILES: I *paid* you the five hundred minae!
    (PSEUDOLUS *reacts*)
Through my agents. Has the money escaped as well?

PSEUDOLUS: There has been a little mistake.
    (*Laughs weakly*)

I was only joking. Lycus will pay you.

> (LYCUS *groans, disappears from window*)

MILES: What?

PSEUDOLUS: I was helping out a friend. Allow me, great captain.

> (*He goes to* LYCUS'*s house, pulls* LYCUS *out*)

Come out here!

> (*To* MILES)

Here is your man!

> (*To* LYCUS)

Tell him! Tell him who I am!

> (HYSTERIUM *enters*)

LYCUS: Everyone knows who you are, *Lycus*.

HYSTERIUM: Of course. He is Marcus Lycus.

PSEUDOLUS: No! No! *He* is Lycus. *This* is his house!

LYCUS (*To* MILES): Look within, sir. You will find none here but hooded men. We are a holy order. An ancient brotherhood of lepers.

> (MILES *backs away*)

Unclean! Unclean! And bless you, Lycus!

> (*He backs offstage*)

MILES: What now, Lycus?

PSEUDOLUS: What?

MILES: I shall tell you what! With axe and pike, my soldiers shall raze this house to the ground!

HYSTERIUM (*Fainting*): Our beautiful house!

MILES: And you, you shall receive the maximum punishment — death!

> (COURTESANS *scream*)

PSEUDOLUS: Please, sir, please! May I be allowed a word?

77

MILES: A word?

PSEUDOLUS: One word.

MILES: It had better be a good one.

PSEUDOLUS: Oh, it is, sir!

MILES: What is it?

PSEUDOLUS (*To audience*): Intermission!

(*Curtain*)

Zero Mostel as Pseudolus

The Proteans: Eddie Phillips, George Reeder, David Evans

"The House of Marcus Lycus"
Lycus (John Carradine) and Courtesans

PSEUDOLUS: "I think it might be of interest to the family that their slave in chief, their pillar of virtue has secreted within the confines of his cubicle Rome's most extensive and diversified collection of erotic pottery."
Pseudolus (Zero Mostel) and Hysterium (Jack Gilford)

"That Dirty Old Man" Hysterium (Jack Gilford) and Domina (Ruth Kobart)

VAN WILLIAMS

"Everybody Ought to Have a Maid" Lycus (John Carradine) Hysterium (Jack Gilford) Senex (David Burns) and Pseudolus (Zero Mostel)

VAN WILLIAMS

Original London Production

ZOE DOMINIC

82

Hysterium (Larry Blyden) and Pseudolus (Phil Silvers)

Domina (Nancy Walker) and Hysterium (Larry Blyden)

Pseudolus (Zero Mostel) and Lycus (Phil Silvers)

Erronius (Buster Keaton)

Hero (Michael Crawford) and Courtesans

Ernie Sabella, Nathan Lane

Nathan Lane, Mark Linn-Baker, Ernie Sabella, Lewis J. Stadlen

Whoopi Goldberg

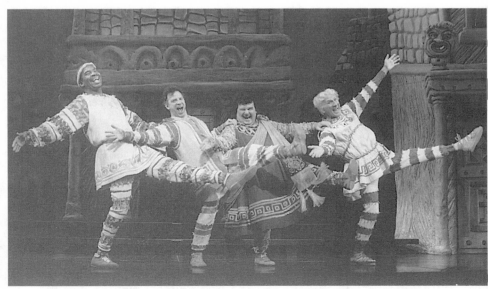

David Alan Grier, Ross Lehman, Ernie Sabella, Dick Latessa

ACT II

The scene is the same as Act I, but now PROLOGUS *is played by* SENEX *rather than by* PSEUDOLUS. *As characters enter, they assume the positions in which we last saw them at the end of Act I.*

PROLOGUS: Welcome again, playgoers. You are about to witness the second half of our play.
(*Signals orchestra, which plays under following*)
Permit me to remind you where we were when last you saw us. The virgin . . .
(PHILIA *enters*)
. . . was waiting . . . that's what they do best . . . waiting here in the house for her captain to claim her. She has refused to drink the potion on religious grounds.
(PHILIA *exits into* SENEX's *house*)
Lycus . . .
(LYCUS *enters*)
. . . skulks about the city, searching for Philia.
(LYCUS *exits*)
Hero . . .
(HERO *enters*)
. . . is at the baths where he sits and soaks.
(HERO *exits*)
His mother . . .
(DOMINA *enters, exits*)

87

. . . is on the way to the country to visit *her* mother. A hundred and four years old, and not one organ in working condition. The courtesans . . .

(COURTESANS *enter*)

. . . Miles Gloriosus and his mighty warriors . . .

(MILES, SOLDIERS *enter*)

. . . Hysterium and Pseudolus are here.

(HYSTERIUM, PSEUDOLUS *enter*)

And I, Senex, await the maid in my neighbor's house, hopefully about to sow my last oat, if memory serves. Let the play continue!

(*Exits into* ERRONIUS*'s house*)

PSEUDOLUS (*To* MILES): Sir! I . . .

MILES (*To* SOLDIERS): Gag him!

> (SOLDIER *grabs* PSEUDOLUS *from behind, clamps hand over his mouth*)

And now I rid Rome of a rascal!

> (*He pulls his sword back, and as he is about to send it into* PSEUDOLUS *at belly level,* PSEUDOLUS *whirls around, and the sword jabs* SOLDIER *in the rear.* SOLDIER *releases* PSEUDOLUS, *jumps away rubbing sore spot.* MILES *advances on* PSEUDOLUS)

You . . .

PSEUDOLUS: Sir!

> (MILES *stalks him, as* PSEUDOLUS *speaks glibly*)

The girl must be near at hand. If you kill me you deprive yourself of seeing a face so fair, a heart so pure, a body so undulating . . .

> (MILES *lowers his sword.* PSEUDOLUS, *sensing success, presses on*)

She is magnificence personified! If you had been born a woman, you would have been she!

MILES: As magnificent as that?

PSEUDOLUS: Yes, sir. Spare me! I am sure she can be found.

MILES: You are?

PSEUDOLUS: Yes, sir. I shall give you a list of ten or twenty places you might look for her.

MILES: *You* shall look for her!

PSEUDOLUS: Me? With this bad leg?
(*Limps horribly.* MILES *grabs him*)

MILES: With that bad leg!

PSEUDOLUS: Yes, it will do it good. And where may I deliver the girl? I mean, where will you be?

MILES (*Points to* SENEX's *house*): Waiting here in your house.

HYSTERIUM: No!

MILES: No?!

HYSTERIUM: I meant "yes," it just came out "no."

MILES (*To* PSEUDOLUS): And to assure your return . . . Men! You are to go with him.

PSEUDOLUS: Sir, before I go, a word with my eunuch.

MILES: Be brief.

PSEUDOLUS: Yes, sir. Come here, eunuch.
(*Pulls* HYSTERIUM *aside*)
Hysterium, this is what you must do. Hide the girl, up on the roof.

HYSTERIUM: Why?
(*They are both stumped, then* PSEUDOLUS *has the answer . . .*)

PSEUDOLUS: Why not? Go.

MILES (*To* SOLDIERS): He is not to stray from your sight.
(HYSTERIUM *exits into* SENEX's *house*)

89

PSEUDOLUS (*To* MILES): My eunuch is making sure the house is fit to receive so illustrious a visitor.

MILES: I have been put off enough for one day!
(*Turns to enter house, stops, as* ERRONIUS *enters*)

ERRONIUS: The second time around!
(*Exits, all watch him*)

MILES: Lycus!

PSEUDOLUS: Yes, sir!
(*Calls*)

Ready?

HYSTERIUM (*From inside* SENEX's *house*): Ready!

PSEUDOLUS: All is ready, sir. There is food and drink within. And the girls will sing and dance for you.
(COURTESANS *exit into* SENEX's *house*)

MILES: You have but one hour. Men, you are to hound his every step.
(*Exits into* SENEX's *house*. PSEUDOLUS *circles stage, followed by* SOLDIERS, *they exit*. SENEX *appears in window of* ERRONIUS's *house*)

SENEX: Hysterium!
(HYSTERIUM *re-enters*)

HYSTERIUM: Yes, sir!

SENEX: Tell the little maid I am almost ready.

HYSTERIUM: Sir, I must say this to you. Abandon this mad adventure! Think of your wife on the way to the country!

SENEX: *That*, Hysterium, is the country's problem.

HYSTERIUM: Yes, sir.

SENEX: Hysterium, one thing more. You know that potion

you prepare that so fills one with passion, one can almost perform miracles?

HYSTERIUM: Yes, sir. We have some left over from your last anniversary.

SENEX: Bring it to me now, slave-in-chief.
(*Exits into house*)

HYSTERIUM: Slave-in-chief! I wonder how many slaves-in-chief have a master in the tub, a house full of courtesans, and a virgin on the roof.
(*Exits into* SENEX*'s house, as* PSEUDOLUS *enters, closely followed by* SOLDIERS. *He does several intricate maneuvers which the* SOLDIERS *carefully follow. The maneuvers become more elaborate.* PANACEA *enters from* SENEX*'s house, and* SOLDIERS *follow her off*)

PSEUDOLUS (*To audience*): Just one hour. Pretending she was dead was the perfect plan. If only Philia had taken one sip . . . It still is the perfect plan, if I can only find a body. A body.
(*An inspiration*)
Gusto! Gusto, the bodysnatcher! He owes me a favor!
(*He runs off, not seeing* DOMINA, *who enters, addresses audience*)

DOMINA: Since sending my husband back to Rome, I have been haunted by the premonition that he is up to something low.
(*Calls*)
Hysterium!

HYSTERIUM (*Entering from* SENEX*'s house with cup*): Coming master . . . mistress! You're home!

DOMINA: And parched with thirst, ever-thoughtful Hysterium.
(*Reaches for cup, he pulls it away*)

HYSTERIUM: No! It's a potion!

DOMINA: What sort of potion?

HYSTERIUM: To make you thirsty. And you're already thirsty, so you don't need it.
                    (*Puts cup near* ERRONIUS*'s house*)

DOMINA: Thirst is the lesser of my problems. Hysterium, on the best of intuition, I believe my husband is fouling the nest.

HYSTERIUM (*Looking nervously at* ERRONIOUS*'s house*): No! Never!

DOMINA: Never? Old friend and confidant, you are talking to a woman who faces facts.
                    (*Sings*)
For over thirty years,
I've cried myself to sleep,
Assailed by doubts and fears
So great the gods themselves would weep!
The moment I am gone,
I wonder where he'll go.
In all your simple honesty,
You can't begin to know . . .
Ohhhh . . .
                    (*Wailing tenderly*)
I want him,
I need him,
Where is he?
                    (*Furiously*)
That dirty old man is here somewhere,
Cavorting with someone young and fair,
Disporting in every shameless whim,
Just wait till I get my hands on him!
                    (*Tenderly*)
I'll hold him,

Enfold him,
Where is he?

(*Furiously*)

That dirty old man, where can he be?
Profaning our vows for all to see,
Complaining how he's misunderstood,
Abusing me (if he only would!)

Oh, love,
Sweet love,
Why hide?
You vermin, you worm, you villain!
Come face,
Embrace
Your bride!
Wherever he is, I know he's still an

Angel,
My angel!
Where is he,
That dirty old man divine?
I love him,
I love him,
That lecherous, lewd, lascivious,
Loathsome, lying, lazy,
Dirty old man of mine!

MILES (*From inside* SENEX*'s house*): Why?

DOMINA: Ah, I hear him now!

MILES: Why must I always be surrounded by fawning admirers?

DOMINA: That is not my husband's voice. Tell me, who is in my house?

HYSTERIUM: I think it's a captain.

DOMINA: A captain?

HYSTERIUM: Yes . . . he thinks that . . . your house . . . is the . . .
I hope you do not object to my offering him your hospi-
tality.

DOMINA: Object? When I, myself, am the daughter of a
Roman general? Hysterium, I must meet him.

HYSTERIUM: You wouldn't like him. He's very vulgar.

DOMINA: All soldiers are, in a grand sort of way.
(MILES *appears in doorway*)

MILES: . . . interminable!
(*Shouts at* HYSTERIUM)
Bring more food and drink, eunuch!

HYSTERIUM (*To* DOMINA): You see?

DOMINA: Captain, I was just coming inside to give you a
proper welcome.
(HYSTERIUM *winces*)

MILES (*Thinking she is one of* LYCUS's *girls*): You are of this
house?

DOMINA: For years and years. You know, Captain, my father
was General Magnus.
(MILES *reacts*)
On the last anniversary of his death, I entertained over
two hundred officers.

MILES: Two hundred? By yourself?

DOMINA: Of course not. Hysterium here was a big help.
(HYSTERIUM *smiles proudly, then reacts painfully*)
But now my business takes me to the Forum, but I shall
return. And for the length of your stay I shall bend over
backwards to please you.

MILES (*Horrified*): That will not be necessary!
(*Exits into* SENEX's *house*)

DOMINA: I do wish I could chat on with him, but I must find out why my husband was so anxious to return to Rome. Hysterium, when next we meet I shall be in some form of disguise. If you recognize me, not a word.

(*Waving to* MILES, *who appears in door of house*)
Until later, Captain.

(MILES *moans, exits into house.* DOMINA *starts off, as* PSEUDOLUS *enters, sees her, starts polishing pillar*)
Ah, Pseudolus, busy as ever.

PSEUDOLUS: Yes, madam.

(*She exits.* PSEUDOLUS *rushes to* HYSTERIUM)
She's back!

HYSTERIUM: Yes!

PSEUDOLUS: What has happened?

HYSTERIUM: What *hasn't* happened?

PSEUDOLUS: All right, what *hasn't* happened? She hasn't found out anything, has she?

HYSTERIUM: No!

PSEUDOLUS: Good!

HYSTERIUM: But she will, and she'll kill me!

PSEUDOLUS: No, she won't!

HYSTERIUM: No, she won't. I'll kill myself! I can do it painlessly. If she does it, it will hurt. I must do it. I have besmirched the honor of my family. My father will turn in his grave.

PSEUDOLUS: Your father is alive.

HYSTERIUM: This will kill him!

PSEUDOLUS: Are you finished? Now, listen to this. I have really shocking news.

HYSTERIUM: What?

PSEUDOLUS: You know Gusto, the bodysnatcher?
>   (HYSTERIUM *nods*)

He died this morning.

HYSTERIUM: No! I saw him only yesterday. When is he to be buried?

PSEUDOLUS: They don't know. Someone snatched the body.

HYSTERIUM: Isn't that a sha — ?
>   (*Does a take*)

Why are we crying over a dead bodysnatcher?!

PSEUDOLUS: Because he could have helped us. He could have lent us a body.
>   (*Puts his hand on* HYSTERIUM*'s shoulder*)

HYSTERIUM: A body?

PSEUDOLUS: A body.
>   (*A gleam comes into his eye, starts running his hand over*
>   HYSTERIUM*'s shoulder and chest*)

A body. Hysterium, would you like everything to be the way it was when you woke up this morning?

HYSTERIUM: In a minute!

PSEUDOLUS: That's all it will take. Come!
>   (*Pulls* HYSTERIUM *to* LYCUS*'s house*)

HYSTERIUM: In here?

PSEUDOLUS: In here!

HYSTERIUM: Where did you get the money?
>   (PSEUDOLUS *pulls* HYSTERIUM *into* LYCUS*'s house.* SENEX
>   *enters from* ERRONIUS*'s house, inhales deeply*)

SENEX: Mmmmmmm.
>   (*To audience*)

Something smells divine, and it's me. I just took the most luxurious bath. The oil, the essences. Oh, spectators, I would love to pass among you so that each and every one might get a good whiff.

(*Calls*)

Philia!

(*To himself*)

Mustn't shout. I have to save every bit of energy.

(*Gently*)

Philia.

(PHILIA *appears on roof of* SENEX's *house*)

PHILIA: Yes, master? Master?

SENEX (*Looks around for her, then sees her on roof*): Ah, my dear. No need to dust up there. Come to me.

PHILIA: I am yours.

SENEX: Yes, my dear. But not on the roof. Join me in this house.

PHILIA: Yes, sir.

(SENEX *exits into* ERRONIUS's *house. As* PHILIA *disappears from roof,* MILES *appears on balcony of* SENEX's *house*)

MILES: Oh, where is he? If he does not bring me my bride he shall see me at the height of my wrath.

(*Looks down, gets dizzy, emits a tiny scream, and staggers back into house.* PHILIA *enters from* SENEX's *house, as* HERO *runs on*)

HERO: Philia!

PHILIA: In time to say farewell.

HERO: Did not Pseudolus give you a beaker of wine?

PHILIA: My religion forbids the drinking of wine.

HERO: Oh, no!

PHILIA: Oh, yes.

HERO: Oh, Philia.

PHILIA: The captain. I must go to him.

HERO: I hate him.

PHILIA: So do I. And I have a way to make him suffer.
(*Sings*)
Let the captain wed me and woo me,
I shall play my part!
Let him make his mad passion to me,
You will have my heart!
He can have the body he paid for,
Nothing but the body he paid for!
When he has the body he paid for,
Our revenge will start!

When I kiss him,
I'll be kissing you,
So I'll kiss him morning and night,
That'll show him!

When I hold him,
I'll be holding you,
So I'll hold him ten times as tight,
That'll show him, too!

I shall coo and tenderly stroke his hair.
Wish that you were there —
You'd enjoy it!

When it's evening
And we're in our tent for two,
I'll sit on his knee,
Get to know him
Intimately,
That'll show him

98

How much I really love you!
                    (PSEUDOLUS *enters from* LYCUS *'s house*)

HERO: Pseudolus!

PSEUDOLUS: What has happened? Why are you not on the . . . ?

HERO: Her captain has come!

PSEUDOLUS: Where is he?

PHILIA (*Points to* ERRONIUS *'s house*): In there.

PSEUDOLUS: In there . . . ?
                    (*Realizes she is referring to* SENEX)
No, no, he *was* in there. He had to go to the Senate for an unexpected ovation.

HERO: Really?

PSEUDOLUS (*Shaking his head no*): Of course.

PHILIA: Does he still want me to wait on the roof?

PSEUDOLUS: Yes.

MILES (*From inside* SENEX *'s house*): Leave me alone!

PSEUDOLUS: No! Wait — uh — in the garden!

PHILIA: In the garden?

PSEUDOLUS: Yes. Behind that large clump of myrrh!

PHILIA: You will tell me when he comes?

PSEUDOLUS: Don't we always?

PHILIA: Oh, Hero, if only you could come buy me from the captain.

PSEUDOLUS: If Hero has the captain's contract, you will go with him?
                    (PHILIA *nods yes*)

It shall be arranged. Into the garden.
> (HERO *and* PHILIA *exit into garden.* PSEUDOLUS *hums
> "Free" as he pushes bench center stage. He calls*)

Come out here! Come on out!
> (HYSTERIUM *enters from* LYCUS*'s house in virginal gown
> and wig*)

HYSTERIUM: You didn't tell me I'd have to be a girl!

PSEUDOLUS: A dead girl! The captain will see you, go on his
way, and all will be well.

HYSTERIUM: No! It won't do!
> (*He starts back into house.* PSEUDOLUS *stops him*)

PSEUDOLUS: Please, Hysterium. We must convince the captain.

HYSTERIUM: That I am a beautiful dead girl?

PSEUDOLUS: Yes.

HYSTERIUM: He'll never believe it.

PSEUDOLUS: He will. You're delicious.

HYSTERIUM: What if he tries to kiss me?

PSEUDOLUS: He won't kiss you.

HYSTERIUM: How can he help it — if I'm so delicious?

PSEUDOLUS: Hysterium, please — just lie on the bench.

HYSTERIUM: He'll never believe I'm a girl. Look at me. Just
look at me.

PSEUDOLUS: I can't take my eyes off you.
> (*Sings*)

You're lovely,
Absolutely lovely,
Who'd believe the loveliness of you?

HYSTERIUM: No!

PSEUDOLUS: Come back!
(*Sings*)
Perfect,
Sweet and warm and winsome,
Radiant as in some dream come true.
Now
Venus will seem tame,
Helen and her thousand ships
Will have to die of shame!
(HYSTERIUM *is becoming convinced;* PSEUDOLUS *presses his advantage*)
You're so lovely,
Frighteningly lovely,
That the world will never seem the same!
(*Gently forces* HYSTERIUM *to lie back on the bench, folds his arms. Speaks*)
Now, lie there, close your eyes, and think dead thoughts.
Good!
(*Starts into* SENEX*'s house, stops, with disgust, as* HYSTERIUM *sits up and sings*)

HYSTERIUM:
I'm lovely,
Absolutely lovely,
Who'd believe the loveliness of me?
Perfect,
Sweet and warm and winsome,
Radiant as in some dream come true.
(PSEUDOLUS *forces him down on bench*)
Now . . .
(*Speaks*)
Shouldn't I have jewelry?

PSEUDOLUS: Jewelry?

101

(*Thinks for a moment, takes* ERRONIUS's *ring from his finger, slips it on* HYSTERIUM)

HYSTERIUM: Flowers.

PSEUDOLUS: What?

HYSTERIUM: I should have flowers.
   (PSEUDOLUS *gives flower to* HYSTERIUM. *Sings*)
I'm so lovely,

PSEUDOLUS:
Literally lovely —

BOTH:
That the world will never seem the same —

PSEUDOLUS:
You look lovely —

BOTH:
That the world will never seem the same!
   (PSEUDOLUS *gets him down on bench once more, covers his face with the veil, and folds his arms*)

PSEUDOLUS: Fold the arms!

HYSTERIUM (*Sitting up*): Any coins he puts in my eyes, I keep!
   (PSEUDOLUS *pushes* HYSTERIUM *down*)

FIRST SOLDIER (*Offstage*): Ho, there!
   (SOLDIERS *run on in pursuit of* PANACEA, *who exits into* SENEX's *house.* PSEUDOLUS *stops* SOLDIERS)

PSEUDOLUS: I have been looking everywhere for you. Here is your captain's bride. Dead!
   (SOLDIERS *crowd around* HYSTERIUM)
Give her air!
   (*They jump back*)
You had best break the sad news to your captain.
   (SOLDIERS *are reluctant.* FIRST SOLDIER *is pushed for-*

ward by others. He enters SENEX's *house fearfully.* PSEU-
DOLUS *looks at* HYSTERIUM, *then to* SOLDIERS)
A virgin. A lot of good it did her.
(MILES enters with FIRST SOLDIER)

MILES: Oh, grievous day. Men, support me!
(SOLDIERS hold him)
How? How did she die?

PSEUDOLUS: Well, she just sort of rolled over and . . .

MILES: Spare me! I cannot control my tears. I must cry.

PSEUDOLUS: Go ahead, you'll feel better. Now that you have
seen her, sir, I suggest you depart and torture yourself no
longer. If you'll give me the contract, I — I shall dispose
of the body.

MILES: Ghoul! I will not leave without the comfort of a proper funeral service!
(HYSTERIUM *shakes his head no.* PSEUDOLUS *blocks* MILES's
view)

PSEUDOLUS: Sir, do you have time for that? I mean, isn't
there a war somewhere you should be — ?

MILES: Silence! I insist on conducting a funeral.

PSEUDOLUS: Yes, sir.

MILES: We need mourners.

PSEUDOLUS: We have them.
(To SOLDIERS)
Hold him firmly.
(SOLDIERS *hold* MILES. PSEUDOLUS *exits into* SENEX's
house)

MILES: The poor girl. To have died so young, without ever
having experienced . . . me.
(PSEUDOLUS re-enters)

PSEUDOLUS: Sir, they will be here presently. While we wait, would you like something to eat?

MILES: No, thank you.
(*Wails, then blubbers*)
Oh, her bridal bower becomes a burial bier of bitter bereavement.

PSEUDOLUS: Very good. Can you say, "Titus, the tailor, told ten tall tales to Titania, the titmouse?"

MILES: Do not try to cheer me. I am inconsolable!
(COURTESANS *enter from* SENEX*'s house, with a bit of black on their near-nakedness*)

PSEUDOLUS: Gather around, handmaidens of sorrow.

MILES (*Sings*):
Sound the flute,
Blow the horn,
Pluck the lute,
Forward . . . mourn!
(SOLDIERS *and* COURTESANS *wail so effectively that even* HYSTERIUM *is affected*)

PSEUDOLUS (*Tragically, over the body*):
All Crete was at her feet,
All Thrace was in her thrall.
All Sparta loved her sweetness and Gaul . . .
And Spain . . .

MILES:
And Greece . . .

PSEUDOLUS:
And Egypt . . .

MILES:
And Syria . . .

PSEUDOLUS:
And Mesopotamia . . .

MOURNERS:
All Crete was at her feet,
All Thrace was in her thrall.
Oh, why should such a blossom fall?
> (COURTESANS *pound on bench, frightening* HYSTERIUM, *who falls to the floor. He scrambles back on bench, lies there, his arms unfolded*)

MILES:
Speak the spells,
Chant the charms,
Toll the bells —

PSEUDOLUS (*To* HYSTERIUM):
Fold the arms!
> (HYSTERIUM *slowly folds his arms*)

Sir, on behalf of the body, I want to thank you for a lovely funeral. I don't know about you, but I've suffered enough. If you will just give me the contract, I shall take the body and . . .

MILES (*Paying him no attention*):
Strew the soil,
Strum the lyre,
Spread the oil,
Build the pyre!

PSEUDOLUS: A pyre? What kind of pyre?

MILES: A pyre of fire!

PSEUDOLUS: Oh, a fire pyre!

MILES: She must be burned!

PSEUDOLUS: Burned? Sir . . .

MILES: I want her ashes!

PSEUDOLUS: Captain, I implore you. It is not for us to destroy such loveliness. The Gods are awaiting her. They would not be happy if we sent up a charred virgin!

MILES: I cannot afford to offend the Gods.

PSEUDOLUS: Who can?

MILES (*Sings*):
 All Crete was at her feet,
 But I shall weep no more.
 I'll find my consolation as before
 Among the simple pleasures of war!
                              (*Speaks*)
 Bring me the contract.
                    (SOLDIER *hands him contract*)
 I give her to the Gods.
                    (*Puts contract on* HYSTERIUM)
 Take her then and lay her to rest. And I shall go my
 melancholy way. Men.
                         (*Starts to go, stops*)
 Wait. A farewell kiss.

PSEUDOLUS: Of course.
                    (*Kisses* MILES *on the cheek*)

MILES: Not you!
          (*Pushes him aside, bends over* HYSTERIUM)

PSEUDOLUS: Sir! You mustn't!

MILES: Why not?

PSEUDOLUS: It could make you very sick. The truth is, she
 died of an illness contracted on Crete.

MILES: What illness?

PSEUDOLUS: The plague!
          (*There is general pandemonium.* COURTESANS *scream
          "The plague, the plague!" and run about wildly, exiting in
          all directions*)

MILES: Silence!

PSEUDOLUS: The plague! The plague! Run for your lives!
                              (*To audience*)
   Don't just sit there! Run!
                       (MILES *grabs* PSEUDOLUS)

MILES: There is no plague!

PSEUDOLUS: What?

MILES: I have returned this day from Crete, and there is no
   plague.

PSEUDOLUS: Then what was everyone yelling about?
                       (LYCUS *enters, hides behind pillar*)

MILES (*Leans over* HYSTERIUM): This girl is alive!

HYSTERIUM (*Jumps up*): And she's going to stay that way!
                              (*Runs off*)

MILES: Stop! After her, men!
                       (SOLDIERS *run off*)

PSEUDOLUS: I'll get her!
                       (*Runs off in opposite direction*)

MILES: Wait!
                       (*Chases* PSEUDOLUS)

LYCUS: Now *all* the courtesans have escaped. Eunuchs! I
   stand to lose a fortune in flesh!
                       (EUNUCH *enters from* LYCUS *'s house*)
   Find the girls! Bring them back!
       (EUNUCH *exits, chattering.* LYCUS *exits.* HYSTERIUM *re-
       enters, hiding face with leafy branch*)

HYSTERIUM: I've got to get out of these clothes! I'm calm,
   I'm calm.
       (SENEX *enters from* ERRONIUS *'s house, spots* HYSTERIUM,
       goes to him)

SENEX: Ah, there you are, my little dove!
>(*Cooing*)
You don't have to be afraid of me.
>(*Leads* HYSTERIUM *to bench, seats him on his lap*)
My slave has prepared a little feast. I want you to serve it to me in there.
>(*Points to* ERRONIUS*'s house*)
Do you understand? Go, then.
>(HYSTERIUM *exits into* SENEX*'s house.* SENEX *exits into* ERRONIUS*'s house, singing "Everybody Ought to Have a Maid."* HYSTERIUM *pokes his head out of door and ducks back into house as he sees* EUNUCH *enter with* VIBRATA. EUNUCH *pushes her into* LYCUS*'s house, exits, chattering.* HYSTERIUM *starts out of house once more as* PSEUDOLUS *runs on, kicks him from behind*)

HYSTERIUM: Pseudolus!

PSEUDOLUS: I ought to give you worse than that! What did you do with the contract?

HYSTERIUM: I gave it to a soldier, He wants to meet me later tonight.

PSEUDOLUS: Well, get it. I need it.

MILES (*Offstage*): He dies!

PSEUDOLUS: Look out!
>(PSEUDOLUS *and* HYSTERIUM *run off in opposite directions.* MILES *runs on, runs off after* HYSTERIUM, *shouting*)

MILES: This way, men! I have found her!
>(SOLDIER *enters and runs off.* DOMINA *enters, disguised as virgin, removes veil from her face, addresses audience*)

DOMINA: If it's a pretty face he wants . . .
>(PSEUDOLUS *enters behind her, gives her a swift kick. She screams. He exits,* LYCUS *enters*)

How dare you!

(*She slaps* LYCUS)

SOLDIER (*Offstage*): Here she is! Men, the virgin!
(SOLDIER *runs on, chases* DOMINA *and* LYCUS *off.* EUNUCH *enters with* PANACEA *and* TINTINABULA, *pushes them into* LYCUS'*s house. He exits, chattering.* MILES *enters, as* DOMINA *re-enters*)

MILES: My virgin!

DOMINA: Sir, I am not anybody's virgin!

MILES: You made that more than clear when last we met!
(*He runs off.* HYSTERIUM *runs on, behind* DOMINA)

HYSTERIUM: The cause of it all!
(*Kicks* DOMINA *in the rear, she screams, he hides behind pillar, as* LYCUS *runs on*)

DOMINA: You, again!
(*Swings at* LYCUS, *misses, chases him off.* HYSTERIUM *runs to* LYCUS'*s house*)

HYSTERIUM: I have to get out of these clothes!
(SENEX *enters from* ERRONIUS'*s house*)

SENEX: No, no, my dear. Wrong house.
(*Chases* HYSTERIUM *around his house*)

HYSTERIUM (*As he comes around the first time*): Leave me alone!

SENEX (*Following him on the run*): Ah, you're beautiful when you're angry!
(HERO *appears on balcony of* SENEX'*s house*)

HERO (*Calls*): Philia! Philia!
(*Exits into house.* HYSTERIUM *re-appears from behind* SENEX'*s house*)

HYSTERIUM: Second time around!

(*Exits into* SENEX's *house.* PSEUDOLUS *runs on, chased by* SOLDIERS. PSEUDOLUS *leads them among the pillars, swings doors open, knocks two of them out and into the wings, trips* THIRD SOLDIER *who falls.* PSEUDOLUS *runs to him, takes contract from his belt.* HERO *appears on balcony*)

HERO: All is lost?

PSEUDOLUS: All is won! The contract! — This is what you must do —
(HERO *exits into house, as* MILES *runs on, sword drawn.* PSEUDOLUS *cowers*)

MILES: You die!
(LYCUS *runs on*)
The leper!

LYCUS: Unclean! Unclean!
(MILES *and* PSEUDOLUS *run off in opposite directions.* LYCUS *runs off.* SENEX *appears on roof of his house, coos*)

SENEX: I know you're up here somewhere, my dear. Philia! Philia!
(*He disappears from roof as* PHILIA *enters from behind* SENEX's *house*)

PHILIA: I thought I heard someone call my name.
(*Exits into* SENEX's *house.* Two EUNUCHS *enter carrying* GEMINAE. *All exit into* LYCUS's *house.* DOMINA *enters, hides behind pillar as* PSEUDOLUS, *disguised as* EUNUCH, *enters, chattering, leading* GYMNASIA, *exits with her into* LYCUS's *house*)

DOMINA: That is where my husband is!
(*Knocks on* LYCUS's *door*)
I know what goes on in there!
(PSEUDOLUS *appears in upper window of* LYCUS's *house*)

PSEUDOLUS: Who doesn't?

(DOMINA *goes to* SENEX's *house, cautiously looks around.
Unseen by her,* HYSTERIUM *enters from same house, looks
around, then* PHILIA *also enters from house, looking about.
They just miss seeing each other as they go in and out of
house. Suddenly they see one another, scream and run
behind* SENEX's *house.* PSEUDOLUS *enters from* LYCUS's
house, runs to SENEX's *house, opens door. As* PHILIA *runs
on from behind house, he pushes her through the doorway.
As* HYSTERIUM *passes,* PSEUDOLUS *kicks him and*
HYSTERIUM *tumbles into* ERRONIUS's *house.* DOMINA *chases after* HYSTERIUM. *She is followed by* SENEX *who catches
her at* ERRONIUS's *door, pushes her in*)

SENEX (*Triumphantly*): At last!

    (HERO *re-appears on balcony*)

PSEUDOLUS: Hero! The contract!

    (*Throws contract to him*)

To the harbor!

HERO: What will happen to you?

PSEUDOLUS: Nothing. Here is what I will do. I shall cause a
diversion. Then I shall drink a potion which will make
me appear as if dead.

    (HERO *exits into house.* SOLDIER *staggers to his feet*)

SOLDIER: You are under arrest!

    (PSEUDOLUS *blows at him,* SOLDIER *falls back down.* DOMI-
NA *enters from* ERRONIUS's *house, followed by* SENEX.
PSEUDOLUS *ducks into* SENEX's *house*)

DOMINA: Dearest Senex, you saw through my disguise!

SENEX: Yes, beloved.

    (*She embraces him. He looks around for* PHILIA)

DOMINA: Forgive me for mistrusting you. My darling, it's
just that you have been a little distant these last twenty-
nine years.

SENEX (*Backing off*): Yes, beloved, yes.
                              (*Exits, as she follows*)

DOMINA: Senex! Senex!

ERRONIUS (*Entering*): Third time around!
       (*Starts for his house, as* HYSTERIUM *is entering from same
       house. Seeing* ERRONIUS, *he runs back in*)
The spirit!
       (*Sneaks over to side of his house.* HYSTERIUM *peeks out of
       door, then tip-toes out, not seeing* ERRONIUS)
Who are you?!
       (HYSTERIUM *trips and falls.* ERRONIUS *helps him up*)
Let me help you.

HYSTERIUM: Thank you. I am quite all right.

ERRONIUS (*Seeing ring*): Wait!

HYSTERIUM: What is it?

ERRONIUS: My dear one! My sweet one! My little one!
                              (*Kisses* HYSTERIUM)

HYSTERIUM: Why do older men find me so attractive?

ERRONIUS: My daughter!

HYSTERIUM: What?

ERRONIUS: You wear the ring with the gaggle of geese!

HYSTERIUM: I am not your daughter!
              (MILES *and* SOLDIERS *run on, spot* HYSTERIUM)

MILES: There she is!

ERRONIUS: Yes!

MILES: My virgin!

HYSTERIUM: I am not a virgin!

ERRONIUS: Those filthy pirates!

112

HYSTERIUM: I am not your daughter! I . . . uh . . . I am an Etrus-
can dancer.

> (*Dances a few steps as* SENEX *re-enters*)

SENEX: Dancing with impatience, my dear?

MILES: Who is it speaks so boldly to my virgin?

SENEX: Your what? She is my maid!

ERRONIUS: She is my daughter!

> (*All tug at* HYSTERIUM)

HYSTERIUM: Please! No fighting! That hurts! Please!
> (*In the tussle, without knowing it,* HYSTERIUM *loses his
> wig*)

MILES: You are not the virgin!

HYSTERIUM (*Walks into* ERRONIUS'*s arms*): Of course not! I am
this old man's baby daughter.

SENEX: Hysterium!

MILES: The eunuch!

ERRONIUS: My daughter is a eunuch?

MILES: Seize that man!
> (*Points to* HYSTERIUM. SOLDIERS *point swords at him*)

DOMINA (*Entering*): Senex!

MILES: You, again?

SENEX: Sir, you are speaking to my wife!

MILES: You are married to that . . . that . . .

SENEX: Yes, I am married to that . . . that! And I shall thank
you to release my slave and remove yourself from in front
of my house!

MILES: Your house? This is the house of Lycus.

DOMINA: Lycus?

(*All babble at once*)

MILES: Quiet! I declare this area under martial law!

PSEUDOLUS (*Entering from* SENEX*'s house, indicating* HYSTERI-UM): Release that man!

MILES: Release that man!

(*Recognizes* PSEUDOLUS)

You!

PSEUDOLUS: Sir, this quivering creature is blameless. It is I, and I alone, who have caused you this grief.

MILES: Men, unseize him and seize him!

(SOLDIERS *surround* PSEUDOLUS)

And now, death by evisceration!

(PSEUDOLUS *reacts horribly*)

HYSTERIUM: Oh, Pseudolus!

PSEUDOLUS: Calm, my friend.

(*To* MILES)

Sir, I believe a doomed man is allowed a final request?

MILES: Yes.

PSEUDOLUS: Allow me to take my own life.

MILES: Sir, I have seen kings with less courage.

PSEUDOLUS: So have I. Hysterium, the potion. You know the one I mean.

HYSTERIUM: The potion?

(*Picks up cup from where he placed it earlier*)

PSEUDOLUS: Thank you, dear friend. Give the hemlock to Socrates.

HYSTERIUM (*To* SOLDIERS): Which one of you is Socrates?

114

PSEUDOLUS: Give me that!

> (*Takes cup, raises it*)

I go to sail on uncharted seas. To the harbor, to the harbor . . .

> (PHILIA *and* HERO *sneak out of* SENEX's *house, exit unseen*)

. . . from which no mariner returns. Farewell.

> (*Drains potion, dies noisily and elaborately.* MILES *leans over him*)

Kiss me!

> (*He apparently has taken the wrong potion. Jumps up*)

Somebody kiss me! Anybody!

> (*To* HYSTERIUM)

I could kill you . . . you darling!

MILES: Seize him!

> (SOLDIER *grabs* PSEUDOLUS)

PSEUDOLUS: Thank you! I needed that!

MILES: Stop that!

> (*Smacks* PSEUDOLUS *in back of head.* LYCUS *enters with* PHILIA. HERO *follows*)

LYCUS: Great Miles Gloriosus! I would not reveal my true identity until I could deliver that which I had promised. Sir, I am Lycus. Philia, go to the man who bought you.

> (PHILIA *sighs, goes to* SENEX. DOMINA *reacts*)

SENEX: No, no.

PHILIA: Aren't you the . . . ?

SENEX (*Whispers*): Quiet! We're under martial law.

LYCUS: *There* is the captain! Captain, here is your virgin.

MILES: And worth the waiting for.

> (*To* PSEUDOLUS)

Out of the great joy of the occasion, forgiveness. You are free.

PSEUDOLUS: Free . . . to be a slave.
(*Slumps against pillar*)

ERRONIUS: I cannot understand it. There was the ring. The ring with the gaggle of geese.

MILES: What did you say, old man?
(MILES *extends his hand*)

ERRONIUS: The ring!

MILES: Father!

ERRONIUS: You've grown!
(*They embrace*)

PHILIA (*Showing ring on chain about her neck*): Are these many geese a gaggle?

ERRONIUS: How long have you had this?

PHILIA: I've had this since, I don't know when I've had this since.

ERRONIUS: My daughter!

MILES: My sister?!

HYSTERIUM: Pseudolus, did you hear that?

PSEUDOLUS: Silence! Stand back, everyone! My dear old man, I take it your daughter is free born?

ERRONIUS: Without a doubt!

PSEUDOLUS: Lycus, as all of us know, the penalty for selling a free-born citizen is to be trampled to death by a water buffalo in heat!

MILES: Seize him!

LYCUS: Careful, I'm a bleeder!

PSEUDOLUS (*To* LYCUS): Bring out those girls!
(*To audience*)

I told you this was to be a comedy!
> (*As* LYCUS *brings* COURTESANS *out of his house*)
Hero!

HERO: Mother and father, I wish to marry.

SENEX (*Aside*): Son, if you are only as happy as your mother and I, my heart will bleed for you.

PSEUDOLUS (*Sings, to audience, indicating* HERO *and* PHILIA):
  Lovers divided
  Get coincided.
  Something for everyone —

HERO *and* PHILIA:
  A comedy tonight!

PSEUDOLUS (*Indicating* SENEX *and* DOMINA):
  Father and mother
  Get one another.

DOMINA:
  Something for everyone —

SENEX:
  A tragedy tonight!

MILES (*Holding the* GEMINAE):
  I get the twins!
  They get the best!

ERRONIUS:
  I get a family . . .

HYSTERIUM:
  I get a rest.

SOLDIERS (*Holding the other* COURTESANS):
  We get a few girls.

LYCUS:
  I'll get some new girls.

PSEUDOLUS:

I get the thing I want to be:
Free!

ALL:

Free! Free! Free! Free! Free!
(PSEUDOLUS *exits joyfully*)
Nothing for kings,
Nothing for crowns,
Something for lovers, liars and clowns!
What is the moral?
Must be a moral.
Here is the moral, wrong or right:

PSEUDOLUS (*Re-enters with* GYMNASIA):

Morals tomorrow!

ALL:

Comedy, comedy, comedy, comedy, comedy, comedy,
Comedy, comedy,
Tonight!

(*Curtain*)

Set and Costume Designs by Tony Walton

Above, the first sketch for the set; *below,* a model of the final set

119

PSEUDOLUS (E)   THE '86 HYSTERIUM & VIRGIN   THE   MILES GLORIOSUS   THE

DOMINA.   THE'8   SENEX (?)   THE GEMINAE   THE

120

ADDITIONAL LYRICS
with Commentary by Stephen Sondheim

"Invocation" and "Love Is in the Air"

"Invocation" was the original opening number for the show, but the director, George Abbott, felt that the tune wasn't hummable enough, so I replaced it with "Love Is in the Air," which we used during the tryout in New Haven and Washington. The problem with "Love Is in the Air" was that it misled the audience into believing that they were going to see a charming vaudeville instead of a knockabout farce. When Jerome Robbins came to Washington to help us out, he suggested to me that the opening number should be a bouncy song with a neutral lyric so that he could stage a collage of low-comedy vignettes against it. The result was "Comedy Tonight," which was staged with brilliant invention and which overnight turned the show from a flop into a hit.

"Invocation"

COMPANY (*To the Gods*):
　　Gods of the theater, smile on us.
　　You who sit up there stern in judgment, smile on us.
　　You who look down on actors (and who doesn't?),
　　Bless our little company and smile on us.
　　Think not about deep concerns,
　　Think not about dark dilemmas.
　　We offer you rites and revels,
　　Smile on us for a while.
　　　　　　(*To the audience*)
　　Gods of the theater, smile on us.
　　You who sit out there stern in judgment, smile on us.
　　Think not about deep concerns,
　　Think not about dark dilemmas.
　　We offer you rites and revels,
　　Bless our play and smile.

　　Forget war, forget woe,
　　Forget matters weighty and great,

121

Allow matters weighty to wait
For a while.
For this moment, this brief time,
Frown on reason, smile on rhyme.

Forget pomp, forget show,
Forget laurels, helmets and crowns,
Receive lovers, liars and clowns
For a while.
For this brief moment, this brief span,
Celebrate the state of man.

Forget war, forget woe,
Forget greed and vengeance and sin
And let mime and mockery in
For a while.

Gods of the theater, smile on us.
Gods of the theater, bless our efforts, smile on us.
We offer you song and dance,
We offer you rites and revels,
Grace and beauty,
Joy and laughter,
Sly disguises,
Wild confusions,
Happy endings.
If we please you,
Bless our play,
Smile our way.
Smile this moment, then at length
Go, and with a new-found strength

Resume war, resume woe,
Resume matters weighty and great,
Resume man's impossible state,
But now smile.
For this moment,
This brief stay,

Bless these players,
Bless this play!

"Love Is in the Air"

PROLOGUS *and* PROTEANS:
Love is in the air
Quite clearly.
People everywhere
Act queerly.
Some are hasty, some are halting,
Some are simply somersaulting,
Love is going around.

Anyone exposed
Can catch it.
Keep your window closed
And latch it.
Leave your house and lose your reason,
This is the contagious season:
Love is going around.

It's spreading each minute
Throughout the whole vicinity,
Step out and you're in it:
With all the fun involved,
Who can stay uninvolved?

Love is in the air
This morning.
Bachelors beware,
Fair warning:
If you start to feel a tingle
And you like remaining single,
Stay home, don't take a breath,
You could catch your death,
'Cause love is around.

"Farewell"

This song was written specifically for Nancy Walker when she agreed to play Domina in the 1971 revival.

Cue into "Farewell":

DOMINA: Senex, lead the way!

SENEX: Yes, dear.

DOMINA: Oversee the slaves.

SENEX: Yes, dear.

DOMINA: And Senex —

SENEX: Yes, dear?

DOMINA: Carry my bust with pride.

SENEX (*To audience*): A lesson for you all. Never fall in love during a total eclipse!

(*Exits*)

DOMINA (*Sings*):
Farewell, beloved son.
(*Kisses* HERO)
Farewell, devoted slave.
(HYSTERIUM *kisses her hem*)
Farewell, my ancestral home.
Farewell, my Rome.

Farewell, you temples and basilicae,
More rich than Athens or Pompeii.
Though country life be more idyllic, I
Could never long stay away.

Farewell, responsive son.
(*Kisses* HERO)
Farewell, respectful slave.
(HYSTERIUM *kisses her hand*)

Farewell, resplendent Rome.
Farewell, my home.
Farewell.

> (*Exits.* HYSTERIUM *starts to rise and* HERO *opens his mouth to talk to him when suddenly* DOMINA *re-enters;* HYSTERIUM *immediately falls to his knees again.* DOMINA *caresses her house*)

Farewell, inestimable domicile.
Farewell, domestic work of art.
Although I journey far, I promise I'll
Keep every portico,
Every pediment,
Every plinth in my heart —
I start.

Farewell, angelic son.
Farewell, efficient slave.
Farewell, exquisite Rome.
Farewell, my home.
Farewell!

> (*Exits. Again,* HYSTERIUM *and* HERO *start to continue the action, but again* DOMINA *re-enters*)

Could anyone conceive a view
More beautiful than this and these?
One look before I take my leave of you:

> (*Sentimentally, to* HYSTERIUM)

So scrub my atrium, leave it stainless.
Wash my architrave when it's rainless.
Keep my progeny chaste and brainless . ∴ .
Please,
No tears . . .

> (*Standing back from them*)

My frieze . . .
My dears . . .
Farewell, beloved son.

> (*Kisses* HERO)

125

Farewell, devoted slave.

> (*Is kissed by* HYSTERIUM)

Farewell, ancestral home.

Farewell, my Rome, farewell.

Farewell.

> (*Exiting, her voice fading into the distance*)

Farewell ... farewell ... farewell ... etc. ...

> (HYSTERIUM *and* HERO *wait until her voice has faded almost into nothingness, then start once more to resume the action only to have* DOMINA *re-enter again, this time from the other side of the stage*)

Farewell!

> (*She exits for good*)

The action continues with Hysterium's speech, "Well, to work, to work!"

"The House of Marcus Lycus"

This was cut down to a minimum because Burt felt strongly that the presentation of the girls from the House of Lycus should be either a dance or a song, but not both — and since there was so much singing in the expository first forty-five minutes of the show, we opted for the dance.

LYCUS (*As* FEMINA *enters and parades*): To make her available to you, I outbid the King of Nubia. Femina. With a face that holds a thousand promises . . . and a body that stands behind each promise.
> (*Sings*)
> Hot-blooded, cool-headed, warm-hearted, sly.
> Light-footed, dark-featured, dim-witted, shy.
> Only recently arrived from Greece,
> Likes her love experimental.
> Every inch of her a masterpiece —
> High standards, low rental . . .
> (*As* VIBRATA *enters, speaks*)
> Now may I present Vibrata. Exotic as a jungle bloom, wondrous as a flamingo, lithe as a panther . . . For the man whose interest is — wild life.
> (*Sings*)
> Uncanny, unnerving, unblemished, untaught,
> Unstinting, unswerving, unselfish, unbought.
> Here's potential that is still untapped,
> Here are fires still unstarted.
> Here are raptures that are still unwrapped,
> Whole sections uncharted . . .

LYCUS:	PSEUDOLUS:
	Hot-blooded, warm-hearted . . .
	Unselfish, uncharted . . .
There is merchandise for	Light-footed, dark-featured . . .
every mood	

127

At the House of Marcus Lycus.
There is latitude and longitude
At the House of Marcus Lycus.
'Neath the cherry-blossom
  and the quince
And the cooing of the dove,
At the House of Marcus Lycus,
Prince of Love.

Unblemished, dim-witted . . .
Cool-headed, low rental . . .
Unstinting, unswerving . . .

(*Speaks, as a very tall girl enters*)

And now — Gymnasia! A stadium of delight. A province
of mystery. A challenge to the intrepid explorer.

(*Sings*)

Expansive, explosive, exquisite and excruciating,
Exceeding exciting, exhausting but exhilarating . . .
Wait until the day she's fully grown —
She'll be useful on safari.
You could purchase her for shade alone
And never be sorry.

(*Speaks*)

What's that you say? "Hold! Enough! I am dazzled!" And
to that I say, but wait . . .

(*As twins enter*)

May I present the Geminae. A matched pair. Either one
a divinely assembled woman, together an infinite number of mathematical possibilities.

(*Sings*)

A banquet, a bargain, placed end to end.
A lifetime's provisions — invite a friend.
Feast until you're fully satisfied,
Gorge on gorgeousness compounded.
Face the future side by side by side,
Completely surrounded . . .

PSEUDOLUS:
Completely . . .

LYCUS:
No taxes . . .

A lifetime's . . .

128

Don't handle . . .

Unblemished . . .

One birthmark . . . A banquet . . .

A bargain . . . Exhausting . . .

Don't *do* that! A lifetime's . . .

GIRLS:
You can feast until
  you're satisfied
At the House of
  Marcus Lycus.
Face the future side
  by side by side
At the House of
  Marcus Lycus.
For a sense of
  sensuality
And a plethora
  thereof . . .

LYCUS:
  One is ecstasy,
  One is mystery,
  One is six foot three,
  Two is company —
  At the House of Marcus Lycus,
  Merchant of Love!

(*Speaks*)

And need I add, as all who are of the House of Lycus,
these beauties are well-versed in the arts, proficient at
needlework and surprised at nothing.

"Your Eyes Are Blue"

*This song was written for Hero and Philia when they first meet
in Act I. We used it during the New Haven tryout, but cut it when
our two young leading players, Pat Fox and Karen Black, were
replaced by Brian Davies and Preshy Marker.*

HERO:

    Once upon a time
    It happened there lived a boy
    Who loved a girl . . .
    Your eyes are blue . . .
    And every single night
    He'd see her across the way.
    I'd want to say —
    He'd want to say,
    "Your eyes are blue
    And I love you."

    But never had they spoken,
    Never had he dared.
    Beautiful as she was,
    I was —
    He was
    Scared.

    Then suddenly one day
    He met her, and he could see
    Her eyes were blue
    As they could be.
    What did he do?
    Well . . .
    You tell me.

    Once upon a time —

PHILIA:

    Let me try —
    "There lived a boy . . . "

HERO:

"Who loved a girl . . . "

PHILIA:

"Whose eyes were —
Blue!"
And every single night
She'd see him across the way.
She hoped he'd say,
"Your eyes are blue
And I love you!"
And yet she knew . . .

There was a wall between them
Built around his heart.
This was their dilemma,
Keeping them apart,
When suddenly one day
She met him . . .
He looked so tall . . .

HERO:

He felt so small . . .

PHILIA:

What did he do

To break the wall?

HERO:

What could he do

To break the wall?

(*They kiss*)

BOTH:

And that was
All.

"*I Do Like You*"

This number was to be sung by Hysterium and Pseudolus in Act I just before Hysterium goes off to the country to snitch on Pseudolus. It never got beyond the early stages of rehearsals for reasons too dimly buried for me to remember. It was replaced by Pseudolus's "erotic pottery" speech.

PSEUDOLUS:
Friend,

Good
Friend and true,

I worship
You.

I
Want to do,
Want to be
Like my
Friend.
Do
What you must.

I'm
Happy just
Being
A copy of the one I
Trust.

HYSTERIUM:
Oh, today it's
"Friend" . . .
Yes,
It's always
"Friend" . . .

When you need a
Friend.

"Friend, friend, friend, friend,
Friend" . . .
That's
What I in-
Tend . . .
Well, goodbye, old
Friend . . .

PSEUDOLUS:
   I like to do like you like to do,
   'Cause I like you . . .

HYSTERIUM:
   Oh, Pseudolus!

PSEUDOLUS:

> You do a deed,
> I follow your lead,
> 'Cause I like you.

HYSTERIUM:

> Oh, Pseudolus!

PSEUDOLUS:

> You climb a tree,
> I climb with you.
> You give a smile,
> I smile.
> You take a journey,
> I'm with you!
> Whatever you'll do,
> I'll.
>
> No one is perfect,
> You have your flaws,
> But I don't care.
> I have the flaws
> That you have because
> I want to share.
> You're all the things
> I most admire,
> All I aspire
> To.
> I do like you
> Because I do like you.

PSEUDOLUS:

And the best you
Have . . .
Yes,
I thought I
Would . . .

HYSTERIUM:

Friend,

You've touched me
So.

I didn't

No, you never
Do . . .

Deeper than you
Think . . .
You don't have to
Die . . .
I know how you
Feel . . .

Know
Such deep devotion
Existed and
Friend,
I'd rather
Die
Than say good-
Bye.
Friend, just as
Soon as I get back I'll cry.

PSEUDOLUS:

    I like to do like you like to do,
    That's how I feel.
    You ruin me, and I ruin you,
    You're my ideal.
    We each have had a fling
    Or two
    Nobody knows but we.
    You tell a little thing
    Or two,
    I tell a thing or three.

    You keep a secret, I keep a secret
    Like I should.
    You tell a secret, I tell a secret
    Twice as good.
    Since you're the model I take after
    That's what I'd have to do.
    I have to do like you like,
    Only because I do like
    You.

PSEUDOLUS *and* HYSTERIUM:

    Reciprocation in the end
    Is why a friend
    Is true.
    How could I ever doubt you?
    Knowing so much about you.
    I do like you
    And still I do like you.

"There's Something About a War"

This never even got into rehearsal. Burt felt that there should be no political or satirical edge to any of the songs, since the show was to be strictly a domestic farce and not a commentary. It was replaced by "Bring Me My Bride" (which, incidentally, used the only line in the show directly translated from Plautus: "I am a parade").

MILES (*Entering, with the* PROTEANS *dressed as* SOLDIERS):
Stand aside there, I take large steps!

SOLDIERS:
One-two, one-two!

MILES:
We not only fought but we won, too!

SOLDIERS:
One-two, one-two!
Left-right, left-right!

MILES:
There's none of the enemy left, right?

SOLDIERS (*Confused*):
Right! Left-right, left-left-uh-right!

MILES:
Halt!
(*Front*)
I don't know how to say it,
But there's something about a war.
Mere words cannot convey it,
But there's something about a war.
It's noisy and it's crowded and you have to stand in line,
But there's something about a war
That's divine!

135

You march until you're bleary,
But there's something about a war.
The company is dreary,
But there's something about a war.
Your fingernails get broken and the food is often vile,
But there's something about a war
Makes you smile.

The rain may rust your armor,
Your straps may be too tight,
But decapitate a farmer
And your heart feels light!

There's something about a war,
Something about a war,
Something about a war
That makes this little old world all right.

MILES *and* SOLDIERS (*Variously*):
    Oh, it's tread, tread, tread
    Through the mud, mud, mud
    And it's shed, shed, shed
    All the blood, blood — yich!

MILES, *then* SOLDIERS:
    There's something about a war.

MILES *and* SOLDIERS (*Variously*):
    Oh, it's plunge, plunge, plunge
    Through the dust, dust, dust
    And it's lunge, lunge, lunge
    And it's thrust, thrust — oooh!

MILES, *then* SOLDIERS:
    There's something about a war.

ALL:
    You know it isn't massacres and laughter all day long,
    Still there's something about a war —

A SOLDIER:

> Like a song!

MILES:

> A warrior's work is never done,
> He never can take a rest.
> There always are lands to overrun
> And people to be oppressed.

SOLDIERS (*Variously*):

> There's always a town to pillage,
> A city to be laid to waste.
> There's always a little village
> Entirely to be erased.
> And citadels to sack, of course,
> And temples to attack, of course,
> Children to annihilate,
> Priestesses to violate,
> Houses to destroy — hey!
> Women to enjoy — hey!
> Statues to deface — hey!
> Mothers to debase — hey!
> Virgins to assault — hey!

MILES:

> Halt — hey!

> (*Front*)
> It's hurry, hurry, hurry,
> But there's something about a war.
> It's worry after worry,
> But there's something about a war.
> It isn't all the drama and heroics it may seem —

ALL:

> But there's something about a war
> That's a scream!

MILES:

> There's never time for reading,

Yet there's something about a war.
The elephants keep breeding,
But there's something about a war.
You frequently feel lonely when the enemy has gone,
Still there's something about a war
That goes on!

ALL:

And on! And on!

MILES:

You sulk when someone's suing
For temporary truce,
Then another war starts brewing
And soon breaks loose!

ALL:

There's something about a war,

MILES, *then* SOLDIERS:

Something about a war —

MILES:

It isn't just the glory or
The groaning or the gorier
Details that cause a warrior
To smirk.

SOLDIERS:

Left-right!

ALL:

It's the knowledge that he'll never be out of work!

"Echo Song"

"Echo Song" was cut in New Haven during the tryout because the whole show wasn't working properly and this number (among many others) didn't make enough impact on the audience. It was replaced by "That'll Show Him," which was transferred from Act I to Act II. Burt Shevelove and I decided to resuscitate "Echo Song" for the 1971 revival, where once again it didn't work. It did seem, however, to be more effective than "That'll Show Him" if for no other reason than that it offered some funny staging opportunities.

Cue into "Echo Song" (replacing the one into "That'll Show Him"):

HERO: I hate him.

PHILIA: So do I.

HERO: What shall we do?

PHILIA: If you ask the Gods for guidance, they sometimes answer you by echoing your words.

HERO: Echoing your words?

PHILIA: Instead of those other things. Like thunder.
                    (*Music under*)

HERO (*Looking at the roof, getting an idea*): Perhaps if you were alone the Gods would listen more closely.

PHILIA: Perhaps. I shall pray.
        (*As she starts to sing, facing front,* HERO *clambers to the roof to answer her hollowly as a god*)
    Tell me . . .
    Dare I ask it? . . .
    Should I love him? . . .
    Shall I leave with him? . . .
    Tell me . . .
    Should I leave right now? . . .
    I hear my heart say,

139

"Let him live with me!"
Should I hear my heart and go?
(Turns away discouraged, tries again)

Tell me . . .   HERO *(Sings)*:
                                       (Tell me . . .)

Dare I ask it? . . .
                                       (Ask it.)

Should I love him? . . .
                                       (Love him!)

Shall I leave with him? . . .
                                       (Leave with him, leave with
                                       him!)

Tell me . . .
                                       (Tell me . . .)

Should I leave
   right now? . . .
                                       (Right now!)

I hear my heart say,
"Let him live with me!"
                                       (Live with me, live with me!)

Should I hear my heart
   and go?
                                       (Go! Go!)

Or should I, worthy, wait here
Till I meet my fate here?
Tell me, tell me, I must know.
                                       (No, no, no . . .)

Tell me . . .
                                       (Tell me . . .)

Should I hold him? . . .
                                       (Hold him!)

Or forget him
                                       (Get him!)

And forego my love?
                                       (Go, my love! Go, my love!)

Thank you!

I believe, now!

I must hurry,

So I'll say goodbye.

Only one more question,
  please —

Does he want me?

Would he miss me?

Must I pay the debt I owe?

Or may I go with Hero,
My beloved Hero?
Tell me yes, so I may know.

(Thank you!)

(Leave now!)

(Hurry!)

(Say goodbye, say goodbye!)

(Please! Please! Please!)

(Does he!)

(Would he!)

(Oh . . . Oh . . .)

(Ye — N — Y- N - Yes!)

(At the end of the song, PHILIA *realizes that it is* HERO *she has been listening to, and looks up to see him)*

PHILIA: Oh, Hero, you have enraged the Gods!

HERO (*Jumping down*): I don't care!

PHILIA: But they will strike you down.

HERO: Oh, let them. I would die for love of you!

PHILIA: You would die for me?

HERO: Die dead.

PHILIA: Oh, Hero, if you could get the contract from the Captain, I would go with you.

HERO: Dare I dare believe what you are saying?

PHILIA: You dare dare.

(PSEUDOLUS *enters from* LYCUS *'s house*)

141

"The Gaggle of Geese"

This song never got into rehearsal. It was cut because the situation that gave rise to it was cut when we were shortening the script. The situation: Pseudolus, for reasons too complicated to explain here, had drunk a knock-out potion and was lying unconscious in front of Erronius's house, wearing the ring with the gaggle of geese. While Hysterium is trying desperately to bring him back to life, Erronius stumbles on, trips over the body, sees the ring and assumes that Pseudolus is his long-lost son, stolen in infancy by pirates.

ERRONIUS (*Suddenly emits a series of inarticulate cries, to music*):
    Eeeeh! Aaaahh!
                    (HYSTERIUM *reacts;* ERRONIUS *staggers*)
    Aaahh! Eeeeh!

HYSTERIUM (*ad lib*): What's the matter?

ERRONIUS:
    Aahh . . . eeehh . . . aahh . . . eeehh . . . eeehh . . . aahh . . .
    The ring! The ring!

HYSTERIUM: What ring?

ERRONIUS:
    He's wearing the ring!
    The ring with the gaggle of geese!

HYSTERIUM: Gaggle of *what?*

ERRONIUS:
    It's proof! You see?
    There only are three!
    They're worn by my children and me!

HYSTERIUM: I don't follow . . .

ERRONIUS:
    The family crest, the gaggle of geese,
    The ring with the galloping gaggle of geese!

142

The Gods above
Have answered my call!
Release every dove
From Carthage to Gaul!
Light welcoming fires, let trumpets and lyres
Proclaim it to one and to all:
THIS IS MY SON!

The gaggle of geese, the gaggle of geese,
It *is* the gaggle of geese,
For years I've sought the gaggle of geese,
And here is the gaggle of geese
At last, the gaggle of geese!

The gaggle of geese, the gaggle of geese!
It's not a covey of quails,
It's not a flight of nightingales,
It isn't a school of whales,
It must be a gaggle of geese!

Sing paeans of jubilation
In celebration!
Send runners with torches burning
To mark my son's returning!

The gaggle of geese, the gaggle of geese!
Ring out . . . the gaggle . . . the bells . . .
The geese . . . My son . . . the gaggle . . . is home . . .
Again . . . with the gaggle . . . he wears . . .
To stay . . . with the gaggle . . .

My heart has joy,
My mind has peace,
I've found my boy
With the gaggle of — look! The gaggle of — see! The
    gaggle of — yes!
The gaggle of — this! The gaggle of — there!
                    (*Speaking, music under*)

143

Hysterium, why are you sitting around?
It isn't enough that my son has been found!
My daughter, my daughter, yes, where is my daughter?
And why is my boy lying down on the ground?
Do something at once! He's obviously
Completely exhausted from searching for me.
Go get a physician!
No, stay with him here and *I'll* get a physician —
No, first I will seek that sayer of sooth —
He'll certainly know where my daughter must be!
My son being here, she ought to be near . . .
Not here . . . but where? . . . Nearby, but where? . . .
He'll know . . . I go . . .
Goodbye . . .
Hello,
My beautiful boy!
  (*Covers the prostrate* PSEUDOLUS *with kisses; a great smile
  spreads over* PSEUDOLUS *'s face*)
The family crest
Was put to the test
And half of my quest
Is done!
I have at long last found my long-lost son!
  (*He starts offstage, bumps into the sundial, pats it affec-
  tionately*)
Forgive me, my child . . . Go back to your game . . .
  (*Continues off, bumps into proscenium, calls into wings*)
Wait for me, daughter, wherever you are! . . .
  (*Exits*)

MAJOR PRODUCTIONS

A Funny Thing Happened on the Way to the Forum was first presented by Harold Prince at the Alvin Theatre, New York City, on May 8, 1962, with the following cast:

(In order of appearance)

PROLOGUS	Zero Mostel
THE PROTEANS	Eddie Phillips, George Reeder, David Evans
SENEX, *a citizen of Rome*	David Burns
DOMINA, *his wife*	Ruth Kobart
HERO, *his son*	Brian Davies
HYSTERIUM, *slave to Senex and Domina*	Jack Gilford
LYCUS, *a dealer in courtesans*	John Carradine
PSEUDOLUS, *slave to Hero*	Zero Mostel
TINTINABULA	Roberta Keith
PANACEA	Lucienne Bridou
THE GEMINAE	Lisa James, Judy Alexander
VIBRATA	Myrna White
GYMNASIA	Gloria Kristy
PHILIA	Preshy Marker
ERRONIUS, *a citizen of Rome*	Raymond Walburn
MILES GLORIOSUS, *a warrior*	Ronald Holgate

Production Directed by George Abbott
Choreography and Musical Staging by Jack Cole
Settings and Costumes by Tony Walton
Lighting by Jean Rosenthal
Orchestrations by Irwin Kostal *and* Sid Ramin
Musical Direction by Harold Hastings
Dance Music Arranged by Hal Schaefer

145

The following songs were cut prior to the New York opening: *"Invocation," "Love Is in the Air," "The House of Marcus Lycus"* (the complete version), *"Your Eyes Are Blue," "I Do Like You," "There's Something About a War," "Echo Song,"* and *"The Gaggle of Geese."*

A Funny Thing Happened on the Way to the Forum gave its first performance at the Shubert Theatre, New Haven, Connecticut, opening on March 31, 1962 and closing on April 7th after 8 performances and 1 preview. The show then moved to the National Theatre, Washington, D.C., opening on April 11th and closing on April 28th after 22 performances. Previews began in New York City on May 2, 1962, and the show opened on May 8th and closed on August 29, 1964 after 964 performances and 7 previews.

AWARDS

Tony Awards: Best Musical, Best Producer of a Musical (Harold Prince), Best Book of a Musical (Burt Shevelove and Larry Gelbart), Best Direction of a Musical (George Abbott), Best Actor in a Musical (Zero Mostel), Best Supporting or Featured Actor in a Musical (David Burns). Also received Tony nominations for Best Supporting or Featured Actor in a Musical (Jack Gilford) and Best Supporting or Featured Actress in a Musical (Ruth Kobart).

A Funny Thing Happened on the Way to the Forum was first presented in London by Harold Prince, Tony Walton and Richard Pilbrow, by arrangement with Send Manor Trust Ltd., at the Strand Theatre on October 3, 1963 for 762 performances, with the following cast:

(In order of appearance)

PROLOGUS	Frankie Howerd
THE PROTEANS	Ben Aris, George Giles, Malcolm Macdonald
SENEX, *a citizen of Rome*	"Monsewer" Eddie Gray
DOMINA, *his wife*	Linda Gray
HERO, *his son*	John Rye
HYSTERIUM, *slave to Senex and Domina*	Kenneth Connor
PSEUDOLUS, *slave to Hero*	Frankie Howerd
LYCUS, *a dealer in courtesans*	Jon Pertwee
TINTINABULA	Norma Dunbar
PANACEA	Christine Child
THE GEMINAE	Marion Horton, Vyvyan Dunbar
VIBRATA	Faye Craig
GYMNASIA	Sula Freeman
PHILIA	Isla Blair
ERRONIUS, *a citizen of Rome*	Robertson Hare
MILES GLORIOSUS, *a warrior*	Leon Greene

Production Directed by George Abbott
Musical Numbers originally staged by Jack Cole *re-staged by* George Martin
Settings and Costumes by Tony Walton
Lighting by Jean Rosenthal
Orchestrations by Irwin Kostal *and* Sid Ramin
Musical Direction by Alyn Ainsworth
Dance Arrangements by Hal Schaefer

147

A Funny Thing Happened on the Way to the Forum was revived by the Center Theatre Group of Los Angeles (Robert Fryer, Managing Director) at the Ahmanson Theatre, Los Angeles, California, October 13 – November 20, 1971 for 47 performances, with the following cast:

PROLOGUS	Phil Silvers
SENEX, *a Roman citizen*	Lew Parker
DOMINA, *his wife*	Nancy Walker
HERO, *his son, in love with Philia*	John Hansen
HYSTERIUM, *slave to Senex and Domina*	Larry Blyden
PSEUDOLUS, *slave to Hero*	Phil Silvers
LYCUS, *a buyer and seller of courtesans*	Carl Ballantine
ERRONIUS, *an old man*	Reginald Owen
MILES GLORIOSUS, *a warrior*	Carl Lindstrom
TINTINABULA, *a courtesan*	Ann Jillian
PANACEA, *a courtesan*	Gloria Mills
THE GEMINAE, *courtesans*	Trish Mahoney, Sonja Haney
VIBRATA, *a courtesan*	Keita Keita
GYMNASIA, *a courtesan*	Charlene Ryan
PHILIA, *a virgin*	Pamela Hall
THE PROTEANS	Marc Breaux, Marc Wilder, Joe Ross

Directed by Burt Shevelove
Choreography by Ralph Beaumont
Settings by James Trittipo
Costumes by Noel Taylor
Lighting by H. R. Poindexter
Orchestrations by Irwin Kostal *and* Sid Ramin
Musical and Vocal Direction by Jack Lee
Dance Music Arranged by Hal Schaefer

148

Additional Dance Music by Richard De Benedictis
Production Associate, Robert Linden

For this revival a new song, *"Farewell,"* was written for Nancy Walker (DOMINA); *"That'll Show Him"* was dropped; *"Echo Song"* was added for PHILIA and HERO.

This production was subsequently presented in New York City by David Black, in association with Seymour Vail and Henry Honeckman, and produced by Larry Blyden at the Lunt-Fontanne Theatre. Prior to its Broadway engagement, the revival played at the McVickers Theatre, Chicago, February 28 – March 25, 1972, and opened in New York on March 30, 1972 and closed August 12, 1972 after 156 performances and 3 previews.

Lizabeth Pritchett replaced Nancy Walker as DOMINA; Lauren Lucas replaced Ann Jillian as TINTINABULA; Bill Starr and Chad Block replaced Marc Breaux and Marc Wilder as two of the PROTEANS; musical and vocal direction was by Milton Rosenstock. The song *"Pretty Little Picture"* was dropped.

AWARDS

Tony Awards: Best Actor in a Musical (Phil Silvers) and Best Supporting or Featured Actor in a Musical (Larry Blyden). Also received a Tony nomination for Best Direction of a Musical (Burt Shevelove).

A Funny Thing Happened on the Way to the Forum was revived in London by Richard Pilbrow, Pamela Hay and Norman Rothstein for Theatre Projects Associates, in association with David Bulasky and Geoffrey Young, at the Piccadilly Theatre, November 14, 1986 for 49 performances, with the following cast:

PSEUDOLUS, *slave to Hero*	Frankie Howerd
SENEX, *a citizen of Rome*	Patrick Cargill
DOMINA, *his wife*	Betty Benfield
HERO, *his son*	Graeme Smith
HYSTERIUM, *slave to Senex and Domina*	Ronnie Stevens
LYCUS, *a buyer and seller of courtesans*	Fred Evans
ERRONIUS, *an old man*	Derek Royle
MILES GLORIOSUS, *a warrior*	Leon Greene
PHILIA, *a virgin*	Lydia Watson
THE PROTEANS	Max Cane, Richard Drabble, Chris Eyden
THE GEMINAE	Julie and Tracy Collins
GYMNASIA	Elizabeth Elvin
TINTINABULA	Claire Lutter
VIBRATA	Sharon Stephens
PANACEA	Billi Wylde

Directed by Larry Gelbart
Choreography and Musical Staging by George Martin
Settings and Costumes by Tony Walton
Lighting by Robert Ornbo
Musical Direction by Godfrey Salmon

150

The motion picture of *A Funny Thing Happened on the Way to the Forum* was produced by Melvin Frank Productions and released through United Artists in October of 1966, with the following cast:

PSEUDOLUS	Zero Mostel
LYCUS	Phil Silvers
HYSTERIUM	Jack Gilford
ERRONIUS	Buster Keaton
HERO	Michael Crawford
PHILIA	Annette Andre
DOMINA	Patricia Jessel
SENEX	Michael Hordern
MILES GLORIOSUS	Leon Greene
GYMNASIA	Inga Neilsen
VIBRATA	Myrna White
PANACEA	Lucienne Bridou
TINTINABULA	Helen Funai
THE GEMINAE	Jennifer and Susan Baker
FERTILLA	Janet Webb
HIGH PRIESTESS	Pamela Brown
GUARD	Alfie Bass

Others: John Bennett, John Bluthal, Ronny Brody, Peter Butterworth, Frank Elliott, Andrew Faulds, Bill Kerr, Roy Kinnear, Beatrix Lehmann, Jack Max, Jon Pertwee, Frank Thornton

Directed by Richard Lester
Screenplay by Melvin Frank *and* Michael Pertwee
Musical Direction and Incidental Music by Ken Thorne
Production and Costumes Designed by Tony Walton

Director of Photography, Nicolas Roeg, B.S.C.
Dances by George and Ethel Martin

MUSICAL NUMBERS

Tibia Solo (Ken Thorne)	Instrumental
"Comedy Tonight"	Zero Mostel, Company
Search for Mare's Sweat (Thorne)	Instrumental
"Lovely"	Annette Andre, Michael Crawford
Tintinabula's Dance (Thorne)	Instrumental
Vibrata's Dance (Thorne)	Instrumental
Roman Emissary (Thorne)	Instrumental
"Everybody Ought to Have a Maid"	Michael Hordern, Zero Mostel, Jack Gilford, Phil Silvers
Riot at the Funeral (Sondheim)	Instrumental
Domina Returns/Fanfare (Thorne)	Instrumental
"Bring Me My Bride"	Leon Greene, Company
Erronius Returns (Thorne)	Instrumental
Orgy Music . . . Roman Style (Thorne)	Instrumental
"Lovely" (Reprise)	Zero Mostel, Jack Gilford
In the Arena (Thorne)	Instrumental
The Dirge and Funeral Sequence	Leon Greene, Company
The Rescue of Philia (Thorne)	Instrumental
The Chase (Sondheim)	Instrumental
"Comedy Tonight"/Playout (Sondheim)	Instrumental

The motion picture is available on video cassette: CBS Fox 4618

A Funny Thing Happened on the Way to the Forum was revived by Jujamcyn Theatres, Scott Rudin/Paramount Pictures, Viertel-Baruch-Frankel Group, Roger Berlind, and Dodger Productions at the St. James Theatre, April 18, 1996 (previews from March 18) - January 4, 1998 for 715 peformances and 35 previews, with the following cast:

(*In order of appearance*)

PROLOGUS (an actor)/PSEUDOLUS	Nathan Lane
PROTEANS	Brad Aspel, Cory English, Ray Roderick
HERO	Jim Stanek
PHILIA	Jessica Boevers
SENEX	Lewis J. Stadlen
DOMINA	Mary Testa
HYSTERIUM	Mark Linn-Baker
LYCUS	Ernie Sabella
TINTINABULA	Pamela Everett
PANACEA	Leigh Zimmerman
THE GEMINAE	Susan Misner, Lori Werner
VIBRATA	Mary Ann Lamb
GYMNASIA	Stephanie Pope
ERRONIUS	William Duell
MILES GLORIOSUS	Cris Groenendaal

SWINGS: Michael Arnold, Kevin Kraft, Kristin Willits

Directed by Jerry Zaks
Choreography by Rob Marshall;
Orchestrations by Jonathan Tunick
Musical Supervision by Edward Strauss
Set/Costumes by Tony Walton;
Dance Arrangements by David Chase

Whoopi Goldberg replaced Nathan Lane as PSEUDOLUS, and was subsequently replaced by David Alan Grier; Dick Latessa re-

153

placed Lewis J. Stadlen as SENEX and was subsequently replaced by Robert Fitch; Ross Lehman replaced Mark Linn-Baker as HYSTERIUM; Bob Amaral replaced Ernie Sabella as LYCUS; Holly Cruikshank replaced Leigh Zimmerman as PANACEA; Tara Nicole replaced Susan Misner as one of the GEMINAE; Pascale Faye replaced Mary Ann Lamb as VIBRATA and was subsequently replaced by Carol Lee Meadows; Kena Tangi Dorsey replaced Stephanie Pope as GYMNASIA. The song *"Pretty Little Picture"* was dropped.

AWARDS

Tony Award: Best Actor in a Musical (Nathan Lane)

SELECTED DISCOGRAPHY

* <u>Original Broadway Cast Recording</u> (1962)
   Capitol Records
   LP WAO (M)/SWAO (S)-1717; reissue W (M)/SW (S)-1717
   Bay Cities Music (1990, reissue)
   CD BCD 3002
   (Also included in Time-Life Records "American Musicals"
   Series: *Stephen Sondheim.* LP STL-AM12, Cassette 4TL-AM12)

<u>Original London Cast Album</u> (1963)
   His Master's Voice/EMI Records (England)
   LP CLP 1685 (M)/CSD 1518 (S)
   DRG Records (reissue)
   LP Stet DS-15028 (S)
   Cassette Stet DSC-15028
   First Night Records (England; reissue)
   LP OCR 3
   Cassette OCR C3

<u>Motion Picture Soundtrack Recording</u> (1966)
   United Artists Records
   LP UAL-4144 (M)/UAS-5144 (S); reissue UA-LA284-G (S)
   Cassette UA-EA284-H

Sondheim: A Musical Tribute (1973)
   Warner Bros. Records
   LP 2WS 2705 (S); 2 record set
   RCA Records (1990, reissue)
   Cassette 60515-4-RC
   CD 60515-2-RC
   Includes: "*Love Is in the Air*"—Larry Blyden, Susan Browning;
   "*Your Eyes Are Blue*"—Pamela Hall, Harvey Evans

* Nominated for the Grammy Award for the Best Original Cast Show
Album

Side by Side by Sondheim/Millicent Martin, Julia McKenzie
and David Kernan (1976)
   RCA Records
      LP CBL2-1851 (S); 2 record set
      Cassette CBK2-1851
      CD 1851-2-RG; 2 disc set
   Includes: "*Comedy Tonight*"/"*Love Is in the Air*"—Millicent Martin,
         Julia McKenzie, David Kernan

Songs of Sondheim (original Irish cast recording of *Side by Side
by Sondheim*, 1977)
   RAM Records
      LP RMLP 1026
   Includes: "*Comedy Tonight*"/"*Love Is in the Air*"—Tony Kenny,
         Loreto O'Connor, Gay Byrne, Denis O'Sullivan, Gemma
         Craven, Jim Doherty

Side by Side by Sondheim (original Australian cast recording, 1977)
   RCA Red Seal (Australia)
      LP VRL2-0156; 2 record set
      Cassette VRK2-0156; 2 tape set
   Includes: "*Comedy Tonight*"/ "*Love Is in the Air*" Jill Perryman,
         Bartholomew John, Geraldine Morrow; "*Everybody
         Ought to Have a Maid*"—John Laws, Bartholomew
         John, Geraldine Morrow, Jill Perryman

A Different Side of Sondheim/Richard Rodney Bennett (1979)
   DRG Records
      LP SL 5182
      Cassette SLC-5182
   Includes: "*I Do Like You*"

Marry Me a Little/Craig Lucas and Suzanne Henry (1981)
   RCA Records
      LP ABL1-4159 (S)
      Cassette ABK1-4159
      CD 7142-2-RG
   Includes: "*Your Eyes Are Blue*"—Craig Lucas, Suzanne Henry

A Stephen Sondheim Collection/Jackie Cain and Roy Kral (1982)
    Finesse Records
      LP FW 38324 (S)
      Cassette FWT 38324
    DRG Records (1990, reissue)
      Cassette DSC 25102
      CD DSCD 25102
    Includes: "*Comedy Tonight*"—Jackie Cain, Roy Kral; "*Love Is in the Air*"—Jackie Cain, Roy Kral; "*I Do Like You*"—Jackie Cain, Roy Kral

A Stephen Sondheim Evening (1983)
    RCA Records
      LP CBL2-4745 (S); 2 record set
      Cassette CBK2-4745; 2 tape set
    Includes: "*Pretty Little Picture*"—Bob Gunton, Liz Callaway, Steven Jacob; "*The House of Marcus Lycus*"—George Hearn, Bob Gunton, Women; "*Echo Song*"—Liz Callaway, Steven Jacob; "*There's Something About a War*"—Cris Groenendaal, Men

A Collector's Sondheim (1985)
    RCA Records
      LP CRL4-5359 (S); 4 record set
      Cassette CRK4-5359; 4 tape set
      CD RCD3-5480; 3 disc set
    Includes: "*Comedy Tonight*"/"*Love Is in the Air*"—Millicent Martin, Julia McKenzie, David Kernan (track from original cast recording of *Side by Side by Sondheim*); "*Pretty Little Picture*"—Bob Gunton, Liz Callaway, Steven Jacob; "*The House of Marcus Lycus*"—George Hearn, Bob Gunton, Women; "*There's Something About a War*"—Cris Groenendaal, Men (all three tracks from *A Stephen Sondheim Evening*); "*Your Eyes Are* Blue"—Craig Lucas, Suzanne Henry (track from original cast recording of *Marry Me a Little* and included on the LP and cassette only of *A Collector's Sondheim*)

Sondheim (1985)
Book-of-the-Month Records
LP 81-7515 (S) ; 5 record set
Cassette 91-7516; 2 tape set
CD 11-7517; 2 disc set
Includes: *"I Do Like You"*—Bob Gunton, Timothy Nolen; *"Comedy Tonight"*—Bob Gunton, Company

Cleo Sings Sondheim/Cleo Laine (1988)
RCA Records
LP 7702-1-RC
Cassette 7702-4-RC
CD 7702-2-RC
Includes: *"I'm Calm"*

Julie Wilson Sings the Stephen Sondheim Songbook (1988)
DRG Records
LP SL 5206
Cassette SLC 5206
CD CDSL 5206
Includes: *"I Do Like You,"* *"Love, I Hear"*

Symphonic Sondheim/Don Sebesky Conducts The London Symphony Orchestra (1990)
WEA Records (London)
LP 9051-72 119-1
Cassette 9051-72 119-4
CD 9051-72 119-2
Includes: *"Comedy Tonight"*

Sondheim: A Celebration at Carnegie Hall (1992)
RCA Victor
CD 09026-61484-2; 2 CD set
Includes: *"Love, I Hear,"* *"Comedy Tonight"*

<u>Broadway Revival Cast Recording</u> (1996)
Broadway Angel
CD 7243 8 52223 2 0

A Little Night Music

•

Music and Lyrics by
Stephen Sondheim

Book by
Hugh Wheeler

Suggested by a Film by Ingmar Bergman

Originally Produced and Directed on Broadway by Harold Prince

Introduction by Jonathan Tunick

Victoria Mallory (Anne Egerman), Garn Stephens (Petra, but replaced prior to the Broadway opening by D. Jamin-Bartlett), George Lee Andrews (Frid), Laurence Guittard (Count Carl-Magnus Malcolm), Patricia Elliott (Countess Charlotte Malcolm), Len Cariou (Fredrik Egerman), Glynis Johns (Desirée Armfeldt) and Hermione Gingold (Madame Armfeldt)

INTRODUCTION

During the course of our preliminary discussions of *A Little Night Music,* Stephen Sondheim remarked that he imagined "the atmosphere to be perfumed—of musk in the air." My immediate reply was, "Plenty of strings." This exchange offers a paradigm of the composer-orchestrator relationship as practiced in the Broadway musical. Although the various textbook definitions of the orchestrator's craft confine themselves strictly to the adaptation for orchestra of music already complete in melody, harmony, and form, but composed for another medium, such as the piano, the theater orchestrator's responsibilities are more far-reaching. It is his function, as indicated by the foregoing anecdote, to translate into practical terms the musical and dramatic conception of the composer, who, unlike Sondheim, may not be a literate, trained musician, or, like him, may conceive his music exclusively on the piano and need to rely upon a specialist in the technique of the orchestra and its various instruments. Sondheim is rare among Broadway composers in that he calls for highly colored and dramatic effects in his accompaniments, but typical in that he is not trained in translating these effects from the medium of the piano to that of the orchestra.

Therefore, the existence of what I have come to regard as an honorable craft and the opportunity for me to have participated in the creation of this most elegant work.

If one imagines the Sondheim-Prince musicals of the 1970s to be the movements of a symphony (*Company:*

161

Allegro; *Follies:* Adagio; *Pacific Overtures*—well I admit that the analogy falters here—how about Intermezzo á l'Orientale; and *Sweeney Todd:* Finale), *A Little Night Music* takes its place as the third, or Scherzo, movement. The Scherzo, introduced by Beethoven as a replacement for the Classical symphony's Minuet, became an integral element of the Romantic symphonies of Schubert, Mendelssohn, and Brahms.

A Little Night Music, like the Scherzo, is light, fast, playful, mysterious, and in triple meter. It swims in the heady, magical atmosphere imagined by its creators and displays all the literacy and wit that we have come to expect from them. The music is rich in melodic invention, contrapuntal development, and harmonic texture. The show's quirky, appealing characters demonstrate satisfying growth during the course of the developing plot, which comes to a rational and gratifying conclusion. It is Prince's most romantic work as well: erotic, charming, and imaginative.

Although easier on the audience than most of Sondheim's musicals, *A Little Night Music* is by no means simplistic. Like all great romantic works, it is classically precise in structure. Hugh Wheeler brought to the material the exactitude of the mystery writer (Sondheim commented that the show is plotted like an Iris Murdoch novel), creating between the various characters an effectively geometrical pattern of interrelationships, based, like the score, upon the number three:

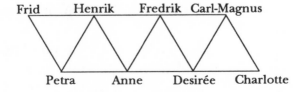

A chain of triangles: in each of these connected relationships, the unstable number three is drawn to the stable two, as the various mismatched couples disengage and find their proper partners.

It was Sondheim's intention that the score be entirely in triple time—a Waltz musical in the style of the turn-of-the-century Viennese operettas. (Strauss, Lehar, and Kálmán, the masters of this genre, never did this—the many waltzes in their scores are balanced by plenty of music in 2/4 and 4/4—polkas, marches, galops, etc.) Though one might quibble about Sondheim's use of a 12/8 Nocturne pattern accompanying "Send in the Clowns," and that there are twelve 2/4 bars in "The Glamorous Life," eighteen more in "The Miller's Son," and an entire passage in 4/4 (No. 22 in the Vocal Score—an underscoring passage), the remainder of the score consists exclusively of various permutations of triple time, utilizing for the main part eighteenth- and nineteenth-century generic forms such as the Waltz ("Soon," "You Must Meet My Wife"), Mazurka ("Remember," "The Glamorous Life"), Sarabande ("Later," "Liaisons"), Polonaise ("In Praise of Women"), Etude ("Now," "Every Day a Little Death"), and Gigue ("A Weekend in the Country").

There is great symmetry of form here as well as in the book. Sondheim tends here toward trios with the characters separated ("Now," "Later," "Soon") and duets regarding a third person ("You Must Meet My Wife," "It Would Have Been Wonderful," "Every Day a Little Death"). These songs of alienation and yearning for cohesion and balance all represent the unstable number three drawn to the stable two—the triangle yearning to be reconciled to the proper couple. This precision of form is combined with a musky romanticism and all-round good humor and warmth. Here is Sondheim at his very best: witty, whimsical, and knowing.

Sondheim's musicals present an unusual challenge to the orchestrator in that he eschews for the most part the familiar melodic, harmonic, and rhythmic conventions of the Broadway musical. *A Little Night Music* is no exception to this principle, presenting as it does some particularly harrowing problems, such as the cross-hand Etude pattern in the accompaniment of "Every Day a Little Death." The syncopated eighthnote pattern was originally assigned to the clarinets, who quickly retitled the piece "Every Page a Little Breath" due to the complete absence of rests in their part. (The company was unusually partial to puns and parodies—I recall with particular pleasure Barbara Lang's "The screens won't move, they keep falling out of their groove" to the tune of "Night Waltz.") For the movie version, I thought better of the situation and scored the passage for the nonbreathing strings.

Sondheim provided his typically complete piano accompaniment for each song, meticulously notated as to melody, harmony, and rhythm—much like an art-song accompaniment—and most effective when performed in its original medium—the piano. Although I have never heard him play a note written by another composer (with the single exception of "Something's Coming" from *West Side Story,* accompanying Larry Kert at a party), Sondheim plays his own compositions most effectively on the piano and sings the parts of the various characters, usually, like Leonard Bernstein, at an octave below pitch. His piano accompaniments, like those of art songs, suggest the dramatic implications of the songs and their appropriate instrumentation through use of rhythmic, contrapuntal, and coloristic devices such as repeated notes, arpeggios, broken chords, and the use of extreme registers.

Because these devices are idiomatic only to the piano, and are ineffective or even impossible to play on orchestral instruments, the accompaniments must be reduced by the orchestrator to a harmonic and rhythmic abstraction and recomposed, utilizing devices suitable to orchestral combinations. This process results in a full orchestral score that bears little visual resemblance to the original piano accompaniment, and when the orchestral score is reduced by the copyist to a short score or piano-conductor part, thereby reversing the orchestration process, the written notes, now reflecting orchestral rather than piano idioms, suffer in effect when played on the piano.

Aside from developing a general familiarity with the score by having it played and sung by the composer in person and on tape recordings and reading it at home, as well as some general research into the musical and historical milieu of the place (in this case the waltzes of Strauss and Lehar, and late Romantic music in general, particularly Russian and Scandinavian—Tchaikovsky, Rachmaninoff, and Grieg), there is little for the orchestrator to do until the rehearsal period begins. Not until then is it decided what keys will be appropriate for the various performers—they are invariably different from those in which the songs are originally written—and the songs are expanded by the director and choreographer, working with the dance music arranger at the piano, into full-length numbers. I have wasted what seem to be cubic miles of breath trying to explain to inexperienced producers that any orchestration done before the rehearsal period will invariably be thrown out. The production must be orchestrated as much as the score, and the rehearsal period is as much a creative process as the writing; it cannot be second-guessed.

During the time before the rehearsal period, the orchestrator may plan his instrumentation. The size of a Broadway orchestra is determined by an agreement between the League of New York Theaters and Local 802 of the American Federation of Musicians, specifying a minimum number of players for each theater. Although it is not unheard of, it is rare indeed for a producer to agree to engage more than the minimum number of players. The minimum, therefore, becomes effectively the maximum.

At the time of *A Little Night Music* the minimum at the Shubert Theater was twenty-five players, a typical number for a Broadway musical. With such a limited number of musicians available, every player counts, and the orchestrator must choose his instrumentation with great care and accuracy, giving particular attention to balance between sections. (To balance seven brass and five saxophones, for example, against six violins and two 'cellos is quite a feat, although it can be and has been done.)

Since *A Little Night Music* is European in setting, turn-of-the-century in time, and romantic in style, and since the score reflects these qualities, containing no musical anachronisms or stylistic deviations, I decided upon a legitimate operetta orchestra, not dependent upon a rhythm section but fully orchestrated in Classical style, and employing traditional combinations of woodwind, brass, string, and percussion instruments, foregoing such inappropriate ones as saxophones and guitars. The score is so delicate that I was tempted to dispense with the trumpets and drums, but decided to include them for safety's sake. It was, after all, a Broadway musical, a field in which no one has ever suffered due to lack of subtlety.

The instrumentation that I planned was that of a typical operetta orchestra, but held to a somewhat inadequate number of strings mandated by Broadway budgets. It is composed of the following:

Five woodwinds: flute, oboe, two clarinets, and bassoon, each player alternating on one or more doubles, or secondary instruments, such as the piccolo, English horn, bass clarinet, and so on. This system of doubling in the woodwinds permits a section of four or five players to do the work of many more. When *Follies* was performed by the New York Philharmonic, for example, seventeen nondoubling woodwind players—four flutes, four clarinets, a bass clarinet, an oboe, an English horn, a bassoon, and five saxophones—were required to execute the parts written for five doublers. The woodwinds—the quirky, temperamental prima donnas of the orchestra—are the most difficult to write for, but they provide essential color and personality to the orchestra and are well worth the trouble.

Three horns were employed. Such a large section is unusual in musicals, although Don Walker used three in *The Most Happy Fella* and *She Loves Me*, as did Russell Bennett in *South Pacific* and *The King and I.* They give an elegant, rounded middle to the ensemble, as well as a brilliant unison in *forte* passages such as my rather blatant quotation from *Der Rosenkavalier* in "A Weekend in the Country."

The brass section consists of two trumpets and a single trombone. Although they are little heard from, they make themselves valuable in the full *tuttis* as well as various mock-military effects (mostly involving Carl-Magnus) and coloristic passages such as the chattering trumpets in "Now." At one period during tryouts there were so few notes in the trombone part (I once counted them at 113) that the instrument was in danger of losing its place in the orchestra. I had this problem in mind as I approached my next assignment, "It Would Have Been Wonderful." Fortunately the number involved the strutting dragoon Carl-Magnus, and I was able to feature the trombone in a solo *obbligato*, making the instrument indispensable and thereby saving its job, for which it has never thanked me.

Although the presence of a piano is dictated by both the score and the script, being necessary to portray Fredrika's piano exercises, the instrument has no place in this type of orchestra and aside from these passages remains tacet, taking no part in the orchestration. The pianist doubles on the celesta, which is liberally used, due to its charming, bell-like tone. The harp, with its intense romantic associations, was assigned an elaborate and necessarily difficult part, particularly complex for the harpist in that the highly chromatic nature of the score requires a virtual tap dance among the pedals that provide the sharps and flats. The harp figures prominently as an accompanying instrument, so evocative of the romantic past and far more idiomatic than the commonplace piano or the homely guitar.

The strings form the most important element of the *Night Music* orchestra, although the minimum of twenty-five players restricted me to six violins, two violas, two 'cellos, and a bass, which is what we laughingly refer to on Broadway as a full string section. Generations of theater orchestrators, however, have over the years developed an arsenal of trick voicings, mostly unknown to classical composers, in order to achieve a fuller resonance from their skimpy string sections. It is customary to double the number of strings in the orchestra for cast recordings, so that the string sound that one hears on cast albums is far richer, sometimes to a fault, than what one hears from the pit.

In Broadway show orchestration, and commercial work in general, string writing is pretty much confined to the following:

1. Melody and countermelody, unison or harmonized
2. Sustained harmonic accompaniment ("footballs")
3. Runs, trills, tremolos, and other decoration
4. The ubiquitous afterbeats, so abhorred by players.

The score demanded more ambitious use of the string group, particularly for rhythmic accompaniment passages, due to the absence of a rhythm section. It was necessary to draw upon my studies of classical and modern music in order to employ such devices as *pizzicato, spiccato,* double and triple stopping, and harmonics, which permitted a wider and more flexible use of the strings as background. They replaced the customary but inappropriate pianos, guitars, and other rhythm instruments, for which I am greatly indebted to Debussy, Mahler, Bartók, and Stravinsky.

168

Customarily the units of the string group (violins, violas, 'cellos) play in unison. In addition to this necessary *tutti* writing, I call for an unusual (for Broadway) number of *divisi* passages as well as solos for the violin, 'cello, and even the viola, and occasional duets and trios for solo string instruments. The 'cello *obbligato* in "Later" stands out, as does the gypsy-like violin solo at the very end of the show—a chromatic scale, quite awkward for the violin, climbing to an *altissimo* E natural. Of all the violinists that I have heard attempt it, none played it better than the toupeed contractor of the tryout orchestra in Boston.

Sondheim's original concept was of a dark, somewhat Chekhovian, yet romantic and erotic musical taking the form of a theme and variations, the first act forming the theme and the second the variations. This idea was to take shape as a farce at the country house, using the device of Madame Armfeldt's dealing the cards each time the plot went wrong, and starting again. Wheeler's book, however, did not support this notion, and some of the darker elements of Sondheim's score were replaced during the rehearsal period by lighter material. Such numbers as "Bang!" and "My Husband the Pig" gave way to the more easygoing "In Praise of Women" and "Every Day a Little Death."

Due to the extensive rewriting required by this change of tone in the show, Sondheim fell behind in his writing schedule and rehearsals had to begin before the score was completed. Sondheim is a systematic, skillful writer, and as rehearsals proceeded such material as the "Night Waltzes," "In Praise of Women," "Every Day a Little Death," "It Would Have Been Wonderful," and "A Weekend in the Country" arrived, and, finally, "Send in the Clowns."

Sondheim finds the amazing success of this song, though most welcome, a little baffling. Most of his shows, he says, have at least one simple romantic ballad, but none of these had received what seems to him the disproportionate acclamation attracted by what he refers to as a *boite* song. Perhaps its appeal lies to some degree in the fact that it is written in short phrases in order to be acted rather than sung; in fact, it was tailor-made to suit the abilities of Glynis Johns, who lacks the vocal power to sustain long phrases, and the song does not actually work very well when sung "correctly" by a trained singer.

"Send in the Clowns" was orchestrated overnight in a hotel room in Boston in between orchestra rehearsals. The orchestration for strings, harp, and solo clarinet is quite conventional, and most of the night was spent in deciding between the solo clarinet and 'cello to play the now familiar unaccompanied introduction and the subsequent *obbligato*. I chose the clarinet for its haunting, lonely effect in its low register and rejected the 'cello, which I felt was too closely associated with another character, Henrik. The reprise is scored for the full orchestra in what I refer to as the "Max Steiner" section, a most gratifying romantic climax in the honored Hollywood tradition. It sounds even better in the movie, with three trombones.

Bobby Short heard the song in Boston, fell in love with it, and asked for a copy. Soon he was performing it in New York, where Judy Collins heard it and invited me to record it with her as orchestrator-conductor. The recording orchestration that I prepared for Judy substituted an English horn for the clarinet, but is otherwise similar to that used in the show. The record soared, providing Sondheim with his biggest hit to date.

A Little Night Music has taken its place among the classics of the musical theater, the most popular, along with *A Funny Thing Happened on the Way to the Forum* and *Sweeney Todd,* of Sondheim's works. It won for its authors a brace of Tony awards, and the cast album has become a staple in the collections of all lovers of musicals. It is a witty and well-constructed work that embraces and uplifts its audience in an atmosphere of warmth and romantic good nature. There is no better example of Sondheim's penchant for an erudite, knowing, whimsical chuckle at the human condition.

Jonathan Tunick

New York
September 1990

CAST OF CHARACTERS

MADAME ARMFELDT

DESIRÉE ARMFELDT, *her daughter, an actress*

FREDRIKA ARMFELDT, *Desirée's daughter*

FREDRIK EGERMAN, *a lawyer*

ANNE EGERMAN, *his second wife*

HENRIK EGERMAN, *his son*

COUNT CARL-MAGNUS MALCOLM, *a dragoon*

COUNTESS CHARLOTTE MALCOLM, *his wife*

PETRA, *the Egerman maid*

FRID, *Madame Armfeldt's butler*

MALLA, *Desirée's maid*

BERTRAND, *Madame Armfeldt's page*

OSA, *Madame Armfeldt's maid*

MR. LINDQUIST

MRS. NORDSTROM

MRS. ANDERSSEN

MR. ERLANSON

MRS. SEGSTROM

MUSICAL NUMBERS

Overture	MR. LINDQUIST, MRS. NORDSTROM, MRS. ANDERSSEN, MR. ERLANSON, MRS. SEGSTROM

ACT I

"Night Waltz"	COMPANY
"Now"	FREDRIK
"Later"	HENRIK
"Soon"	ANNE, HENRIK, FREDRIK
"The Glamorous Life"	FREDRIKA, DESIRÉE, MALLA, MADAME ARMFELDT, MRS. NORDSTROM, MRS. SEGSTROM, MRS. ANDERSSEN, MR. LINDQUIST, MR. ERLANSON
"Remember?"	MR. LINDQUIST, MRS. NORDSTROM, MRS. SEGSTROM, MR. ERLANSON, MRS. ANDERSSEN
"You Must Meet My Wife"	FREDRIK, DESIRÉE
"Liaisons"	MADAME ARMFELDT
"In Praise of Women"	CARL-MAGNUS
"Every Day a Little Death"	CHARLOTTE, ANNE
"A Weekend in the Country"	COMPANY

ACT II

"The Sun Won't Set"	MRS. ANDERSSEN, MRS. SEGSTROM, MRS. NORDSTROM, MR. LINDQUIST, MR. ERLANSON
"It Would Have Been Wonderful"	FREDRIK, CARL-MAGNUS
"Night Waltz II"	MRS. NORDSTROM, MR. ERLANSON, MR. LINDQUIST, MRS. SEGSTROM, MRS. ANDERSSEN
"Perpetual Anticipation"	MRS. NORDSTROM, MRS. SEGSTROM, MRS. ANDERSSEN
"Send in the Clowns"	DESIRÉE
"The Miller's Son"	PETRA
Finale	COMPANY

Time: Turn of the Century
Place: Sweden

Overture

Before the houselights are down, MR. LINDQUIST *appears and sits at the piano. He removes his gloves, plunks a key, and begins to vocalize.* MRS. NORDSTROM *enters, hits a key on the piano, and vocalizes with him.* MRS. ANDERSSEN, MR. ERLANSON *and* MRS. SEGSTROM *come out and join the vocalizing.*

MEN:	WOMEN:
La, la la la	La, la la la
La, la la la	La, la la la

MRS. NORDSTROM:
  The old deserted beach that we walked —
  Remember?

MR. ERLANSON:
  Remember?
  The café in the park where we talked —
  Remember?

MRS. ANDERSSEN:
  Remember?
  The tenor on the boat that we chartered,
  Belching "The Bartered
  Bride" —

175

ALL:

Ah, how we laughed,
Ah, how we cried,

MR. LINDQUIST:

Ah, how you promised
And
Ah, how
I lied.

OTHER MEMBERS OF QUINTET:

La, la la la

Ah . . .
Lie . . . lie . . . lie . . .

MRS. SEGSTROM:

That dilapidated inn —
Remember, darling?

MR. ERLANSON:

The proprietress's grin,
Also her glare.

MRS. NORDSTROM:

Yellow gingham on the bed —
Remember, darling?

MR. LINDQUIST:

And the canopy in red,
Needing repair.

ALL:

Soon, I promise.
Soon I won't shy away,
Dear old —
Soon. I want to.
Soon, whatever you say.
Even

WOMEN:

Now,
When we're close and
We

MEN:

Now, when we touch,

176

Touch,   Touching my brow,
And you're kissing my
Brow,   Ahhhh . . .
I don't mind it
Too much.
And you'll have to

ALL:

Admit I'm endearing,
I help keep things humming,
I'm not domineering,
What's one small shortcoming?

And

Unpack the luggage, la la la
Pack up the luggage, la la la
Unpack the luggage, la la la
Hi-ho, the glamorous life!

Unpack the luggage, la la la
Pack up the luggage, la la la
Unpack the luggage, la la la
Hi-ho, the glamorous life!

MR. LINDQUIST: OTHER MEMBERS OF QUINTET:
Ahhhhh . . .   Unpack the luggage, la la la
                                Pack up the luggage, la la la

MRS. NORDSTROM: OTHER MEMBERS OF QUINTET:
Ahhhh . . .   Unpack the luggage, la la la
                                Hi-ho, the glamorous life!

ALL:

Bring up the curtain, la la la
Bring down the curtain, la la la
Bring up the curtain, la la la
Hi-ho, hi-ho
For the glamorous life!

(After the applause, the QUINTET *starts to waltz. The show curtain flies out revealing the main characters doing a strangely surreal waltz ["Night Waltz"] of their own, in which partners change partners and recouple with others. The* QUINTET *drifts up into the waltzing couples, and reappears to hum accompaniment for the last section of the dance.* FREDRIKA *wanders through the waltz, too, watching)*

ACT I

Prologue

At the end of the opening waltz, MADAME ARMFELDT *is brought on in her wheelchair by her butler,* FRID. *In her lap is a tray containing a silver cigarette box, a small vase with four yellow bud-roses, and the cards with which she is playing solitaire. She is watched by* FREDRIKA ARMFELDT, *13 — a grave, very self-contained and formal girl with the precise diction of the convent-trained.*

FREDRIKA: If you cheated a little, it would come out.

MADAME ARMFELDT (*Continuing to play*): Solitaire is the only thing in life that demands absolute honesty. As a woman who has numbered kings among her lovers, I think my word can be taken on that point.
(*She motions to* FRID, *who crosses down and lights her cigarette*)
What was I talking about?

FREDRIKA: You said I should watch.

MADAME ARMFELDT: Watch — what?

FREDRIKA: It sounds very unlikely to me, but you said I should watch for the night to smile.

MADAME ARMFELDT: Everything is unlikely, dear, so don't let

that deter you. Of course the summer night smiles. Three times.

FREDRIKA: But how does it smile?

MADAME ARMFELDT: Good heavens, what sort of nanny did you have?

FREDRIKA: None, really. Except Mother, and the other actresses in the company — and the stage manager.

MADAME ARMFELDT: Stage managers are not nannies. They don't have the talent.

FREDRIKA: But if it happens — how does it happen?

MADAME ARMFELDT: You get a feeling. Suddenly the jasmine starts to smell stronger, then a frog croaks — then all the stars in Orion wink. Don't squeeze your bosoms against the chair, dear. It'll stunt their growth. And then where would you be?

FREDRIKA: But why does it smile, Grandmother?

MADAME ARMFELDT: At the follies of human beings, of course. The first smile smiles at the young, who know nothing.
        (*She looks pointedly at* FREDRIKA)
The second, at the fools who know too little, like Desirée.

FREDRIKA: Mother isn't a fool.

MADAME ARMFELDT (*Going right on*): Um-hum. And the third at the old who know too much — like me.
        (*The game is over without coming out. Annoyed at the cards,* MADAME ARMFELDT *scatters them at random, and barks at* FRID)
Frid, time for my nap.

FREDRIKA (*Intrigued in spite of herself, gazes out at the summer night*): Grandmother, might it really smile tonight?

MADAME ARMFELDT: Why not? Now, practice your piano, dear, preferably with the soft pedal down. And as a treat tonight at dinner, I shall tell you amusing stories about my liaison with the Baron de Signac, who was, to put it mildly, peculiar.

(FRID *wheels her off and* FREDRIKA *goes to sit at the piano*)

Scene 1

THE EGERMAN ROOMS

Two rooms: the parlor and the master bedroom, indicated on different levels. ANNE EGERMAN, *a ravishingly pretty girl of 18, is on the bed. She goes to the vanity table, toys with her hair, and then enters the parlor.* HENRIK EGERMAN, *her stepson, a brooding young man of 19, is seated on the sofa, playing his cello. Beside him on the sofa is a book with a ribbon marker.* ANNE *looks at* HENRIK, *then leans over the sofa to get his attention.*

ANNE: Oh Henrik, dear, don't you have anything less gloomy to practice?

HENRIK: It isn't gloomy, it's profound.

ANNE (*Reaches down, takes* HENRIK's *book, and begins reading from it*): " . . . in discussing temptation, Martin Luther says: 'You cannot prevent the birds from flying over your head, but you can prevent them from nesting in your hair.'" Oh dear, that's gloomy too! Don't they teach you anything at the seminary a little more cheerful?

HENRIK (*Grand*): A man who's going to serve in God's Army must learn all the ruses and stratagems of the Enemy.

ANNE (*Sitting, giggling*): And which of your professors made that historic statement?

HENRIK (*Caught out*): Pastor Ericson, as a matter of fact. He says we're like generals learning to win battles against the devil.

> (*Her ball of silk falls off her lap*)

ANNE: Oh dear, my ball!

> (HENRIK *bends down to pick up the ball. He stands beside her, obviously overwhelmed by her nearness.* ANNE *pats her lap*)

You can put it there, you know. My lap isn't one of the Devil's snares.

> (*Flushing,* HENRIK *drops the ball into her lap and moves away from her*)

HENRIK: Anne, I was wondering — could we go for a walk?

ANNE: Now?

HENRIK: I've so much to tell you. What I've been thinking, and everything.

ANNE: Silly Henrik, don't you realize it's almost tea-time? And I think I hear your father.

> (*She rises, puts down the ball of silk*)

I'm sure you've made the most wonderful discoveries about life, and I long to talk, but — later.

> (FREDRIK *enters, followed by* PETRA, *21, the charming, easy-going maid*)

Fredrik, dear!

HENRIK (*Mutters to himself*): Later.

ANNE: Look who's come home to us — holier than ever.

FREDRIK: Hello, son. How was the examination?

HENRIK: Well, as a matter of fact . . .

FREDRIK (*Breaking in*): You passed with flying colors, of course.

ANNE: First on the list.

HENRIK (*Trying again*): And Pastor Ericson said . . .

FREDRIK (*Breaking in*): Splendid — you must give us a full report. Later.

ANNE: He'd better be careful or he'll go straight to heaven before he has a chance to save any sinners.

FREDRIK: Don't tease him, dear.

ANNE: Oh, Henrik likes to be teased, don't you, Henrik? Fredrik, do you want your tea now?

FREDRIK: Not now, I think. It's been rather an exhausting day in Court and as we have a long evening ahead of us, I feel a little nap is indicated.
(*He produces theater tickets from his pocket*)

ANNE (*Grabbing at them, delighted as a child*): Tickets for the theater!

FREDRIK: It's a French comedy. I thought it might entertain you.

ANNE: It's *Woman of the World,* isn't it? With Desirée Armfeldt! She's on all the posters! Oh, Fredrik, how delicious!
(*To* HENRIK, *teasing*)
What shall I wear? My blue with the feathers —
(FREDRIK *pours water*)
genuine angel's feathers — ? Or the yellow? Ah, I know. My pink, with the bosom. And Henrik, you can do me up in the back.
(*She goes into the bedroom*)

FREDRIK: I'm sorry, son. I should have remembered you were coming home and got a third ticket. But then per-

184

haps a French comedy is hardly suitable.

(FREDRIK *takes a pill*)

HENRIK (*Outburst*): Why does everyone laugh at me? Is it so ridiculous to want to do some good in this world?

FREDRIK: I'm afraid being young in itself can be a trifle ridiculous. Good has to be so good, bad so bad. Such superlatives!

HENRIK: But to be old, I suppose, is not ridiculous.

FREDRIK (*Sigh*): Ah, let's not get into that. I love you very much, you know. So does Anne — in her way. But you can't expect her to take your mother's place. She's young too; she has not yet learned . . .

HENRIK: . . . to suffer fools gladly?

FREDRIK (*Gentle*): You said that, son. Not I.

ANNE: Fredrik!

(*As* FREDRIK *moves into the bedroom,* HENRIK *picks up his book and reads.* ANNE *is sitting on the bed, buffing her nails*)

You were sweet to think of the theater for me.

FREDRIK: I'll enjoy it too.

ANNE: Who wouldn't — when all the posters call her The One And Only Desirée Armfeldt?

(FREDRIK *begins to try to kiss her. She rattles on*)

I wonder what it would feel like to be a One and Only! The One and Only — Anne Egerman!

(*She leaves* FREDRIK *on the bed and moves to the vanity table. As aware as he is of her rejection*)

Poor Fredrik! Do I still make you happy? After eleven months? I know I'm foolish to be so afraid — and you've been so patient, but, soon — I promise. Oh, I know you think I'm too silly to worry, but I do . . .

185

(*As* FREDRIK *looks up to answer, she gives a little cry*)
Oh no! For heaven's sakes, can that be a pimple coming?
(FREDRIK, *deflated, begins to sing as he undresses*)

FREDRIK:
  Now, as the sweet imbecilities
  Tumble so lavishly
  Onto her lap . . .

ANNE: Oh Fredrik, what a day it's been! Unending drama!
  While Petra was brushing my hair, the doorbell . . .
  (*Throughout the song, she continues chattering in pan-
  tomime when not actually speaking*)

FREDRIK:
  Now, there are two possibilities:
  A, I could ravish her,
  B, I could nap.

ANNE: . . . that grumpy old Mrs. Nordstrom from next door.
  Her sister's coming for a visit . . .

FREDRIK:
  Say it's the ravishment, then we see
  The option
  That follows, of course:

ANNE: . . . do hope I'm imperious enough with the servants.
  I try to be. But half the time I think they're laughing at
  me . . .

FREDRIK:
  A, the deployment of charm, or B,
  The adoption
  Of physical force.

  Now B might arouse her,
  But if I assume
  I trip on my trouser
  Leg crossing the room . . .

Her hair getting tangled,
Her stays getting snapped,
My nerves will be jangled,
My energy sapped . . .

Removing her clothing
Would take me all day
And her subsequent loathing
Would turn me away —
Which eliminates B
And which leaves us with A.

ANNE: Could you ever be jealous of me? . . .

FREDRIK:

Now, insofar as approaching it,
What would be festive
But have its effect?

ANNE: Shall I learn Italian? I think it would be amusing, if
the verbs aren't too irregular . . .

FREDRIK:

Now, there are two ways of broaching it:
A, the suggestive
And B, the direct.

ANNE: . . . but then French is a much chic-er language. Everyone says so. Parlez-vous Français? . . .

FREDRIK:

Say that I settle on B, to wit,
A charmingly
Lecherous mood . . .

A, I could put on my nightshirt or sit
Disarmingly,
B, in the nude . . .
That might be effective,

My body's all right,
But not in perspective
And not in the light . . .

I'm bound to be chilly
And feel a buffoon,
But nightshirts are silly
In midafternoon . . .

Which leaves the suggestive,
But how to proceed?
Although she gets restive,
Perhaps I could read . . .

In view of her penchant
For something romantic,
De Sade is too trenchant
And Dickens too frantic,
And Stendhal would ruin
The plan of attack,
As there isn't much blue in
The Red and the Black.

De Maupassant's candor
Would cause her dismay.
The Brontës are grander
But not very gay.
Her taste is much blander,
I'm sorry to say,
But is Hans Christian Ander-
Sen ever risqué?
Which eliminates A.

(*Exits upstage*)

ANNE: And he said, "You're such a pretty lady!" Wasn't that
silly? . . .

FREDRIK (*As he walks back on in nothing but his long underwear*):
Now, with my mental facilities

188

Partially muddied
And ready to snap . . .

ANNE (*At the jewel box now*): . . . I'm sure about the bracelet.
But earrings, earrings! *Which* earrings? . . .

FREDRIK:
Now, though there are possibilities
Still to be studied,
I might as well nap . . .

ANNE: Mother's rubies? . . . Oh, the diamonds are — Agony!
I know . . .

FREDRIK (*Getting into bed*):
Bow though I must
To adjust
My original plan . . .

ANNE: Desirée Armfeldt — I just know she'll wear the most
glamorous gowns! . . .

FREDRIK:
How shall I sleep
Half as deep
As I usually can? . . .

ANNE: Dear, distinguished old Fredrik!

FREDRIK:
When now I still want and/or love you,
Now, as always,
Now,
Anne?
   (FREDRIK *turns over and goes to sleep. They remain frozen.*
   PETRA *enters the parlor*)

PETRA: Nobody rang. Doesn't he want his tea?

HENRIK (*Still deep in book*): They're taking a nap.

PETRA (*Coming up behind him, teasingly ruffling his hair*): You
smell of soap.

HENRIK (*Pulling his head away*): I'm reading.

PETRA (*Caressing his head*): Do those old teachers take a scrubbing brush to you every morning and scrub you down like a dray horse?
>
> (*Strokes his ear*)

HENRIK (*Fierce*): Get away from me!

PETRA (*Jumping up in mock alarm*): Oh what a wicked woman I am! I'll go straight to hell!
>
> (*Starting away, she goes toward the door, deliberately wiggling her hips*)

HENRIK (*Looking up, even fiercer*): And don't walk like that!

PETRA (*Innocent*): Like — what?
>
> (*Wiggles even more*)

Like this?

HENRIK (*Pleadingly*): Stop it. Stop it!
>
> (*He rises, goes after her, clutches her, and starts savagely, clumsily, to kiss her and fumble at her breasts. She slaps his hand*)

PETRA: Careful!
>
> (*Breaks away*)

That's a new blouse! A whole week's wages and the lace extra!
>
> (*Looks at him*)

Poor little Henrik!
>
> (*Then affectionately pats his cheek*)

Later! You'll soon get the knack of it!
>
> (*She exits.* HENRIK *puts down the book, gets his cello and begins to sing, accompanying himself on the cello*)

HENRIK:

Later . . .

When is later? . . .

All you ever hear is "Later, Henrik! Henrik, later . . ."

"Yes, we know, Henrik.
Oh, Henrik —
Everyone agrees, Henrik —
Please, Henrik!"
You have a thought you're fairly bursting with,
A personal discovery or problem, and it's
"What's your rush, Henrik?
Shush, Henrik —
Goodness, how you gush, Henrik —
Hush, Henrik!"
You murmur,
"I only . . .
It's just that . . .
For God's sake!"
"Later, Henrik . . . "

"Henrik" . . .
Who is "Henrik"? . . .
Oh, that lawyer's son, the one who mumbles —
Short and boring,
Yes, he's hardly worth ignoring
And who cares if he's all dammed —
                    (*Looks up*)
— I beg your pardon —
Up inside?
As I've
Often stated,
It's intolerable
Being tolerated.
"Reassure Henrik,
Poor Henrik.
Henrik, you'll endure
Being pure, Henrik."

Though I've been born, I've never been!
How can I wait around for later?

191

I'll be ninety on my deathbed
And the late, or rather later,
Henrik Egerman!

Doesn't anything begin?
(ANNE, *in the bedroom, gets up from the vanity table and
stands near the bed, singing to* FREDRIK)

ANNE:
Soon, I promise.
Soon I won't shy away,
Dear old —
(*She bites her lip*)
Soon. I want to.
Soon, whatever you say.
Even now,
When you're close and we touch,
And you're kissing my brow,
I don't mind it too much.
And you'll have to admit
I'm endearing,
I help keep things humming,
I'm not domineering,
What's one small shortcoming?
And think of how I adore you,
Think of how much you love me.
If I were perfect for you,
Wouldn't you tire of me
Soon,
All too soon?
Dear old —
(*The sound of* HENRIK*'s cello.* FREDRIK *stirs noisily in bed.*
ANNE *goes into the parlor*)
Henrik! That racket! Your father's sleeping!
(*She remains, half-innocent, half-coquettish, in her neg-
ligee. For a second,* ANNE *watches him. She closes her night-
gown at the neck and goes back into the bedroom*)

192

ANNE (*Back at the bed*):
  Soon —

HENRIK:
  "Later" . . .

ANNE:
  I promise.

HENRIK:
  When is "later?"

(*Simultaneously*)

ANNE:	HENRIK:
Soon	"Later, Henrik, later."
I won't shy	All you ever hear is,
Away,	"Yes, we know, Henrik, oh,
	Henrik,
Dear old —	Everyone agrees, Henrik,
	please, Henrik!"

(FREDRIK *stirs. Simultaneously*)

ANNE:	HENRIK:	FREDRIK:
Soon.		
I want to.	"Later" . . .	Now,
	When is "later"?	As the sweet
		imbecilities
	All you ever	Trip on my trouser leg,
Soon,		
	Hear is	
Whatever you		
Say.	"Later, Henrik,	
		Stendhal
		eliminates
	Later."	A,
	As I've often	
	Stated:	But
	When?	When?

Even	Maybe	Maybe
Now,		
When you're close	Soon, soon	Later.
And we touch	I'll be ninety	
	And	
And you're kissing	Dead.	When I'm kissing
My brow,		Your brow
I don't mind it	I don't mind it	And I'm stroking
		your head,
Too much,	Too much,	
		You'll come into
		my bed.
And you'll have	Since I have to	And you have to
to admit	Admit	Admit
I'm endearing,	I find peering	I've been hearing
I help		
Keep things	Through life's	All those tremu-
		lous cries
Humming, I'm	Gray windows	
	Impatiently	Patiently,
Not domineering,	Not very cheering.	Not interfering
What's one small	Do I fear death?	With those tremu-
		lous thighs.
Shortcoming?	Let it	Come to me
And	Come to me	Soon,
Think of how	Now,	
I adore you,		
Think of how	Now,	Soon,
Much you love me.		
If I were perfect	Now,	Soon,
For you,		
Wouldn't you tire	Now.	Soon.
Of me		
Later?	Come to me	Come to me
	Soon. If I'm	Soon,

```
                    Dead,
We will,            I can
Later.              Wait.            Straight to me,
                                       never mind
                    How can I        How.
We will . . .       Live until       Darling,
Soon.               Later?           Now —
                                     I still want and/or
                    Later . . .      Love
                                     You,

Soon.
                                     Now, as
                    Later . . .      Always,
Soon.                                Now,
                                       (He does a kiss)
                                     Desirée.
```

(ANNE *stares out, astonished, as the lights go down and the bedroom and parlor roll off.* FREDRIKA, *still at the piano, is playing scales*)

FREDRIKA (*Sings*):

Ordinary mothers lead ordinary lives:
Keep the house and sweep the parlor,
Cook the meals and look exhausted.
Ordinary mothers, like ordinary wives,
Fry the eggs and dry the sheets and
Try to deal with facts.

Mine acts.

(DESIRÉE *sweeps on with* MALLA, *her maid, in tow.* MALLA *carries a wig box, suitcase, and parasol*)

DESIRÉE (*As* FREDRIKA *reads a letter from her*):

Darling, I miss you a lot
But, darling, this has to be short
As Mother is getting a plaque
From the Halsingborg Arts Council

Amateur Theatre Group.
Whether it's funny or not,
I'll give you a fuller report
The minute they carry me back
From the Halsingborg Arts Council
Amateur Theatre Group . . .
Love you . . .

(*The* QUINTET *appears*)

QUINTET:
Unpack the luggage, la la la
Pack up the luggage, la la la
Unpack the luggage, la la la
Hi-ho, the glamorous life!

MRS. SEGSTROM:
Ice in the basin, la la la

MR. ERLANSON:
Cracks in the plaster, la la la

MRS. ANDERSSEN:
Mice in the hallway, la la la

ALL THE QUINTET:
Hi-ho, the glamorous life!

MEN:
Run for the carriage, la la la

WOMEN:
Wolf down the sandwich, la la la

ALL THE QUINTET:
Which town is this one? La la la
Hi-ho, the glamorous life!

(FRID *wheels* MADAME ARMFELDT *onstage*)

MADAME ARMFELDT:
Ordinary daughters ameliorate their lot,

Use their charms and choose their futures,
Breed their children, heed their mothers.
Ordinary daughters, which mine, I fear, is not,
Tend each asset, spend it wisely
While it still endures . . .

Mine tours.

DESIRÉE (*As* MADAME ARMFELDT *reads a letter from her*):
Mother, forgive the delay,
My schedule is driving me wild.
But, Mother, I really must run,
I'm performing in Rottvik,
And don't ask where is it, please.
How are you feeling today
And are you corrupting the child?
Don't. Mother, the minute I'm done
With performing in Rottvik,
I'll come for a visit

And argue.

MEN:
Mayors with speeches, la la la

WOMEN:
Children with posies, la la la

MEN:
Half-empty houses, la la la

ALL THE QUINTET:
Hi-ho, the glamorous life!

MRS. NORDSTROM:
Cultural lunches,

ALL THE QUINTET:
La la la

MRS. ANDERSSEN:
   Dead floral tributes,

ALL THE QUINTET:
   La la la

MR. LINDQUIST:
   Ancient admirers,

ALL THE QUINTET:
   La la la
   Hi-ho, the glamorous life!

FREDRIKA:
   Mother's romantic, la la la

MADAME ARMFELDT:
   Mother's misguided, la la la

DESIRÉE:
   Mother's surviving, la la la
   Leading the glamorous life!
                    (*Holds up a mirror*)
   Cracks in the plaster, la la la
   Youngish admirers, la la la
   Which one was that one? La la la
   Hi-ho, the glamorous life!

DESIRÉE *and* QUINTET:
   Bring up the curtain, la la la
   Bring down the curtain, la la la
   Bring up the curtain, la la la
   Hi-ho, the glamorous . . .
   Life.

Scene 2

STAGE OF LOCAL THEATER

The show curtain is down. Two stage boxes are visible. Sitting in one are MR. LINDQUIST, MRS. NORDSTROM, *and* MR. ERLANSON. ANNE *and* FREDRIK *enter, and speak as they walk to their box.*

ANNE: Does she look like her pictures?

FREDRIK: Who, dear?

ANNE: Desirée Armfeldt, of course.

FREDRIK: How would I know, dear?

ANNE (*Pause*): I only thought . . .

FREDRIK: You only thought — what?

ANNE: Desirée is not a common name. I mean, none of your typists and things are called Desirée, are they?

FREDRIK: My typists and things in descending order of importance are Miss Osa Svensen, Miss Ona Nilsson, Miss Gerda Bjornson, *and* Mrs. Amalia Lindquist.

(A PAGE *enters, and knocks three times with the staff he is carrying. The show curtain rises revealing the stage*

199

behind it, a tatty Louis XIV "salon," as PAGE *exits. For a moment it is empty. Then two* LADIES, *in rather shabby court costumes, enter)*

FIRST LADY (MRS. SEGSTROM): Tell me something about this remarkable Countess, Madame.

SECOND LADY (MRS. ANDERSSEN): I shall try as best I can to depict the personality of the Countess, Madame, although it is too rich in mysterious contradictions to be described in a few short moments.

FIRST LADY: It is said that her power over men is most extraordinary.

SECOND LADY: There is a great deal of truth in that, Madame, and her lovers are as many as the pearls in the necklace which she always wears.

FIRST LADY: Your own husband, Madame, is supposed to be one of the handsomest pearls, is he not?

SECOND LADY: He fell in love with the Countess on sight. She took him as a lover for three months and after that I had him back.

FIRST LADY: And your marriage was crushed?

SECOND LADY: On the contrary, Madame! My husband had become a tender, devoted, admirable lover, a faithful husband and an exemplary father. The Countess's lack of decency is most moral.

(*The* PAGE *re-enters)*

PAGE: The Countess Celimène de Francen de la Tour de Casa.

(*The* COUNTESS — DESIRÉE — *makes her sensational entrance. A storm of applause greets her.* FREDRIK *claps.* ANNE *does not as she glares at the stage. During the applause,* DESIRÉE *makes a deep curtsey, during which, old pro that*

200

she is, she cases the house. Her eye falls on FREDRIK. *She does a take and instantly all action freezes*)

MR. LINDQUIST (*Sings*):
Remember?

MRS. NORDSTROM (*Sings*):
Remember?
(MR. LINDQUIST *and* MRS. NORDSTROM *leave the stage box*)
The old deserted beach that we walked —
Remember?

MR. LINDQUIST:
Remember?
The café in the park where we talked —
Remember?

MRS. NORDSTROM:
Remember?

MR. LINDQUIST:
The tenor on the boat that we chartered,
Belching "The Bartered
Bride" —

BOTH:
Ah, how we laughed,
Ah, how we cried.

MR. LINDQUIST:
Ah, how you promised and
Ah, how I lied.

MRS. NORDSTROM:
That dilapidated inn —
Remember, darling?

MR. LINDQUIST:
The proprietress's grin,
Also her glare . . .

MRS. NORDSTROM:
Yellow gingham on the bed —
Remember, darling?

MR. LINDQUIST:
And the canopy in red,
Needing repair?

BOTH:
I *think* you were there.
(*They return to the stage box and the action continues*)

ANNE (*Fierce, to* FREDRIK): She looked at us. Why did she look at us?

DESIRÉE (*To* SECOND LADY): Dear Madame Merville, what a charming mischance to find you here this evening.

FREDRIK: I don't think she looked especially at us.

ANNE:	SECOND LADY:
She did! She peered,	Charming, indeed, dear
then she smiled.	Celimène.

SECOND LADY: May I be permitted to present my school friend from the provinces? Madame Vilmorac — whose husband, I'm sure, is in dire need of a little expert polishing.

FIRST LADY: Oh, dear Countess, you are all but a legend to me. I implore you to reveal to me the secret of your success with the hardier sex!

ANNE: She smiled at us!
(*Grabs* FREDRIK's *opera glasses and studies the stage*)

DESIRÉE: Dear Madame, that can be summed up in a single word —

ANNE: She's ravishingly beautiful.

FREDRIK: Make-up.

DESIRÉE: — dignity.

TWO LADIES: Dignity?

ANNE (*Turning on* FREDRIK): How can you be sure — if you've never seen her?

FREDRIK: Hush!

DESIRÉE (*Playing her first-act set speech*): Dignity. We women have a right to commit any crime toward our husbands, our lovers, our sons, as long as we do not hurt their dignity. We should make men's dignity our best ally and caress it, cradle it, speak tenderly to it, and handle it as our most delightful toy. Then a man is in our hands, at our feet, or anywhere else we momentarily wish him to be.

ANNE (*Sobbing*):	FREDRIK:
I want to go home!	Anne!

ANNE: I want to go home!

FREDRIK: Anne!

(*She runs off,* FREDRIK *following*)

Scene 3

THE EGERMAN ROOMS

> *In the parlor,* PETRA, *lying on the couch, is calmly re-arranging her blouse.* HENRIK, *in a storm of tension, is pulling on his trousers. On the floor beside them is a bottle of champagne and two glasses.*

HENRIK: We have sinned, and it was a complete failure!
> (*Struggling with his fly buttons*)

These buttons, these insufferable buttons!

PETRA: Here, dear, let me.
> (*She crosses, kneels in front of him, and starts to do up the fly buttons*)

Don't you worry, little Henrik. Just let it rest a while.
> (*She pats his fly*)

There. Now you put on your sweater and do a nice little quiet bit of reading.
> (*She gets his sweater from the back of a chair and helps him into it.* ANNE *enters, still crying. She sees* HENRIK *and* PETRA, *lets out a sob, and runs into the bedroom.* FREDRIK *enters. Perfectly calm, to* FREDRIK)

My, that was a short play.

FREDRIK: My wife became ill; I had to bring her home.

(*He gives* HENRIK *a look, sizing up the situation approvingly, before following* ANNE *into the bedroom*)
Anne!
(HENRIK *starts again toward* PETRA, *who avoids him*)

PETRA: No, lamb. I told you. Give it a nice rest and you'll be surprised how perky it'll be by morning.
(*She wiggles her way out.* FREDRIK *has now entered the bedroom;* ANNE *is no longer visible — as if she had moved into an inner room. In the parlor,* HENRIK *picks up the champagne bottle and glasses and puts them on the table*)

ANNE (*Off, calling*): Fredrik!

FREDRIK: Yes, dear.

ANNE: Did you have many women between your first wife and me? Sometimes when I think of what memories you have, I vanish inside.

FREDRIK: Before I met you I was quite a different man. Many things were different. Better?
(ANNE *comes back into the bedroom*)
Worse? Different, anyway.

ANNE: Do you remember when I was a little girl and you came to my father's house for dinner and told me fairy tales? Do you remember?

FREDRIK: Yes, I remember.

ANNE (*Sitting on* FREDRIK'*s lap*): Then you were "Uncle Fredrik" and now you're my husband. Isn't that amusing? You were so lonely and sad that summer. I felt terribly sorry for you, so I said: "Poor thing, I'll marry him." Are you coming to bed yet?

FREDRIK: Not just yet. I think I'll go for a breath of fresh air.

ANNE: That wasn't an amusing play, was it?

205

FREDRIK: We didn't see that much of it.

ANNE: I wonder how old that Armfeldt woman can be. At least fifty — don't you think?

FREDRIK: I wouldn't say that old.

ANNE: Well, goodnight.

FREDRIK: Goodnight.
(*As* FREDRIK *moves into the parlor,* MR. LINDQUIST *and* MRS. NORDSTROM *appear. There is a musical sting and* FREDRIK *and* HENRIK *freeze*)

MRS. NORDSTROM (*Sings*):
Remember?

MR. LINDQUIST (*Sings*):
Remember?

BOTH:
Remember?
Remember?
(FREDRIK *unfreezes, clasps his hands together and goes into the parlor.* HENRIK *looks anxiously at his father*)

HENRIK: Is she all right now?

FREDRIK: Oh yes, she's all right.

HENRIK: It wasn't anything serious?

FREDRIK: No, nothing serious.

HENRIK: You don't think — a doctor? I mean, it would be terrible if it was something — serious.

FREDRIK: Pray for her, son. Correction — pray for me. Goodnight.

HENRIK: Goodnight, father.

(FREDRIK *exits, and* MRS. NORDSTROM *and* MR. LINDQUIST *sweep downstage*)

MRS. NORDSTROM (*Sings*):
The local village dance on the green —
Remember?

MR. LINDQUIST (*Sings*):
Remember?
The lady with the large tambourine —
Remember?

MRS. NORDSTROM:
Remember?
The one who played the harp in her boa
Thought she was so a-
Dept.

BOTH:
Ah, how we laughed,
Ah, how we wept.
Ah, how we polka'd

MRS. NORDSTROM:
And ah, how we slept.
How we kissed and how we clung —
Remember, darling?

MR. LINDQUIST:
We were foolish, we were young —

BOTH:
More than we knew.

MRS. NORDSTROM:
Yellow gingham on the bed,
Remember, darling?
And the canopy in red —

MR. LINDQUIST:

Or was it blue?

(MRS. NORDSTROM *and* MR. LINDQUIST *are joined by* MRS. SEGSTROM, MRS. ANDERSSEN *and* MR. ERLANSON, *who appear downstage*)

MRS. SEGSTROM:

The funny little games that we played —
Remember?

MR. ERLANSON:

Remember?
The unexpected knock of the maid —
Remember?

MRS. ANDERSSEN:

Remember?
The wine that made us both rather merry
And, oh, so very
Frank —

ALL:

Ah, how we laughed.
Ah, how we drank.

MR. ERLANSON:

You acquiesced

MRS. ANDERSSEN:

And the rest is a blank.

MR. LINDQUIST:

What we did with your perfume —

MR. ERLANSON:

Remember, darling?

MRS. SEGSTROM:

The condition of the room
When we were through . . .

MRS. NORDSTROM:

Our inventions were unique —
Remember, darling?

MR. LINDQUIST:

I was limping for a week,
You caught the flu . . .

ALL:

I'm *sure* it was —
You.

> (*They drift off as* DESIRÉE'*s digs come on*)

Scene 4

DESIRÉE'S DIGS

> FREDRIK *walks on, as* DESIRÉE, *in a robe, enters, munching
> a sandwich and carrying a glass of beer.*

FREDRIK: They told me where to find you at the theater.

DESIRÉE: Fredrik!

FREDRIK: Hello, Desirée.
> (*For a moment they gaze at each other*)

DESIRÉE: So it *was* you! I peered and peered and said: "Is it
. . . ? Can it be . . . ? Is it possible?" And then, of course,
when you walked out after five minutes, I was sure.

FREDRIK: Was my record that bad?

DESIRÉE: Terrible. You walked out on my Hedda in Halsingborg. And on my sensational Phaedra in Ekilstuna.

FREDRIK (*Standing, looking at her*): Fourteen years!

DESIRÉE: Fourteen years!

FREDRIK: No rancor?

DESIRÉE: Rancor? For a while, a little. But now — no rancor,
not a trace.

210

> (*Indicating a plate of sandwiches*)
Sandwich?

FREDRIK (*Declining*): Hungry as ever after a performance, I see.

DESIRÉE: Worse. I'm a wolf. Sit down.
> (*Pouring him a glass of schnapps*)
Here. You never said no to schnapps.
> (FREDRIK *sits down on the love seat. She stands, looking at him*)

FREDRIK: About *this* walking out! I'd like to explain.

DESIRÉE: The girl in the pink dress, I imagine.

FREDRIK: You still don't miss a thing, do you?

DESIRÉE: Your wife.

FREDRIK: For the past eleven months. She was so looking forward to the play, she got a little overexcited. She's only eighteen, still almost a child.
> (*A pause*)
I'm waiting.

DESIRÉE: For what?

FREDRIK: For you to tell me what an old fool I've become to have fallen under the spell of youth, beginnings, the blank page.
> (*Very coolly,* DESIRÉE *opens the robe, revealing her naked body to him*)

DESIRÉE: The page that has been written on — *and* rewritten.

FREDRIK (*Looking, admiring*): With great style. Some things — schnapps, for example — improve with age.

DESIRÉE: Let us hope that proves true of your little bride.
> (*She closes the wrapper and stands, still very cool, looking at him*)

211

So you took her home and tucked her up in her cot with her rattle and her woolly penguin.

FREDRIK: Figuratively speaking.

DESIRÉE: And then you came to me.

FREDRIK: I wish you'd ask me why.

DESIRÉE (*Dead pan*): Why did you come to me?

FREDRIK: For old times' sake? For curiosity? To boast about my wife? To complain about her? Perhaps — Hell, why am I being such a lawyer about it?
(*Pause*)
This afternoon when I was taking my nap . . .

DESIRÉE: So you take afternoon naps now!

FREDRIK: Hush! . . . I had the most delightful dream.

DESIRÉE: About . . . ?

FREDRIK: . . . you.

DESIRÉE: Ah! What did we do?

FREDRIK: Well, as a matter of fact, we were in that little hotel in Malmö. We'd been basking in the sun all day.

DESIRÉE (*Suddenly picking it up*): When my back got so burned it was an agony to lie down so you . . . ?

FREDRIK: As vivid as . . . Well, *very* vivid! So you see. My motives for coming here are what might be called — mixed.
(DESIRÉE *suddenly bursts into laughter. Tentative*)
Funny?

DESIRÉE (*Suddenly controlling the laughter, very mock solemn*): No. Not at all.
(*There is a pause, distinctly charged with unadmitted sex*)

FREDRIK (*Looking around, slightly uncomfortable*): How familiar all this is.

DESIRÉE: Oh yes, nothing's changed. Uppsala one week. Örebro the next. The same old inevitable routine.

FREDRIK: But it still has its compensations?

DESIRÉE: Yes — no — no — yes.

FREDRIK: That's a rather ambiguous answer.
(*Pause*)
You must, at least at times, be lonely.

DESIRÉE (*Smiling*): Dear Fredrik, if you're inquiring about my love life, rest assured. It's quite satisfactory.

FREDRIK: I see. And — if I may ask — at the moment?

DESIRÉE: A dragoon. A very handsome, very married dragoon with, I'm afraid, the vanity of a peacock, the brain of a pea, but the physical proportions . . .

FREDRIK: Don't specify the vegetable, please. I am easily deflated.
(*They both burst into spontaneous laughter*)
Oh, Desirée!

DESIRÉE: Fredrik!
(*Another charged pause.* FREDRIK *tries again*)

FREDRIK: Desirée, I . . .

DESIRÉE: Yes, dear?

FREDRIK: I — er . . . That is . . .
(*Loses his nerve again*)
Perhaps a little more schnapps?

DESIRÉE : Help yourself.
(FREDRIK *crosses to the writing desk, where, next to the schnapps, is a framed photograph of* FREDRIKA. *He notices it*)

FREDRIK: Who's this?

DESIRÉE (*Suddenly rather awkward*): That? Oh — my daughter.

FREDRIK: Your daughter? I had no idea . . .

DESIRÉE: She happened.

FREDRIK: She's charming. Where is she now?

DESIRÉE: She's with my mother in the country. She used to
tour with me, and then one day Mother swept up like the
Wrath of God and saved her from me — You never knew
my mother! She always wins *our* battles.
> (*Wanting to get off the subject*)
I think perhaps a little schnapps for me too.

FREDRIK: Oh yes, of course.
> (FREDRIK *pours a second schnapps. The charged pause
> again*)

DESIRÉE (*Indicating the room*): I apologize for all this squalor!

FREDRIK: On the contrary, I have always associated you very
happily with — chaos.
> (*Pause*)
So.

DESIRÉE: So.

FREDRIK (*Artificially bright*): Well, I think it's time to talk
about my wife, don't you?

DESIRÉE: Boast or complain?

FREDRIK: Both, I expect.
> (*Sings*)
She lightens my sadness,
She livens my days,
She bursts with a kind of madness
My well-ordered ways.
My happiest mistake,
The ache of my life:
You must meet my wife.

She bubbles with pleasure,

214

She glows with surprise,
Disrupts my accustomed leisure
And ruffles my ties.
I don't know even now
Quite how it began.
You must meet my wife, my Anne.

One thousand whims to which I give in,
Since her smallest tear turns me ashen.
I never dreamed that I could live in
So completely demented,
Contented
A fashion.

So sunlike, so winning,
So unlike a wife.
I do think that I'm beginning
To show signs of life.
Don't ask me how at my age
One still can grow —
If you met my wife,
You'd know.

DESIRÉE: Dear Fredrik, I'm just longing to meet her. Sometime.

FREDRIK:
She sparkles.

DESIRÉE:
How pleasant.

FREDRIK:
She twinkles.

DESIRÉE:
How nice.

FREDRIK:
Her youth is a sort of present —

DESIRÉE:
Whatever the price.

FREDRIK:
The incandescent — what? — the —

DESIRÉE (*Proffering a cigarette*):
Light?

FREDRIK (*Lighting it*):
— Of my life!
You must meet my wife.

DESIRÉE:
Yes, I must, I really must. Now —

FREDRIK:
She flutters.

DESIRÉE:
How charming.

FREDRIK:
She twitters.

DESIRÉE:
My word!

FREDRIK:
She floats.

DESIRÉE:
Isn't that alarming?
What is she, a bird?

FREDRIK:
She makes me feel I'm — what? —

DESIRÉE:
A very old man?

FREDRIK:
Yes — no!

DESIRÉE:
No.

FREDRIK:
But —

DESIRÉE:
I must meet your Gertrude.

FREDRIK:
My Anne.

DESIRÉE:
Sorry — Anne.

FREDRIK:
She loves my voice, my walk, my mustache,
The cigar, in fact, that I'm smoking.
She'll watch me puff until it's just ash,
Then she'll save the cigar butt.

DESIRÉE:
Bizarre, but
You're joking.

FREDRIK:
She dotes on —

DESIRÉE:
Your dimple.

FREDRIK:
My snoring.

DESIRÉE:
How dear.

FREDRIK:
The point is, she's really simple.

DESIRÉE (*Smiling*):
Yes, that much seems clear.

FREDRIK:
   She gives me funny names.

DESIRÉE:
   Like — ?

FREDRIK:
   "Old dry-as-dust."

DESIRÉE:
   Wouldn't she just?

FREDRIK:
   You must meet my wife.

DESIRÉE:
   If I must —
            (*Looks over her shoulder at him and smiles*)
   Yes, I must.

FREDRIK:
   A sea of whims that I submerge in,
   Yet so lovable in repentance.
   Unfortunately, still a virgin,
   But you can't force a flower —

DESIRÉE (*Rises*):
   Don't finish that sentence!
   She's monstrous!

FREDRIK:
   She's frightened.

DESIRÉE:
   Unfeeling!

FREDRIK:
   Unversed.
   She'd strike you as unenlightened.

DESIRÉE:
   No, I'd strike her first.

FREDRIK:
Her reticence, her apprehension —

DESIRÉE:
Her crust!

FREDRIK:
No!

DESIRÉE:
Yes!

FREDRIK:
No!

DESIRÉE:
Fredrik . . .

FREDRIK:
You must meet my wife.

DESIRÉE:
Let me get my hat and my knife.

FREDRIK:
What was that?

DESIRÉE:
I must meet your wife.

FREDRIK: DESIRÉE:
Yes, you must.   Yes, I must.

DESIRÉE (*Speaks*): A virgin.

FREDRIK: A virgin.

DESIRÉE: Eleven months?

FREDRIK: Eleven months.

DESIRÉE: No wonder you dreamed of me!

FREDRIK: At least it was you I dreamed of, which indicates a
kind of retroactive fidelity, doesn't it?

DESIRÉE: At least.

FREDRIK (*Suddenly very shy*): Desirée, I —

DESIRÉE: Yes?

FREDRIK: Would it seem insensitive if I were to ask you — I can't say it!

DESIRÉE: Say it, darling.

FREDRIK: Would you . . .
>   (*He can't*)

DESIRÉE: Of course. What are old friends for?
> (*She rises, holds out her hand to him. He takes her hand, rises, too*)

Wait till you see the bedroom! Stockings all over the place, a rather rusty hip-bath — and the Virgin Mary over the headboard.
> (*They exit, laughing, into the bedroom.* MADAME ARM-
> FELDT *appears and sings, with one eye on the room*)

MADAME ARMFELDT:
At the villa of the Baron de Signac,
Where I spent a somewhat infamous year,
At the villa of the Baron de Signac
I had ladies in attendance,
Fire-opal pendants . . .

Liaisons! What's happened to them,
Liaisons today?
Disgraceful! What's become of them?
Some of them
Hardly pay their shoddy way.

What once was a rare champagne
Is now just an amiable hock,
What once was a villa at least
Is "digs."

What once was a gown with train
Is now just a simple little frock,
What once was a sumptuous feast
Is figs.
No, not even figs — raisins.
Ah, liaisons!

Now let me see . . . Where was I? Oh, yes . . .

At the palace of the Duke of Ferrara,
Who was prematurely deaf but a dear,
At the palace of the Duke of Ferrara
I acquired some position
Plus a tiny Titian . . .

Liaisons! What's happened to them,
Liaisons today?
To see them — indiscriminate
Women, it
Pains me more than I can say,
The lack of taste that they display.

Where is style?
Where is skill?
Where is forethought?
Where's discretion of the heart,
Where's passion in the art,
Where's craft?
With a smile
And a will,
But with more thought,
I acquired a chateau
Extravagantly o-
Verstaffed.

Too many people muddle sex
With mere desire,
And when emotion intervenes,

The nets descend.
It should on no account perplex,
Or worse, inspire.
It's but a pleasurable means
To a measurable end.
Why does no one comprehend?
Let us hope this lunacy is just a trend.

Now let me see . . . Where was I? Oh, yes . . .

In the castle of the King of the Belgians
We would visit through a false chiffonier.
In the castle of the King of the Belgians
Who, when things got rather touchy,
Deeded me a duchy . . .

Liaisons! What's happened to them,
Liaisons today?
Untidy — take my daughter, I
Taught her, I
Tried my best to point the way.
I even named her Desirée.

In a world where the kings are employers,
Where the amateur prevails and delicacy fails to pay,
In a world where the princes are lawyers,
What can anyone expect except to recollect
Liai . . .

(*She falls asleep.* FRID *appears and carries her off. A beat*)

CARL-MAGNUS (*Off*): All right, all right. It's broken down. So
do something! Crank it up — or whatever it is!
(FREDRIK *and* DESIRÉE *appear at the bedroom door,* FRED-
RIK *in a bathrobe,* DESIRÉE *in a negligee*)

FREDRIK: What can it be?

DESIRÉE: It can't!

FREDRIK: The dragoon?

DESIRÉE: Impossible. He's on maneuvers. Eighty miles away. He couldn't . . .

CARL-MAGNUS (*Off, bellowing*): A garage, idiot! That's what they're called.

DESIRÉE: He could.

FREDRIK: Is he jealous?

DESIRÉE: Tremendously.
>(*Suppresses a giggle*)
This shouldn't be funny, should it?

FREDRIK: Let him in.

DESIRÉE: Fredrik . . .

FREDRIK: I am not a lawyer — nor are you an actress — for nothing. Let him in.
>(DESIRÉE *goes to open the door.* CARL-MAGNUS *enters, immaculate but brushing imaginary dust from his uniform. He is carrying a bunch of daisies*)

DESIRÉE (*With tremendous poise*): Carl-Magnus! What a delightful surprise!
>(*Totally ignoring* FREDRIK, CARL-MAGNUS *bows stiffly and kisses her hand*)

CARL-MAGNUS: Excuse my appearance. My new motorcar broke down.
>(*Hand kiss. Presents the daisies*)
From a neighboring garden.

DESIRÉE (*Taking them*): How lovely! Will you be staying long?

CARL-MAGNUS: I have twenty hours leave. Three hours coming here, nine hours with you, five hours with my wife and three hours back.
>(*Still ignoring* FREDRIK)
Do you mind if I take off my uniform and put on my robe?

223

DESIRÉE: Well — at the moment it's occupied.

CARL-MAGNUS (*Not looking at* FREDRIK): So I see.

DESIRÉE: Mr. Egerman — Count Malcolm.

FREDRIK: Sir.

CARL-MAGNUS (*Still ignoring* FREDRIK): Sir.

FREDRIK: I feel I should give you an explanation for what may seem to be a rather unusual situation.
(*With tremulous aplomb*)
For many years, I have been Miss Armfeldt's mother's lawyer and devoted friend. A small lawsuit of hers — nothing major, I'm happy to say — comes up in Court tomorrow morning and at the last minute I realized that some legal papers required her daughter's signature. Although it was late and she had already retired . . .

DESIRÉE: I let him in, of course.

CARL-MAGNUS (*Turning the icy gaze on her*): And then?

DESIRÉE: Ah, yes, the — the robe. Well, you see . . .

FREDRIK: Unfortunately, sir, on my way to the water-closet — through Miss Armfeldt's darkened bedroom — I inadvertently tripped over her hip-bath and fell in. Miss Armfeldt generously loaned me this garment while waiting for my clothes to dry in the bedroom.

CARL-MAGNUS: In that case, Miss Armfeldt, I suggest you return to the bedroom and see whether this gentleman's clothes are dry by now.

DESIRÉE: Yes. Of course.
(*She crosses between* FREDRIK *and* CARL-MAGNUS *and exits. Pacing,* CARL-MAGNUS *begins to whistle a military march.* FREDRIK *counters by whistling a bit of Mozart*)

CARL-MAGNUS: Are you fond of duels, sir?

FREDRIK: I don't really know. I haven't ever tried.

CARL-MAGNUS: I have duelled seven times. Pistol, rapier, foil. I've been wounded five times. Otherwise fortune has been kind to me.

FREDRIK: I must say I'm impressed.

CARL-MAGNUS (*Picking up fruit knife*): You see this fruit knife? The target will be that picture. The old lady. Her face. Her eye.
> (*Throws knife, which hits target*)

FREDRIK (*Clapping*): Bravo.

CARL-MAGNUS: Are you being insolent, sir?

FREDRIK: Of course — sir.
> (DESIRÉE *returns from the bedroom. She is carrying* FREDRIK's *clothes in a soaking wet bundle. She has dipped them in the hip-bath*)

DESIRÉE: They're not *very* dry.

FREDRIK: Oh dear me, they're certainly not, are they?

CARL-MAGNUS: A predicament.

FREDRIK: Indeed.

CARL-MAGNUS: I imagine, Miss Armfeldt, you could find this gentleman one of my nightshirts.

FREDRIK: Thank you, thank you. But I think I'd prefer to put on my own — er — garments.
> (FREDRIK *takes the wet bundle from* DESIRÉE)

CARL-MAGNUS: Unfortunately, sir, you will not have the time for that.
> (*To* DESIRÉE)
Perhaps you could tell him where to look.

DESIRÉE: Oh yes, yes. The left hand — no, the right hand

bottom drawer of the — er —
>
> (*Indicating a chest of drawers*)

. . . thing.

> (FREDRIK *gives her the wet clothes*)

FREDRIK (*Hesitating, then*): Thank you.

> (*He goes into the bedroom. While he is away,* DESIRÉE *and* CARL-MAGNUS *confront each other in near-silence:* CARL-MAGNUS *whistles a bit of the march that he whistled at* FREDRIK *earlier.* FREDRIK *returns in a nightshirt, carrying the robe, which he holds out to* CARL-MAGNUS)

Your robe, sir.

> (CARL-MAGNUS *receives it in silence.* FREDRIK *puts on the nightcap that goes with the nightshirt*)

Well — er — goodnight. Miss Armfeldt, thank you for your cooperation.

> (FREDRIK *takes the wet bundle from* DESIRÉE *and exits*)

CARL-MAGNUS (*Sings, to himself*):
She wouldn't . . .
Therefore they didn't . . .
So then it wasn't . . .
Not unless it . . .
Would she?
She doesn't . . .
God knows she needn't . . .
Therefore it's not.

He'd never . . .
Therefore they haven't . . .
Which makes the question absolutely . . .
Could he?
She daren't . . .
Therefore I mustn't . . .
What utter rot!

Fidelity is more than mere display,

It's what a man expects from life.
   (*The unit that* DESIRÉE *is sitting on starts to ride off as*
   CHARLOTTE, *seated at her breakfast table, rides on*)
Fidelity like mine to Desirée
And Charlotte, my devoted wife.

Scene 5

BREAKFAST ROOM IN MALCOLM COUNTRY HOUSE

Breakfast for one (CHARLOTTE's) — *and an extra coffee cup* — *stands on an elegant little table. Music under.*

CHARLOTTE: How was Miss Desirée Armfeldt? In good health, I trust?

CARL-MAGNUS: Charlotte, my dear. I have exactly five hours.

CHARLOTTE (*Dead pan*): Five hours this time? Last time it was four. I'm gaining ground.

CARL-MAGNUS (*Pre-occupied*): She had a visitor. A lawyer in a nightshirt.

CHARLOTTE: Now, *that* I find interesting. What did you do?

CARL-MAGNUS: Threw him out.

CHARLOTTE: In a nightshirt?

CARL-MAGNUS: In *my* nightshirt.

CHARLOTTE: What sort of lawyer? Corporation, maritime, criminal — testamentary?

CARL-MAGNUS: Didn't your sister's little school friend Anne Sorensen marry a Fredrik Egerman?

CHARLOTTE: Yes, she did.

CARL-MAGNUS: Fredrik Egerman . . .
>   (*Sings*)
> The papers,
> He mentioned papers,
> Some legal papers
> Which I didn't see there . . .
> Where were they,
> The goddamn papers
> She had to sign?
>
> What nonsense!
> He brought her papers,
> They were important,
> So he had to be there . . .
> I'll kill him . . .
> Why should I bother?
> The woman's mine!
>
> Besides, no matter what one might infer,
> One must have faith to some degree.
> The least that I can do is trust in her
> The way that Charlotte trusts in me.
>   (*Speaks*)
> What are you planning to do today?

CHARLOTTE: *After* the five hours?

CARL-MAGNUS: Right now. I need a little sleep.

CHARLOTTE: Ah! I see. In that case, my plans will have to be changed. What will I do?
>   (*Sudden mock radiance*)
> I know! Nothing!

CARL-MAGNUS: Why don't you pay a visit to Marta's little school friend?

CHARLOTTE: Ah ha!

CARL-MAGNUS: She probably has no idea what *her* husband's up to.

CHARLOTTE: And I could enlighten her. Poor Carl-Magnus, are you *that* jealous?

CARL-MAGNUS: A civilized man can tolerate his wife's infidelity, but when it comes to his mistress, a man becomes a tiger.

CHARLOTTE: As opposed, of course, to a goat in rut. Ah, well, if I'm back in two hours, that still leaves us three hours. Right?

CARL-MAGNUS (*Unexpectedly smiling*): You're a good wife, Charlotte. The best.

CHARLOTTE: That's a comforting thought to take with me to town, dear. It just may keep me from cutting my throat on the tram.

(CHARLOTTE *exits*)

CARL-MAGNUS:
Capable, pliable . . .
Women, women . . .
Undemanding and reliable,
Knowing their place.
Insufferable, yes, but gentle,
Their weaknesses are incidental,
A functional but ornamental
                     (*Sips coffee*)
Race.
Durable, sensible . . .
Women, women . . .
Very nearly indispensable
Creatures of grace.
God knows the foolishness about them,

But if one had to live without them,
The world would surely be a poorer,
If purer,
Place.

The hip-bath . . .
About that hip-bath . . .
How can you slip and trip into a hip-bath?
The papers . . .
Where were the papers?
Of course, he might have taken back the papers . . .
She wouldn't . . .
Therefore they didn't . . .
The woman's mine!

(He strides off)

Scene 6

THE EGERMAN ROOMS

In the bedroom, ANNE, *in a negligee, sits on the bed while* PETRA *combs her hair.*

ANNE: Oh, that's delicious. I could purr. Having your hair brushed is gloriously sensual, isn't it?

PETRA: I can think of more sensual things.

ANNE (*Giggles, then suddenly serious*): Are you a virgin, Petra?

PETRA: God forbid.

ANNE (*Sudden impulse*): I am.

PETRA: I know.

ANNE (*Astonished and flustered*): How on earth can you tell?

PETRA: Your skin, something in your eyes.

ANNE: Can everyone see it?

PETRA: I wouldn't think so.

ANNE: Well, that's a relief.

(*Giggles*)

How old were you when —

PETRA: Sixteen.

ANNE: It must have been terrifying, wasn't it? *And* disgusting.

PETRA: Disgusting? It was more fun than the rolly-coaster at the fair.

ANNE: Henrik says that almost everything that's fun is automatically vicious. It's so depressing.

PETRA: Oh him! Poor little puppy dog!

ANNE (*Suddenly imperious*): Don't you dare talk about your employer's son that way.

PETRA: Sorry, Ma'am.

ANNE: I forbid anyone in this house to tease Henrik.
> (*Giggles again*)

Except me.
> (ANNE *goes to the vanity, sits, opens the top of her robe, studies her reflection in the table-mirror*)

It's quite a good body, isn't it?

PETRA: Nothing wrong there.

ANNE: Is it as good as yours?
> (*Laughing, she turns and pulls at* PETRA, *trying to undo* PETRA*'s uniform*)

Let me see!
> (*For a moment,* PETRA *is shocked. Laughing,* ANNE *continues;* PETRA *starts laughing too. They begin struggling playfully together*)

If I was a boy, would I prefer you or me? Tell me, tell me!
> (*Still laughing and struggling they stumble across the room and collapse in a heap on the bed*)

You're a boy! You're a boy!

PETRA (*Laughing*): God forbid!

(As they struggle, the front doorbell rings)

ANNE *(Sits up)*: Run, Petra, run. Answer it.

> *(PETRA climbs over ANNE to get off of the bed. As PETRA hurries into the parlor and exits to answer the door, ANNE peers at herself in the mirror)*

Oh dear, oh dear, my hair! My — everything!

> *(PETRA returns to the parlor with CHARLOTTE)*

PETRA: Please have a seat, Countess. Madame will be with you in a minute.

> *(CHARLOTTE looks around the room — particularly at FREDRIK's picture. PETRA hurries into the bedroom. Hissing)*

It's a Countess!

ANNE: A Countess?

PETRA: Very grand.

ANNE: How thrilling! Who on earth can she be?

> *(After a final touch at the mirror, she draws herself up with great dignity and, with PETRA behind her, sweeps into the parlor. At the door, she stops and stares. Then delighted, runs to CHARLOTTE)*

Charlotte Olafsson! It is, isn't it? Marta's big sister who married that magnificent Count Something or Other — and I was a flower girl at the wedding.

CHARLOTTE: Unhappily without a time-bomb in your Lilly-of-the-Valley bouquet.

ANNE *(Laughing)*: Oh, Charlotte, you always did say the most amusing things.

CHARLOTTE: I still do. I frequently laugh myself to sleep contemplating my own future.

ANNE: Petra. Ice, lemonade, cookies.

> *(PETRA leaves. Pause)*

CHARLOTTE: Well, dear, how are you? And how is your marriage working out?

ANNE: I'm in bliss. I have all the dresses in the world and a maid to take care of me and this charming house and a husband who spoils me shamelessly.

CHARLOTTE: That list, I trust, is in diminishing order of priority.

ANNE: How dreadful you are! Of course it isn't. And how's dear Marta?

CHARLOTTE: Ecstatic. Dear Marta has renounced men and is teaching gymnastics in a school for retarded girls in Bettleheim. Which brings me or . . .
(*Glancing at a little watch on her bosom*)
. . . rather should bring me, as my time is strictly limited — to the subject of men. How do you rate your husband as a man?

ANNE: I — don't quite know what you mean.

CHARLOTTE: I will give you an example. As a man, my husband could be rated as a louse, a bastard, a conceited, puffed-up, adulterous egomaniac. He constantly makes me do the most degrading, the most humiliating things like . . . like . . .
(*Her composure starts to crumble. She opens a little pocketbook and fumbles*)

ANNE: Like?

CHARLOTTE: Like . . .
(*Taking tiny handkerchief from purse, dabbing at her nose and bursting into tears*)
Oh, why do I put up with it? Why do I let him treat me like — like an intimidated corporal in his regiment? Why? Why? Why? I'll tell you why. I despise him! I hate

235

him! I *love* him! Oh damn that woman! May she rot forever in some infernal dressing room with lipstick of fire and scalding mascara! Let every billboard in hell eternally announce: Desirée Armfeldt in — in — in *The Wild Duck!*
(*Abandons herself to tears*)

ANNE: Desirée Armfeldt? But what has she done to you?

CHARLOTTE: What has she *not* done? Enslaved my husband — enslaved yours . . .

ANNE: Fredrik!

CHARLOTTE: He was there last night in her bedroom — in a nightshirt. My husband threw him out into the street and he's insanely jealous. He told me to come here and tell you . . . and I'm actually *telling* you! Oh what a monster I've become!

ANNE: Charlotte, is that the truth? Fredrik was there — in a nightshirt?
(CHARLOTTE *sobs*)

CHARLOTTE: My husband's nightshirt!

ANNE: Oh I knew it! I was sure he'd met her before. And when she *smiled* at us in the theater . . .
(*She begins to weep*)

CHARLOTTE: Poor Anne!
(PETRA *enters with the tray of lemonade and cookies and stands gazing at the two women in astonishment*)

PETRA: The lemonade, Ma'am.

ANNE: (*Looking up, controlling herself with a great effort, to the weeping* CHARLOTTE): Lemonade, Charlotte?

CHARLOTTE (*Looking up too, seeing the lemonade*): Lemonade! It would choke me!
(*Sings*)

Every day a little death
In the parlor, in the bed,
In the curtains, in the silver,
In the buttons, in the bread.
Every day a little sting
In the heart and in the head.
Every move and every breath,
And you hardly feel a thing,
Brings a perfect little death.

He smiles sweetly, strokes my hair,
Says he misses me.
I would murder him right there,
But first I die.
He talks softly of his wars,
And his horses
And his whores,
I think love's a dirty business!

ANNE: So do I!

CHARLOTTE:	ANNE:
I'm before him	So do I . . .
On my knees	
And he kisses me.	

CHARLOTTE:
He assumes I'll lose my reason,
And I do.
Men are stupid, men are vain,
Love's disgusting, love's insane,
A humiliating business!

ANNE:
Oh, how true!

CHARLOTTE:
Ah, well . . .
Every day a little death,

ANNE:

Every day a little death,

CHARLOTTE:

In the parlor, in the bed,

ANNE:

On the lips and in the eyes,

CHARLOTTE:
In the curtains,
In the silver,
In the buttons,
In the bread.

ANNE:
In the murmurs,
In the pauses,
In the gestures,
In the sighs.

Every day a little sting
In the heart
And in the head.

Every day a little dies,

In the looks and in
The lies.

Every move and
Every breath,
And you hardly feel a
Thing,
Brings a perfect little
Death.

And you hardly feel a
Thing,
Brings a perfect little
Death.

> (*After the number,* HENRIK *enters, taking off his hat and scarf*)

HENRIK: Oh, excuse me.

ANNE (*Trying to rise to the occasion*): Charlotte, this is Henrik Egerman.

HENRIK (*Bows and offers his hand*): I am happy to make your acquaintance, Madame.

CHARLOTTE: Happy! Who could ever be happy to meet *me?*

(*Holding* HENRIK's *hand, she rises and then drifts out.* ANNE *falls back sobbing on the couch.* HENRIK *stands, gazing at her*)

HENRIK: Anne, what is it?

ANNE: Nothing.

HENRIK: But what did that woman say to you?

ANNE: Nothing, nothing at all.

HENRIK: That can't be true.

ANNE: It is! It is! She — she merely told me that Marta Olafsson, my dearest friend from school is — teaching gymnastics . . .
> (*Bursts into tears again, falls into* HENRIK's *arms.* HENRIK *puts his arms around her slowly, cautiously*)

HENRIK: Anne! Poor Anne! If you knew how it destroys me to see you unhappy.

ANNE: I am not unhappy!

HENRIK: You know. You must know. Ever since you married Father, you've been more precious to me than . . .

ANNE (*Pulls back, suddenly giggling through her tears*): . . . Martin Luther?
> (HENRIK, *cut to the quick, jumps up*)

HENRIK: Can you laugh at me even now?

ANNE (*Rises*): Oh dear, I'm sorry. Perhaps, after all, I am a totally frivolous woman with ice for a heart. Am I, Henrik? Am I?
> (PETRA *enters*)

MADAME ARMFELDT (*Off*): Seven of Hearts on the Eight of Spades.

ANNE (*Laughing again*): Silly Henrik, get your book, quick,

239

and denounce the wickedness of the world to me for at least a half an hour.

(ANNE *runs off as the bedroom and parlor go.* HENRIK *follows her, as does* PETRA, *carrying the lemonade tray*)

MADAME ARMFELDT (*Off*): The Ten of Hearts! Who needs the Ten of Hearts!!

Scene 7

ARMFELDT TERRACE

> MADAME ARMFELDT *is playing solitaire, with* FRID *standing behind her.* FREDRIKA *sits at the piano, playing scales.*

MADAME ARMFELDT: Child, I am about to give you your advice for the day.

FREDRIKA: Yes, Grandmother.

MADAME ARMFELDT: Never marry — or even dally with — a Scandinavian.

FREDRIKA: Why not, Grandmother?

MADAME ARMFELDT: They are all insane.

FREDRIKA: All of them?

MADAME ARMFELDT: Uh-hum. It's the latitude. A winter when the sun never rises, a summer when the sun never sets, are more than enough to addle the brain of any man. Further off, further off. You practically inhaled the Queen of Diamonds.

DESIRÉE (*Off*): Who's home?

FREDRIKA (*Jumps up, thrilled*): Mother!

(DESIRÉE *enters and* FREDRIKA *rushes to her, throwing herself into* DESIRÉE's *arms*)

DESIRÉE: Darling, you've grown a mile; you're much prettier, you're irresistible! Hello, Mother.

MADAME ARMFELDT (*Continuing to play, unfriendly*): And to what do I owe the honor of this visit?

DESIRÉE: I just thought I'd pop out and see you both. Is that so surprising?

MADAME ARMFELDT: Yes.

DESIRÉE: You're in one of your bitchy moods, I see.

MADAME ARMFELDT: If you've come to take Fredrika back, the answer is no. I do not object to the immorality of your life, merely to its sloppiness. Since I have been tidy enough to have acquired a sizeable mansion with a fleet of servants, it is only common sense that my granddaughter should reap the advantages of it.
> (*To* FREDRIKA)

Isn't that so, child?

FREDRIKA: I really don't know, Grandmother.

MADAME ARMFELDT: Oh yes you do, dear. Well, Desirée, there must be something you want or you wouldn't have "popped out." What is it?

DESIRÉE: All right. The tour's over for a while, and I was wondering if you'd invite some people here next weekend.

MADAME ARMFELDT: If they're actors, they'll have to sleep in the stables.

DESIRÉE: Not actors, Mother. Just a lawyer from town and his family — Fredrik Egerman.

242

MADAME ARMFELDT: In my day, one went to lawyers' offices but never consorted with their *families*.

DESIRÉE: Then it'll make a nice change, dear, won't it?

MADAME ARMFELDT: I am deeply suspicious, but very well.

DESIRÉE (*Producing a piece of paper*): Here's the address.

MADAME ARMFELDT (*Taking it*): I shall send 'round a formal invitation by hand.
> (*She snaps her fingers for* FRID. *As he wheels her off*)
Needless to say, I shall be polite to your guests. However, they will not be served my best champagne. I am saving that for my funeral.
> (FREDRIKA *runs to* DESIRÉE; *they embrace, and freeze in that pose. We see, in another area,* PETRA *bringing* ANNE *an invitation on a small silver tray*)

PETRA:
> Look, Ma'am,
> An invitation.
> Here, Ma'am,
> Delivered by hand.
> And, Ma'am,
> I notice the station-
> Ery's engraved and very grand.

ANNE:
> Petra, how too exciting!
> Just when I need it!
> Petra, such elegant writing,
> So chic you hardly can read it.
> What do you think?
> Who can it be?
> Even the ink —
> No, here, let me . . .
> "Your presence . . . "

Just think of it, Petra!
"Is kindly . . . "
It's at a chateau!
"Requested . . . "
Et cet'ra, et cet'ra,
". . . Madame Leonora Armf — "
Oh, no!
A weekend in the country!

PETRA:
We're invited?

ANNE:
What a horrible plot!
A weekend in the country!

PETRA:
I'm excited.

ANNE:
No, you're not!

PETRA:
A weekend in the country!
Just imagine!

ANNE:
It's completely depraved.

PETRA:
A weekend in the country!

ANNE:
It's insulting!

PETRA:
It's engraved.

ANNE:
It's that woman,
It's that Armfeldt . . .

PETRA:
Oh, the actress . . .

ANNE:
No, the ghoul.
She may hope to
Make her charm felt,
But she's mad if she thinks
I would be such a fool
As to weekend in the country!

PETRA (*Ironically*):
How insulting!

ANNE:
And I've nothing to wear!

BOTH:
A weekend in the country!

ANNE:
Here!
(ANNE *gives the invitation back to* PETRA)
The last place I'm going is there!
(ANNE *and* PETRA *exit*. DESIRÉE *and* FREDRIKA *unfreeze
and begin to move downstage*)

DESIRÉE: Well, dear, are you happy here?

FREDRIKA: Yes. I think so. But I miss us.

DESIRÉE: Oh, so do I!
(*Pause*)
Darling, how would you feel if we had a home of our very
own with me only acting when I felt like it — and a man
who would make you a spectacular father?

FREDRIKA: Oh I see. The lawyer! Mr. Egerman!

DESIRÉE: Dear child, you're uncanny.

245

(DESIRÉE *and* FREDRIKA *freeze once again.* FREDRIK, ANNE, *and* PETRA *enter*)

PETRA (*To* FREDRIK):
  Guess what, an invitation!

ANNE:
  Guess who, begins with an "A" . . .
  Armfeldt —
  Is that a relation
  To the decrepit Desirée?

PETRA:
  Guess when we're asked to go, sir —
  See, sir, the date there?
  Guess where — a fancy chateau, sir!

ANNE:
  Guess, too, who's lying in wait there,
  Setting her traps,
  Fixing her face —

FREDRIK:
  Darling,
  Perhaps a change of pace . . .

ANNE:
Oh, no!

FREDRIK:
A weekend in the country
Would be charming,
And the air would be fresh.

ANNE:
  A weekend
  With that woman . . .

FREDRIK:
  In the country . . .

ANNE:
  In the flesh!

FREDRIK:

I've some business
With her mother.

PETRA:

See, it's business!

ANNE:

. . . Oh, no doubt!
But the business
With her mother
Would be hardly the business I'd worry about.

FREDRIK *and* PETRA:

Just a weekend in the country,

FREDRIK:

Smelling jasmine . . .

ANNE:

Watching little things grow.

FREDRIK *and* PETRA:

A weekend in the country . . .

ANNE:

Go!

FREDRIK:

My darling,
We'll simply say no.

ANNE:

Oh.

(*They exit.* FREDRIKA *and* DESIRÉE *unfreeze*)

FREDRIKA: Oh, Mother, I know it's none of my business, but
. . . that dragoon you wrote me about — with the mustache?

DESIRÉE: Oh, him! What I ever saw in him astounds me.

He's a tin soldier — arms, legs, brain — tin, tin, tin!
(*They freeze on the downstage bench.* ANNE *and* CHAR-
LOTTE *enter*)

ANNE:
A weekend!

CHARLOTTE:
How very amusing.

ANNE:
A weekend!

CHARLOTTE:
But also inept.

ANNE:
A weekend!
Of course, we're refusing.

CHARLOTTE:
Au contraire,
You must accept.

ANNE:
Oh, no!

CHARLOTTE:
A weekend in the country . . .

ANNE:
But it's frightful!

CHARLOTTE:
No, you don't understand.
A weekend in the country
Is delightful
If it's planned.
Wear your hair down
And a flower,
Don't use make-up,

248

Dress in white.
She'll grow older
By the hour
And be hopelessly shattered by
Saturday night.
Spend a weekend in the country.

ANNE:
We'll accept it!

CHARLOTTE:
I'd a feeling
You would.

BOTH:
A weekend in the country!

ANNE:
Yes, it's only polite that we should.

CHARLOTTE:
Good.

> (ANNE *and* CHARLOTTE *disappear.* DESIRÉE *and* FREDRIKA *unfreeze*)

FREDRIKA: Count Malcolm's insanely jealous, isn't he? You don't suppose he'll come galloping up on a black stallion, brandishing a sword?

DESIRÉE: Oh dear, I hadn't thought of that. But no, no, thank heavens. It's his wife's birthday this weekend — sacred to domesticity. At least we're safe from him.

> (*They freeze.* CARL-MAGNUS *enters;* CHARLOTTE *follows opposite to meet him*)

CARL-MAGNUS:
Well?

CHARLOTTE:
I've an intriguing little social item.

CARL-MAGNUS:
    What?

CHARLOTTE:
    Out at the Armfeldt family manse.

CARL-MAGNUS:
    Well, what?

CHARLOTTE:
    Merely a weekend,
    Still I thought it might am-
    Use you to know who's invited to go,
    This time with his pants.

CARL-MAGNUS:
    You don't mean — ?

CHARLOTTE:
    I'll give you three guesses.

CARL-MAGNUS:
    She wouldn't!

CHARLOTTE:
    Reduce it to two.

CARL-MAGNUS:
    It can't be . . .

CHARLOTTE:
    It nevertheless is . . .

CARL-MAGNUS:
    Egerman!

CHARLOTTE:
    Right! Score one for you.

CARL-MAGNUS (*Triumphantly*):
    Aha!

CHARLOTTE (*Triumphantly*):
 Aha!

CARL-MAGNUS (*Thoughtfully*):
 Aha!

CHARLOTTE (*Worriedly*):
 Aha?

CARL-MAGNUS:
 A weekend in the country . . .
 We should try it —

CHARLOTTE:
 How I wish we'd been asked.

CARL-MAGNUS:
 A weekend in the country . . .
 Peace and quiet —

CHARLOTTE:
 We'll go masked.

CARL-MAGNUS:
 A weekend in the country . . .

CHARLOTTE:
 Uninvited —
 They'll consider it odd.

CARL-MAGNUS:
 A weekend in the country —
 I'm delighted!

CHARLOTTE:
 Oh, my God.

CARL-MAGNUS:
 And the shooting should be pleasant
 If the weather's not too rough.
 Happy Birthday,
 It's your present.

CHARLOTTE:
    But —

CARL-MAGNUS:
    You haven't been getting out nearly enough,
    And a weekend in the country —

CHARLOTTE:
    It's perverted!

CARL-MAGNUS:
    Pack my quiver and bow.

BOTH:
    A weekend in the country —

CARL-MAGNUS:
    At exactly 2:30, we go.

CHARLOTTE:
    We can't.

CARL-MAGNUS:
    We shall.

CHARLOTTE:
    We shan't.

CARL-MAGNUS:
    I'm getting the car
    And we're motoring down.

CHARLOTTE:
    Yes, I'm certain you are
    And I'm staying in town.
                    (ANNE, FREDRIK, *and* PETRA *appear*)

CARL-MAGNUS:	ANNE:
Go and pack my suits!	We'll go.
CHARLOTTE:	PETRA:
I won't!	Oh, good!

252

CARL-MAGNUS:
My boots!
Pack everything I own
That shoots.

CHARLOTTE:
No!

CARL-MAGNUS:
Charlotte!

CHARLOTTE:
I'm thinking it out.

CARL-MAGNUS:
Charlotte!

CHARLOTTE:
There's no need to shout.

CARL-MAGNUS:
Charlotte!

CHARLOTTE:
All right, then,

BOTH:
We're off on our way,

FREDRIK:
We will?

ANNE:
We should.
Pack everything white.

PETRA:
Ma'am, it's wonderful news!

FREDRIK:
Are you sure it's all right?

ANNE:
We'd be rude to refuse.

FREDRIK:
Then we're off!

PETRA:
We are?

FREDRIK:
We'll take the car.

ALL THREE:
We'll bring champagne
And caviar!
We're off on our way,

What a beautiful day   What a beautiful day
For   For

ALL:
   A weekend in the country,
   How amusing,
   How delightfully droll.
   A weekend in the country
   While we're losing our control.
   A weekend in the country,
   How enchanting
   On the manicured lawns.
   A weekend in the country,
   With the panting and the yawns.
   With the crickets and the pheasants
   And the orchards and the hay,
   With the servants and the peasants,
   We'll be laying our plans
   While we're playing croquet
   For a weekend in the country,
   So inactive that one has to lie down.
   A weekend in the country
   Where . . .

                 (HENRIK *enters*)

HENRIK:
   A weekend in the country,
   The bees in their hives,
   The shallow, worldly figures,
   The frivolous lives.
   The devil's companions
   Know not whom they serve.
   It might be instructive
   To observe.

        (DESIRÉE *and* FREDRIKA *unfreeze*)

DESIRÉE: However, there is one tiny snag.

254

FREDRIKA: A snag?

DESIRÉE: Lawyer Egerman is married.

FREDRIKA: That could be considered a snag.

DESIRÉE: Don't worry, my darling. I was not raised by your
Grandmother for nothing.

(DESIRÉE *holds out her arm, and* FREDRIKA *runs to her.*
Together, they walk upstage as we see, for the first time, the
facade of the Armfeldt mansion. FRID *stands at the door,*
and once DESIRÉE *and* FREDRIKA *have entered, he closes it*
behind them)

CARL-MAGNUS: Charlotte!	FREDRIK: We're off!	HENRIK: A weekend in the Country, The bees in their Hives . . .
CHARLOTTE: I'm thinking it out.	PETRA: We are?	
CARL-MAGNUS: Charlotte!	FREDRIK *and* ANNE: We'll take the car.	
CHARLOTTE: There's no need To shout.	ALL THREE: We'll bring Champagne and Caviar!	MRS. SEGSTROM *and* MRS. ANDERSSEN: We're off! We are? We'll take the car.
MRS. NORDSTROM *and* MR. ERLANSON: A weekend of playing Croquet A weekend of strolling The lawns,	MR. LINDQUIST: Confiding our motives And hiding our yawns,	MRS. ANDERSSEN *and* MRS. SEGSTROM: We'll Bring Champagne And caviar!

255

CARL-MAGNUS, CHARLOTTE,
FREDRIK, ANNE, *and* PETRA:
We're off and away,
What a beautiful day!

QUINTET:
The weather is spectacular!

ALL:
With riotous laughter
We quietly suffer
The season in town,
Which is reason enough for
A weekend in the country,
How amusing,
How delightfully droll!
A weekend in the country,
While we're losing our control.
A weekend in the country,
How enchanting
On the manicured lawns.
A weekend in the country,
With the panting and the yawns.
With the crickets and the pheasants
And the orchards and the hay,
With the servants and the peasants,
We'll be laying our plans
While we're playing croquet
For a weekend in the country,
So inactive that one has to lie down.
A weekend in the country
Where . . .
We're twice as upset as in
Twice as upset as in
Twice as upset as in
Twice as upset as in . . .
                    (*All, simultaneously*)

QUINTET:
Twice as upset as in,

Twice as upset as in,
Twice as upset as in,
Twice as upset as in,
Twice as upset as in,
Twice as upset as in,
Twice as upset as in,
Twice as upset as in,
Twice as upset as in —

ANNE:
Twice as upset as in town.
A weekend!
A weekend!
A weekend!
A weekend!
A weekend!
A weekend out of —

CHARLOTTE:
Twice as upset . . .
We're uninvited,
Uninvited,
Uninvited —
We should stay in —

PETRA:
Twice as upset . . .
A weekend!
A weekend!
A weekend!
A weekend!
A weekend!
A weekend!
A weekend out of —

ALL:
  Town!

FREDRIK:
Twice as upset . . .
Are you sure you want to go?
Are you sure you want to go?
Are you sure you want to go
Away and leave,
Go and leave — ?

CARL-MAGNUS:
Twice as upset . . .
Charlotte, we're going,
Charlotte, we're going,
Charlotte, we're going,
Charlotte, out of —

HENRIK:
Shallow, worldly
People going,
Shallow people
Going out of —

(*Curtain*)

Glynis Johns as Desirée Armfeldt

Victoria Mallory as Anne Egerman

Frid (George Lee Andrews), Fredrika Armfeldt (Judy
Kahan) and Madame Armfeldt (Hermione Gingold)

259

"Later"
Henrik Egerman (Mark Lambert)

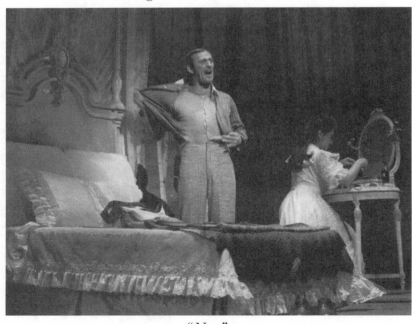

"Now"
Fredrik (Len Cariou) and Anne (Victoria Mallory)

260

Len Cariou as Fredrik Egerman

"In Praise of Women"
Count Carl-Magnus Malcolm (Laurence
Guittard) and Desirée (Glynis Johns)

"Every Day a Little Death"
Countess Charlotte Malcolm (Patricia Elliot)
and Anne (Victoria Mallory)

"Liaisons"
Madame Armfeldt (Hermione Gingold)

263

Desirée (Glynis Johns) and Fredrik (Len Cariou)

New York City Opera Production

Sally Ann Howes as
Desirée Armfeldt

CAROL ROSEGG

CAROL ROSEGG

Regina Resnik as
Madame Armfeldt

CAROL ROSEGG

George Lee Andrews as Fredrik Egerman and
Michael Maguire as Count Carl-Magnus Malcolm

265

Jean Simmons as Desirée Armfeldt

Fredrik Egerman (Joss Ackland), Desirée Armfeldt (Jean Simmons), Anne Egerman (Veronica Page), Madame Armfeldt (Hermione Gingold), Henrik Egerman (Terry Mitchell), Count Carl-Magnus Malcolm (David Kernan) and Countess Charlotte Malcolm (Maria Aitken)

ACT II

Entr'acte

After a musical entr'acte, the QUINTET *enters.*

MRS. ANDERSSEN:
   The sun sits low,
   Diffusing its usual glow.
   Five o'clock . . .
   Twilight . . .
   Vespers sound,
   And it's six o'clock . . .
   Twilight
   All around,

ALL:
   But the sun sits low,
   As low as it's going to go.

MR. ERLANSON:
   Eight o'clock . . .

MR. LINDQUIST:
   Twilight . . .

WOMEN:
   How enthralling!

267

MR. ERLANSON:
   It's nine o'clock . . .

MR. LINDQUIST:
   Twilight . . .

WOMEN:
   Slowly crawling
   Towards

MR. ERLANSON:
   Ten o'clock . . .

MR. LINDQUIST:
   Twilight . . .

WOMEN:
   Crickets calling,

ALL:
   The vespers ring,
   The nightingale's waiting to sing.
   The rest of us wait on a string.
   Perpetual sunset
   Is rather an unset-
   Tling thing.
                    (*The show curtain rises on Scene 1*)

Scene 1

THE ARMFELDT LAWN

> FRID *is serving champagne to* DESIRÉE *and* MALLA. FREDRIKA, *upstage, is playing croquet with the help of* BERTRAND, MADAME ARMFELDT*'s page.* FRID *returns to* MADAME ARMFELDT. OSA, MADAME ARMFELDT*'s maid, passes with a tray of cookies, and* FREDRIKA *takes one.* DESIRÉE *gets a mallet and begins to play croquet.*

MADAME ARMFELDT: To lose a lover or even a husband or two during the course of one's life can be vexing. But to lose one's teeth is a catastrophe. Bear that in mind, child, as you chomp so recklessly into that ginger snap.

FREDRIKA: Very well, Grandmother.

MADAME ARMFELDT (*Holding up her glass to* FRID): More champagne, Frid.
> (FRID *gets a fresh bottle*)
One bottle the less of the Mumms '87 will not, I hope, diminish the hilarity at my wake.
> (DESIRÉE *sits on the rise.* FRID *opens the bottle with a loud pop!*)

QUINTET:
The sun won't set.

269

It's useless to hope or to fret.
It's dark as it's going to get.
The hands on the clock turn,
But don't sing a nocturne
Just yet.

> (*Off, we hear a car-horn*)

DESIRÉE: They're coming!

MADAME ARMFELDT: Nonsense!

DESIRÉE: But they are!

MADAME ARMFELDT: Impossible. No guest with the slightest grasp of what is seemly would arrive before five-fifteen on a Friday afternoon.
> (*We hear the car-horn again, and this time it's louder*)
Good God, you're right!

DESIRÉE: Malla!
> (DESIRÉE *runs up into the house, followed closely by* MALLA *and* OSA. BERTRAND *exits with the croquet set*)

MADAME ARMFELDT: Frid! We cannot be caught squatting on the ground like Bohemians!
> (FRID *scoops her up and carries her into the house.* FREDRIKA *follows. The* QUINTET *runs on to collect the furniture and props left on stage. They freeze for a moment at the sound of the car-horn, and then all run off. A beat later,* CARL-MAGNUS's *sports car drives on.* CARL-MAGNUS *is driving;* CHARLOTTE *sits beside him.* CARL-MAGNUS *stops the car and gets out*)

CHARLOTTE (*Looking around*): Happy birthday to me!

CARL-MAGNUS (*Inspecting a wheel*): What was that?

CHARLOTTE: I merely said . . . oh, never mind.

CARL-MAGNUS: If that damn lawyer thinks he's going to get away with something — Haha!

270

CHARLOTTE: Haha! indeed, dear.

> (CARL-MAGNUS *helps* CHARLOTTE *out of the car*)

CARL-MAGNUS: Watch him, Charlotte. Watch them both like a . . .

CHARLOTTE: Hawk. I know, dear. You're a tiger, I'm a hawk. We're our own zoo.

> (*As she speaks, a touring car sweeps on from the opposite side. It is driven rather erratically by* FREDRIK *with* ANNE *beside him.* HENRIK *and* PETRA *are in the back seat with a pile of luggage. The car only just misses* CARL-MAGNUS's *car as it shudders to a stop. Recognition comes.* FREDRIK *gets out of his car*)

FREDRIK: Good day, sir. I was not aware that you were to be a fellow guest.

> (FREDRIK *opens the car door and helps* ANNE *out.* HENRIK *helps* PETRA *out of the back seat*)

CARL-MAGNUS: Neither is Miss Armfeldt. I hope our arrival will in no way inconvenience you.

FREDRIK: Not at all, not at all. I am happy to see that you have gotten through yet another week without any serious wounds.

CARL-MAGNUS: What's that? Wounds, sir?

FREDRIK: Rapier? Bow and arrow? Blow dart?

> (*At this point,* ANNE *and* CHARLOTTE *see each other. They run together. On the way,* ANNE *drops her handkerchief*)

ANNE (*Hissing*):	CHARLOTTE (*Hissing*):
So you did come?	So you did come?
(*Pause*)	(*Pause*)
Talk later.	Talk later.

> (HENRIK, *tremendously solicitous, holds out the handkerchief to* ANNE)

HENRIK: Your handkerchief, Anne.

ANNE (*Taking it, moving away*): Thank you.

HENRIK: You must have dropped it.
(PETRA *taps* HENRIK *on the shoulder*)

PETRA: Your book, Master Henrik.

HENRIK (*Taking it*): Thank you.

PETRA (*With soupy mock-solicitousness*): You must have dropped it.
(PETRA *moves to get the luggage.* FRID, *seeing and imme-diately appreciating* PETRA, *goes to her*)

FRID: Here. Let me.

PETRA (*Handing him two suitcases*): Let you — what?
(PETRA, *with one suitcase, enters the house, followed by* FRID, *who is carrying two.* HENRIK *is moodily drifting away as* DESIRÉE *emerges from the house. She is followed by* FREDRIKA, *and smiling dazzingly for the* EGERMANS)

DESIRÉE: Ah, here you all are . . .
(CARL-MAGNUS *clears his throat noisily. The smile dies*)
Count Malcolm!

CARL-MAGNUS (*Bowing frigidly over her hand*): My wife and I were in the neighborhood to visit her cousin. Unhappily, on arrival, we discovered the chateau was quarantined for . . .
(*Snaps his fingers at* CHARLOTTE)

CHARLOTTE: Plague.

CARL-MAGNUS: Since I am due back to maneuvers by dawn, we venture to propose ourselves for the night.

DESIRÉE (*Concealing no little fluster*): Well, yes. Indeed. Why not? Mother will be honored! — surprised, but honored.
(DESIRÉE *crosses to* CHARLOTTE, *and sweeps past her, bare-ly touching her hand*)
Countess Malcolm, I presume?

272

CHARLOTTE (*As* DESIRÉE *sweeps past her*): You do indeed, Miss Armfeldt.

DESIRÉE: And Mr. Egerman! How kind of you all to come. Mother will be overjoyed.

FREDRIK (*Bending over her hand*): It is your mother who is kind in inviting us. Allow me to present my rather anti-social son, Henrik.
(*Points to the drifting away* HENRIK, *who turns to acknow-ledge her*)
And this is my wife.
(*He presents* ANNE)

DESIRÉE: How do you do?

ANNE (*Icy*): How do you do?

DESIRÉE (*Indicating* FREDRIKA): And this is *my* daughter.
(*Pause*)
You must all be exhausted after your journeys; my daughter will show you to your rooms. Mother likes dinner at nine.
(FREDRIKA *leads them into the house:* CHARLOTTE, *then* ANNE, *then* HENRIK, *then* OSA. FREDRIKA *returns to the terrace. Simultaneously, both* FREDRIK *and* CARL-MAGNUS *turn, both with the same idea: to get* DESIRÉE *alone*)

CARL-MAGNUS *and* FREDRIK: Where shall I put the car?
(*They exchange a hostile glare*)

DESIRÉE (*Even more flustered*): Ah, the cars, the cars! Now let me see.

CARL-MAGNUS (*Hissing*): I must speak to you at once!

DESIRÉE (*Whispering*): Later.
(*Out loud*)
How about the stables? They're straight ahead.

FREDRIK (*Hissing*): I must speak to you at once!

DESIRÉE (*Whispering*): Later.
> (*Reassured,* CARL-MAGNUS *and* FREDRIK *return to their cars.
> Calling after him*)

You can't miss them, Mr. Egerman. Just look for the weather vane. A huge tin cockerel.
> (*Spinning to* FREDRIKA, *pulling her downstage*)

Disaster, darling!

FREDRIKA: But what are you going to do? The way he glared at Mr. Egerman! He'll kill him!

DESIRÉE: Let us keep calm.
> (FREDRIK *and* CARL-MAGNUS, *both with auto-cranks in
> hand, start back toward* DESIRÉE)

FREDRIKA (*Noticing*): They're coming back!

DESIRÉE (*Totally losing her calm*): Oh no! Oh God!
> (DESIRÉE *starts to run up to the house*)

FREDRIKA (*Calling after her*): But what should I say?

DESIRÉE: Anything!
> (*She runs into the house, as* FREDRIK *and* CARL-MAGNUS,
> *gazing after* DESIRÉE *in astonishment, come up to* FREDRIKA)

FREDRIKA (*On the spot but gracious, seemingly composed*): Mr. Egerman — Count Malcolm . . . Mother told me to tell you that she suddenly . . .
> (*She breaks*)

. . . oh dear, oh dear.
> (*She scurries up into the house. The two men react, then,
> ignoring each other, return to their cars. They each crank
> their cars and get into them. The cars back out offstage.*
> MR. ERLANSON *and* MRS. NORDSTROM *enter*)

MRS. NORDSTROM:
The sun sits low
And the vespers ring,

274

MR. ERLANSON:
  And the shadows grow
  And the crickets sing,
  And it's . . .

MRS. NORDSTROM:
  Look! Is that the moon?

MR. ERLANSON:
  Yes.
  What a lovely afternoon!

MRS. NORDSTROM:
  Yes.

MR. ERLANSON:
  The evening air
  Doesn't feel quite right

MRS. NORDSTROM:
  In the not-quite glare
  Of the not-quite night,
  And it's . . .
  Wait! Is that a star?

MR. ERLANSON:
  No.
  Just the glow of a cigar.

MRS. NORDSTROM:
  Oh.

                              (*They exit*)

Scene 2

ANOTHER PART OF THE GARDEN

ANNE *leads* CHARLOTTE *on. Both women carry parasols.*

ANNE: . . . After I spoke to you, I thought: I will go! I won't!
Then I thought: Why not? We'll go to that awful woman's
house and I'll say to her: "How dare you try to steal my
husband? At your age you should have acquired at least
some moral sense." And then — then in the motorcar
coming here, I thought: Oh dear, I'll never have the
courage and maybe it's all my fault. And oh, I want to go
home.
> (*Bursts into sobs*)

CHARLOTTE: Have no fears. Miss Armfeldt has met her
match.

ANNE (*Astonished, even through tears*): She has? Who?

CHARLOTTE: Me. When I told my husband, he instantly
became a tiger — his word, of course — and then, as if
from heaven, a plan flashed into my mind.
> (*Pause*)

Do you feel up to hearing my plan, dear?
> (ANNE *gives a little nod*)

I shall make love to your husband.

ANNE (*Aghast*): You too?

CHARLOTTE: Confident of my own charms, I shall throw myself into your husband's arms. He will succumb. Why not? Carl-Magnus, in a storm of jealousy, will beg my forgiveness and swear eternal fidelity. And as for Miss Desirée Armfeldt, she will be back peddling her dubious commodities elsewhere. At least, that is the plan.

ANNE (*Suddenly forgetful of her tears*): Oh how amusing. How extremely amusing. Poor old Fredrik. And it serves him right, too.

CHARLOTTE: I am not sure I appreciate that remark, dear.
>>(FREDRIK *appears, walking toward them*)

FREDRIK: Ah, here you are, ladies.

CHARLOTTE (*Sudden devastating smile at* FREDRIK): Oh, Mr. Egerman! If you'll pardon my saying so, that's a simply ravishing cravat.

FREDRIK (*Slightly bewildered*): It is?

CHARLOTTE (*Taking* FREDRIK's *left arm;* ANNE *takes his right arm*): I can't remember when I have seen so seductive a cravat.
>>(*As* ANNE *suppresses giggles, they all walk off together. As* ANNE, CHARLOTTE, *and* FREDRIK *exit,* MR. LINDQUIST *and* MRS. SEGSTROM *appear*)

MR. LINDQUIST:
The atmosphere's becoming heady,
The ambiance thrilling,

MRS. SEGSTROM:
The spirit unsteady,
The flesh far too willing.

MR. LINDQUIST:
　　To be perpetually ready
　　Is far from fulfilling . . .

MRS. SEGSTROM:
　　But wait —
　　The sun
　　Is dipping.

MR. LINDQUIST:
　　Where?
　　You're right.
　　It's dropping.
　　Look — !
　　At last!
　　It's slipping.

MRS. SEGSTROM:
　　Sorry,
　　My mistake,
　　It's stopping.

　　　　　　　　　　　　(*They exit*)

Scene 2A

ANOTHER PART OF THE GARDEN

FREDRIKA *enters.*

FREDRIKA: Oh, I do agree that life at times can seem complicated.

(HENRIK *enters behind her*)

HENRIK: Complicated! If only you knew! Oh, Miss . . . Miss . . .

FREDRIKA: Armfeldt. I am not legitimate.

HENRIK: I see. Oh, Miss Armfeldt, all my life, I've made a fiasco of everything. If you knew how poor an opinion I have of myself! If you knew how many times I wish I had been one of the spermatazoa that never reached the womb.

(*He breaks from her*)

There, there! You see? I've done it again!

FREDRIKA: Mr. Egerman, I have toured with mother, you know. I'm broadminded.

HENRIK: You are? Then in that case, might I make a confession to you?

FREDRIKA: Of course.

279

HENRIK: I hate to burden you on so slight an acquaintance, but bottling it up inside of me is driving me insane.
> (*Pause. With great effort*)

Oh, Miss Armfeldt, for the past eleven months, although I am preparing to enter the Ministry, I —
> (*He can't get it out*)

FREDRIKA: What, Mr. Egerman?

HENRIK: I have been madly, hopelessly in love with my step-mother. Do you realize how many mortal sins that involves? Oh, damn everything to hell! I beg your pardon.
> (*They link arms and walk off.* MR. LINDQUIST, MRS. SEGSTROM, MR. ERLANSON, MRS. ANDERSSEN *and* MRS. NORDSTROM *enter and sing*)

QUINTET:
  The light is pink
  And the air is still
  And the sun is slinking
  Behind the hill.
  And when finally it sets,
  As finally it must,
  When finally it lets
  The moon and stars adjust,
  When finally we greet the dark
  And we're breathing Amen —

MRS. ANDERSSEN:
  Surprise of surprises,
  It instantly rises
  Again.
> (*The* QUINTET *exits*)

Scene 3

ARMFELDT TERRACE

> *Both dressed for dinner,* FREDRIK *and* CARL-MAGNUS *are discovered;* FREDRIK *downstage,* CARL-MAGNUS *pacing on the porch.* FREDRIK *has a cigar and a small liqueur glass;* CARL-MAGNUS *carries a champagne glass.*

FREDRIK (*Sings, to himself*):
I should never have
Gone to the theatre.
Then I'd never have come
To the country.
If I never had come
To the country,
Matters might have stayed
As they were.

CARL-MAGNUS (*Nods*): Sir . . .

FREDRIK (*Nods*): Sir . . .
>   (*To himself again*)
If she'd only been faded,
If she'd only been fat,
If she'd only been jaded
And bursting with chat,

281

If she'd only been perfectly awful,
It would have been wonderful.
If . . . if . . .
If she'd been all a-twitter
Or elusively cold,
If she'd only been bitter,
Or better, looked passably old,
If she'd been covered with glitter
Or even been covered with mold,
It would have been wonderful.

But the woman was perfection,
To my deepest dismay.
Well, not quite perfection,
I'm sorry to say.
If the woman were perfection,
She would go away,
And that would be wonderful.
                    (*To* CARL-MAGNUS)
Sir . . .

CARL-MAGNUS: Sir . . .
If she'd only looked flustered
Or admitted the worst,
If she only had blustered
Or simpered or cursed,
If she weren't so awfully perfect,
It would have been wonderful.
If . . .
If . . .
If she'd tried to be clever,
If she'd started to flinch,
If she'd cried or whatever
A woman would do in a pinch,
If I'd been certain she never
Again could be trusted an inch,

It would have been wonderful.

But the woman was perfection,
Not an action denied,
The kind of perfection
I cannot abide.
If the woman were perfection,
She'd have simply lied,
Which would have been wonderful.

FREDRIK:
If she'd only been vicious . . .

CARL-MAGNUS:
If she'd acted abused . . .

FREDRIK:
Or a bit too delicious . . .

CARL-MAGNUS:
Or been even slightly confused . . .

FREDRIK:
If she had only been sulky . . .

CARL-MAGNUS:
Or bristling . . .

FREDRIK:
Or bulky . . .

CARL-MAGNUS:
Or bruised . . .

BOTH:
It would have been wonderful.

CARL-MAGNUS:
If . . .

BOTH:
If . . .

FREDRIK:
If she'd only been willful . . .

CARL-MAGNUS:
If she only had fled . . .

FREDRIK:
Or a little less skillful . . .

CARL-MAGNUS:
Insulted, insisting . . .

FREDRIK:
In bed . . .

CARL-MAGNUS:
If she had only been fearful . . .

FREDRIK:
Or married . . .

CARL-MAGNUS:
Or tearful . . .

FREDRIK:
Or dead . . .

BOTH:
It would have been wonderful.
But the woman was perfection,
And the prospects are grim.
That lovely perfection
That nothing can dim.
Yes, the woman was perfection,
So I'm here with him . . .

CARL-MAGNUS: Sir . . .

FREDRIK: Sir . . .

BOTH:
It would have been wonderful.

284

(FREDRIKA *enters from the house*)

FREDRIKA: Excuse me, Count Malcolm, but Mother says she would like a word with you in the green salon.

(CARL-MAGNUS, *glaring triumphantly at* FREDRIK, *strides into the house.* FREDRIKA *stands and grins shyly at* FREDRIK, *then follows* CARL-MAGNUS *into the house.* DESIRÉE *enters*)

DESIRÉE: Fredrik, you wanted a moment alone with me, I believe. Here it is.

FREDRIK (*Puzzled*): But that child said . . .

DESIRÉE: Oh, that was just Fredrika's little stratagem.

FREDRIK: Fredrika? Your child is called Fredrika?

DESIRÉE: Yes.

FREDRIK: Ah!

DESIRÉE: Really, Fredrik, what vanity. As if you were the only Fredrik in the world.

(*Brisk*)

Now, what is it you want to tell me?

FREDRIK: As a matter of fact, I thought you should know that my wife has no inkling of the nightshirt episode. So we should be discreet.

DESIRÉE: Dear Fredrik, of course. I wouldn't dream of giving that enchanting child a moment's anxiety.

FREDRIK: Then you do see her charm?

DESIRÉE: How could anyone miss it? How lovely to see you, Fredrik.

FREDRIK: In spite of Count Malcolm's invasion? You're sure we're not complicating . . .

CARL-MAGNUS (*Off*): Desirée!

FREDRIK: Oh God! Something tells me I should make myself scarce.

CARL-MAGNUS (*Off*): Desirée!

FREDRIK: Later, perhaps?

DESIRÉE: Any time.

FREDRIK: In your room?

DESIRÉE: In my room.
(FREDRIK *looks around for a place to hide. He finds the statue, puts his glass on it, and hides behind it. He douses his cigar in another glass resting on the statue*)

CARL-MAGNUS (*Comes out of the house*): Desirée!

DESIRÉE (*Calling, excessively sweet*): Here, dear!

CARL-MAGNUS: That child said the green salon.

DESIRÉE: She did? How extraordinary.

CARL-MAGNUS: Where's that goddamn lawyer?

DESIRÉE (*Airy*): Mr. Egerman? Oh, somewhere about, no doubt.

CARL-MAGNUS: What's he doing here anyway?

DESIRÉE: He's visiting my mother, of course. He told you. They're the most devoted old friends.

CARL-MAGNUS: That had better be the truth. If I catch him so much as touching you, I'll call him out — with rapiers!
(*Glares*)
Where is your bedroom? Readily accessible, I trust.

DESIRÉE (*Aghast*): But, Carl-Magnus!
(FRID *enters from the house, crosses downstage*)
With your *wife* here . . . !

CARL-MAGNUS: Charlotte is irrelevant. I shall visit your bedroom at the earliest opportunity tonight.

FRID: Madame, Count Malcolm! Dinner is served.
(*As he moves past them to pick up* FREDRIK*'s glass, he sees* FREDRIK *behind the statue. Totally unaware of complications*)
Dinner is served, Mr. Egerman.
(FRID *exits up into the house*)

DESIRÉE (*Rising to it*): Ah, there you are, Mr. Egerman!
(FREDRIK *comes out from behind the statue, laughing*)
Gentlemen, shall we proceed?
(*Gives one arm to each as they start up into the house and freeze in place*)

Scene 4

THE DINING ROOM

As the dining room table and guests come on, MRS. NORD-
STROM, MRS. SEGSTROM *and* MRS. ANDERSSEN *sing.*

MRS. NORDSTROM:
Perpetual antici-
   pation is
Good for the soul   MRS. SEGSTROM:
But it's bad for the   Perpetual antici-
   heart.   Pation is good for
It's very good for
   practicing
                  The
Self-control.   Soul, but it's bad
It's very good for   For the
Morals,   Heart.
But bad for morale.   It's very good for
It's very bad.   Practicing self-
It can lead to   Control. It's very   MRS. ANDERSSEN:
                  good for   Per-
Going quite mad.   Morals but bad   Petual antici-
It's very good for   For morale. It's   pation is good

		For
Reserve and	Too unnerving.	The soul, but It's
Learning to do	It's very good,	Bad for the Heart.
What one should. It's very good.	Though, to have Things to contem-	It's Very good, Though, To learn to Wait.
Perpetual antici- pation's A delicate art.	Plate. Perpetual antici- pation's a	Perpetual Anticipation's A
Playing a role,	Delicate art.	Delicate art.
Aching to start,	Playing a role,	Playing a role,
Keeping control	Aching to start,	Aching to start,
While falling apart,	Keeping control	Keeping control
Perpetual antici- pation is	While falling Apart,	While falling Apart,
Good for the soul	Perpetual antici- pation is good	Perpetual Anticipation Is bad for
But it's bad for The heart.	But it's bad for The heart.	The heart.

(*The dining room table has moved onstage with* MADAME ARMFELDT *already seated in place, facing the audience in*

289

solitary splendor. The table is elaborately dressed with fruit and floral pieces and expensive dinnerware. There are also two large candelabra, one at each end of the table. Parallel to the table and upstage of it, the line of servants has come on: BERTRAND, OSA, PETRA, *and* FRID. OSA *and* PETRA *stand with trays as* FRID *and* BERTRAND *light the candelabra.*

Once the table is in place, FREDRIK *and* CARL-MAGNUS *move up to it with* DESIRÉE. FREDRIK *pulls out a chair for* DESIRÉE *and she sits.* FREDRIK *gets* ANNE *and seats her.* CHARLOTTE *enters,* CARL-MAGNUS *seats her on the extreme right end of the table. He then moves to the extreme left, and sits down next to* DESIRÉE. HENRIK *sits between* DESIRÉE *and* ANNE, FREDRIK *between* ANNE *and* CHARLOTTE. *The guests all sit facing upstage.* FRID *and* BERTRAND *pour, and* MADAME ARMFELDT *raises her glass. The others follow her. When the glasses come down, there is a burst of laughter and noise from the guests.* FREDRIKA, *seated at the piano, "accompanies" the scene)*

DESIRÉE: . . . So you won the case after all, Mr. Egerman! How splendid!

FREDRIK: I was rather proud of myself.

DESIRÉE: And I'm sure you were tremendously proud of him too, Mrs. Egerman.

ANNE: I beg your pardon? Oh, I expect so, although I don't seem to remember much about it.
    (CHARLOTTE *extends her glass;* BERTRAND *fills it)*

FREDRIK: I try not to bore my wife with my dubious victories in the courtroom.

DESIRÉE: How wise you are. I remember when I was her age, anything less than a new dress, or a ball, or a thrilling piece of gossip bored me to tears.

290

FREDRIK: That is the charm of youth.

CHARLOTTE: Dearest Miss Armfeldt, do regale us with more fascinating reminiscences from your remote youth.

CARL-MAGNUS: Charlotte, that is an idiotic remark.

FREDRIK: A man's youth may be as remote as a dinosaur, Countess, but with a beautiful woman, youth merely accompanies her through the years.

CHARLOTTE: Oh, Mr. Egerman, that is too enchanting!
(*Leaning over her chair*)
Anne, dear, where on earth did you find this simply adorable husband?

ANNE (*Leans. In on the "plan," of course, giggling*): I'm glad you approve of him.

CHARLOTTE (*To* HENRIK): Your father . . .
(HENRIK *leans*)
is irresistible.
(CARL-MAGNUS *leans*)
I shall monopolize him for the entire weekend.
(DESIRÉE *leans. Then, to* ANNE)
Will you lease him to me, dear?

ANNE (*Giggling*): Freely. He's all yours.
(FREDRIK *looks at* ANNE, *then at* CHARLOTTE, *then leans*)
. . . unless, of course, our hostess has other plans for him.

DESIRÉE (*Smooth, getting out of her seat*): I had thought of seducing him into rolling the croquet lawn tomorrow, but I'm sure he'd find the Countess less exhausting.

CHARLOTTE (*Rising*): I wouldn't guarantee that!
(*Clapping her hand over her mouth*)
Oh, how could those wicked words have passed these lips!

CARL-MAGNUS (*Astonished, rising*): Charlotte!

CHARLOTTE: Oh, Carl-Magnus, dear, don't say you're bristling!

(*To* FREDRIK, *who has also risen. From here the two of them move to the music in a stylized fashion*)

My husband, Mr. Egerman, is a veritable porcupine. At the least provocation he is all spines — or is it quills? Beware. I am leading you down dangerous paths!

CARL-MAGNUS (*Frigid*): I apologize for my wife, sir. She is not herself tonight.

FREDRIK (*Both amused and gracious*): If she is this charming when she is *not* herself, sir, I would be fascinated to meet her when she *is*.

CHARLOTTE: Bravo, bravo! My champion!
(HENRIK *and* ANNE *get up from the table and join the stylized dance*)
May tomorrow find us thigh to thigh pushing the garden roller in tandem.

FREDRIK (*Turning it into a joke*): That would depend on the width of the rollers.
(*To* DESIRÉE)
Miss Armfeldt, as a stranger in this house, may I ask if your roller . . .

CARL-MAGNUS (*Instantly picking this up*): Stranger, sir? How can you call yourself a stranger in *this* house?

FREDRIK (*Momentarily bewildered*): I beg your pardon?

CARL-MAGNUS (*Triumphantly sure he has found* FREDRIK *and* DESIRÉE *out, to* MADAME ARMFELDT): I understand from your daughter, Madame, that Mr. Egerman is an old friend of yours and consequently a frequent visitor to this house.

MADAME ARMFELDT (*Vaguely aware of him, peering through a lorgnette*): Are you addressing me, sir? Whoever you may be.

CARL-MAGNUS: I am, Madame.

MADAME ARMFELDT: Then be so kind as to repeat yourself.

DESIRÉE (*Breaking in*): Mother, Count Malcolm —

MADAME ARMFELDT (*Overriding this, ignoring her, to* CARL-MAGNUS): Judging from the level of the conversation so far, young man, you can hardly expect me to have been paying attention.
> (CARL-MAGNUS *is taken aback*)

CHARLOTTE: Splendid! The thrust direct! I shall commandeer that remark and wreak havoc with it at all my husband's regimental dinner parties!
> (*The guests waltz slowly for a moment. Finally* MADAME ARMFELDT *tings on a glass with her fork for silence*)

MADAME ARMFELDT (*As* FRID *and* BERTRAND *serve*): Ladies and gentlemen, tonight I am serving you a very special dessert wine. It is from the cellars of the King of the Belgians who — during a period of intense intimacy — presented me with all the bottles then in existence. The secret of its unique quality is unknown, but it is said to possess the power to open the eyes of even the blindest among us . . .
> (*Raising her glass*)

To Life!
> (*The guests all raise their glasses*)

THE GUESTS: To Life!

MADAME ARMFELDT: And to the only other reality — Death!
> (*Only* MADAME ARMFELDT *and* CHARLOTTE *drink. A sudden chilly silence descends on the party as if a huge shadow had passed over it. The guests slowly drift back to the table in silence. At length the silence is broken by a little tipsy giggle from* CHARLOTTE)

CHARLOTTE: Oh I *am* enjoying myself! What an unusual sensation!

(*Raises her glass to* DESIRÉE)

Dearest Miss Armfeldt, at this awe-inspiring moment — let me drink to *you* who have made this evening possible. The One and Only Desirée Armfeldt, beloved of hundreds — regardless of course of their matrimonial obligations!

(*Hiccups*)

CARL-MAGNUS: Charlotte, you will go to your room immediately.

(*There is general consternation*)

FREDRIK: Miss Armfeldt, I'm sure the Countess —

ANNE: Oh dear, oh dear, I am beside myself.

HENRIK (*Suddenly jumping up, shouting, smashing his glass on the table*): Stop it! All of you! Stop it!

(*There is instant silence*)

FREDRIK: Henrik!

HENRIK (*Swinging to glare at him*): Are *you* reproving *me?*

FREDRIK: I think, if I were you, I would sit down.

HENRIK: Sit, Henrik. Stand, Henrik. Am I to spend the rest of my life at your command, like a lapdog? Am I to respect a man who can permit such filthy pigs' talk in front of the purest, the most innocent, the most wonderful . . . ? I despise you all!

ANNE (*Giggling nervously*): Oh, Henrik! How comical you look!

DESIRÉE (*Smiling, holding out her glass to him*): Smash this, too. Smash every glass in the house if you feel like it.

HENRIK (*Bewildered and indignant*): And you! You're an artist! You play Ibsen and — and Racine! Don't any of the great truths of the artists come through to you at all? Are you no better than the others?

DESIRÉE: Why don't you just laugh at us all, my dear? Wouldn't that be a solution?

HENRIK: How can I laugh, when life makes me want to vomit?

> (*He runs out of the room*)

ANNE: Poor silly Henrik. Someone should go after him.

> (*She gets up from the table, starts away*)

FREDRIK (*Standing, very authoritative*): Anne. Come back.

> (*Meekly*, ANNE *obeys, sitting down again at the table. Total silence.* FREDRIK *sits. Then, after a beat, a hiccup from* CHARLOTTE)

DESIRÉE: Dear Countess, may I suggest that you try holding your breath — for a very long time?

> (*The lights go down on the scene, and the table moves off*)

Scene 5

ARMFELDT GARDEN

> HENRIK *runs on and stands near the bench in despair.*
> FREDRIKA, *at the piano, sees him.*

FREDRIKA (*Stops playing*): Mr. Egerman!
> (HENRIK *ignores her*)
Mr. Egerman?
> (HENRIK *looks up*)

HENRIK: I have disgraced myself — acting like a madman, breaking an expensive glass, humiliating myself in front of them all.

FREDRIKA: Poor Mr. Egerman!

HENRIK (*Defending himself in spite of himself*): They laughed at me. Even Anne. She said, "Silly Henrik, how comical you look!" Laughter! How I detest it! Your mother — everyone — says, "Laugh at it all." If all you can do is laugh at the cynicism, the frivolity, the lack of heart — then I'd rather be dead.

ANNE (*Off*): Henrik!

HENRIK: Oh God! There she is!
> (*He runs off*)

ANNE (*Off*): Henrik, dear!

FREDRIKA (*Calls after him*): Mr. Egerman! Please don't do
anything rash!
(ANNE *runs on*)
Oh, Mrs. Egerman, I'm so terribly worried.

ANNE: You poor dear. What about?

FREDRIKA: About Mr. Egerman — Junior, that is.

ANNE: Silly Henrik! I was just coming out to scold him.

FREDRIKA: I am so afraid he may do himself an injury.

ANNE: How delightful to be talking to someone younger
than myself. No doubt he has been denouncing the
wickedness of the world — and quoting Martin Luther?
Dearest Fredrika, all you were witnessing was the latest
crisis in his love affair with God.

FREDRIKA: Not with God, Mrs. Egerman — with you!

ANNE (*Totally surprised*): Me!

FREDRIKA: You may not have noticed, but he is madly, hopelessly in love with you.

ANNE: Is that really the truth?

FREDRIKA: Yes, he told me so himself.

ANNE (*Thrilled, flattered, perhaps more*): The poor dear boy!
How ridiculous of him — and yet how charming. Dear
friend, if you knew how insecure I constantly feel, how
complicated the marriage state seems to be. I adore old
Fredrik, of course, but . . .

FREDRIKA (*Interrupting*): But Mrs. Egerman, he ran down
towards the lake!

ANNE (*Laughing*): To gaze over the ornamental waters! How
touching! Let us go and find him.

297

(ANNE *takes* FREDRIKA*'s arm and starts walking off with her*)

Such a good looking boy, isn't he? Such long, long lashes . . .

(*They exit giggling, arm-in-arm*)

Scene 5A

ANOTHER PART OF THE GARDEN

> FRID *runs on from behind a screen, followed by a more leisurely* PETRA. *They have a bottle of wine and a small bundle of food with them.*

PETRA: Who needs a haystack? Anything you've got to show, you can show me right here — that is, if you're in the mood.

FRID (*Taking her into his arms*): When am I not in the mood?

PETRA (*Laughing*): I wouldn't know, would I? I'm just passing through.

FRID: I'm in the mood.
>   (*Kiss*)
> I'm in it twenty-four hours a day.
>   (*Kiss.* FREDRIKA *runs across stage*)

FREDRIKA: Mr. Egerman!

PETRA: Private here, isn't it?
>   (ANNE *runs across stage*)

ANNE: Henrik! Henrik!

PETRA: What *are* they up to?

FRID: Oh, them! What are they ever up to?

(ANNE *runs back across*)

ANNE: Henrik!

(FREDRIKA *runs back across*)

FREDRIKA: Mr. Egerman!

FRID: You saw them all at dinner, dressed up like waxworks, jabbering away to prove how clever they are. And never knowing what they miss.

(*Kiss*)

ANNE (*Off*): Henrik!

FRID: Catch one of them having the sense to grab the first pretty girl that comes along — and do her on the soft grass, with the summer night just smiling down.

(*Kiss*)

Any complaints yet?

PETRA: Give me time.

FRID: You've a sweet mouth — sweet as honey.

(*The lights dim on them as they lower themselves onto the grass. We now see* HENRIK, *who has been watching them make love. After an anguished moment, he runs straight up into the house, slamming the doors behind him*)

Scene 6

DESIRÉE'S BEDROOM

DESIRÉE sits on the bed, her long skirt drawn up over her knees, expertly sewing up a hem. FREDRIK enters and clears his throat.

FREDRIK: Your dragoon and his wife are glowering at each other in the green salon, and all the children appear to have vanished, so when I saw you sneaking up the stairs . . .

DESIRÉE: I ripped my hem on the dining room table in all that furore.

FREDRIK (*Hovering*): Is this all right?

DESIRÉE: Of course. Sit down.
(Patting the bed beside her, on which tumbled stockings are strewn)

FREDRIK: *On* the stockings?

DESIRÉE: I don't see why not.
(There is a long pause)
Well, we're back at the point where we were so rudely interrupted last week, aren't we?

301

FREDRIK: Not quite. If you'll remember, we'd progressed a step further.

DESIRÉE: How true.

FREDRIK: I imagine neither of us is contemplating a repeat performance.

DESIRÉE: Good heavens, with your wife in the house, and my lover and his wife and my daughter . . .

FREDRIK: . . . and my devoted old friend, your mother.
(*They both laugh*)

DESIRÉE (*During it, like a naughty girl*): Isn't my dragoon awful?

FREDRIK (*Laughs*): When you told me he had the brain of a pea, I think you were being generous.
(*They laugh more uproariously*)

DESIRÉE: What in God's name are we laughing about? Your son was right at dinner. We don't fool that boy, not for a moment. The One and Only Desirée Armfeldt, dragging around the country in shoddy tours, carrying on with someone else's dim-witted husband. And the Great Lawyer Egerman, busy renewing his unrenewable youth.

FREDRIK: Bravo! Probably that's an accurate description of us both.

DESIRÉE: Shall I tell you why I really invited you here? When we met again and we made love, I thought: Maybe here it is at last — a chance to turn back, to find some sort of coherent existence after so many years of muddle.
(*Pause*)
Of course, there's your wife. But I thought: Perhaps — just perhaps — you might be in need of rescue, too.

FREDRIK: From renewing my unrenewable youth?

DESIRÉE (*Suddenly tentative*): It was only a thought.

FREDRIK: When my eyes are open and I look at you, I see a woman that I have loved for a long time, who entranced me all over again when I came to her rooms . . . who gives me such genuine pleasure that, in spite of myself, I came here for the sheer delight of being with her again. The woman who could rescue me? Of course.

(*Pause*)

But when my eyes are not open — which is most of the time — all I see is a girl in a pink dress teasing a canary, running through a sunlit garden to hug me at the gate, as if I'd come home from Timbuktu instead of the Municipal Courthouse three blocks away . . .

DESIRÉE (*Sings*):
Isn't it rich?
Are we a pair?
Me here at last on the ground,
You in mid-air.
Send in the clowns.

Isn't it bliss?
Don't you approve?
One who keeps tearing around,
One who can't move.
Where are the clowns?
Send in the clowns.

Just when I'd stopped
Opening doors,
Finally knowing
The one that I wanted was yours,
Making my entrance again
With my usual flair,
Sure of my lines,
No one is there.

(FREDRIK *rises*)

Don't you love farce?
My fault, I fear.
I thought that you'd want what I want —
Sorry, my dear.
But where are the clowns?
Quick, send in the clowns.
Don't bother, they're here.

FREDRIK: Desirée, I'm sorry. I should never have come. To flirt with rescue when one has no intention of being saved . . . Do try to forgive me.

(*He exits*)

DESIRÉE:

Isn't it rich?
Isn't it queer?
Losing my timing this late
In my career?
And where are the clowns?
There ought to be clowns.
Well, maybe next year . . .

(*The lights iris out on* DESIRÉE)

Scene 7

THE TREES

As DESIRÉE's *bedroom goes off,* HENRIK *emerges from the house, carrying a rope. He runs downstage with it.* ANNE *and* FREDRIKA *run on; when* HENRIK *hears them, he runs behind a tree to hide.*

ANNE (*As she runs on*): Henrik!
>   (*To* FREDRIKA)
Oh, I'm quite puffed! Where can he be?
>   (*Noticing* FREDRIKA's *solemn face*)
Poor child, that face! Don't look so solemn. Where would you go if you were he?

FREDRIKA: Well, the summer pavilion? And then, of course, there's the stables.

ANNE: Then you go to the stables and I'll take the summer pavilion.
>   (*Laughing*)
Run!
>   (*She starts off*)
Isn't this exciting after that stodgy old dinner!
>   (*They run off, and* HENRIK *runs back on. He stops at the tree, stands on the marble bench, and, after circling the*

305

*noose around his neck, throws the other end of the rope up
to the tree limb.* ANNE *can be heard calling "Henrik!"* HEN-
RIK *falls with a loud thud, as* ANNE *enters*)

ANNE: What an extraordinary . . . ! Oh, Henrik — how comical you look!
>(*Pulling him up by the noose still around his neck*)

Oh, no! You didn't!
>(*Pause*)

For me?
>(*She gently removes the noose from his neck*)

Oh, my poor darling Henrik.
>(*She throws herself into his arms*)

Oh, my poor boy! Oh, those eyes, gazing at me like a lost
Saint Bernard . . .
>(*They start to kiss passionately*)

HENRIK: I love you! I've actually *said* it!

ANNE (*Returning his kisses passionately*): Oh how scatter-
brained I was never to have realized. Not Fredrik . . . not
poor old Fredrik . . . not Fredrik at all!
>(*They drop down onto the ground and start to make pas-
sionate love. The trees wipe them out, revealing* PETRA *and*
FRID. FRID *is asleep*)

PETRA (*Sings*):
I shall marry the miller's son,
Pin my hat on a nice piece of property.
Friday nights, for a bit of fun,
We'll go dancing.
Meanwhile . . .

It's a wink and a wiggle
And a giggle in the grass
And I'll trip the light Fandango,
A pinch and a diddle
In the middle of what passes by.

It's a very short road
From the pinch and the punch
To the paunch and the pouch and the pension.
It's a very short road
To the ten-thousandth lunch
And the belch and the grouch and the sigh.
In the meanwhile,
There are mouths to be kissed
Before mouths to be fed,
And a lot in between
In the meanwhile.
And a girl ought to celebrate what passes by.

Or I shall marry the businessman,
Five fat babies and lots of security.
Friday nights, if we think we can,
We'll go dancing.
Meanwhile . . .

It's a push and a fumble
And a tumble in the sheets
And I'll foot the Highland Fancy,
A dip in the butter
And a flutter with what meets my eye.
It's a very short fetch
From the push and the whoop
To the squint and the stoop and the mumble.
It's not much of a stretch
To the cribs and the croup
And the bosoms that droop and go dry.
In the meanwhile,
There are mouths to be kissed
Before mouths to be fed,
And there's many a tryst
And there's many a bed
To be sampled and seen

In the meanwhile.
And a girl has to celebrate what passes by.

Or I shall marry the Prince of Wales —
Pearls and servants and dressing for festivals.
Friday nights, with him all in tails,
We'll have dancing.
Meanwhile . . .

It's a rip in the bustle
And a rustle in the hay
And I'll pitch the Quick Fantastic,
With flings of confetti
And my petticoats away up high.
It's a very short way
From the fling that's for fun
To the thigh pressing under the table.
It's very short day
Till you're stuck with just one
Or it has to be done on the sly.
In the meanwhile,
There are mouths to be kissed
Before mouths to be fed,
And there's many a tryst
And there's many a bed.
There's a lot I'll have missed
But I'll not have been dead when I die!
And a person should celebrate everything
Passing by.

And I shall marry the miller's son.
            (*She smiles, as the lights fade on her*)

Scene 8

ARMFELDT HOUSE AND GARDEN

> FREDRIKA *is lying on the grass reading.* MADAME ARMFELDT
> *is seated in a huge wingchair upstage.* DESIRÉE, *on the bed,*
> *is writing in her diary.* CARL-MAGNUS *paces on the terrace*
> *and then goes into the house.* MRS. SEGSTROM *and* MR.
> LINDQUIST *are behind trees,* MR. ERLANSON *and* MRS.
> ANDERSSEN *are behind opposite trees.* CHARLOTTE *sits*
> *downstage on a bench. After a beat,* FREDRIK *enters, sees*
> *the figure on the bench. Is it* ANNE? *He hurries toward her.*

FREDRIK: Anne? — Oh, forgive me, Countess. I was looking
for my wife.

CHARLOTTE (*Looking up, through sobs*): Oh, Mr. Egerman, how
can I face you after that exhibition at dinner? Throwing
myself at your head!

FREDRIK: On the contrary, I found it most morale-building.
> (*Sits down next to her*)
It's not often these days that a beautiful woman does me
that honor.

CHARLOTTE: I didn't.

FREDRIK: I beg your pardon?

309

CHARLOTTE: I didn't do you that honor. It was just a charade. A *failed* charade! In my madness I thought I could make my husband jealous.

FREDRIK: I'm afraid marriage isn't one of the easier relationships, is it?

CHARLOTTE: Mr. Egerman, for a woman it's impossible!

FREDRIK: It's not all that possible for men.

CHARLOTTE: Men! Look at you — a man of an age when a woman is lucky if a drunken alderman pinches her derriere at a village fete! And yet, you have managed to acquire the youngest, prettiest . . . I hate you being happy. I hate *anyone* being happy!
    (HENRIK *and* ANNE *emerge from the house, carrying suitcases. They start stealthily downstage*)

HENRIK: The gig should be ready at the stables.

ANNE (*Giggling*): Oh Henrik, darling, I do hope the horses will be smart. I so detest riding in a gig when the horses are not smart.
    (HENRIK *stops, pulls her to him. They kiss*)

MRS. SEGSTROM (*Turns, looking onstage, sings*):
    Think of how I adore you,
    Think of how much you love me.
    If I were perfect for you,
    Wouldn't you tire of me
    Soon . . . ?

HENRIK: Let all the birds nest in my hair!

ANNE: Silly Henrik! Quick, or we'll miss the train!
    (*They are now downstage. Unaware of* FREDRIK *and* CHARLOTTE, *they move past them. For a long moment,* FREDRIK *and* CHARLOTTE *sit, while* FREDRIK's *world tumbles around his ears*)

CHARLOTTE: It was, wasn't it?

FREDRIK: It was.

CHARLOTTE: Run after them. Quick. You can catch them at the stables.

FREDRIK (*Even more quiet*): After the horse has gone?
 (*Pause*)
How strange that one's life should end sitting on a bench in a garden.

MR. ERLANSON (*Leans, looking onstage, sings*):
She lightens my sadness,
She livens my days,
She bursts with a kind of madness
My well-ordered ways.
My happiest mistake,
The ache of my life . . .
 (FREDRIK *and* CHARLOTTE *remain seated as the lights come up on* DESIRÉE*'s bedroom.* CARL-MAGNUS *enters*)

DESIRÉE: Carl-Magnus, go away!

CARL-MAGNUS (*Ignoring her, beginning to unbutton his tunic*): I'd have been here half an hour ago if I hadn't had to knock a little sense into my wife.

DESIRÉE: Carl-Magnus, do not take off your tunic!

CARL-MAGNUS (*Still ignoring her*): Poor girl. She was somewhat the worse for wine, of course. Trying to make me believe that she was attracted to that asinine lawyer fellow.

DESIRÉE: Carl-Magnus, listen to me! It's over. It was never anything in the first place, but now it's OVER!

CARL-MAGNUS (*Ignoring this, totally self-absorbed*): Of all people — that lawyer! Scrawny as a scarecrow and without a hair on his body, probably.
 (*He starts removing his braces*)

311

DESIRÉE (*Shouting*): Don't take off your trousers!

CARL-MAGNUS (*Getting out of his trousers*): Poor girl, she'd slash her wrists before she'd let any other man touch her. And even if, under the influence of wine, she did stray a bit, how ridiculous to imagine I would so much as turn a hair!

> (*As he starts to get out of his trouser leg, he stumbles so that he happens to be facing the "window." He stops dead, peering out*)

Good God!

DESIRÉE: What is it?

CARL-MAGNUS (*Peering*): It's her! And him! Sitting on a bench! She's touching him! The scoundrel! The conniving swine! Any man who thinks he can lay a finger on *my* wife!

> (*Pulling up his pants and grabbing his tunic as he hobbles out*)

DESIRÉE: Carl-Magnus, what are you doing?

CARL-MAGNUS: My duelling pistols!

> (*And he rushes out.* DESIRÉE *runs after him*)

DESIRÉE: Carl-Magnus!

> (*The bed rolls off and the lights go down on the bedroom and up on* MADAME ARMFELDT *and* FREDRIKA)

MADAME ARMFELDT: A great deal seems to be going on in this house tonight.

> (*Pause*)

Child, will you do me a favor?

FREDRIKA: Of course, Grandmother.

MADAME ARMFELDT: Will you tell me what it's all for? Having outlived my own illusions by centuries, it would be soothing at least to pretend to share some of yours.

FREDRIKA (*After thought*): Well, I think it must be worth it.

MADAME ARMFELDT: Why?

FREDRIKA: It's all there is, isn't it? Oh, I know it's often discouraging, and to hope for something too much is childish, because what you want so rarely happens.

MADAME ARMFELDT: Astounding! When I was your age I wanted everything — the moon — jewels, yachts, villas on the Riviera. And I got 'em, too, — for all the good they did me.
>   (*Music. Her mind starts to wander*)
There was a Croatian Count. He was my first lover. I can see his face now — such eyes, and a mustache like a brigand. He gave me a wooden ring.

FREDRIKA: A wooden ring?

MADAME ARMFELDT: It had been in his family for centuries, it seemed, but I said to myself: a wooden ring? What sort of man would give you a wooden ring, so I tossed him out right there and then. And now — who knows? He might have been the love of my life.
>   (FREDRIKA *falls asleep, resting her head against* MADAME ARMFELDT'*s knee. In the garden,* FREDRIK *and* CHARLOTTE *pause*)

CHARLOTTE: To think I was actually saying: How I hate you being happy! It's — as if I carry around some terrible curse.
>   (CARL-MAGNUS *enters from house, runs down steps*)
Oh, Mr. Egerman . . . I'm sorry.
>   (CHARLOTTE *breaks from* FREDRIK *with a little cry.* FREDRIK, *still dazed, merely turns, gazing vaguely at* CARL-MAGNUS)

CARL-MAGNUS (*Glaring, clicks his heels*): Sir, you will accompany me to the pavilion.

(CHARLOTTE *looks at the pistol. Slowly the wonderful truth begins to dawn on her. He really cares! Her face breaks into a radiant smile*)

CHARLOTTE: Carl-Magnus!

CARL-MAGNUS (*Ignoring her*): I think the situation speaks for itself.

CHARLOTTE (*Her ecstatic smile broadening*): Carl-Magnus, dear, you won't be *too* impulsive, will you?

CARL-MAGNUS: Whatever the provocation, I remain a civilized man.
(*Flourishing the pistol*)
The lawyer and I are merely going to play a little Russian Roulette.

CHARLOTTE: Russian Roulette?

CARL-MAGNUS (*To* FREDRIK): Well, sir? Are you ready, sir?

FREDRIK (*Still only half aware*): I beg your pardon. Ready for what??

CHARLOTTE (*Thrilled*): Russian Roulette!

FREDRIK: Oh, Russian Roulette. That's with a pistol, isn't it? And you spin the . . .
(*Indicating*)
Well, why not?
(*Very polite, to* CHARLOTTE)
Excuse me, Madame.
(CARL-MAGNUS *clicks his heels and struts off.* FREDRIK *follows him off slowly*)

MR. LINDQUIST (*Sings*):
A weekend in the country . . .

MR. LINDQUIST *and* MRS. ANDERSSEN:
So inactive

MR. LINDQUIST, MRS. ANDERSSEN *and* MR. ERLANSON:
That one has to lie down.

ALL THE QUINTET:
A weekend in the country
Where . . .
> (FRID *and* PETRA *enter, unobserved, and lean against a tree. Gunshot*)

We're twice as upset as in town!
> (*The* QUINTET *scatters and runs off, except for* MRS. ANDERSSEN, *who stands behind a tree.* DESIRÉE *runs out of the house and down to* CHARLOTTE)

DESIRÉE: What is it? What's happened?

CHARLOTTE: Oh, dear Miss Armfeldt, my husband and Mr. Egerman are duelling in the pavilion!

DESIRÉE: Are you insane? You let them do it?
> (*She starts to run to the pavilion.* CARL-MAGNUS *enters, carrying* FREDRIK *over one shoulder. Quite roughly, he tosses him down on the grass, where* FREDRIK *remains motionless*)

DESIRÉE: You lunatic! You've killed him! Fredrik!

CHARLOTTE: Carl-Magnus!

CARL-MAGNUS: My dear Miss Armfeldt, he merely grazed his ear. I trust his performance in the Law Courts is a trifle more professional.
> (*He clears his throat. To* CHARLOTTE)

I am prepared to forgive you, dear. But I feel this house is no longer a suitable place for us.

CHARLOTTE: Oh yes, my darling, I agree!

CARL-MAGNUS: You will pack my things and meet me in the stables. I will have the car ready.

CHARLOTTE: Yes, dear. Oh, Carl-Magnus! You became a tiger for me!

(They kiss)

MRS. ANDERSSEN *(Sings)*:
   Men are stupid, men are vain,
   Love's disgusting, love's insane,
   A humiliating business . . .

MRS. SEGSTROM:
   Oh, how true!
      (CARL-MAGNUS *and* CHARLOTTE *break the kiss.* CARL-
      MAGNUS *exits.* CHARLOTTE *runs up to the house)*

MRS. ANDERSSEN:
   Aaaah,
            (When CHARLOTTE *closes the house doors)*
   Well . . .

DESIRÉE: Fredrik? Fredrik!

FREDRIK *(Stirs, opens his eyes, looks dazedly around)*: I don't
   suppose this is my heavenly reward, is it?

DESIRÉE: Hardly, dear, with *me* here.

FREDRIK *(Trying to sit up, failing, remembering)*: Extraordinary,
   isn't it? To hold a muzzle to one's temple — and yet to
   miss! A shaky hand, perhaps, is an asset after all.

DESIRÉE: Does it hurt?

FREDRIK: It hurts — spiritually. You've heard, I imagine,
   about the evening's other event?

DESIRÉE: No, what?

FREDRIK: Henrik and Anne — ran off together.

DESIRÉE: Fredrik!

FREDRIK: Well, I think I should get up and confront the
   world, don't you?

DESIRÉE *(Sings)*:
   Isn't it rich?

316

FREDRIK:
Are we a pair?
You here at last on the ground.

DESIRÉE:
You in mid-air.
(*Speaks*)
Knees wobbly?

FREDRIK: No, no, it seems not. In fact, it's hardly possible, but . . .

DESIRÉE (*Sings*):
Was that a farce?

FREDRIK:
My fault, I fear.

DESIRÉE:
Me as a merry-go-round.

FREDRIK:
Me as King Lear.
(*Speaks*)
How unlikely life is! To lose one's son, one's wife, and practically one's life within an hour and yet to feel — relieved. Relieved, and, what's more, considerably less ancient.
(*He jumps up on the bench*)
Aha! Desirée!

DESIRÉE: Poor Fredrik!

FREDRIK: No, no, no. We will banish "poor" from our vocabulary and replace it with "coherent."

DESIRÉE (*Blank*): Coherent?

FREDRIK: Don't you remember your manifesto in the bedroom? A coherent existence after so many years of muddle? You and me, and of course, Fredrika . . .

317

(*They kiss. The music swells. Sings*)
Make way for the clowns.

DESIRÉE:
Applause for the clowns.

BOTH:
They're finally here.
                    (*The music continues*)

FREDRIK: How does Malmö appeal to you? It'll be high sun-
burn season.

DESIRÉE: Why not?

FREDRIK: Why not?

DESIRÉE: Oh God!

FREDRIK: What is it?

DESIRÉE: I've got to do Hedda for a week in Halsingborg.

FREDRIK: Well, what's wrong with Purgatory before Paradise?
I shall sit through all eight performances.
                    (*They go slowly upstage.* FREDRIKA *wakes up*)

FREDRIKA: Don't you think you should go to bed, Grandmother?

MADAME ARMFELDT: No, I shall stay awake all night for fear of
missing the first cock-crow of morning. It has come to be
my only dependable friend.

FREDRIKA: Grandmother —

MADAME ARMFELDT: What, dear?

FREDRIKA: I've watched and watched, but I haven't noticed
the night smiling.

MADAME ARMFELDT: Young eyes are not ideal for watching.
They stray too much. It has already smiled. Twice.

318

FREDRIKA: It has? Twice? For the young — and the fools?

MADAME ARMFELDT: The smile for the fools was particularly broad tonight.

FREDRIKA: So there's only the last to come.

MADAME ARMFELDT: Only the last.

(MADAME ARMFELDT *dies. We become more aware of the underscoring, the same used under the opening waltz.* HENRIK *and* ANNE *suddenly waltz on, and then all of the other couples, at last with their proper partners, waltz through the scene. The trees close in, and* MR. LINDQUIST *appears at the piano. He hits one key of the piano, just as he did at the opening. And the play is over*)

Costume Designs by Florence Klotz

Anne Egerman

Countess Celimène de Frances de la Tour de Casa

Desirée Armfeldt

Desirée Armfeldt

Two of Boris Aronson's Set Models for
the original Broadway production

ROBERT GALBREATH

ADDITIONAL LYRICS
with Commentary by Stephen Sondheim

"Two Fairy Tales"

Written for the characters of Henrik and Anne Egerman to sing in the first act, "Two Fairy Tales" was cut during the first days of rehearsals as the act was running overlong.

ANNE:
Once upon a time

There lived a princess

Who was exceedingly
  beloved,
Who had a kingdom

Which was perfect,

Which was carpeted with
  jewels.

She was beset on every side

With handsome princes

And lesser nobles

Bearing gifts and begging
  marriage.

She would spurn them,

And they would kill them-
  selves in duels.

HENRIK:
Once upon a time

There lived a knight

Who was devout,

In a kingdom

Which was wretched,

Which was under someone's
  curse.

On every side it was beset

With giant trolls,

And with dragons,

Bringing famine.

He would pray,

And it constantly got worse.
Of course the knight was
  much inspired

324

But the princess soon
   grew tired

By the misery at hand.

Of all the fires she had
   fanned.

And as time went on,

As time went on,

He thought,

She thought, "I must wed
   someone

"I must do something
To alleviate the sorrow
   in the land."

To alleviate the sorrow
   in the land."

Now there were three

There were three

Princes

Dragons
In particular named

In particular named
Virtue,

Falsehood,

Kindness,

Greed,

And Excellence,

And Lust.

But she could not

He could not

Choose

Refuse the call.

At all.

He bade his wife

She bade the three appear.

Farewell, for go he must.
Then to the west

She got her wizard to
   suggest

A sort of test.

At her behest

The princely suitors did
    their best,

And who'd have guessed?

All three were tested and
    they passed.

She was depressed,

To say the least,

But she got dressed

And served a feast
Where she was faced

With princes
Virtue,

Kindness,

And Excellence.

After many years

The king her father,

Who'd been abroad in
    search of truth,

The knight set off upon his
    quest.

He bore his crest

As if possessed,

Nor did he rest!

He was obsessed.

He found a priest,

He made a fast and was
    confessed.

He never ceased,

Until at last he had laid waste

And turned to dust
The dragons

Falsehood,

Greed,

And Lust.

After many years

The noble knight,

Returned to find

The kingdom wretched,

All activity suspended.

To his dismay,
He also found

His daughter mad

With indecision.

She had lapsed into
a coma,

While her suitors

Had grown restless and
offended.

And so the king to ease
her sorrow

Passed a curious decree

That she could marry all
three suitors.

Did she feel guilty?
No,

Who'd lost an arm,

Returned to find

The kingdom perfect,

All activity resumed.

He also found,
To his dismay,

His wife had died

With the waiting

And his children,

Left alone,

Had been starving and were
doomed.

So the court upon the
morrow

Proclaimed a holiday to be,

And the day was named for
him.
Did he feel guilty?

Oh yes,

327

And it was wonderful
  to see!
So she lived

Ever after

With Virtue,

Kindness,

And Excellence.

That's a tale

Which was read me by
  my father,

And it was wonderful
  to see!
So he lived —
Not for long —

Ever watchful for

Falsehood,

Greed,

And Lust.

That's a tale
Which was read me by
  my mother,

BOTH:
And there's probably
A moral to be
Pointedly discussed,
But it's always been
My favorite,
And I read it when I'm gloomy,
And though fairy tales are
Foolish, that's a
Fairy tale to trust.

"Silly People"

This number, sung in Scene 5A of Act II, was cut during the show's Boston tryout because it was felt that the character it was written for, Frid, wasn't important enough to spend some four minutes with.

FRID:

Lie here with me on the grass.
Let the wind be our words
As the night smiles down.
Don't they know, don't they?
No, they don't, do they?
Silly people, silly people, silly people.

Voices glide by, let them pass.
Let them float in their words
Till they slowly drown.
Don't they know, don't they,
What they want?
Silly, silly people!
Patient and polite,
Crying in their teacups,
Shying from the night —

When now it smiles it smiles for lovers.
When next it smiles it smiles for fools.
The last it smiles it smiles for them,
The others, the rememberers,
The truly silly people.
Them and us and all . . .

Lie then with me, closer still.
You can float in my arms
Till we gently drown.
Don't they know, don't they,
What it means, dying?

Silly people, silly people . . .
Float and flow,
And down we go
To drown.

"Bang!"

To have been sung by Count Carl-Magnus and Desirée in Desirée's digs, this song was cut in rehearsal because it didn't have the transition Hal Prince needed to make the set change that would get the Count from Desiree's digs to his next scene with Charlotte. "Bang!" was replaced by "In Praise of Women," which neatly moved the scene to Charlotte's breakfast nook.

CARL-MAGNUS (*To himself, eyeing Desirée*):
The war commences, the
   enemy awaits
In quivering expectancy.
The poor defenses, the pene-
   trable gates,
How terrible to be a woman.
The time is here,
The game is there.
The smell of fear,
Like musk, pervades the air.
The bugle sounding,
The pistol steady,
The blood is pounding,
Take aim and ready . . .
(*Unbuttoning his tunic, one but-
   ton at a time, with each
   "Bang!"*)
Bang!
Twenty minutes small talk,
Thirty at the most.
Bang!
Two or three to pour the
   schnapps.
Bang! Bang! Bang!
Half a minute to propose

The necessary toast.
Bang!
The tunic opens,
Bang!
The trousers fall,
Bang!
The foe is helpless,
Back against the wall.
Bang!
An hour and a quarter over
 all,
And bang!

Bang!

Bang! Bang! Bang!

Bang!

Bang!

Bang!

Bang!

Bang!

Bang! Bang!

The battle rages.

DESIRÉE (*To herself*):
Twenty minutes to arrange
Those bloody awful flowers.

Can I get away with more?

Then I have to brush my
 hair,
And that could take me
 hours.

A fit of vapors —

No, that's too quaint.

A wracking cough,
And then a graceful
 faint . . .

A lengthy lecture

On self-restraint . . .

QUINTET:
Bang! Bang! Bang! Bang!

                                        Bang!
Whatever ground I gain
I fortify remorselessly.
                                        Bang! Bang!

The foe engages
                                        Bang!

By shifting the terrain —
How pitiful to be a woman.
                                        Bang!

Attack,
                                        Bang!

Retreat,
                                        Bang!

Lay back,
                                        Bang!

Reform.
                                        Bang! Bang!

Outflank,
                                        Bang!

Deplete,
                                        Bang!

Move up and then restorm.
                                        Bang! Bang! Bang! Bang!

The siege succeeding,
                                        Bang!

The time grows shorter,
                                        Bang!

She lies there pleading,
                                        Bang!

I give no quarter . . .
Bang!   Bang!
Foray at the elbow,
Salvo at the knee!
Bang!   Bang!
Fusillades at breast
And thigh!
Bang! Bang! Bang!   Bang! Bang! Bang!
Then when she's exhausted,

Bang!
A fresh sortie!

I taste the conquest,

The taste is sweet.

She lays her arms down,
Welcoming defeat.

Both sides, content,

Secure

Positions.

All passion spent,

Discuss

Conditions.
How terrible,

How pitiful,

How glorious to be a
  woman.

The quarry senses
A momentary pang.

The war commences.
Bang!

Bang!

Bang!

Bang! Bang!

Bang! Bang!

Bang!

Bang!

Bang! Bang! Bang!

Bang!

Bang!

Bang!

Bang!

DESIRÉE:
He is a peacock,
I keep forgetting . . .

It's all so foolish —
Why am I sweating?

"My Husband the Pig"

"My Husband the Pig" was written to be sung in Act I, Scene 5 by Charlotte, angrily trying to enjoy her breakfast after Carl-Magnus has ordered her to pay a visit to the Egerman household. It was replaced by the second half of "In Praise of Women."

CHARLOTTE:

Fop.
Lout.
What am I, a prop
To order about?
Adulterous lowlife!
He seems to assume I have no life
Of my own.
Well, he isn't alone!

I lie on the shelf at my station
To bolster his self-adulation.
I have no objection
To passing inspection,
But who can contend with an endless erection
That falls on its knees when it sees its reflection?

My husband, the pig,
The swaggering bore
I'll do anyting for,
What a pig!
The air of disdain is appalling,
The level of decency nil.
If he thinks that I'll always come crawling,
Ha! I will.

My husband, the pig.
I worship the ground
That he kicks me around
On, the pig.

A stunted affront to humanity,
A vat of gelatinous vanity,
The stamp of my rampant insanity:
My husband the —

Ugh!
There's a clot in the cream
And a fly in the jam
And I think that I'm going to scream. . . . .
Yes, I am!
But would anyone here give a damn?
No.

Ah, well.
Every day a little death
In the parlor, in the bed,
In the curtains, in the silver,
In the buttons, in the bread.
Every day a little sting
In the heart and in the head.
Every move and every breath,
And you hardly feel a thing,
Brings a perfect little death.

Every day a little death,
On the lips and in the eyes
In the murmurs, in the pauses,
In the gestures, in the sighs.
Every day a little dies
In the looks and in the lies,
And you hardly feel a thing . . .

Ugh!
There's a leaf in the cup
And a crack in the pot
And I think I'm about to throw up.
But I'm not,

'Cause I have to go out, and for what?

A pat on the hand and I'm suet.
I don't understand why I do it.
While I'm in abstention
In every dimension,
His horse and his whores and his wars get attention
And I decompose like a rose with a pension!

My husband, the pig.
I loathe and deplore
Every bone I adore,
He's a pig!
He throws me a crumb to be cruel
And then expects humble delight.
Does he think a duet is a duel?
Ha! He's right!

My husband, the pig!
My swain is a swine
Or, to further refine
It, a pig!
It's ghastly and vastly ironical,
A cynical, clinical chronicle:
"The woman who married a monocle."
My husband, the pig!
Ugh!

"Night Waltz" ("Love Takes Time")

As the opening for the motion picture, these lyrics were written for "Night Waltz."

DESIRÉE, CHARLOTTE, ANNE, PETRA, MADAME ARMFELDT,
FREDERICKA, ERICH, FREDERICK:

Love takes time,
Entirely too much but sublime.
Frightening, love is.
Full of quicksand,
Enlightening, love is,
Full of tricks and
It does take time,
Which really is rather a crime.

Curious, love is,
Self-tormenting,
Embarrassing, love is,
Unrelenting,
A labyrinth, love is.
Just resenting
The time love takes
Compounds the confusion it makes.
One muddles the facts with the fakes.
And love is a lecture
On how to correct your
Mistakes.
                    (*Individual voices*)
What shall I wear?
Where is my parasol?
Do I compare?
                    (*Overlapping*)
Have I missed it?
Will I ever?

Did he notice?
What will they say?
Should I care?
How does one start it up again?
Why can't we stay just the way — ?
Will I ever?
Was I ever?
Can I ever?

MADAME ARMFELDT: I have no questions . . .

OTHERS:
Love comes first.
It matters the most at its worst.
You always feel underrehearsed.
One sets the conditions,
Then finds the positions
Reversed.
The time love takes
Awakens the heart that it breaks.
Consider the new friends it makes.
Yes, love is a lecture
On how to correct your
Mistakes.
                    (*Overlapping*)
What shall I wear?
Where is my parasol?
Do I compare?
Would she dare?
Have I missed it?
Will I ever?

MADAME ARMFELDT: I have no time . . .

OTHERS (*All overlapping, gradually fading*):
Why did she smile? Will she remember?
Why are we laughing? What will he want?

Are you ever? Do you ever?
When will I learn?
Am I too late?
Why did I say that? Is there time? Am I too late?
Have I the right? What are the chances?
Where is my parasol? . . .

"The Glamorous Life"

In the stage version of Night Music, *"The Glamorous Life" is a song about Desirée's life as an actress on the road, with three different points of view — Fredrika's, Desirée's and Madame Armfeldt's — but it was felt that this would be too convoluted and confusing for the film version, and the song was rewritten preserving only the verse of the number (with new lyrics) and employing only one point of view, Fredericka's.*

FREDERICKA:
> Ordinary mothers lead ordinary lives,
> Mop the floors and chop the parsley,
> Mend the clothes and tend the children.
> Ordinary mothers, like ordinary wives,
> Make the beds and bake the pies
> And wither on the vine —
> Not mine.
>
> Dying by inches
> Every night,
> What a glamorous life!
> Pulled on by winches
> To recite —
> What a glamorous life!
>
> Ordinary mothers never get the flowers
> And ordinary mothers never know the joys,
> But ordinary mothers couldn't cough for hours,
> Maintaining their poise.
>
> Sandwiches only,
> But she eats
> What she wants when she wants.
> Sometimes it's lonely,

But she meets
Many handsome gallants.

Ordinary mothers don't live out of cases
But ordinary mothers don't go different places,
Which ordinary mothers can't do,
Being mothers all day.
Mine's away in a play
And she's realer than they . . .

What if her brooch is only glass
And her costumes unravel?
What if her coach is second class?
She at least gets to travel.

And some time this summer,
Meaning soon,
She'll be travelling to me!
Some time this summer —
Maybe June —
I'm the new place she'll see!

Ordinary daughters may think life is better
With ordinary mothers near them when they choose,
But ordinary daughters seldom get a letter
Enclosing reviews!

Gay and resilient,
With applause —
What a glamorous life!
Speeches are brilliant —
When they're Shaw's —
What a glamorous life!

Ordinary mothers needn't meet committees,

But ordinary mothers don't get keys to cities.
No, ordinary mothers merely see their children all year —
Which is lovely, I hear,
But it does interfere
With the glamorous . . .

I am the princess, guarded by dragons
Snorting and grumbling and rumbling in wagons.
She's in her kingdom, wearing disguises,
Living a life that is full of surprises,

And some time this summer
She'll come galloping over the green!
Some time this summer,
To my rescue, my mother the queen!

Ordinary mothers thrive on being private,
But ordinary mothers somehow can survive it,
And ordinary mothers never know they're just standing
    still,
With the kettles to fill,
While they're missing the thrill
Of the glamorous life!

"Send in the Clowns"

For Barbra Streisand's recording of this song on her Broadway
Album, *the lyrics were slightly revised, and a new lyric written for
a second release.*

Isn't it rich?
Are we a pair?
Me here at last on the ground,
You in mid-air.
Send in the clowns.

Isn't it bliss?
Don't you approve?
One who keeps tearing around,
One who can't move.
Where are the clowns?
Send in the clowns.

Just when I'd stopped
Opening doors,
Finally knowing
The one that I wanted was yours,
Making my entrance again
With my usual flair,
Sure of my lines,
No one is there.

Don't you love farce?
My fault, I fear.
I thought that you'd want what I want —
Sorry, my dear.
But where are the clowns?
There ought to be clowns.
Quick, send in the clowns.

What a surprise!

Who could foresee
I'd come to feel about you
What you felt about me?
Why only now when I see
That you've drifted away?
What a surprise . . .
What a cliché . . .

Isn't it rich?
Isn't it queer?
Losing my timing this late
In my career?
And where are the clowns?
Quick, send in the clowns!
Don't bother, they're here.

MAJOR PRODUCTIONS

A *Little Night Music* was first presented by Harold Prince, in association with Ruth Mitchell, at the Sam S. Shubert Theatre, New York City, on February 25, 1973, with the following cast:

(in order of appearance)

MR. LINDQUIST	Benjamin Rayson
MRS. NORDSTROM	Teri Ralston
MRS. ANDERSSEN	Barbara Lang
MR. ERLANSON	Gene Varrone
MRS. SEGSTROM	Beth Fowler
FREDRIKA ARMFELDT	Judy Kahan
MADAME ARMFELDT	Hermione Gingold
FRID, *her butler*	George Lee Andrews
HENRIK EGERMAN	Mark Lambert
ANNE EGERMAN	Victoria Mallory
FREDRIK EGERMAN	Len Cariou
PETRA	D. Jamin-Bartlett
DESIRÉE ARMFELDT	Glynis Johns
MALLA, *her maid*	Despo
BERTRAND, *a page*	Will Sharpe Marshall
COUNT CARL-MAGNUS MALCOLM	Laurence Guittard
COUNTESS CHARLOTTE MALCOLM	Patricia Elliott
OSA	Sherry Mathis

Production Directed by Harold Prince
Choreography by Patricia Birch
Scenic Production Designed by Boris Aronson
Costumes Designed by Florence Klotz
Lighting Designed by Tharon Musser
Orchestrations by Jonathan Tunick
Musical Direction by Harold Hastings

The following songs were cut prior to the New York opening: *"Silly People," "Two Fairy Tales," "My Husband the Pig,"* and *"Bang!"*

A Little Night Music gave its first performance at the Colonial Theatre in Boston, opening on January 23, 1973 and closing on February 10th after 23 performances. Previews began in New York City on February 14, 1973, and the show opened on February 25th and closed on August 3, 1974 after 601 performances and 12 previews.

AWARDS

New York Drama Critics Circle Award — Best Musical

Tony Awards: Best Musical, Best Book of a Musical (Hugh Wheeler), Best Music and Lyrics (Stephen Sondheim), Best Actress in a Musical (Glynis Johns), Best Supporting Actress in a Musical (Patricia Elliott), Best Costume Design (Florence Klotz). Also received Tony nominations for Best Direction of a Musical (Harold Prince), Best Actor in a Musical (Len Cariou), Best Supporting Actor in a Musical (Laurence Guittard), Best Supporting Actress in a Musical (Hermione Gingold), Best Scenic Design (Boris Aronson) and Best Lighting Design (Tharon Musser).

A *Little Night Music* was first presented in London by Ruth Mitchell, Frank Milton, Eddie Kulukundis and Richard Pilbow, in association with Bernard Delfont, at the Adelphi Theatre on April 15, 1975 for 406 performances, with the following cast:

(in order of appearance)

MR. LINDQUIST	John J. Moore
MRS. NORDSTROM	Chris Melville
MRS. ANDERSSEN	Liz Robertson
MR. ERLANSON	David Bexon
MRS. SEGSTROM	Jacquey Chappell
FREDRIKA ARMFELDT	Christine McKenna
MADAME ARMFELDT	Hermione Gingold
FRID, *her butler*	Michael Harbour
HENRIK EGERMAN	Terry Mitchell
ANNE EGERMAN	Veronica Page
FREDRIK EGERMAN	Joss Ackland
PETRA	Diane Langton
DESIRÉE ARMFELDT	Jean Simmons
BERTRAND, *a page*	Christopher Beeching
COUNT CARL-MAGNUS MALCOLM	David Kernan
COUNTESS CHARLOTTE MALCOLM	Maria Aitken
OSA	Penelope Potter

Production Directed by Harold Prince
Choreography by Patricia Birch
Production Supervised by George Martin
Scenic Production Designed by Boris Aronson
Costumes Designed by Florence Klotz
Lighting Designed by Tharon Musser
Orchestrations by Jonathan Tunick
Musical Direction by Ray Cook
Sound by David Collison

AWARD: London Standard Drama Award for Best Musical

A Little Night Music was revived in London by H. M. Tennent Ltd., by arrangement with the Chichester Festival Theatre, John Gale, Executive Producer, at the Piccadilly Theatre, October 6, 1989 – February 17, 1990 for 144 performances, with the following cast:

MADAME ARMFELDT	Lila Kedrova
DESIRÉE ARMFELDT, *her daughter*	Dorothy Tutin
FREDRIKA ARMFELDT, *her granddaughter*	Debra Beaumont
FRID, *her manservant*	David Hitchen
FREDRIK EGERMAN, *a lawyer*	Peter McEnery
HENRIK EGERMAN, *his son*	Alexander Hanson
ANNE EGERMAN, *his second wife*	Deborah Poplett
PETRA, *their maid*	Sara Weymouth
COUNT CARL-MAGNUS MALCOLM	Eric Flynn
COUNTESS CHARLOTTE MALCOLM, *his wife*	Susan Hampshire
MALLA	Mandi Martin
OSA	Susan Paule

The Liebeslieder Singers

MRS. NORDSTROM	Dinah Harris
MRS. ANDERSSEN	Hilary Western
MRS. SEGSTROM	Susan Flannery
MR. ERLANSON	Michael Bulman
MR. LINDQUIST	Martin Nelson

Directed by Ian Judge
Designed by Mark Thompson
Choreography by Anthony Van Laast
Lighting by Nick Chelton
Sound by Matthew Gale
Music Supervised by John Owen Edwards
Musical Director, Roger Ward

A Little Night Music was presented by the New York City Opera (Christopher Keene, General Director) at the New York State Theatre, New York City, August 3, 1990, with the following cast:

MR. LINDQUIST	Ron Baker
MRS. NORDSTROM	Lisa Saffer
MRS. ANDERSSEN	Barbara Shirvis
MR. ERLANSON	Michael Rees Davis
MRS. SEGSTROM	Susanne Marsee
FREDRIKA ARMFELDT	Danielle Ferland
MADAME ARMFELDT	Regina Resnik
FRID, *her butler*	David Comstock
HENRIK EGERMAN	Kevin Anderson
ANNE EGERMAN	Beverly Lambert
FREDRIK EGERMAN	George Lee Andrews
PETRA	Susan Terry
DESIRÉE ARMFELDT	Sally Ann Howes
MALLA, *her maid*	Raven Wilkinson
BERTRAND, *a page*	Michael Rees Davis
COUNT CARL-MAGNUS MALCOLM	Michael Maguire
COUNTESS CHARLOTTE MALCOLM	Maureen Moore
OSA	Judith Jarosz

SERVANTS: Michael Cornell, Ernest Foederer, Kent A. Heacock, Ronald Kelley, Brian Michaels, Brian Quirk, Christopher Shepherd, John Henry Thomas.

Conducted by Paul Gemignani
Directed by Scott Ellis
Orchestrations by Jonathan Tunick
Scenery Designed by Michael Anania
Costumes Designed by Lindsay W. Davis
Lighting Designed by Dawn Chiang
Choreography by Susan Stroman
Sound Designed by Abe Jacob

The motion picture of *A Little Night Music* was produced by New World/Sascha-Wien Films, in association with Elliott Kastner, and released in March of 1978, with the following cast:

DESIRÉE ARMFELDT	Elizabeth Taylor
CHARLOTTE MITTELHEIM	Diana Rigg
FREDERICK EGERMAN	Len Cariou
ANNE EGERMAN	Lesley-Anne Down
MME. ARMFELDT	Hermione Gingold
CARL-MAGNUS MITTELHEIM	Laurence Guittard
ERICH EGERMAN	Christopher Guard
FREDERICKA ARMFELDT	Chloe Franks
KURT	Heins Marecek
PETRA	Lesley Dunlop
CONDUCTOR	Jonathan Tunick
FRANZ	Herbert Tscheppe
BAND CONDUCTOR	Rudolph Schrympf
THE MAYOR	Franz Schussler
THE MAYORESS	Johanna Schussler
BOX OFFICE LADY IN THEATRE	Jean Sincere
FIRST LADY	Dagmar Koller
SECOND LADY	Ruth Brinkman
CONCIERGE	Anna Veigl
UNIFORMED SARGEANT	Stefan Paryla
FIRST WHORE	Eva Dvorska
SECOND WHORE	Lisa De Cohen
MAJOR DOMO	Kurt Martynow
COOK	Gerty Barek
FOOTMAN	James De Groat

(Note: For the film the locale was changed from Sweden to Vienna, and some of the character names were Germanized.)

Directed by Harold Prince
Screenplay by Hugh Wheeler
Edited by John Jympson
Photographed by Arthur Ibbetson, B.S.C.
Costumes Designed by Florence Klotz
Choreography by Patricia Birch
Music Scored and Supervised by Jonathan Tunick
Musical Direction by Paul Gemignani
Executive Producer, Heinz Lazek
Presented by Roger Corman — A New World Picture

MUSICAL NUMBERS

"Overture"/"Night Waltz" (*"Love Takes Time"*)	Company
"The Glamorous Life"	Chloe Franks
"Now"/"Soon"/"Later"	Len Cariou, Lesley-Anne Down, Christopher Guard
"You Must Meet My Wife"	Len Cariou, Elizabeth Taylor
"Every Day a Little Death"	Diana Rigg
Night Waltz	Instrumental
"A Weekend in the Country"	Company
"Send in the Clowns"	Elizabeth Taylor
"It Would Have Been Wonderful"	Len Cariou, Laurence Guittard
Finale: "Send in the Clowns"/"Night Waltz"	Len Cariou, Elizabeth Taylor, Company

The motion picture is available on video cassette: Embassy Home Entertainment 00103.

SELECTED DISCOGRAPHY

* Original Broadway Cast Recording (1973)
    Columbia Records
      LP KS (S)/SQ (Q)-32265
      Cassette ST 32265
      CD CK 32265
    (Also included in Time-Life Records "American Musicals" series:
    Stephen Sondheim. LP STL–AM12, Cassette 4TL–AM12)
      (Although recorded for the original cast album, *"Night Waltz II"*
      was not included on the final original cast recording)

+ Original London Cast Recording (1975)
    RCA Records
      LP LRL1-5090 (S)
      Cassette CRK1-5090; reissue 5090-4-RG
      CD RCD1-5090; reissue 5090-2-RG

Motion Picture Soundtrack Recording (1978)
    Columbia Records
      LP JS 35333 (S)
      Cassette JST 35333

A Little Night Music (studio cast recording, 1990)
    That's Entertainment Records (England)
      Cassette ZCTER 1179
      CD CDTER 1179
      (Includes *"Night Waltz II"*)

Sondheim: A Musical Tribute (1973)
    Warner Bros. Records
      LP 2WS 2705 (S); 2 record set
    RCA Records (1990 reissue)
      Cassette 60515-4
      CD 60515-2
      Includes: *"Silly People"*—George Lee Andrews; *"Two Fairy*
          Tales"—Mark Lambert, Victoria Mallory

* Winner of the Grammy Award for Best Original Cast Show Album
+ Nominated for the Grammy Award for Best Original Cast Show Album
Note: *"Send in the Clowns"* won the 1975 Grammy for Song of the Year,
     with the award going to Mr. Sondheim as the composer/lyricist.

Side by Side by Sondheim/Millicent Martin, Julia McKenzie and David Kernan (1976)

> RCA Records
> > LP CBL2–1851 (S); 2 record set
> > Cassette CBK2–1851; reissue 1851-4-RG
> > CD 1851-2-RG; 2 disc set
>
> Includes: *"You Must Meet My Wife"*—David Kernan, Millicent Martin; *"Send in the Clowns"*—Millicent Martin

Songs of Sondheim (original Irish cast recording of *Side by Side by Sondheim,* 1977)

> RAM Records
> > LP RMLP 1026
>
> Includes: *"Send in the Clowns"*—Gemma Craven

Side by Side by Sondheim (original Australian cast recording, 1977)

> RCA Red Seal (Australia)
> > LP VRL2–0156; 2 record set
> > Cassette VRK2–0156; 2 tape set
>
> Includes: *"You Must Meet My Wife"*—Bartholomew John, Jill Perryman; *"Send in the Clowns"*—Jill Perryman

A Different Side of Sondheim/Richard Rodney Bennett (1979)

> DRG Records
> > LP SL 5182
> > Cassette SLC–5182
>
> Includes: *"You Must Meet My Wife," "Night Waltz I"*

Marry Me a Little/Craig Lucas and Suzanne Henry (1981)

> RCA Records
> > LP ABL1–4159 (S)
> > Cassette ABK1–4159; reissue 7142-4-RG
> > CD 7142-2-RG
>
> Includes: *"Two Fairy Tales"*—Craig Lucas, Suzanne Henry; *"Bang!"*—Craig Lucas, Suzanne Henry; *"Silly People"*—Craig Lucas

Evelyn Lear Sings Sondheim and Bernstein (1981)
Mercury Records Golden Imports
   LP MR 75136
   Cassette MRI 75136
Includes: *"Send in the Clowns"*

A Stephen Sondheim Collection/Jackie Cain and Roy Kral (1982)
Finesse Records
   LP FW 38324 (S)
   Cassette FWT 38324
DRG Records (1990 reissue)
   Cassette DSC 25102
   CD DSCD 25102
Includes: *"Send in the Clowns"*—Jackie Cain

A Stephen Sondheim Evening (1983)
RCA Records
   LP CBL2–4745 (S); 2 record set
   Cassette CBK2–4745; 2 tape set
Includes: *"Send in the Clowns"*—Angela Lansbury; *"The Miller's Son"*
         —Liz Callaway

A Little Sondheim Music/Los Angeles Vocal Arts Ensemble (1984)
Angel Records
   LP EMI DS-37347 (S)
   Cassette EMI 4DS-37347
Includes: *"Overture"*—Michael Gallup, Darlene Romano, Delcina
         Stevenson, Jeffrey Araluce, Rickie Weiner-Gole; *"Night
         Waltz I"*/*"Night Waltz II"*—Janet Smith, Darlene Romano,
         Paul Johnson, Rickie Weiner-Gole, Michael Gallup; *"In
         Praise of Women"*—Michael Gallup; *"A Weekend in the
         Country"*—Janet Smith, Michael Gallup, Ensemble; *"Send in
         the Clowns"* —Rickie Weiner-Gole, Dale Morich

The Broadway Album/Barbra Streisand (1985)
Columbia Records
LP OC 40092
Cassette OCT 40092
CD CK 40092
Includes: *"Send in the Clowns"* (with Sondheim's revised lyric)

A Collector's Sondheim (1985)
RCA Records
LP CRL4–5359 (S); 4 record set
Cassette CRK4–5359; 4 tape set
CD RCD3–5480; 3 disc set
Includes: *"Overture"/"Night Waltz I"*—Orchestra/John J. Moore, Chris Melville, Liz Robertson, David Bexon, Jacquey Chappell; *"The Glamorous Life"*—Christine McKenna, Jean Simmons, John J. Moore, Chris Melville, Liz Robertson, David Bexon, Jacquey Chappell, Hermione Gingold; *"In Praise of Women"*—David Kernan; *"A Weekend in the Country"*—Diane Langton, Veronica Page, Joss Ackland, Maria Aitken, David Kernan, Terry Mitchell; *"Liaisons"*—Hermione Gingold; *"The Miller's Son"*—Diane Langton (all six tracks from original London cast recording); *"Two Fairy Tales"*—Craig Lucas, Suzanne Henry; *"Silly People"*—Craig Lucas (not included on CD release); *"Bang!"*—Craig Lucas, Suzanne Henry (all three tracks from original cast recording of *Marry Me a Little*); *"The Glamorous Life"* (The Letter Song)—Elaine Tomkinson (track from the motion picture soundtrack); *"Night Waltz II"*—Teri Ralston, Gene Varrone, Benjamin Rayson, Beth Fowler, Barbara Lang (out-take from original Broadway cast recording); *"Send in the Clowns"*—Angela Lansbury (track from *A Stephen Sondheim Evening*)

Sondheim (1985)
Book-of-the-Month Records
LP 81–7515 (S); 3 record set
Cassette 91–7516; 2 tape set
CD 11–7517; 2 disc set
Includes: *"Liaisons"*—Chamber Ensemble; *"Send in the Clowns"*—Joyce Castle; *"You Must Meet My Wife"*—Chamber Ensemble; *"The Glamorous Life"* (The Letter Song)—Betsy Joslyn (the motion picture version)

355

Old Friends/Geraldine Turner Sings the Songs of Stephen Sondheim (1986)
Larrikin Records (Australia)
LP LRF-169
Cassette TC-LRF-169
Includes: *"The Miller's Son"*
(This album was reissued by Silva Screen Records [London] under the title *The Stephen Sondheim Songbook*: LP Song 001, Cassette Song C001, CD Song CD001)

Cleo Sings Sondheim/Cleo Laine (1988)
RCA Records
LP 7702–1–RC
Cassette 7702–4–RC
CD 7702–2–RC
Includes: *"Liaisons," "Send in the Clowns," "The Miller's Son"*

Julie Wilson Sings the Stephen Sondheim Songbook (1988)
DRG Records
LP SL 5206
Cassette SLC 5206
CD CDSL 5206
Includes: *"Send in the Clowns"*

The Other Side of Sondheim/Jane Harvey (1988)
Atlantic Records
LP 81833-1
Cassette 81833-4
CD 81833-2
Includes: *"Send in the Clowns"*

Symphonic Sondheim/Don Sebesky Conducts The London Symphony Orchestra (1990)
WEA Records (London)
LP 9031-72 119-1
Cassette 9031-72 119-4
CD 9031-72 119-2
Includes: *"Send in the Clowns"*

Sondheim: A Celebration at Carnegie Hall (1992)
  RCA Victor
    CD 09026-61484-2; 2 disc set
    Includes: *"Send in the Clowns," "Remember?"*

A Little Night Music (Royal National Theatre Recording, 1995)
  Tring Records
    CD TRING001

Stephen Sondheim's A Little Night Music/Terry Trotter (1997)
  Varèse Sarabande
    CD VSD-5819

Sweeney Todd

The Demon Barber of Fleet Street

MUSIC AND LYRICS BY
STEPHEN SONDHEIM

BOOK BY
HUGH WHEELER

FROM AN ADAPTATION BY CHRISTOPHER BOND

INTRODUCTION BY
CHRISTOPHER BOND

Dorothy Loudon, who replaced Angela
Lansbury in the role of Mrs. Lovett

INTRODUCTION

For me there is only one rule in the theater: Does it work? And by that I don't mean will the show run for twenty years or make X million dollars, but have I come out of the theater feeling more alive than when I went in? Has my imagination been fired, my emotions been aroused, my brain kick-started into life? Is my heart pounding and my mind racing; and, if the show is a musical, do a series of discordant and Neanderthal groans issue from my mouth? (This is known as Chris hums the score.) When I see *Sweeney Todd* all these things usually happen.

My involvement with the show goes back to 1968—I wrote the play on which Stephen Sondheim based his musical, have directed four productions of the musical in England and Scandinavia, and seen a further six or seven productions around the world. What follows is a highly subjective and partial history that will almost certainly be inaccurate in places—I am writing this entirely from memory as I am in Sweden directing a show and have no access to any notes, diaries, books, or records. A perfect opportunity to be a theater critic for a day and try to force the facts to fit my own prejudices . . .

HISTORY

Sweeney Todd is pure fiction. Plenty of unhinged and vindictive malcontents have worked in Fleet Street over the last two hundred years (until very recently most English

361

newspapers had their offices there), but no one has ever succeeded in finding a shred of evidence as to the existence of a Demon Barber thereabouts. There was one in revolutionary Paris—a Jacobin who cut his customers' throats, though whether for profit or because of political differences is unclear. In seventeenth-century Scotland there are accounts of a family of robbers led by one Sawney Bean who are said to have eaten their victims. Shakespeare's Titus Andronicus kills and bakes two brothers in a pie before serving them up to their mother, Tamora, Queen of the Goths; and every culture has tales of cannibalism from the Gilgamesh of Babylon through Transylvania to the present day. Some would claim that a benign form of cannibalism remains with us in ritualized form in the communion service of the Catholic Church.

It's against this background that Sweeney Todd started life in the 1830s in London. He was the creation of George Dibden-Pitt, a freelance journalist who wrote an account of Sweeney's life and crimes for a "penny dreadful," a broadsheet that sold for a penny and was roughly equivalent to the more preposterous of our present-day tabloids. "Aliens Bonked My Mother-in-Law!" "Vicar Eats Royal Gerbil—Shock Horror!" etc. Sweeney was a psychopath who killed for profit and Mrs. Lovett a harridan who baked the bodies. The story was widely believed to be true, and aroused such interest that George immediately adapted it for the stage, where it became an instant success.

MELODRAMA

The theaters George's play was performed in were known as "Blood Tubs" on account of the fact that their repertoire was almost exclusively devoted to shows of the most lurid and sensational kind. Large helpings of sex and violence, with a perfunctory spoonful of Christian humbug at the end. The atmosphere these shows were performed in was rough and boisterous, and whilst we can speculate on the standard of the performances when measured against today's menu at the bourgeois culture trough, there is no doubt that they possessed at least some of the essential ingredients that go to make good theater: energy and commitment crackling between the stage and the audience; involvement; passion and fun. Nowadays the word *melodrama* is usually used pejoratively, as if there were something inherently cheap and phony about it, and modern revivals usually seek to poke fun at the form rather than attempt to get to grips with the subject matter. Such exercises seem to me to be pointless and depressing; mocking and distorting the past may make us feel superior, but it can give us no understanding of the present. Having said that, there is no doubt that on the printed page most melodramas seem lifeless and stilted and give very few clues as to how they must have been in action. And the original script of *Sweeney Todd* is no exception.

THE PLAY

In 1968 I was working as an actor at the Victoria Theatre, Stoke-on-Trent, an excellent repertory theater in the Midlands—the center of England. The theater announced *Sweeney Todd* as a forthcoming attraction; no one had read the script but another melodrama, *A Ticket-of-Leave Man,* had been a success two seasons before, and we thought that if the script needed doctoring we could sort it out in rehearsals. Due to a series of cock-ups we didn't get hold of a copy of the play until two weeks before rehearsals were due to begin, and on the page the show was crude, repetitive, and simplistic—hardly any plot and less character development. It didn't need doctoring, it needed a heart transplant. And preferably new lungs and balls as well. I had had a novel published the year before and with the optimism/arrogance of youth (I was twenty-three), cheerfully volunteered to write my first play: It would retain the title, the razors, the pies, and the trick chair and be delivered in a week's time. Fortunately it wrote itself. I crossed Dumas's *The Count of Monte Cristo* with Tourneur's *The Revenger's Tragedy* for a plot; added elements of pastiche Shakespeare in a sort of blank-ish verse for Sweeney, the Judge, and the lovers to talk; borrowed the name of the author of *The Prisoner of Zenda* for my sailor boy; remembered some market patter I'd learnt as a child; and adapted the wit and wisdom of Brenda, who ran the greengrocer's shop opposite my house, for Mrs. Lovett's ruminations upon life, death, and the state of her sex life. I met my deadline with a couple of hours to spare and started rehearsals playing Tobias Ragg, which I'd written for myself, a week later. The show was well received and was subsequently produced several times in various theaters in England, and eventually, due to the efforts of my agent, Blanche Marvin, at the Theatre Royal, Stratford East in London in the mid-seventies. It was there that Stephen Sondheim saw it. And perhaps that's where the real story begins because whilst I have great affection for the play, until Steve performed his alchemical miracle on it, it remained a neat pastiche that worked well if performed with sufficient panache, but base metal nevertheless. But the transformation to pure gold was about to begin.

SONDHEIM

Blanche told me that someone named Stephen Sondheim had seen the show—I'm ashamed to say I'd never heard of him at that time. There had been talk of doing the play in New York, but the American producers who were interested in the project, Richard Barr and Charles Woodward, were now asking if we would be willing to shelve that idea in favor of a possible musical that Steve would write. Blanche was

364

very enthusiastic about the idea. I took her advice. I remember two meetings round about that time but can't remember which order they came in.

I think the first was with Steve's agent, Flora Roberts, and I'm fairly certain I was drunk (a semi-permanent state until 1984 when I knocked it on the head and joined AA). I remember being terrified of her (I still am) and thinking that she reminded me of a cross between Mae West and a New York version of Lady Bracknell. She was extremely direct and straightforward and in attempting to match these qualities I swore a lot and ended up by saying (expletives deleted): "Look, if he [Steve] is any good, and she [Blanche] says he is, then let him do what he likes with it [my play]." Which with the benefit of hindsight is one of the more spectacularly sensible things I've said in my life.

The other meeting was with Steve at the Granada studios in Manchester where they were filming numbers from *Side by Side by Sondheim* for TV. I was moving house at that time, and, since I was driving a large lorry full of furniture, was sober for once. We talked about the play in some detail and what struck me most forcibly was his complete lack of bullshit. "What a lovely bloke," I remember thinking. "What's he doing working in the theater?" I find it difficult to write about someone whom I admire so much without it sounding soppy; suffice it to say that since I've become familiar with his work I find it difficult to sit through a show that isn't by Stephen Sondheim without wishing that it was. I have also been known to pick fist-fights with people who complain that his work has no heart. For their information the heart is a large and powerful muscle that pumps blood, a singularly inappropriate organ to tie up in a pink ribbon or fit with a neat attachment for wearing on the sleeve. And from "Being Alive" to "No One Is Alone" and at all points in between I hear the double thump of a heart as big as a house. And if in *Sweeney* the blood it pumps is sometimes black with bile it nevertheless remains hot, strong, and foaming with life. Steve has always been generous about my contribution to *Sweeney*: it's nice to be able to say thanks.

THE MUSICAL

Steve's original intention was to write a sung-through show without dialogue, but when this proved impractical he approached Hugh Wheeler, with whom he had collaborated on previous shows, including *A Little Night Music* and *Pacific Overtures*, to write the book for the show. It's no secret that Hugh Wheeler and I had our differences: professional rather than personal, but since he died in 1987 I don't feel it's appropriate to discuss them here as there were doubtless faults on both sides, and he's unable to put his point of view. What is indisputable is that *Sweeney Todd* is a book-heavy musical. Its storyline and character development run directly parallel to those in the play; the plot and subplots are complicated and all major characters interlock and interrelate. Indeed, were one feeling pretentious one could even subtitle the piece *Aspects of Love*, for that is what everyone in the show is looking for. It is Sweeney's love for his wife and daughter that sustains him through his fifteen-year exile and brings him back to London; it is Mrs. Lovett's love for Sweeney that makes her keep his razors and forges anew their fatal partnership. Judge Turpin and Anthony both love Johanna in their different ways; and Johanna reciprocates. The Beggar Woman once loved and now "loves" professionally. Tobias has never known love but desires it above all else. Add to all this Sweeney's relationship with his razors and Mrs. Lovett's with the coin of the realm and you have just about covered the entire spectrum from necrophilia through rape and filial duty to romance. We care about the characters in *Sweeney* because they care so passionately about each other; and on a good night we plunge headlong to triumph and disaster with them. The music sees to that.

I'm not competent to comment on the score (I've been known to ask a conductor if he could cut three and a half bars of Verdi to help me stage an aria; when the wind is from the north I can still feel a piece of his baton lodged somewhere up my left nostril) beyond saying that for me it perfectly mirrors and distills the particular people and precise situations in the show. And lifts them to another plane.

SWEENEY *IN PERFORMANCE*

My only quarrel with Hal Prince's original Broadway production at the Uris Theatre is that it was at the Uris Theatre. It seems a strange place to tell stories in; and that's what we do, isn't it? But then I have very seldom enjoyed a show in a venue that seats many more than a thousand people. A lot depends upon the architecture, but generally speaking if you go much beyond that number I find it difficult to get involved in what's happening. The sets get larger, the amplification gets greater, the hype begins, the tickets get more expensive to pay for it all, the hype increases, and eventually the event begins to take on all the subtlety and humanity of a Roman circus. Theater is a personal and human activity and I think it's usually best on a human scale. It's a tribute to everyone concerned with the original production that it worked so brilliantly, but I've always felt it did so in spite of, rather than because of, where it opened.

As with any worthwhile and complex show there are many ways of interpreting it and balancing its component parts. There is no right or wrong way, only, "Does the end result add up to a graphic realization of the authors' intentions? Does it successfully tell their story here and now?" Within these parameters directors, designers, actors, and technicians make the choices that give their particular production its particular emphasis and dynamics. What follows are some highly personal preferences.

The people in *Sweeney* are fuelled by basic and simple

human emotions: greed, lust, vengeance, and a desire to love and be loved in return. They inhabit a corrupt, unjust, and dangerous world, but this should tend to intensify their humanity rather than destroy it. To overemphasize the elements of the show encapsulated most clearly in the lines:

"The engine roared, the motor hissed,
And who could see how the road would twist . . .?"

is in some ways to deny the audience's total involvement with the people and events in the story, and is ultimately too Brechtian an approach for me. If the people are dehumanized for any reason we cease to care about them. Paradoxically, when I have directed the show I have always shifted the emphasis of the first two scenes of Act II by having grotesquely frock-coated and crinolined figures in half-masks as Mrs. Lovett's customers and Sweeney's anonymous victims because I don't want people involved with them. Visually, this ties up with the dumb-show rape of Sweeney's wife in Act I, and I like the idea that the pie shop and barber shop have become a chic venue for the gentry to attend—the white folks slumming it in Harlem, so to speak. The masks also seem to fit well with Sweeney's almost dreamlike state during the "Quartet" and maybe add another layer of meaning to the line:

"Those above will serve those down below . . ."

The other major shift that I have attempted in production is in the middle section of Act I. The first act is very long and it was found necessary in the original production to cut the Judge's song; this seems unfortunate as it tends to reduce him to an all-purpose baddie, and I have found it more satisfactory to introduce Anthony into the market scene to get across swiftly such plot points as are important, follow the market scene with the Judge's song, and then cut almost the entire scene in the barber's shop up to Pirelli's entrance, retaining just enough lines to reestablish the Beggar Woman's presence in the street and Sweeney's growing impatience that the Beadle has not yet come for a shave. It is also possible to keep Pirelli's song in the market intact; it is long, but if the scene can be staged so that he sings as he shaves and pulls teeth, then it holds.

These and other minor alterations I made when I first directed the show at the Liverpool Playhouse in 1981. With a cast of ten and an orchestra of five. Which I think is the minimum it should be attempted with! I think it worked: It certainly did for the punter who, when Sweeney's razor was poised over the disguised Johanna's neck, leapt to his feet and yelled: "Don't kill 'er, yer soft get; she's yer daughter!" He subsequently became aware of where he was and sat down in confusion. But maybe melodrama isn't completely dead and buried. I hope not. Now read on. Bon Appetit.

Chris Bond

Karlstad, Sweden
October 1990

(Upper left) Sarah Rice (Johanna) and Victor Garber (Anthony) and *(from lower left)* Joaquin Romaguera (Pirelli), Len Cariou (Sweeney Todd), Angela Lansbury (Mrs.

Lovett), Jack Eric Williams (the Beadle) and Edmund Lyndeck (Judge Turpin) in the original Broadway production of *Sweeney Todd, the Demon Barber of Fleet Street*

Len Cariou

Angela Lansbury

(Lower left) Jim Walton (Anthony) and Gretchen Kingsl___
(Johanna) and *(from upper left)* Michael McCarty (t___
Beadle), Bill Nabel (Pirelli), Bob Gunton (Sweeney Tod___
David Baron (Judge Turpin), Beth Fowler (Mrs. Lovett) a___
Eddie Korbich (Tobias) in the 1989 Circle-in-the-Squa___
revival of *Sweeney Todd*

Bob Gunton

To Flora and Janet Roberts

Time: The 19th Century
Place: London: Fleet Street and environs

CAST OF CHARACTERS

ANTHONY HOPE
SWEENEY TODD
BEGGAR WOMAN
MRS. LOVETT
JUDGE TURPIN
THE BEADLE
JOHANNA
TOBIAS RAGG
PIRELLI
JONAS FOGG
TOWNSPEOPLE, LORDS, LADIES,
    POLICEMEN, LUNATICS, ETC.

"Sweeney Todd,
The Demon Barber of Fleet Street"
was originally produced on Broadway by
Richard Barr, Charles Woodward,
Robert Fryer, Mary Lea Johnson, Martin Richards

MUSICAL NUMBERS

ACT I

"The Ballad of Sweeney Todd"	COMPANY
"No Place Like London"	ANTHONY, TODD, BEGGAR WOMAN
"The Barber and His Wife"	TODD
"The Worst Pies in London"	MRS. LOVETT
"Poor Thing"	MRS. LOVETT
"My Friends"	TODD, MRS. LOVETT
"Green Finch and Linnet Bird"	JOHANNA
"Ah, Miss"	ANTHONY, BEGGAR WOMAN
"Johanna"	ANTHONY
"Pirelli's Miracle Elixir"	TOBIAS, TODD, MRS. LOVETT, COMPANY
"The Contest"	PIRELLI
"Johanna"	JUDGE TURPIN
"Wait"	MRS. LOVETT
"Kiss Me"	JOHANNA, ANTHONY
"Ladies in Their Sensitivities"	THE BEADLE
"Kiss Me"	JOHANNA, ANTHONY, THE BEADLE, JUDGE TURPIN
"Pretty Women"	TODD, JUDGE TURPIN
"Epiphany"	TODD
"A Little Priest"	TODD, MRS. LOVETT

ACT II

"God, That's Good!"	TOBIAS, MRS. LOVETT, TODD, BEGGAR WOMAN, CUSTOMERS
"Johanna"	ANTHONY, TODD, JOHANNA, BEGGAR WOMAN
"By the Sea"	MRS. LOVETT
Wigmaker Sequence	TODD, ANTHONY, QUINTET
"The Letter"	TODD, QUINTET
"Not While I'm Around"	TOBIAS, MRS. LOVETT
"Parlor Songs"	THE BEADLE, MRS. LOVETT, TOBIAS
"City on Fire"	LUNATICS, JOHANNA, ANTHONY
"Searching"	MRS. LOVETT, TODD, BEGGAR WOMAN, ANTHONY, JOHANNA
Final Sequence	MRS. LOVETT, TODD, BEGGAR WOMAN, JUDGE TURPIN
"The Ballad of Sweeney Todd"	COMPANY

378

Prologue

As the audience enters, an organist takes his place at a huge eccentric organ to the side of the stage and begins to play funeral music. Before a front drop depicting in a honeycombed beehive the class system of mid-19th century England two gravediggers appear, carrying shovels, and begin to dig a grave downstage center. As they dig they disappear six feet into the earth, leaving piles of dirt on the upstage side.

At curtain time a police warden appears, looks at his watch, hurrying them. Two workmen enter. They pull down the drop. The deafeningly shrill sound of a factory whistle. Blackout.

The lights come up to reveal the company. A man steps forward and sings.

MAN:
Attend the tale of Sweeney Todd.
His skin was pale and his eye was odd.
He shaved the faces of gentlemen
Who never thereafter were heard of again.
He trod a path that few have trod,
Did Sweeney Todd,
The Demon Barber of Fleet Street.

ANOTHER MAN:

He kept a shop in London town,
Of fancy clients and good renown.
And what if none of their souls were saved?
They went to their maker impeccably shaved
By Sweeney,
By Sweeney Todd,
The Demon Barber of Fleet Street.

(A blinding light cuts down the stage as an upstage iron door opens. Two men enter. They carry a body in a bag, tied at both ends with rope. They are followed by a woman carrying a tin canister marked "Flour." They walk to the edge of the grave and unceremoniously dump the body in it. The woman opens the canister and pours black ashes into the hole. This action covers the next verse of the song)

COMPANY:

Swing your razor wide, Sweeney!
Hold it to the skies!
Freely flows the blood of those
Who moralize!

(Various members of the company step forward and sing)

SOLOISTS:

His needs were few, his room was bare:
A lavabo and a fancy chair,
A mug of suds and a leather strop,
An apron, a towel, a pail and a mop.
For neatness he deserves a nod,
Does Sweeney Todd,

COMPANY:

The Demon Barber of Fleet Street.

WOMEN:

Inconspicuous Sweeney was,
Quick and quiet and clean 'e was.

Back of his smile, under his word,
Sweeney heard music that nobody heard.
Sweeney pondered and Sweeney planned,
Like a perfect machine 'e planned.
Sweeney was smooth, Sweeney was subtle,
Sweeney would blink and rats would scuttle.
  (*The men join in singing, voices overlapping, in a gradu-
  al crescendo*)
Sweeney was smooth, Sweeney was subtle,
Sweeney would blink and rats would scuttle.
Inconspicuous Sweeney was,
Quick and quiet and clean 'e was,
Like a perfect machine 'e was,
Was Sweeney!
Sweeney!
Sweeney!
Sweeeeeneeeeey!
  (TODD *rises out of the grave and sings as the company
  repeats his words*)

TODD *and* COMPANY:
Attend the tale of Sweeney Todd.
He served a dark and a vengeful god.

TODD:
What happened then — well, that's the play,
And he wouldn't want us to give it away,
Not Sweeney,

TODD *and* COMPANY:
Not Sweeney Todd,
The Demon Barber of Fleet Street . . .
  (*The scene blacks out. The bells of a clock tower chime.
  Early morning light comes up . . .*)

ACT I

A street by the London docks. A small boat appears from the back. In it are SWEENEY TODD, ANTHONY HOPE *and the pilot.* ANTHONY *is a cheerful country-born young ship's first mate with a duffel bag slung over his shoulder.* TODD *is a heavy-set, saturnine man in his forties who might, say, be a blacksmith or a dockhand. There is about him an air of brooding, slightly nerve-chilling self-absorption.*

ANTHONY (*Sings*):
   I have sailed the world, beheld its wonders
   From the Dardanelles
   To the mountains of Peru,
   But there's no place like London!
   I feel home again.

   I could hear the city bells
   Ring whatever I would do.
   No, there's no pl —

TODD (*Sings grimly*):
   No, there's no place like London.

ANTHONY (*Surprised at the interruption*): Mr. Todd, sir?

TODD (*Sings*):
   You are young.
   Life has been kind to you.
   You will learn.

(*They step out of the boat, music under*)
It is here we go our several ways. Farewell, Anthony, I will not soon forget the good ship *Bountiful* nor the young man who saved my life.

ANTHONY: There's no cause to thank me for that, sir. It would have been a poor Christian indeed who'd have spotted you pitching and tossing on that raft and not given the alarm.

TODD: There's many a Christian would have done just that and not lost a wink's sleep for it, either.
(*A ragged* BEGGAR WOMAN *suddenly appears*)

BEGGAR WOMAN (*Approaching, holding out bowl to* ANTHONY, *sings*):
Alms! . . . Alms! . . .
For a miserable woman
On a miserable chilly morning . . .
             (ANTHONY *drops a coin in her bowl*)
Thank yer, sir, thank yer.
             (*Softly, suddenly leering in a mad way*)
'Ow would you like a little squiff, dear,
A little jig jig,
A little bounce around the bush?
Wouldn't you like to push me crumpet?
It looks to me, dear,
Like you got plenty there to push.
    (*She grabs at him. As* ANTHONY *starts back in embarrassment, she turns instantly and pathetically to* TODD, *who tries to keep his back to her*)
Alms! . . . Alms! . . .
For a pitiful woman
Wot's got wanderin' wits . . .
Hey, don't I know you, mister?
             (*She peers intently at him*)

TODD: Must you glare at me, woman? Off with you, off, I say!

BEGGAR WOMAN (*Smiling vacantly*):
Then 'ow would you like to fish me squiff, mister?
We'll go jig jig,
A little —

TODD (*Making a gesture as if to strike her*): Off, I said. To the devil with you!
(*She scuttles away, turns to give him a piercing look, then wanders off*)

BEGGAR WOMAN (*Singing as she goes*):
Alms! . . . Alms! . . .
For a desperate woman . . .
(*Music continues under*)

ANTHONY (*A little bewildered*): Pardon me, sir, but there's no need to fear the likes of her. She was only a half-crazed beggar woman. London's full of them.

TODD (*Half to himself, half to* ANTHONY): I beg your indulgence, boy. My mind is far from easy, for in these once-familiar streets I feel the chill of ghostly shadows everywhere. Forgive me.

ANTHONY: There's nothing to forgive.

TODD: Farewell, Anthony.

ANTHONY: Mr. Todd, before we part —

TODD (*Suddenly fierce*): What is it?

ANTHONY: I have honored my promise never to question you. Whatever brought you to that sorry shipwreck is your affair. And yet, during those many weeks of the voyage home, I have come to think of you as a friend and, if trouble lies ahead for you in London . . . if you need help — or money . . .

TODD (*Almost shouting*): No!

(ANTHONY *starts, perplexed;* TODD *makes a placating ges-*
ture, sings quietly and intensely)
There's a hole in the world
Like a great black pit
And the vermin of the world
Inhabit it
And its morals aren't worth
What a pig could spit
And it goes by the name of London.

At the top of the hole
Sit the privileged few,
Making mock of the vermin
In the lower zoo,
Turning beauty into filth and greed.
I too
Have sailed the world and seen its wonders,
For the cruelty of men
Is as wondrous as Peru,
But there's no place like London!
        (*Pause, music under, then as if in a trance*)
There was a barber and his wife,
And she was beautiful.
A foolish barber and his wife.
She was his reason and his life,
And she was beautiful.
And she was virtuous.
And he was —
                (*Shrugs*)
Naive.

There was another man who saw
That she was beautiful,
A pious vulture of the law
Who with a gesture of his claw
Removed the barber from his plate.

Then there was nothing but to wait
And she would fall,
So soft,
So young,
So lost,
And oh, so beautiful!
                    (*Pauses, music under*)

ANTHONY: And the lady, sir — did she — succumb?

TODD:
Oh, that was many years ago . . .
I doubt if anyone would know.
                    (*Speaks, music under*)
Now, leave me, Anthony, I beg of you. There's somewhere
I must go, something I must find out. Now. And alone.

ANTHONY: But surely we will meet again before I'm off to
Plymouth!

TODD: If you want, you may well find me. Around Fleet
Street, I wouldn't wonder.

ANTHONY: Well, until then, Mr. Todd.

(ANTHONY *starts off down the street.* TODD *stands a moment alone in thought, then starts down the street in the
opposite direction*)

TODD (*Sings*):
There's a hole in the world
Like a great black pit
And it's filled with people
Who are filled with shit
And the vermin of the world
Inhabit it . . .

(*As* TODD *disappears, we see* MRS. LOVETT*'s pieshop. Above
it is any empty apartment which is reached by an outside
staircase.* MRS. LOVETT, *a vigorous, slatternly woman in*

387

her forties, is flicking flies off the trays of pies with a dirty rag as she sings or hums. TODD *appears at the end of the street and moves slowly toward the pieshop, looking around as if remembering. Seeing the pieshop he pauses a moment at some distance, gazing at it and at* MRS. LOVETT, *who has now picked up a wicked-looking knife and starts chopping suet. After a beat,* TODD *moves toward the shop, hesitates and then enters.* MRS. LOVETT *does not notice him until his shadow passes across her. She looks up, knife in air, and screams, freezing him in his tracks)*

MRS. LOVETT: A customer!
> (TODD *has started out in alarm.* MRS. LOVETT *sings)*
Wait! What's yer rush? What's yer hurry?
> (*She sticks the knife into the counter)*
You gave me such a —
> (*She wipes her hands on her apron)*
Fright. I thought you was a ghost.
Half a minute, can'tcher?
Sit! Sit ye down!
> (*Forcing him into a chair)*
Sit!
All I meant is that I
Haven't seen a customer for weeks.
Did you come here for a pie, sir?
> (TODD *nods. She flicks a bit of dust off a pie with her rag)*
Do forgive me if me head's a little vague —
Ugh!
> (*She plucks something off a pie, holds it up)*
What is *that?*
But you'd think we had the plague —
> (*She drops it on the floor and stamps on it)*
From the way that people —
> (*She flicks something off a pie with her finger)*
Keep avoiding —
> (*Spotting it moving)*

No you don't!
(She smacks it with her hand)
Heaven knows I try, sir!
(Lifts her hand, looks at it)
Ick!
(She wipes it on the edge of the counter)
But there's no one comes in even to inhale —
Tsk!
(She blows the last dust off the pie as she brings it to him)
Right you are, sir. Would you like a drop of ale?
(TODD nods)
Mind you, I can't hardly blame them —
(Pouring a tankard of ale)
These are probably the worst pies in London.
I know why nobody cares to take them —
I *should* know,
I make them.
But good? No,
The worst pies in London —
Even that's polite.
The worst pies in London —
If you doubt it, take a bite.
(He does)
Is that just disgusting?
You have to concede it.
It's nothing but crusting —
Here, drink this, you'll need it —
(She puts the ale in front of him)
The worst pies in London —
(During the following, she slams lumps of dough on the counter and rolls them out, grunting frequently as she goes)
And no wonder with the price of meat
What it is
(Grunt)

When you get it.
>   (*Grunt*)

Never
>   (*Grunt*)

Thought I'd live to see the day men'd think it was a treat
Finding poor
>   (*Grunt*)

Animals
>   (*Grunt*)

Wot are dying in the street.
Mrs. Mooney has a pie shop,
Does a business, but I notice something weird —
Lately all her neighbors' cats have disappeared.
>   (*Shrugs*)

Have to hand it to her —
Wot I calls
Enterprise,
Popping pussies into pies.
Wouldn't do in my shop —
Just the thought of it's enough to make you sick.
And I'm telling you them pussy cats is quick.
No denying times is hard, sir —
Even harder than
The worst pies in London.
Only lard and nothing more —
>   (As TODD *gamely tries another mouthful*)

Is that just revolting?
All greasy and gritty,
It looks like it's molting,
And tastes like —
Well, pity
A woman alone
With limited wind
And the worst pies in London!
>   (*Sighs heavily*)

Ah sir,
Times is hard. Times is hard.
> (*She finishes one of the crusts with a flourish, then notices* TODD *having difficulty with his pie, speaks*)

Spit it out, dear. Go on. On the floor. There's worse things than that down there.
> (*As he does*)

That's my boy.

TODD: Isn't that a room up there over the shop? If times are so hard, why don't you rent it out? That should bring in something.

MRS. LOVETT: Up there? Oh, no one will go near it. People think it's haunted. You see — years ago, something happened up there. Something not very nice.
> (*Sings*)

There was a barber and his wife,
And he was beautiful,
A proper artist with a knife,
But they transported him for life.
> (*Sighs*)

And he was beautiful . . .
> (*Speaks, music continuing under*)

Barker, his name was — Benjamin Barker.

TODD: Transported? What was his crime?

MRS. LOVETT: Foolishness.
> (*Sings*)

He had this wife, you see,
Pretty little thing.
Silly little nit
Had her chance for the moon on a string —
Poor thing. Poor thing.
> (*As she sings, her narration is acted out. First we see the pretty young* WIFE *in the empty upstairs room dancing her household chores. During the following the* JUDGE *and his obse-*

quious assistant, the BEADLE, *approach the house, gazing up
at the* WIFE *lecherously. The* WIFE *remains demure, sewing*)

There were these two, you see,
Wanted her like mad,
One of 'em a Judge,
T'other one his Beadle.
Every day they'd nudge
And they'd wheedle.
But she wouldn't budge
From her needle.
Too bad. Pure thing.

(*Far upstage, in very dim light, shapes appear. A swirl of
cloth, glints of jewels, the faces of people masked as animals
and demons. During the following lyric, the* WIFE *takes an
imaginary baby from an imaginary cot and sits on the
floor, cradling it in her arms as she sobs*)

So they merely shipped the poor bugger off south,
    they did,
Leaving her with nothing but grief and a year-old kid.
Did she use her head even then? Oh no, God forbid!
Poor fool.
Ah, but there was worse yet to come —
(*Intake of breath*)
Poor thing.

(*Again the shapes appear, this time a bit more distinctly.*
MRS. LOVETT *speaks, musingly*)

Johanna, that was the baby's name . . . Pretty little Johanna . . .
(*Drifts off in reminiscence*)

TODD (*Tensely*): Go on.

MRS. LOVETT (*Eyeing* TODD *sharply*): My, you do like a good
story, don't you?
(*The* BEADLE *reappears, gazing up at the* WIFE, *miming in
a solicitous manner for her to come down.* MRS. LOVETT,
warming to the tale, sings)

Well, Beadle calls on her, all polite,
Poor thing, poor thing.
The Judge, he tells her, is all contrite,
He blames himself for her dreadful plight,
She must come straight to his house tonight!
Poor thing, poor thing.
                    (*Excited, almost gleeful*)
Of course, when she goes there,
Poor thing, poor thing.
They're havin' this ball all in masks.
    (*The shapes are now clear. A ball is in progress at the*
    JUDGE's *house: the company, wearing grotesque masks, is*
    dancing a slow minuet. The BEADLE, *leading the* WIFE,
    appears, moving with her through the dancers. He gives
    her champagne. She looks dazedly around, terrified)
There's no one she knows there,
Poor dear, poor thing.
She wanders tormented, and drinks,
Poor thing.
The Judge has repented, she thinks,
Poor thing.
"Oh, where is Judge Turpin?" she asks.
    (*During the following, the* JUDGE *appears, tears off his*
    mask, then his cloak, revealing himself naked. The WIFE
    screams as he reaches for her, struggling wildly as the BEA-
    DLE *hurls her to the floor. He holds her there as the* JUDGE
    mounts her and the masked dancers pirouette around the
    ravishment, giggling)
He was there, all right —
Only not so contrite!
She wasn't no match for such craft, you see,
And everyone thought it so droll.
They figured she had to be daft, you see,
So all of 'em stood there and laughed, you see.
Poor soul!
Poor thing!

TODD (*A wild shout*): Would no one have mercy on her? (*The dumb show vanishes. Music stops.* TODD *and* MRS. LOVETT *gaze at each other*)

MRS. LOVETT (*Coolly*): So it is you — Benjamin Barker.

TODD (*Frighteningly vehement*): Not Barker! Not Barker! Todd now! Sweeney Todd! Where is she?

MRS. LOVETT: So changed! Good God, what did they do to you down there in bloody Australia or wherever?

TODD: Where is my wife? Where's Lucy?

MRS. LOVETT: She poisoned herself. Arsenic from the apothecary on the corner. I tried to stop her but she wouldn't listen to me.

TODD: And my daughter?

MRS. LOVETT: Johanna? He's got her.

TODD: He? Judge Turpin?

MRS. LOVETT: Even he had a conscience tucked away, I suppose. Adopted her like his own. You could say it was good luck for her . . . almost.

TODD: Fifteen years sweating in a living hell on a trumped up charge. Fifteen years dreaming that, perhaps, I might come home to a loving wife and child.
(*Strikes ferociously on the pie counter with his fists*)
Let them quake in their boots — Judge Turpin and the Beadle — for their hour has come.

MRS. LOVETT (*Awed*): You're going to — get 'em? You? A bleeding little nobody of a runaway convict? Don't make me laugh. You'll never get His 'igh and Mightiness! Nor the Beadle neither. Not in a million years.
(*No reaction from* TODD)
You got any money?

(Still no reaction)
Listen to me! You got any money?

TODD: No money.

MRS. LOVETT: Then how you going to live even?

TODD: I'll live. If I have to sweat in the sewers or in the plague hospital, I'll live — and I'll have them.

MRS. LOVETT: Oh, you poor thing! You poor thing!
(A sudden thought)
Wait!
(She disappears behind a curtained entrance leading to her parlor. For a beat TODD *stands alone, almost exalted.* MRS. LOVETT *returns with a razor case. She holds it out to him)*
See! It don't have to be the sewers or the plague hospital. When they come for the little girl, I hid 'em. I thought, who knows? Maybe the poor silly blighter'll be back again someday and need 'em. Cracked in the head, wasn't I? Times as bad as they are, I could have got five, maybe ten quid for 'em, any day. See? You can be a barber again.
(Music begins. She opens the case for him to look inside.
TODD *stands a long moment gazing down at the case)*
My, them handles is chased silver, ain't they?

TODD: Silver, yes.
(Quietly, looking into the box, sings)
These are my friends.
See how they glisten.
(Picks up a small razor)
See this one shine,
How he smiles in the light.
My friend, my faithful friend.
(Holding it to his ear, feeling the edge with his thumb)
Speak to me, friend.
Whisper, I'll listen.
(Listening)

I know, I know —
You've been locked out of sight
All these years —
Like me, my friend.
Well, I've come home
To find you waiting.
Home,
And we're together,
And we'll do wonders,
Won't we?

(MRS. LOVETT, *who has been looking over his shoulder,*
starts to feel his other ear lightly, absently, in her own
trance. TODD *lays the razor back in the box and picks out a*
larger one. They sing simultaneously)

TODD:

You there, my friend.
Come, let me hold you.

Now, with a sigh
You grow warm
In my hand,
My friend,
My clever friend.
(*Putting it back*)
Rest now, my friends.
Soon I'll unfold you.
Soon you'll know splendors

You never have dreamed

All your days,
My lucky friends.
Till now your shine
Was merely silver.
Friends,

MRS. LOVETT:

I'm your friend too, Mr. Todd.
If you only knew, Mr. Todd —
Ooh, Mr. Todd,
You're warm
In my hand.
You've come home.
Always had a fondness for you,
I did.

Never you fear, Mr. Todd,
You can move in here,
    Mr. Todd.
Splendors you never have
    dreamed
All your days
Will be yours.
I'm your friend.
Don't they shine beautiful?
Silver's good enough for me,

396

You shall drip rubies,   Mr. T. . . .
You'll soon drip precious
Rubies . . .

> (TODD *holds up the biggest razor to the light as the music
> soars sweetly, then stops. He speaks into the silence*)

TODD: My right arm is complete again!

> (*Lights dim except for a scalding spot on the razor as
> music blares forth from both the organ and the orchestra.
> The company, including the* JUDGE *and the* BEADLE, *ap-
> pears and sings*)

COMPANY:
Lift your razor high, Sweeney!
Hear it singing, "Yes!"
Sink it in the rosy skin
Of righteousness!
>   (*Variously*)
His voice was soft, his manner mild.
He seldom laughed but he often smiled.
He'd seen how civilized men behave.
He never forgot and he never forgave,
Not Sweeney,
Not Sweeney Todd,
The Demon Barber of Fleet Street . . .

> (*They disappear. There is a moment of darkness in which
> we hear the trilling and twittering of songbirds. Light comes
> up on the facade of* JUDGE TURPIN*'s mansion. A* BIRD SELL-
> ER *enters carrying a bizarre construction of little wicker
> birdcages tied together. It is in these that the birds are
> singing. At an upper level of the* JUDGE*'s mansion appears
> a very young, exquisitely beautiful girl with a long mane of
> shining blonde hair. This is* JOHANNA. *For a moment she
> stands disconsolate, then her eyes fall on the birds*)

JOHANNA: And how are they today?

BIRD SELLER: Hungry as always, Miss Johanna.
(*He lifts the cages up to her*)

JOHANNA (*Sings*):
Green finch and linnet bird,
Nightingale, blackbird,
How is it you sing?
How can you jubilate,
Sitting in cages,
Never taking wing?
Outside the sky waits,
Beckoning, beckoning,
Just beyond the bars.
How can you remain,
Staring at the rain,
Maddened by the stars?
How is it you sing
Anything?
How is it you sing?

Green finch and linnet bird,
Nightingale, blackbird,
How is it you sing?
Whence comes this melody constantly flowing?
Is it rejoicing or merely halloing?
Are you discussing or fussing
Or simply dreaming?
Are you crowing?
Are you screaming?

Ringdove and robinet,
Is it for wages,
Singing to be sold?
Have you decided it's
Safer in cages,
Singing when you're told?

(ANTHONY *enters. Instantly he sees her and stands trans-fixed by her beauty*)
My cage has many rooms,
Damask and dark.
Nothing there sings,
Not even my lark.
Larks never will, you know,
When they're captive.
Teach me to be more adaptive.

Green finch and linnet bird,
Nightingale, blackbird,
Teach me how to sing.
If I cannot fly,
Let me sing.
(*She gazes into the middle distance disconsolately*)

ANTHONY (*Gazing at her, sings softly*):
I have sailed the world,
Beheld its wonders,
From the pearls of Spain
To the rubies of Tibet,
But not even in London
Have I seen such a wonder . . .
(*Breathlessly*)
Lady look at me look at me miss oh
Look at me please oh
Favor me favor me with your glance.
Ah, miss,
What do you what do you see off
There in those trees oh
Won't you give won't you give me a chance?

Who would sail to Spain
For all its wonders,
When in Kearney's Lane

399

Lies the greatest wonder yet?

Ah, miss,
Look at you look at you pale and
Ivory-skinned oh
Look at you looking so sad so queer.
Promise
Not to retreat to the darkness
Back of your window
Not till you not till you look down here.
Look at

ANTHONY:	JOHANNA:
Me!	Green finch and linnet bird,
Look at	Nightingale, blackbird,
Me!	Teach me how to sing.
	If I cannot fly,
Look at me . . .	Let me sing . . .

(*As* JOHANNA *turns back to go inside, their eyes meet and the song dies on their lips. A hushed moment. Then suddenly a clawlike hand darts out from a pile of trash.* ANTHONY *jumps and looks down to see the* BEGGAR WOMAN, *who has been sleeping in the garbage under a discarded shawl, thrusting her bowl at him.* JOHANNA, *frightened, slips back out of sight*)

BEGGAR WOMAN (*Sings*):
  Alms! . . . Alms! . . .
  For a miserable woman . . .
    (ANTHONY *hurriedly digs out a coin and drops it in her bowl; she peers at him*)
  Beg your pardon, it's you, sir . . .
  Thank yer . . . Thank yer kindly . . .
    (ANTHONY *turns back to discover* JOHANNA *gone and the window shut. The* BEGGAR WOMAN *starts off*)

ANTHONY: One moment, mother.
    (*She turns*)

Perhaps you know whose house this is?

BEGGAR WOMAN: That! That's the great Judge Turpin's house, that is.

ANTHONY: And the young lady who resides there?

BEGGAR WOMAN: Ah, her! That's Johanna, his pretty little ward.
> (*Slyly confidential*)

But don't you go trespassing there, young man. Not if you value your hide.
> (*She nods her head*)

Tamper there and it's a good whipping for you — or any other youth with mischief on his mind.
> (*Leers at him, sings*)

Hey! Hoy! Sailor boy!
Want it snugly harbored?
Open me gate, but dock it straight,
I see it lists to starboard.
> (*She grabs at his crotch and starts to dance around him grotesquely, lifting her skirts.* ANTHONY *is appalled. He pulls coins out of his pocket and tosses them to her*)

ANTHONY: Here and here and here. Take it and off with you. Off!
> (*The* BEGGAR WOMAN, *cackling, collects the coins and scampers off.* ANTHONY *turns back to the house, gazes up at the window. The noise has frightened the birds, who start screeching.* ANTHONY *becomes aware of them and moves over to the now sleeping* BIRD SELLER, *shakes him awake, and inspects the cages. Music continues under*)

Which one sings the sweetest?

BIRD SELLER: All's the same, sir. Six pence and cheap at the price.
> (ANTHONY *selects one, gives the man a coin, holds up the cage*)

ANTHONY: He sings bravely.

(*Watches the cage*)

But why does he batter his wings so wildly against the bars?

BIRD SELLER: We blind 'em, sir. That's what we always does. Blind 'em and, not knowing night from day, they sing and sing without stopping, pretty creatures.

(*He gets up, slinging the cages on his back, and starts off*)

Have pleasure of the bird, sir.

(*He exits.* JOHANNA *reappears at the window.* ANTHONY *holds up the cage, indicating it is a present and she should come down to get it. She hesitates, smiles, nods, disappears from the window. He waits. Shyly, almost furtively,* JOHANNA *slips out of the door and stands there. He moves toward her, holding out the cage. Slowly her hand goes out toward him. Their fingers touch*)

ANTHONY (*Sings softly*):

I feel you,
Johanna,
I feel you.
I was half convinced I'd waken,
Satisfied enough to dream you.
Happily I was mistaken,
Johanna!
I'll steal you,
Johanna,
I'll steal you . . .

(*They stand so absorbed with each other that they do not notice the approach of* JUDGE TURPIN, *followed by the* BEADLE)

JUDGE (*Shouting*): Johanna! Johanna!

JOHANNA: Oh dear!

(*Forgetting the bird cage,* JOHANNA *scurries toward the house.* ANTHONY *turns to find the* JUDGE *glaring at him*)

JUDGE: If I see your face again on this or any other neighbor street, you'll rue the day you were born. Is that plain enough speaking for you?

ANTHONY: But, sir, I swear to you there was nothing in my heart but the most respectful sentiments of —

JUDGE (*To* BEADLE): Dispose of him!
(*He strides toward the house*)

JOHANNA: Oh dear! I knew!

BEADLE (*Fondling the truncheon, to* ANTHONY): You heard His Worship.

ANTHONY: But, friend, I have no fight with you.
(*The* BEADLE *takes the cage from him, opens its door, takes out the bird, wrings its neck and then tosses it away*)

BEADLE: Get the gist of it, friend? Next time it'll be *your* neck!
(*He starts after the* JUDGE *and* JOHANNA)

JUDGE: Johanna, if I were to think you encouraged that young rogue . . .

JOHANNA: Oh father, I hope always to be obedient to your commands.

JUDGE (*Relenting, patting her cheek*): Dear child.
(*Gazing at her lustfully*)
How sweet you look in that light muslin gown.
(*She runs into the house, the* JUDGE *after her. The* BEADLE *follows.* ANTHONY *is left alone, the empty cage in his hand*)

ANTHONY (*Sings*):
I'll steal you,
Johanna,
I'll steal you!
Do they think that walls can hide you?

Even now I'm at your window.
I am in the dark beside you,
Buried sweetly in your yellow hair.

I feel you,
Johanna,
And one day
I'll steal you.
Till I'm with you then,
I'm with you there,
Sweetly buried in your yellow hair . . .

> (*He smashes the cage, throws it away and exits as lights fade*)

> (*Lights come up to reveal St. Dunstan's Marketplace. A hand-drawn caravan, painted like a Sicilian donkey cart, stands on the street. On its side is written in ornate script: "Signor Adolfo Pirelli — Haircutter-Barber-Toothpuller to His Royal Majesty the King of Naples," and under this: "Banish Baldness with Pirelli's Miracle Elixir."* TODD *and* MRS. LOVETT *enter.* TODD *is carrying his razor case.* MRS. LOVETT *has a shopping basket*)

TODD (*Pointing at the caravan*): That's him? Over there?

MRS. LOVETT: Yes, dear. He's always here Thursdays.

TODD (*Reading the sign*): Haircutter, barber, toothpuller to His Royal Majesty the King of Naples.

MRS. LOVETT: Eyetalian. All the rage, he is.

TODD: Not for long.

MRS. LOVETT: Oh Mr. T., you really think you can do it?

TODD: By tomorrow they'll all be flocking after me like sheep to be shorn.

MRS. LOVETT (*Sees* BEADLE): Oh no! Look. The Beadle — Beadle Bamford.

TODD: So much the better.

MRS. LOVETT: But what if he recognizes you? Hadn't we better — ?

TODD: I will do what I have set out to do, woman.

MRS. LOVETT: Oops. Sorry, dear, I'm sure.
(TOBIAS, PIRELLI*'s adolescent, simple-minded assistant,
appears through a curtain at the rear of the caravan, beating on a tin drum. A factory whistle blows and a crowd of
people comes running on, gathering around him)*

TOBIAS (*Sings*):
Ladies and gentlemen!
May I have your attention, perlease?
Do you wake every morning in shame and despair
To discover your pillow is covered with hair
Wot ought not to be there?

Well, ladies and gentlemen,
From now on you can waken at ease.
You need never again have a worry or care,
I will show you a miracle marvelous rare.
Gentlemen, you are about to see something wot rose
    from the dead!
    (*A woman gasps — he smiles and wiggles his finger no*)
On the top of my head.

Scarcely a month ago, gentlemen,
I was struck with a 'orrible
Dermatologic disease.
Though the finest physicians in London were called,
I awakened one morning amazed and appalled
To discover with dread that my head was as bald
As a novice's knees.
I was dying of shame
Till a gentleman came,

405

An illustrious barber, Pirelli by name.
He give me a liquid as precious as gold,
I rubbed it in daily like wot I was told,
And behold!
>   (*Doffs his cap dramatically, revealing mountains of hair
>   which cascade to his shoulders*)

Only thirty days old!

'Twas Pirelli's
Miracle Elixir,
That's wot did the trick, sir,
True, sir, true.
Was it quick, sir?
Did it in a tick, sir,
Just like an elixir
Ought to do!
>   (*To* 1ST MAN)

How about a bottle, mister?
Only costs a penny, guaranteed.
>   (*Crowd, overlapping*)

1ST MAN:
>   Penny buys a bottle, I don't know . . .

2ND MAN:
>   You don't need —

1ST MAN:
>   Ah, let's go!
>
>   (*Starts to leave*)

TOBIAS (*To* 3RD MAN):
>   Go ahead and tug, sir.

3RD MAN:
>   Penny for a bottle, is it?

TOBIAS:
>   Go ahead, sir, harder . . .

TOBIAS (*Stopping the* 1ST MAN, *who's quite bald, by pouring a drop on his head*):
Does Pirelli's
Stimulate the growth, sir?
You can have my oath, sir,
'Tis unique.
> (*Takes the man's hand and gently applies it to the wet spot*)
Rub a minute.
Stimulatin', i'n' it?
Soon you'll have to thin it
Once a week!
Penny buys a bottle, guaranteed!
> (*Crowd, overlapping*)

1ST MAN (*To* 2ND MAN):
Penny buys a bottle, might as well . . .
> (*Looks hesitantly to* 2ND MAN)

3RD MAN:
Wotcher think?

2ND WOMAN:
Go ahead and try it, wot the hell . . .

TOBIAS (*To others*):
How about a sample? Have you ever smelled a cleaner smell?

1ST WOMAN (*To* 3RD MAN):
Isn't it a crime they let these urchins clog the pavement?

4TH MAN:
Penny buys a bottle, does it?

TOBIAS (*To* 2ND MAN):
That's enough, sir, ample.

TOBIAS:
Gently dab it.

Gets to be a habit.
Soon there'll be enough, sir,
Somebody can grab it.
>> (*Points to a man standing nearby*)
See that chap with
Hair like Shelley's?
You can tell 'e's
Used Pirelli's!
>> (*Crowd, overlapping*)

1ST MAN:
Let me have a bottle.

2ND MAN:
Make that two.
>> (1ST MAN *buys bottles for both, gets change*)

3RD WOMAN:
Come to think of it, I could get some for Harry . . .

4TH WOMAN:
Nothing works on Harry, dear. Bye bye.

TOBIAS:
Go ahead and feel, mum.
Absolutely real, mum . . .

2ND MAN (*To* 1ST MAN):
How about a beer?

1ST MAN:
You know a pub?

2ND MAN:
There's one close by.

1ST WOMAN (*To* 2ND WOMAN):
You got all the hair you need now.

3RD MAN:
That's no lie.

4TH MAN:
  Pass it by.

2ND WOMAN:
  I'm just passing by.

TODD (*Loudly to* MRS. LOVETT):
  Pardon me, ma'am, what's that awful stench?

MRS. LOVETT:
  Are we standing in an open trench?

TODD:
  Must be standing near an open trench!

TOBIAS (*Distracting the crowd's attention*):
  Buy Pirelli's Miracle Elixir:
  Anything wot's slick, sir,
  Soon sprouts curls.
  Try Pirelli's!
  When they see how thick, sir,
  You can have your pick, sir,
  Of the girls!
                    (*To* 4TH WOMAN)
  Want to buy a bottle, missus?
                    (*Crowd, overlapping*)

TODD (*Sniffing* 1ST MAN*'s bottle*):
  What is this?

MRS. LOVETT (*Examining* 3RD MAN*'s bottle*):
  What is this?

1ST MAN:
  Propogates the hair, sir.

4TH MAN:
  I'll take one!

TODD (*Hands bottle back distastefully*):
  Smells like piss.

MRS. LOVETT:
  Smells like — phew!

2ND MAN:
  He says it smells like piss.

TODD:
  Looks like piss.

MRS. LOVETT:
  Wouldn't touch it if I was you, dear!

2ND MAN (*To* 3RD MAN):
  Wotcher think?

TODD (*Nods*):
  This is piss. Piss with ink.

5TH MAN *and* WOMEN:
  Says it smells like piss or something.

TOBIAS:
  Penny for a bottle . . .
  Have you ever smelled a cleaner smell?
  How about a sample? . . .
  How about a sample, mister? . . .

1ST WOMAN:
  Give us back our money!

2ND WOMAN:
  Give us back our money!

1ST WOMAN:
  Did you ever — ?
  Give us back our money!

3RD WOMAN:
  Glad I didn't buy one, I can tell you!

4TH WOMAN (*To* TOBIAS):
  If you think that piss can fool a lady, you're mistaken!

MRS. LOVETT:
Give 'em back their money!
Did you ever — ?
Give 'em back their money!

3RD WOMAN:
Give 'em back their money, I say!
Give 'em back their money!

TOBIAS (*Trying to calm them, gesturing to* TODD):
Never mind that madman, mister . . .
Never mind the madman . . .

TODD *and* MRS. LOVETT:
Where is this Pirelli?

CROWD:
Where is this Pirelli?
                    (*Variously, overlapping*)
What about my money, laddie?
Yes, what about the money?
Hand it back!
We don't want no piss, boy!
Give it here . . .

TOBIAS (*Desperately, beating the drum out of rhythm*):
Let Pirelli's
Activate your roots, sir —

TODD:
Keep it off your boots, sir —
Eats right through.

CROWD:
Go and get Pirelli!

TOBIAS:
Yes, get Pirelli's!
Use a bottle of it!
Ladies seem to love it —

411

MRS. LOVETT:
> Flies do, too!

>> (*Crowd laughs uproariously*)

CROWD:
> Hand the bloody money over!
> Hand the bloody money over!

TOBIAS (*Frenetically fast, looking desperately toward the curtain*):
> See Pirelli's
> Miracle Elixir
> Grow a little wick, sir,
> Then some fuzz.
> *The* Pirelli's
> Soon'll make it thick, sir,
> Like a good elixir
> Always does!
>
> Trust Pirelli's!
> If your hair is sick, sir,
> Fix it in the nick, sir,
> Don't look grim.
> Just Pirelli's
> Miracle Elixir,
> That'll do the trick, sir —

1ST MAN:
> What about the money?

TOBIAS:
> If you've got a kick, sir —

CROWD (*Individuals, building to a shout*):
> What about the money?
> Where is this Pirelli?
> Go and get Pirelli!
> What about our money?

TOBIAS:
> Tell it to the mixer

Of the Miracle Elixir —
If you've got a kick, sir — !
> (*Desperately yanks the curtain aside, revealing* PIRELLI, *an excessively flamboyant Italian with a glittering suit, thick wavy hair and a dazzling smile — the crowd falls silent, stunned.* TOBIAS *collapses, exhausted*)

Talk to him!

PIRELLI (*Bows and poses splendidly for a moment, in one hand an ornate razor, in the other a sinister-looking tooth-extractor; sings*):
I am Adolfo Pirelli,
Da king of da barbers, da barber of kings,
E buon giorno, good day,
I blow you a kiss!
> (*He does*)

And I, da so-famous Pirelli,
I wish-a to know-a
Who has-a da nerve-a to say
My elixir is piss!
Who says this?

TODD: I do.
> (*He holds up the bottle of elixir*)

I am Mr. Sweeney Todd and I have opened a bottle of Pirelli's Elixir, and I say to you it is nothing but an arrant fraud, concocted from piss and ink.
> (MRS. LOVETT *takes the bottle from* TODD, *sniffs it*)

MRS. LOVETT: He's right. Phew! Better to throw your money down the sewer.
> (*She tosses the bottle to the ground. The onlookers "ooh" and "aah" with shocked excitement*)

TOBIAS (*Beating agitatedly on the drum, shouting*): Ladies and gentlemen, pay no attention to that madman. Who's to be the first for a magnificent shave?

TODD (*Breaking in*): And furthermore . . .

(*Glaring at* PIRELLI)

I have serviced no kings, yet I wager that I can shave a cheek and pull a tooth with ten times more dexterity than any street mountebank!

(*He holds up his razor case for the crowd to see*)

You see these razors?

MRS. LOVETT: The finest in England.

TODD (*To* PIRELLI): I lay them against five pounds you are no match for me. You hear me, sir? Either accept my challenge or reveal yourself as a sham.

MRS. LOVETT: Bravo, bravo.

(*The crowd laughs and cheers, obviously on* TODD*'s side.* PIRELLI, *as imposing as ever, holds up a hand for silence. Slowly he swaggers toward* TODD, *takes the razor case, opens it and examines the razors carefully*)

PIRELLI (*He speaks with a fairly obvious put-on foreign accent, barely concealing an Irish underlay*): Zees are indeed fine razors. Instruments like zees once seen cannot be soon forgotten.

(*Takes out a tooth-extractor*)

And a fine extractor, too! You wager zees against five pounds, sir?

TODD: I do.

PIRELLI (*Addressing the crowd*): You hear zis foolish man? Watch and see how he will regret his folly. Five pounds it is!

(*Music starts*)

TODD (*Surveying the crowd*): Friends, neighbors, who's for a free shave?

1ST MAN (*Stepping forward eagerly*): Me, Mr. Todd, sir.

2ND MAN (*Stepping forward eagerly, too*): And me, Mr. Todd, sir.

TODD: Over here. Bring me a chair.

PIRELLI (*To* TOBIAS): Boy, bring ze basins, bring ze towels!

TOBIAS: Yes, sir . . .

PIRELLI: Quick!
> (*He kicks* TOBIAS. *The boy hurries off into the caravan*)

TODD: Will Beadle Bamford be the judge?

BEADLE: Glad, as always, to oblige my friends and neighbors.
> (*As another man comes on with a wooden chair and* TOBIAS *emerges from the caravan with basins, towels, etc., the* BEADLE *instantly takes over. To man, indicating where to set the chair*)

Put it there.
> (1ST MAN *sits on* TODD's *chair. The* 2ND MAN *is ensconced on* PIRELLI's *chair.* PIRELLI *shakes out a fancy bib with a flourish and covers his man.* TODD *takes a towel and tucks it around his man's neck*)

Ready?

PIRELLI: Ready!

TODD: Ready!

BEADLE: The fastest, smoothest shave is the winner.
> (*He blows his whistle. The music becomes agitated. The contest begins.* PIRELLI *strops his razor quickly,* TODD *in a leisurely manner.* PIRELLI *keeps glancing at* TODD *in various paranoid ways throughout, frightened of* TODD's *progress. He starts whipping up lather rapidly*)

PIRELLI (*Sings to crowd while mixing, furiously*):
Now, signorini, signori,
We mix-a da lather
But first-a you gather
Around, signor-
Ini, signori,
You looking a man
Who have had-a da glory

To shave-a da Pope!
Mr. Sweeney-so-smart —
(*Sarcastic bow to* TODD)
Oh, I beg-a you pardon — 'll
Call me a lie, was-a only a cardinal —
Nope!
It was-a da Pope!
(*Looks over shoulder, sees* TODD *still stropping slowly,
gains confidence, starts to lather his man's face*)
Perhaps, signorini, signori,
You like-a I tell-a
Da famous-a story
Of Queen Isabella,
Da Queen of-a Polan'
Whose toot' was-a swollen,
I pull it so nice from her mout'
That-a though to begin
She's-a screaming-a murder,
She's later-a swoon-a wid
Bliss an' was heard-a
To shout:
"Pull all of 'em out!"
(*Unexpectedly,* TODD *still shows no sign of starting to
shave his man. He merely watches* PIRELLI*'s performance.*
PIRELLI, *now feeling that he can take his time, sings lyri-
cally as he shaves with rhythmic scrapes and elaborate ges-
tures of wiping the razor*)
To shave-a da face,
To pull-a da toot',
Require da grace
And not-a da brute,
For if-a you slip,
You nick da skin,
You clip-a da chin,
You rip-a da lip a bit
And dat's-a da trut'!

(TODD *strops his razor slowly and deliberately, disconcert-*
ing PIRELLI *and drawing the crowd's attention*)
To shave-a da face
Or even a part
Widout it-a smart
Require da heart.
It take-a da art —
I show you a chart —
    (*Pulls down an elaborate chart with many anatomical*
    views of the face and closeups of follicles, etc.)
I study-a starting in my yout'!
            (TODD *starts slowly mixing his lather*)
To cut-a da hair,
To trim-a da beard,
To make-a da bristle
Clean like a whistle,
Dis is from early infancy
Da talent give to me
By God!
It take-a da skill,
It take-a da brains,
It take-a da will
To take-a da pains,
It take-a da pace,
It take-a da grace —
    (*While* PIRELLI *holds this note elaborately,* TODD, *with a*
    few deft strokes, quickly lathers his man's face, shaves him
    and signals the BEADLE *to examine the job*)

BEADLE (*Blowing whistle*):
The winner is Todd.

MRS. LOVETT (*Feeling the customer's cheek*): Smooth as a baby's
arse!
    (*The crowd "oohs" and "ahhs"*)

TODD (*Looks around*): And now, who's for a tooth pulling —
free without charge!

417

MAN WITH HEAD TIED UP IN RAG: Me, sir. Me, sir.
> (*He runs to the chair vacated by the shaved man*)

TODD (*Looking around*): Who else?
> (*There is silence from the crowd*)

No one?
> (*Turning to the* BEADLE)

Then, sir, since there is no means to test the second skill, I claim the five pounds!

MRS. LOVETT: To which he is entitled!
> (*To crowd*)

Right?
> (*The crowd applauds*)

PIRELLI: Wait! One moment. Wait!
> (*He turns to* TOBIAS)

You, boy. Get on that chair.

TOBIAS (*In terror*): Me, signor? Oh, not a tooth, sir, I beg of you! I ain't got a twinge — not the tiniest pain. I —

PIRELLI (*Giving him a stinging blow on the cheek*): You do now!
> (*Forces him into the chair. Turning to the crowd*)

We see who is zee victor now. Zis Mister Todd — or zee great Pirelli!

BEADLE: Ready?

PIRELLI: Ready!

TODD: Ready!
> (*The* BEADLE *blows his whistle. While* TODD, *even more nonchalant than before, merely stands by his patient,* PIRELLI *forces open the mouth of* TOBIAS, *brandishing his extractor. He peers in, selects a tooth, thrusts the extractor into the mouth and starts to tug while singing with pretended ease. During the song,* TOBIAS *starts moaning, then screaming — musically*)

418

PIRELLI (*Sings*):
　　To pull-a da toot'
　　Widout-a da skill
　　Can damage da root —
　　　　　　　　(*As* TOBIAS *squirms*)
　　Now hold-a da still!
　　An' if-a you slip
　　You grip a bit,
　　You hit da pit of it
　　Or chip-a da tip
　　And have-a to fill!

　　To pull-a da toot'
　　Widout-a da grace,
　　You leave-a da space
　　All over da place.
　　You try to erase
　　Widout-a da trace . . .
　　　　　　　　(*Glaring archly at* TODD)
　　Sometimes is da case
　　You even-a kill.
　　　(TODD *still watches;* PIRELLI *is having trouble,* TOBIAS'*s
　　　wails are becoming louder*)
　　To hold-a da clamp
　　Widout-a da cramp,
　　Wid all dat saliva,
　　It could-a drive-a
　　You crazy — !
　　　　　　　　(*To* TOBIAS, *who is groaning*)
　　Don' mutter,
　　Or back-a you go to da gutter —
　　　　　　　　(*To the crowd, forcing a smile*)
　　My touch is as light as a butter-a
　　Cup!

　　I take-a da pains,

419

I learn-a da art,
I use-a da brains,
I give-a da heart,
I have-a da grace,
I win-a da race — !

> (*While again* PIRELLI *holds the note,* TODD *stands watching. Then in one swift move, he tugs the rag off his patient's head, neatly opens the mouth, looks in, and with a single deft motion of the extractor, gives a tiny tug and, turning to the crowd, holds up the extracted tooth. The* BEADLE *blows his whistle. The crowd roars its approval.* PIRELLI, *cut off again in the middle of his high note, sees that* TODD *has extracted his customer's tooth, and droops*)

I give-a da up.

MAN (*Jumping up from chair*): Not a twinge of pain! Not a twinge!

MRS. LOVETT: The man's a bloody marvel!

BEADLE (*Beaming at* TODD): The two-time winner — Mr. Sweeney Todd!

> (PIRELLI *leaves the tooth unpulled in* TOBIAS's *mouth and, still retaining his imposing dignity, moves over to* TODD)

PIRELLI (*With profound bow*): Sir, I bow to a skill far defter than my own.

TODD: The five pounds.

PIRELLI (*Produces a rather flamboyant purse, and from it takes five pounds*): Here, sir. And may the good Lord smile on you —
> (*With a sinister smile*)

— until we meet again. Come, boy.
> (*Bows to crowd*)

Signori! Bellissime signorini! Buon giorno! Buon giorno a tutti!

> (*Kicking* TOBIAS *ahead of him, he returns to the caravan which* TOBIAS, *like a horse, pulls off*)

MRS. LOVETT (*To* TODD): Who'd have thought it, dear! You pulled it off!
> (*The crowd clusters around* TODD)

MAN WITH CAP: Oh, sir, Mr. Todd, sir, do you have an establishment of your own?

MRS. LOVETT: He certainly does. Sweeney Todd's Tonsorial Parlor — above my meat pieshop on Fleet Street.
> (*The* BEADLE *strolls somewhat menacingly over to them*)

BEADLE: Mr. Todd . . . Strange, sir, but it seems your face is known to me.

MRS. LOVETT (*Concealing agitation*): Him? That's a laugh — him being my uncle's cousin and arrived from Birmingham yesterday.

TODD (*Very smooth*): But already, sir, I have heard Beadle Bamford spoken of with great respect.

BEADLE (*Whatever dim suspicions he may have had allayed by the flattery*): Well, sir, I try my best for my neighbors.
> (*To* MRS. LOVETT)

Fleet Street? Over your pieshop, ma'am?

MRS. LOVETT: That's it, sir.

BEADLE: Then, Mr. Todd, you will surely see me there before the week is out.

TODD (*Expressionless*): You will be welcome, Beadle Bamford, and I guarantee to give you, without a penny's charge, the closest shave you will ever know.
> (MRS. LOVETT *takes* TODD*'s arm and starts with him offstage as the scene blacks out. The factory whistle. In limbo, the* BEGGAR WOMAN *appears with other members of the company. They sing*)

MEMBERS OF THE COMPANY:
Sweeney pondered and Sweeney planned.

421

Like a perfect machine 'e planned,
Barbing the hook, baiting the trap,
Setting it out for the Beadle to snap.

Slyly courted 'im, Sweeney did,
Set a sort of a scene, 'e did.
Laying the trail, showing the traces,
Letting it lead to higher places . . .
Sweeney . . .

(*The lights shift to a room in* JUDGE TURPIN's *house. The* JUDGE *is in his judicial clothes, a Bible in his hand. In the adjoining room,* JOHANNA *sits sewing*)

JUDGE (*Sings*):
Mea culpa, mea culpa,
Mea maxima culpa,
Mea maxima maxima culpa!
God deliver me! Release me!
Forgive me! Restrain me! Pervade me!
(*He peers through the keyhole of the door to* JOHANNA's *room*)
Johanna, Johanna,
So suddenly a woman,
The light behind your window —
It penetrates your gown . . .
Johanna, Johanna,
The sun — I see the sun through your —
(*Ashamed, he stops peering*)
No!
God!
Deliver me!
(*Sinks to his knees*)
Deliver me!
(*Starts tearing off his robes*)
Down!

Down.
Down . . .
   (*Now naked to the waist, he picks up a scourge from the table*)
Johanna, Johanna,
I watch you from the shadows.
You sigh before your window
And gaze upon the town . . .
Your lips part, Johanna,
So young and soft and beautiful —
                   (*Whips himself*)
God!
            (*Again and again, as he continues*)
Deliver me!
Filth
Leave me!
Johanna!
Johanna!
I treasured you in innocence
And loved you like a daughter.
You mock me, Johanna,
You tempt me with your innocence,
You tempt me with those quivering —
                   (*Whips himself*)
No!
            (*Again and again*)
God!
Deliver me!
It will —
Stop —
Now! It will —
Stop —
Right —
Now.
Right —

Now.
Right —
Now . . .
    (*Calm again, having kneed his way over to the door, he peers through the keyhole*)
Johanna, Johanna,
I cannot keep you longer.
The world is at your window,
You want to fly away.
You stir me, Johanna,
So suddenly a woman,
I cannot watch you one more day — !
        (*Again whips himself into a frenzy*)
God!
Deliver me!
God!
Deliver me!
God!
Deliver —
            (*Climaxes*)
God!!
    (*Panting, he relaxes; when he is in control again, he starts to dress*)
Johanna, Johanna,
I'll keep you here forever,
I'll wed you on the morrow.
Johanna, Johanna,
The world will never touch you,
I'll wed you on the morrow!
As years pass, Johanna,
You'll tend me in my solitude,
No longer as a daughter,
As a woman.
        (*He is fully dressed again*)
Johanna, Johanna,

I'll hold you here forever then,
You'll keep away from windows and
You'll
Deliver me,
Johanna,
From this
Hot
Red
Devil
With your
Soft
White
Cool
Virgin
Palms . . .

> (*Magisterial again, picking up the Bible, he produces a key and opens the door, the key forgotten, still in the lock.* JOHANNA *jumps up*)

JOHANNA: Father!

JUDGE: Johanna, I trust you've not been near the window again.

JOHANNA (*During this speech her eyes fall on the key in the lock*): Hardly, dear father, when it has been shuttered and barred these last three days.

JUDGE: How right I was to insist on such a precaution, for once again he has come, that conscienceless young sailor. Ten times has he been driven from my door and yet . . .
> (*Breaks off, gazing at her, smitten with lust*)
How sweet you look in that light muslin gown.

JOHANNA: 'Tis nothing but an old dress, father.

JUDGE: But fairer on your young form than wings on an angel . . . oh, if I were to think . . .

JOHANNA (*Demurely, moving to the door*): Think what, dear father?

JUDGE: If I were to think you encouraged this young rogue . . .

JOHANNA (*During this speech, she slips the key from the lock, hides it in her dress*): I? A maid trained from the cradle to find in modesty and obedience the greatest of all virtues? Dear father, when have you ceased to warn me of the wickedness of men?

JUDGE: Venal young men of the street with only one thought in their heads. But there are men of different and far higher breed. I have one in mind for you.

JOHANNA: You have?

JUDGE: A gentle man, who would shield you from all earthly cares and guide your faltering steps to the sober warmth of womanhood — a husband — a protector — and yet an ardent lover too. It is a man who through all the years has surely earned your affection.
(*Drops to his knees*)

JOHANNA (*Staggered*): You?!!!
(*The scene blacks out*)

(*Light comes up on* MRS. LOVETT*'s pieshop and the apartment above, which now is sparsely furnished with a washstand and a long wooden chest. At the foot of the outside staircase is a brand-new barber's pole. Attached to the first banister of the staircase is an iron bell.* TODD *is pacing in the apartment above.* MRS. LOVETT *comes hurrying out of the shop, carrying a wooden chair. As she does so, the* BEGGAR WOMAN *shuffles up to her*)

BEGGAR WOMAN (*Sings*):
Alms . . . alms . . .

MRS. LOVETT (*Imitating her nastily, sings*):
Alms . . . alms . . .

(*Music continues*)

How many times have I told you? I'll not have trash from the gutter hanging around my establishment!

BEGGAR WOMAN: Not just a penny, dear? Or a pie? One of them pies that give the stomach cramps to half the neighborhood?
(*A cackling laugh*)
Come on, dear. Have a heart, dear.

MRS. LOVETT: Off. Off with you or you'll get a kick on the rump that'll make your teeth chatter!

BEGGAR WOMAN: Stuck up thing! You and your fancy airs!
(*Shuffling off into the wings, sings*)
Alms . . . alms . . .
For a desperate woman . . .
(*Exits. Music continues.* MRS. LOVETT *rings the bell to indicate her approach and starts climbing the stairs. At the sound of the bell,* TODD *alerts and snatches up a razor. The music becomes agitated. As* MRS. LOVETT *appears, he relaxes somewhat.* MRS. LOVETT *is now very proprietary towards him*)

MRS. LOVETT: It's not much of a chair, but it'll do till you get your fancy new one. It was me poor Albert's chair, it was. Sat in it all day long he did, after his leg give out from the dropsy.
(*Surveying the room, music under*)
Kinda bare, isn't it? I never did like a bare room. Oh, well, we'll find some nice little knickknacks.

TODD: Why doesn't the Beadle come? "Before the week is out," that's what he said.

MRS. LOVETT: And who says the week's out yet? It's only Tuesday.
(*As* TODD *paces restlessly, sings*)
Easy now.

427

Hush, love, hush.
Don't distress yourself,
What's your rush?
Keep your thoughts
Nice and lush.
Wait.
               (TODD *continues to pace*)
Hush, love, hush.
Think it through.
Once it bubbles,
Then what's to do?
Watch it close.
Let it brew.
Wait.
       (*Looking round, cheerfully, as* TODD *grows calmer*)
I've been thinking, flowers —
Maybe daisies —
To brighten up the room.
Don't you think some flowers,
Pretty daisies,
Might relieve the gloom?
              (*As* TODD *doesn't respond*)
Ah, wait, love, wait.
             (*Music continues under*)

TODD (*Intensely*): And the Judge? When will I get him?

MRS. LOVETT: Can't you think of nothing else? Always brood-in' away on yer wrongs what happened heaven knows how many years ago —
           (TODD *turns away violently with a hiss*)
Slow, love, slow.
Time's so fast.
Now goes quickly —
See, now it's past!
Soon will come.
Soon will last.

Wait.

> (TODD *grows calm again*)

Don't you know,
Silly man,
Half the fun is to
Plan the plan?
All good things come to
Those who can
Wait.

> (*Looking around the room again*)

Gillyflowers, maybe,
'Stead of daisies . . .
I don't know, though . . .
What do you think?

TODD (*Docilely*): Yes.

MRS. LOVETT (*Gently taking the razor from him*): Gillyflowers,
I'd say. Nothing like a nice bowl of gillies.

> (*Music stops. During the above, we have seen* ANTHONY
> *moving down the street. He sees the sign and stops. He goes
> to the bell and rings it, then starts running up the stairs.
> The effect on* TODD *is electric. Even* MRS. LOVETT, *affected
> by his tension, alerts. She hastily gives him back the razor.*
> ANTHONY *bursts in enthusiastically*)

TODD: Anthony.

ANTHONY: Mr. Todd. I've paced Fleet Street a dozen times
with no success. But now the sign! In business already.

TODD: Yes.

ANTHONY: I congratulate you.

> (*Turning to* MRS. LOVETT)

And . . . er . . .

MRS. LOVETT: Mrs. Lovett, sir.

ANTHONY: A pleasure, ma'am. Oh, Mr. Todd, I have so much

to tell you. I have found the fairest and most loving maid that any man could dream of! And yet there are problems. She has a guardian so tyrannical that she is kept shut up from human eye. But now this morning this key fell from her shuttered window.

(*He holds up* JOHANNA's *key*)

The surest sign that Johanna loves me and . . .

MRS. LOVETT: Johanna?

ANTHONY: That's her name, ma'am, and Turpin that of the abominable parent. A judge, it seems. But, as I said, a monstrous tyrant. Oh Mr. Todd, once the Judge has gone to court, I'll slip into the house and plead with her to fly with me tonight. Yet when I have her — where can I bring her till I have hired a coach to speed us home to Plymouth? Oh Mr. Todd, if I could lodge her here just for an hour or two!

(*He gazes at the inscrutable* TODD)

MRS. LOVETT (*After a beat*): Bring her, dear.

ANTHONY: Oh thank you, thank you, ma'am.

(*To* TODD)

I have your consent, Mr. Todd?

TODD (*After a pause*): The girl may come.

(ANTHONY *grabs his hand and pumps it, then turns to grab* MRS. LOVETT's)

ANTHONY: I shall be grateful for this to the grave. Now I must hurry, for surely the Judge is off to the Old Bailey.

(*Turning at the door*)

My thanks! A thousand blessings on you both!

(*He hurries out and down the stairs*)

MRS. LOVETT: Johanna! Who'd have thought it! It's like Fate, isn't it? You'll have her back before the day is out.

TODD: For a few hours? Before he carries her off to the other end of England?

MRS. LOVETT: Oh, that sailor! Let him bring her here and then, since you're so hot for a little . . .
> (*Makes a throat-cutting gesture*)

. . . that's the throat to slit, dear. Oh Mr. T., we'll make a lovely home for her. You and me. The poor thing! All those years and not a scrap of motherly affection! I'll soon change that, I will, for if ever there was a maternal heart, it's mine.
> (*During this speech* PIRELLI, *accompanied by* TOBIAS, *has appeared on the street. They see the sign and start up the stairs without ringing the bell. Now, as* MRS. LOVETT *goes to* TODD *coquettishly,* PIRELLI *and* TOBIAS *suddenly appear at the door.* TODD *pulls violently away from* MRS. LOVETT)

PIRELLI (*With Italianate bow*): Good morning, Mr. Todd — and to you, bellissima signorina.
> (*He kisses* MRS. LOVETT*'s hand*)

MRS. LOVETT: Well, 'ow do you do, signor, I'm sure.

PIRELLI: A little business with Mr. Todd, signora. Perhaps if you will give the permission?

MRS. LOVETT: Oh yes, indeed, I'll just pop on down to my pies.
> (*Surveying* TOBIAS)

Oh lawks, look at it now! Don't look like it's had a kind word since half past never!
> (*Smiling at him*)

What would you say, son, to a nice juicy meat pie, eh? Your teeth is strong, I hope?

TOBIAS: Oh yes, ma'am.

MRS. LOVETT (*Taking his hand*): Then come with me, love.
> (*They start down the stairs to the shop*)

PIRELLI: Mr. Todd.

TODD: Signor Pirelli.

PIRELLI (*Reverting to Irish*): Ow, call me Danny, Daniel O'Higgins' the name when it's not perfessional.
(*Looks around the shop*)
Not much, but I imagine you'll pretty it up a bit.
(*Holds out his hand*)
I'd like me five quid back, if'n ya don't mind.

TODD: Why?
(*In the shop*, MRS. LOVETT *pats a stool for* TOBIAS *to sit down and hands him a piece of pie. He starts to eat greedily*)

MRS. LOVETT: That's my boy. Tuck in.

PIRELLI: It'll hold me over till your customers start coming. Then it's half your profits you'll hand over to me every week on a Friday, share and share alike. All right . . . Mr. Benjamin Barker?

TODD (*Very quiet*): Why do you call me that?

MRS. LOVETT (*Stroking* TOBIAS's *luxurious locks*): At least you've got a nice full head of hair on you.

TODD: Well, ma'am, to tell the truth, ma'am —
(*He reaches up and pulls off the "locks" which are a wig, revealing his own short-cropped hair*)
— gets awful 'ot.
(*He continues to eat the pie.* PIRELLI *strolls over to the washstand, picks up the razor, flicks it open*)

PIRELLI: You don't remember me. Why should you? I was just a down and out Irish lad you hired for a couple of weeks — sweeping up hair and such like —
(*Holding up razor*)
but I remember these — and you. Benjamin Barker, later transported to Botany Bay for life. So, Mr. Todd — is it a

432

deal or do I run down the street for me pal Beadle
Bamford?

> (*For a long moment* TODD *stands gazing at him*)

PIRELLI (*Sings, nastily*):
You t'ink-a you smart,
You foolish-a boy.
Tomorrow you start
In my-a employ!
You unner-a-stan'?
You like-a my plan — ?

> (*Once again he hits his high note, and once again he is
> interrupted —* TODD *knocks the razor out of his hand and
> starts, in a protracted struggle, to strangle him*)

TOBIAS (*Downstairs, unaware of this*): Oh gawd, he's got an
appointment with his tailor. If he's late and it's my fault
— you don't know him!

> (*He jumps up and starts out*)

MRS. LOVETT: I wouldn't want to, I'm sure, dear.

> (TODD *violently continues with the strangling*)

TOBIAS (*Calling on the stairs*): Signor! It's late! The tailor, sir.

> (*Remembering*)

Oh, me wig!

> (*Runs back for it. Upstairs,* TODD *stops dead at the sound
> of the voice. He looks around wildly, sees the chest, runs to
> it, opens the lid and then drags* PIRELLI *to it and tumbles
> him in, slamming the lid shut just as* TOBIAS *enters. It is
> at this moment that we realize that one of* PIRELLI*'s hands
> is dangling out of the chest*)

Signor, I did like you said. I reminded you . . . the tailor
. . . Ow, he ain't here.

TODD: Signor Pirelli has been called away.

TOBIAS: Where did he go?

TODD: He didn't say. You'd better run after him.

TOBIAS: Oh no, sir. Knowing him, sir, without orders to the contrary, I'd best wait for him *here.*

(*He crosses to the chest and sits down on it, perilously near* PIRELLI*'s hand, which he doesn't notice.* TODD *at this moment does, however. Suddenly he is all nervous smiles*)

TODD: So Mrs. Lovett gave you a pie, did she, my lad?

TOBIAS: Oh yes, sir. She's a real kind lady. One whole pie.

(*As he speaks, his hand moves very close to* PIRELLI*'s hand*)

TODD (*Moving toward him*): A whole pie, eh? That's a treat. And yet, if I know a growing boy, there's still room for more, eh?

TOBIAS: I'd say, sir.

(*Patting his stomach*)

An aching void.

(*Once again his hand is on the edge of the chest, moving toward* PIRELLI*'s hand. Slowly now, we see the fingers of* PIRELLI*'s hand stirring, feebly trying to clutch* TOBIAS*'s hand. When it has almost reached him,* TODD *grabs* TOBIAS *up off the chest*)

TODD: Then why don't you run downstairs and wait for your master there? There'll be another pie in it for you, I'm sure.

(*Afterthought*)

And tell Mrs. Lovett to give you a nice big tot of gin.

TOBIAS: Oo, sir! Gin, sir! Thanking you, sir, thanking you kindly. Gin! You're a Christian indeed, sir!

(*He runs down the stairs to* MRS. LOVETT)

Oh, ma'am, the gentleman says to give me a nice tot of gin, ma'am.

MRS. LOVETT: Gin, dear? Why not?

(*Upstairs, with great ferocity,* TODD *opens the chest, grabs the screaming* PIRELLI *by the hair, tugs him up from the*

chest and slashes his throat as, downstairs, MRS. LOVETT
pours a glass of gin and hands it to TOBIAS. *He takes it.*
The tableau freezes, then fades)

THREE TENORS (*Enter and sing*):
His hands were quick, his fingers strong.
It stung a little but not for long.
And those who thought him a simple clod
Were soon reconsidering under the sod,
Consigned there with a friendly prod
From Sweeney Todd,
The Demon Barber of Fleet Street.

See your razor gleam, Sweeney,
Feel how well it fits
As it floats across the throats
Of hypocrites . . .

> (*The ballad ends on a crashing chord as the singers black
> out and light comes up on* JUDGE TURPIN *in full panoply
> of wig, robe, etc. He is about to convict a young boy*)

JUDGE: This is the fourth time, sir, that you have been
brought before this bench. Though it is my earnest wish
ever to temper justice with mercy, your persistent dedica-
tion to a life of crime is such an abomination before God
and man that I have no alternative but to sentence you to
hang by the neck until you are dead.
> (*He produces the black cap and puts it on his head. As he
> does so the condemned prisoner is led away*)
Court adjourned.
> (*During the following, the* JUDGE *removes cap, wig, and
> gown. To the* BEADLE)
It is perhaps remiss of me to close the court so early, but
the stench of those miserable wretches at the bar was so
offensive to my nostrils I feared my eagerness for fresher
air might well impair the soundness of my judgement.

(Light dims on the court and finds the JUDGE *and the* BEA-DLE *now walking down a street together)*

BEADLE: Well, sir, the adjournment is fortunate for me, sir, for it's today we celebrate my sweet little Annie's birthday, and to have her daddy back so soon to hug and kiss her will be her crowning joy on such a happy day.

JUDGE: It is a happy moment for me, too. Walk home with me for I have news for you. In order to shield her from the evils of this world, I have decided to marry Johanna next Monday.

BEADLE: Ah, sir, happy news indeed.

JUDGE: Strange, when I offered myself to her, she showed a certain reluctance. But that's natural enough in a young girl. Now that she has had time for reflection, I'm sure she will greet my proposal in a more sensible frame of mind.

(Light leaves them and comes up on JOHANNA *and* ANTHONY *in* JOHANNA *'s room. She is pacing in agitation and fear)*

JOHANNA (*Sings*):
He means to marry me Monday,
What shall I do? I'd rather die.

ANTHONY (*Sings*):
I have a plan —

JOHANNA:
I'll swallow poison on Sunday,
That's what I'll do, I'll get some lye.

ANTHONY:
I have a plan —

JOHANNA (*Stops pacing suddenly*):
Oh, dear, was that a noise?

ANTHONY:
    A plan —

JOHANNA:
    I think I heard a noise.

ANTHONY:
    A plan!

JOHANNA:
    It couldn't be,
    He's in court,
    He's in court today,
    Still that was a noise,
    Wasn't that a noise?
    You must have heard that —

ANTHONY:
    Kiss me.

JOHANNA (*Shyly*):
    Oh, sir . . .

ANTHONY:
    Ah, miss . . .

JOHANNA:
    Oh, sir . . .
                          (*She turns away, agitatedly*)
    If he should marry me Monday,
    What shall I do? I'll die of grief.

ANTHONY:
    We fly tonight —

JOHANNA:
    'Tis Friday, virtually Sunday,
    What can we do with time so brief?

ANTHONY:
    We fly tonight —

JOHANNA:
Behind the curtain — quick!

ANTHONY:
Tonight —

JOHANNA:
I think I heard a click!

ANTHONY:
Tonight!

JOHANNA:	
It was a gate!	
It's the gate!	ANTHONY:
We don't have a gate.	It's not a gate.
Still there was a — Wait!	There's no gate,
There's another click!	You don't have a gate.
You must have heard that —	If you'd only listen, miss, and —

ANTHONY:
Kiss me!

JOHANNA:
Tonight?

ANTHONY:
Kiss me.

JOHANNA:
You mean tonight?

ANTHONY:
The plan is made.

JOHANNA:
Oh, sir!

ANTHONY:
So kiss me.

JOHANNA:
I feel a fright.

ANTHONY:
Be not afraid.

JOHANNA:	ANTHONY:
Sir, I did	Tonight I'll
Love you even as I	Steal
Saw you, even as it	You,
Did not matter that I	Johanna,
Did not know your name.	I'll steal you . . .

ANTHONY:
It's me you'll marry on Monday,
That's what you'll do!

JOHANNA:
And gladly, sir.

ANTHONY:
St. Dunstan's, noon.

JOHANNA:
I knew I'd be with you one day,
Even not knowing who you were.
I feared you'd never come,
That you'd been called away,
That you'd been killed,
Had the plague,
Were in debtor's jail,
Trampled by a horse,
Gone to sea again,
Arrested by the —

ANTHONY:
Ah, miss,
Marry me, marry me, miss,
Oh, marry me Monday!
Favor me, favor me
With your hand.
Promise,
Marry me, marry me, please,
Oh, marry me Monday —

JOHANNA:
Kiss me!

ANTHONY:
Of course.

JOHANNA:
Quickly!

ANTHONY:
  You're sure?

JOHANNA:
  Kiss me!

ANTHONY (*Taking her in his arms*):
  I shall!

JOHANNA:
  Kiss me!
  Oh, sir . . .

> (*Lights dim on them but remain; light rises on the* JUDGE
> *and the* BEADLE, *still walking together. Music continues
> under*)

JUDGE (*Strolling with* BEADLE): Yes, yes, but surely the respect
  that she owes me as her guardian should be sufficient to
  kindle a more tender emotion.

BEADLE (*Sings*):
  Excuse me, my lord.
  May I request, my lord,
  Permission, my lord, to speak?
  Forgive me if I suggest, my lord,
  You're looking less than your best, my lord,
  There's powder upon your vest, my lord,
  And stubble upon your cheek.
  And ladies, my lord, are weak.
                (*Music continues*)

JUDGE: Perhaps if she greets me cordially upon my return, I
  should give her a small gift . . .

BEADLE (*Winces delicately*):
  Ladies in their sensitivities, my lord,
  Have a fragile sensibility.
  When a girl's emergent,

Probably it's urgent
You defer to her gent-
Ility, my lord.
Personal disorder cannot be ignored,
Given their genteel proclivities.
Meaning no offense, it
Happens they resents it,
Ladies in their sensit-
Ivities, my lord.

JUDGE (*Feeling his chin*): Stubble, you say? Perhaps at times I am a little overhasty with my morning ablutions . . .

BEADLE:
Fret not though, my lord,
I know a place, my lord,
A barber, my lord, of skill.
Thus armed with a shaven face, my lord,
Some eau de cologne to grace my lord
And musk to enhance the chase, my lord,
You'll dazzle the girl until
She bows to your every will.

JUDGE: That may well be so.
                    (*They have reached the* JUDGE*'s house*)

BEADLE: Well, here we are, sir. I bid you good day.

JUDGE: Good day.
                    (*He muses, turns*)
And where is this miraculous barber?

BEADLE: In Fleet Street, sir.

JUDGE: Perhaps you may be right. Take me to him.
          (*They start off. Light up on* JOHANNA*'s room.* JOHANNA
          and ANTHONY *get up from a couch*)

BEADLE (*Sings*):
The name is Todd . . .

441

JUDGE:
 Todd, eh?

ANTHONY:
 We'd best not wait until Monday

  JOHANNA:
Sir, I concur,   BEADLE:
And fully, too.   Sweeney Todd.

ANTHONY:
 It isn't right.
 We'd best be married on Sunday.

JOHANNA:
 Saturday, sir,
 Would also do.

ANTHONY:
 Or else tonight.
  (*The* JUDGE *and the* BEADLE *move past the house*)

JOHANNA:
 I think I heard a noise.

ANTHONY:
 Fear not.

JOHANNA:
 I mean another noise!

ANTHONY:
 Like what?

  JOHANNA:
Oh, never mind,
Just a noise
Just another noise,   ANTHONY:
Something in the street,   You mustn't mind,
I'm a silly little   It's a noise,
Ninnynoddle —   Just another noise,
                                        Something in the street,
                                        You silly —

BOTH (*Falling into each other's arms*):
  Kiss me!

JOHANNA:
  Oh, sir . . .

ANTHONY:
  We'll go to Paris on Monday.

JOHANNA:
  What shall I wear?
  I daren't pack!

ANTHONY:
  We'll ride a train . . .

JOHANNA:
  With you beside me on Sunday,
  What will I care
  What things I lack?

ANTHONY:
  Then sail to Spain . . .

JOHANNA:	ANTHONY:
I'll take my reticule.	
I need my reticule.	Why take your reticule?
You mustn't think	We'll buy a reticule.
Me a fool	I'd never think
But my reticule	You a fool,
Never leaves my side,	But a reticule —
It's the only thing	Leave it all aside
My mother gave me —	And begin again and
Kiss me!	Kiss me!
Kiss me!	
	I know a place where we can go
	Tonight.
We'll go there,	Kiss me!
Kiss me!	
We have a place where we can	We have a place where we can

443

Go . . .   Go tonight.

BEADLE (*Simultaneously with the above*):
   The name is Todd.

JUDGE:
   Todd?

BEADLE:
   Todd. Sweeney Todd.

JUDGE:
   Todd . . .

BEADLE:
   Todd.

JOHANNA:	ANTHONY:
I loved you	I loved you
Even as I saw you,	Even as I saw you,
Even as it does not	Even as it did not
Matter that I still	Matter that I did
Don't know your name, sir,	Not know your name . . .
Even as I saw you,	
Even as it does not	Johanna . . .
Matter that I still	Johanna . . .
Don't know your name . . .	Johanna . . .

BEADLE (*Simultaneously with above*):
   Todd . . . Sweeney Todd.

JUDGE *and* BEADLE:
   Sweeney Todd.

ANTHONY: Anthony . . .

JUDGE: Todd . . .

BEADLE: Todd.

JOHANNA: Anthony . . .

JUDGE: Todd, eh?

JOHANNA:	ANTHONY:
I'll marry Anthony Sunday,	You marry Anthony Sunday,
That's what I'll do,	That's what you'll do,
No matter what!	No matter what!
I knew you'd come for me one day,	I knew I'd come for you one day
Only afraid that you'd forgot.	Only afraid that you'd forgot.

BEADLE (*Simultaneously with above*):

Ladies in their sensitivities, my lord . . .

JUDGE:

Pray lead the way.

BEADLE:

Have a fragile sensibility . . .

JUDGE:

Just as you say.

JOHANNA:	ANTHONY:
I feared you'd never come,	Marry me, marry me, miss,
That you'd been called away,	You'll marry me Sunday.
That you'd been killed,	Favor me, favor me
Had the plague,	With your hand.
Were in debtor's jail,	Promise,
Trampled by a horse,	Marry me, marry me,
Gone to sea again,	That you'll marry me —
Arrested by the . . .	Enough of all this . . .

(*He crushes her to him; they kiss*)

BEADLE (*Simultaneously with above*):

When a girl's emergent,
Probably it's urgent . . .
Ladies in their sensitivities . . .

JUDGE:

Todd . . .

JOHANNA (*As she sinks to the floor with* ANTHONY):
Oh, sir . . .

ANTHONY:
Ah, miss . . .

JOHANNA:

Oh, sir . . .	ANTHONY:
Oh, sir . . .	Ah, miss . . .
Oh, sir . . .	Ah, miss . . .
Oh, sir . . .	Ah, miss . . .
Oh, sir . . .	Ah, miss . . .
Oh, sir . . .	Ah, miss . . .

(*Light leaves them, comes up on the pieshop-tonsorial parlor. Upstairs,* TODD *is silently cleaning his razor. In the shop,* MRS. LOVETT *and* TOBIAS *unfreeze from the position in which they were last seen*)

MRS. LOVETT: Maybe you should run along, dear.

TOBIAS: Oh no, ma'am, I daren't budge till he calls for me.

MRS. LOVETT: I'll pop up and see what Mr. Todd says.
(*Humming,* MRS. LOVETT *starts climbing the stairs. As she enters the parlor*)
Ah me, my poor knees is not what they was, dear.
(*She sits down on the chest*)
How long before the Eyetalian gets back?

TODD (*Still impassively cleaning the razor*): He won't be back.

MRS. LOVETT (*Instantly suspicious*): Now, Mr. T., you didn't!
(TODD *nods toward the chest. Realizing,* MRS. LOVETT *jumps up. For a moment she stands looking at the chest, then, gingerly, she lifts the lid. She gazes down, then spins to* TODD)
You're crazy mad! Killing a man wot done you no harm?
And the boy downstairs?

TODD: He recognized me from the old days. He tried to

blackmail me, half my earnings forever.

MRS. LOVETT: Oh well, that's a different matter! What a relief, dear! For a moment I thought you'd lost your marbles.
(*Turns to peer down again into the chest*)
Ooh! All that blood! Enough to make you come all over gooseflesh, ain't it. Poor bugger. Oh, well!
(*She starts to close the lid, sees something, bends to pick it up. It is* PIRELLI*'s purse. She looks in it*)
Three quid! Well, waste not, want not, as I always say.
(*She takes out the money and puts it down her bosom. She is about to throw the purse away when something about it attracts her. She slips it too down her dress. She shuts the chest lid and, quite composed again, sits down on it*)
Now, dear, we got to use the old noggin.
(*As she sits deep in thought, we see the* JUDGE *and* BEADLE *coming up the street*)

BEADLE (*Pointing*): There you are, sir. Above the pieshop, sir.

JUDGE: I see. You may leave me now.

BEADLE: Thank you, sir. Thank you.
(*He starts off as the* JUDGE *approaches the parlor*)

MRS. LOVETT (*Coming out of her pondering*): Well, first there's the lad.

TODD: Send him up here.

MRS. LOVETT: Him, too! Now surely one's enough for today, dear. Shouldn't indulge yourself, you know. Now let me see, he's half seas over already with the gin . . .
(*As she speaks, downstairs the* JUDGE *clangs the bell.* TODD *runs to the landing and peers down the stairs. The* BEADLE *is still visible, exiting*)

TODD: Providence is kind!

MRS. LOVETT: Who is it?

TODD: Judge Turpin.

MRS. LOVETT (*Flustered*): Him, him? The Judge? It can't be! It —

TODD: Quick, leave me!

MRS. LOVETT: What are you going to do?

TODD (*Roaring*): Leave me, I said!

MRS. LOVETT: Don't worry, dear. I'm — out!
(*She scuttles out of the tonsorial parlor and starts down the stairs as the* JUDGE *ascends. They meet halfway. She gives him a deep curtsy*)
Excuse me, your Lordship.
(*She hurries back to* TOBIAS *in the shop*)

JUDGE: Mr. Todd?

TODD: At your service, sir. An honor to receive your patronage, sir.

MRS. LOVETT (*To* TOBIAS): Now, dear, seems like your guvnor has gone and left you high and dry. But don't worry. Your Aunt Nellie will think of what to do with you.
(*Picks up the bottle of gin and pours some more into his glass. Still holding the bottle, she leads him toward the curtains*)
Come on into my lovely back parlor.
(*They disappear through the curtain*)

JUDGE (*Looking around*): These premises are hardly prepossessing and yet the Beadle tells me you are the most accomplished of all the barbers in the city.

TODD: That is gracious of him, sir. And you must please excuse the modesty of my establishment. It's only a few days ago that I set up quarters here and some necessaries are yet to come.
(*Indicating chair*)

448

Sit, sir, if you please, sir. Sit.
> (*The* JUDGE *settles into the chair; music under as* MRS.
> LOVETT, *still holding the gin bottle, enters her back parlor
> with* TOBIAS)

MRS. LOVETT: See how nice and cozy it is? Sit down, dear, sit.
> (*She starts to pour him more gin*)

Oh, it's empty. Now you just sit there, dear, like a good
quiet boy while I get a new bottle from the larder.
> (*She leaves him alone*)

TODD: And what may I do for you, sir? A stylish trimming of
the hair? A soothing skin massage?

JUDGE (*Sings*):
You see, sir, a man infatuate with love,
Her ardent and eager slave.
So fetch the pomade and pumice stone
And lend me a more seductive tone,
A sprinkling perhaps of French cologne,
But first, sir, I think — a shave.

TODD: The closest I ever gave.
> (*He whips the sheet over the* JUDGE, *then tucks the bib in.
> The* JUDGE *hums, flicking imaginary dust off the sheet;
> TODD whistles gaily*)

JUDGE: You are in a merry mood today, Mr. Todd.

TODD (*Sings, mixing lather*):
'Tis your delight, sir, catching fire
From one man to the next.

JUDGE:
'Tis true, sir, love can still inspire
The blood to pound, the heart leap higher.

BOTH:
What more, what more can man require —

JUDGE:

Than love, sir?

TODD:

More than love, sir.

JUDGE:

What, sir?

TODD:

Women.

JUDGE:

Ah yes, women.

TODD:

Pretty women.

(*The* JUDGE *hums jauntily;* TODD *whistles and starts stropping his razor rhythmically. He then lathers the* JUDGE*'s face. Still whistling, he stands back to survey the* JUDGE, *who is now totally relaxed, eyes closed. He picks up the razor and sings to it*)

Now then, my friend.
Now to your purpose.
Patience, enjoy it.
Revenge can't be taken in haste.

JUDGE (*Opens his eyes*):

Make haste, and if we wed,
You'll be commended, sir.

TODD (*Bows*):

My lord . . .

(*Goes to him*)

And who, may it be said,
Is your intended, sir?

JUDGE:

My ward.

450

(TODD *freezes; the* JUDGE *closes his eyes, settles comfortably, speaks*)
And pretty as a rosebud.

TODD (*Music rising*): As pretty as her mother?

JUDGE (*Mildly puzzled*): What? What was that?
(*As the music reaches a shrill crescendo,* TODD *is slowly bringing the razor toward the* JUDGE*'s throat when suddenly the* JUDGE *opens his eyes and starts to twist around in curiosity*)

TODD (*Musingly, lightly*): Oh, nothing, sir. Nothing. May we proceed?
(*Starts to shave the* JUDGE, *sings*)
Pretty women . . .
Fascinating . . .
Sipping coffee,
Dancing . . .
Pretty women
Are a wonder.
Pretty women.

Sitting in the window or
Standing on the stair,
Something in them
Cheers the air.

Pretty women . . .

JUDGE:
Silhouetted . . .

TODD:
Stay within you . . .

JUDGE:
Glancing . . .

TODD:
Stay forever . . .

JUDGE:
  Breathing lightly . . .

TODD:
  Pretty women . . .

BOTH:
  Pretty women!
  Blowing out their candles or
  Combing out their hair . . .

JUDGE:
Then they leave . . .
Even when they leave you
And vanish, they somehow
Can still remain
There with you,
There with you.

TODD:
Even when they leave,
They still
Are
There.
They're there.

BOTH:
  Ah,
  Pretty women . . .

TODD:
  At their mirrors . . .

JUDGE:
  In their gardens . . .

TODD:
  Letter-writing . . .

JUDGE:
  Flower-picking . . .

TODD:
  Weather-watching . . .

BOTH:
  How they make a man sing!

Proof of heaven
As you're living —
Pretty women, sir!

JUDGE:	TODD:
Pretty women, yes!	Pretty women, here's to
Pretty women, sir!	Pretty women, all the
Pretty women!	Pretty women . . .
Pretty women, sir!	

    (TODD *raises his arm in a huge arc and is about to slice the razor across the* JUDGE*'s throat when* ANTHONY *bursts in*)

ANTHONY (*Singing*):
She says she'll marry me Sunday,
Everything's set, we leave tonight — !

JUDGE (*Jumping up, spilling the basin and knocking the razor from* TODD*'s hand*): You!

ANTHONY: Judge Turpin!

JUDGE: There is indeed a Higher Power to warn me thus in time.
    (*As* ANTHONY *retreats, he jumps on him and grabs him by the arm*)
Johanna elope with you? Deceiving slut — I'll lock her up in some obscure retreat where neither you nor any other vile, corrupting youth shall ever lay eyes on her again.

ANTHONY (*Shaking himself free*): But, sir, I beg of you —

JUDGE (*To* TODD): And as for you, barber, it is all too clear what company you keep. Service them well and hold their custom — for you'll have none of mine.
    (*He strides out and down the stairs*)

ANTHONY: Mr. Todd!

TODD (*Shouting*): Out! Out, I say!

453

(Bewildered, ANTHONY *leaves. Music begins under, very agitated.* TODD *stands motionless, in shock. As the* JUDGE *hurries off down the street,* MRS. LOVETT, *with a new bottle of gin in her hand, sees him. She glances after him, then goes into the back parlor where* TOBIAS *is now asleep. She looks at him, puts down the bottle and hurries out and up the stairs to* TODD)

MRS. LOVETT: All this running and shouting. What is it now, dear?

TODD: I had him — and then . . .

MRS. LOVETT: The sailor busted in. I saw them both running down the street and I said to myself: "The fat's in the fire, for sure!"

TODD (*Interrupting, sings*):
I had him!
His throat was bare
Beneath my hand — !

MRS. LOVETT (*Alarmed, pacifying*): There, there, dear. Don't fret.

TODD:
No, I had him!
His throat was there,
And he'll never come again!

MRS. LOVETT:
Easy now.
Hush, love, hush.
I keep telling you —

TODD (*Violently*):
When?

MRS. LOVETT:
What's your rush?

TODD:

Why did I wait?
You told me to wait!
Now he'll never come again!
    (*Music becomes ferocious.* TODD *'s insanity, always close to*
    the surface, explodes finally)
There's a hole in the world
Like a great black pit
And it's filled with people
Who are filled with shit
And the vermin of the world
Inhabit it —
But not for long!

They all deserve to die!
Tell you why, Mrs. Lovett,
Tell you why:
Because in all of the whole human race, Mrs. Lovett,
There are two kinds of men and only two.
There's the one staying put
In his proper place
And the one with his foot
In the other one's face —
Look at me, Mrs. Lovett,
Look at you!

No, we all deserve to die!
Tell you why, Mrs. Lovett,
Tell you why:
Because the lives of the wicked should be —
                  (*Slashes at the air*)
Made brief.
For the rest of us, death
Will be a relief —
We all deserve to die!
            (*Keening*)

And I'll never see Johanna,
No, I'll never hug my girl to me —
Finished!

> (*Turns on the audience*)

All right! You, sir,
How about a shave?

> (*Slashes twice*)

Come and visit
Your good friend Sweeney — !
You, sir, too, sir —
Welcome to the grave!
I will have vengeance,
I will have salvation!

Who, sir? You, sir?
No one's in the chair —
Come on, come on,
Sweeney's waiting!
I want you bleeders!
You, sir — anybody!
Gentlemen, now don't be shy!
Not one man, no,
Nor ten men,
Nor a hundred
Can assuage me —
I will have you!

> (*To* MRS. LOVETT)

And I *will* get him back
Even as he gloats.
In the meantime I'll practice
On less honorable throats.

> (*Keening again*)

And my Lucy lies in ashes
And I'll never see my girl again,
But the work waits,
I'm alive at last

(Exalted)

And I'm full of joy!

(He drops down into the barber's chair in a sweat, panting)

MRS. LOVETT *(Who has been watching him intently)*: That's all very well, but all that matters now is him!

(She points to the chest. TODD *still sits motionless. She goes to him, peers at him)*

Listen! Do you hear me? Can you hear me? Get control of yourself.

(She slaps his cheek. After a long pause, TODD, *still in a half-dream, gets to his feet)*

What are we going to do about him? And there's the lad downstairs. We'd better go and have a look and be sure he's still there. When I left him he was sound asleep in the parlor.

(She starts downstairs)

Come on!

*(*TODD *follows. She disappears into the back parlor and re-emerges)*

No problem there. He's still sleeping. He's simple as a baby lamb. Later I can fob him off with some story easy. But him!

(Indicating the tonsorial parlor above)

What are we going to do with him?

TODD *(Disinterestedly)*: Later on, when it's dark, we'll take him to some secret place and bury him.

MRS. LOVETT: Well, of course, we could do that. I don't suppose there's any relatives going to come poking around looking for him. But . . .

(Pause. Chord)

You know me. Sometimes ideas just pop into me head and I keep thinking . . .

(Sings)

Seems a downright shame . . .

457

TODD: Shame?

MRS. LOVETT:

Seems an awful waste . . .
Such a nice plump frame
Wot's-his-name
Has . . .
Had . . .
Has . . .
Nor it can't be traced.
Business needs a lift —
Debts to be erased —
Think of it as thrift,
As a gift . . .
If you get my drift . . .

> (TODD *stares into space*)

No?

> (*She sighs*)

Seems an awful waste.
I mean,
With the price of meat what it is,
When you get it,
If you get it —

TODD (*Becoming aware, chuckling*): Ah!

MRS. LOVETT:

Good, you got it.

> (*Warming to it*)

Take, for instance,
Mrs. Mooney and her pie shop.
Business never better, using only
Pussycats and toast.
And a pussy's good for maybe six or
Seven at the most.
And I'm sure they can't compare
As far as taste —

458

TODD:
Mrs. Lovett,
What a charming notion,
Eminently practical and yet
Appropriate, as always.
Mrs. Lovett
How I've lived without you
All these years I'll never know!
How delectable!
Also undetectable.

How choice!
How rare!

MRS. LOVETT:
Well, it does seem a
Waste . . .

It's an idea . . .
Think about it . . .
Lots of other gentlemen'll
Soon be coming for a shave
Won't they?
Think of
All them
Pies!

TODD:
For what's the sound of the world out there?

MRS. LOVETT:
What, Mr. Todd,
What, Mr. Todd,
What is that sound?

TODD:
Those crunching noises pervading the air?

MRS. LOVETT:
Yes, Mr. Todd,
Yes, Mr. Todd,
Yes, all around —

TODD:
It's man devouring man, my dear,
And who are we
To deny it in here?

MRS. LOVETT:
Then who are we
To deny it in here?

TODD: These are desperate times, Mrs. Lovett, and desperate measures are called for.

(She goes to the counter and comes back with an imaginary pie)

MRS. LOVETT: Here we are, hot from the oven.
(She holds it out to him)

TODD:
What is that?

MRS. LOVETT:
It's priest.
Have a little priest.

TODD:
Is it really good?

MRS. LOVETT:
Sir, it's too good,
At least.
Then again, they don't commit sins of the flesh,
So it's pretty fresh.

TODD *(Looking at it)*:
Awful lot of fat.

MRS. LOVETT:
Only where it sat.

TODD:
Haven't you got poet
Or something like that?

MRS. LOVETT:
No, you see the trouble with poet
Is, how do you know it's
Deceased?
Try the priest.

TODD *(Tasting it)*: Heavenly.
(MRS. LOVETT giggles)

Not as hearty as bishop, perhaps, but not as bland as
curate, either.

MRS. LOVETT: And good for business — always leaves you
wanting more. Trouble is, we only get it in Sundays . . .
(TODD *chuckles.* MRS. LOVETT *presents another imaginary pie*)
Lawyer's rather nice.

TODD:
If it's for a price.

MRS. LOVETT:
Order something else, though, to follow,
Since no one should swallow
It twice.

TODD:
Anything that's lean.

MRS. LOVETT:
Well, then, if you're British and loyal,
You might enjoy Royal
Marine.
(TODD *makes a face*)
Anyway, it's clean.
Though, of course, it tastes of wherever it's been.

TODD (*Looking past her at an imaginary oven*):
Is that squire
On the fire?

MRS. LOVETT:
Mercy no, sir,
Look closer,
You'll notice it's grocer.

TODD:
Looks thicker.
More like vicar.

461

MRS. LOVETT:
No, it has to be grocer — it's green.

TODD:
The history of the world, my love —

MRS. LOVETT:
Save a lot of graves,
Do a lot of relatives favors . . .

TODD:
— is those below serving those up above.

MRS. LOVETT:
Everybody shaves,
So there should be plenty of flavors . . .

TODD:
How gratifying for once to know —

BOTH:
— that those above will serve those down below!

MRS. LOVETT: Now, let's see . . .
   (*Surveying an imaginary tray of pies on the counter*)
We've got tinker . . .

TODD (*Looking at it*): Something pinker.

MRS. LOVETT: Tailor?

TODD (*Shaking his head*): Paler.

MRS. LOVETT: Butler?

TODD: Subtler.

MRS. LOVETT: Potter?

TODD (*Feeling it*): Hotter.

MRS. LOVETT: Locksmith?
   (TODD *shrugs, defeated.* MRS. LOVETT *offers another imaginary pie*)

Lovely bit of clerk.

TODD:
Maybe for a lark . . .

MRS. LOVETT:
Then again, there's sweep
If you want it cheap
And you like it dark.
                    (*Another*)
Try the financier.
Peak of his career.

TODD:
That looks pretty rank.

MRS. LOVETT:
Well, he drank.
It's a bank
Cashier.
Last one really sold.
                    (*Feels it*)
Wasn't quite so old.

TODD:
Have you any Beadle?

MRS. LOVETT:
Next week, so I'm told.
Beadle isn't bad till you smell it
And notice how well it's
Been greased.
Stick to priest.
                    (*Offers another pie*)
Now this may be a bit stringy, but then, of course, it's fid-
dle player.

TODD: This isn't fiddle player. It's piccolo player.

MRS. LOVETT: How can you tell?

TODD: It's piping hot.

(Giggles)

MRS. LOVETT (Snorts with glee): Then blow on it first.

(TODD guffaws)

TODD:
The history of the world, my sweet —

MRS. LOVETT:
Oh, Mr. Todd,
Ooh, Mr. Todd,
What does it tell?

TODD:
— is who gets eaten and who gets to eat.

MRS. LOVETT:
And, Mr. Todd,
Too, Mr. Todd,
Who gets to sell.

TODD:
But fortunately, it's also clear —

TODD:	MRS. LOVETT:
That everybody	But everybody
Goes down well with beer.	Goes down well with beer.

MRS. LOVETT: Since marine doesn't appeal to you, how about rear admiral?

TODD: Too salty. I prefer general.

MRS. LOVETT: With or without his privates? "With" is extra.

(TODD chortles)

TODD (As MRS. LOVETT offers another pie):
What is that?

MRS. LOVETT:
It's fop.

464

Finest in the shop.
Or we have some shepherd's pie peppered
With actual shepherd
On top.
And I've just begun.
Here's the politician — so oily
It's served with a doily —
>   (TODD *makes a face*)
Have one.

TODD:
>   Put it on a bun.
>   (*As she looks at him quizzically*)
>   Well, you never know if it's going to run.

MRS. LOVETT:
>   Try the friar.
>   Fried, it's drier.

TODD:
>   No, the clergy is really
>   Too coarse and too mealy.

MRS. LOVETT:
>   Then actor —
>   That's compacter.

TODD:
>   Yes, and always arrives overdone.
>   I'll come again when you
>   Have Judge on the menu . . .

MRS. LOVETT: Wait! True, we don't have Judge — yet — but would you settle for the next best thing?

TODD: What's that?

MRS. LOVETT (*Handing him a butcher's cleaver*): Executioner.
(TODD *roars, and then, picking up her wooden rolling pin, hands it to her*)

TODD:
Have charity toward the world, my pet —

MRS. LOVETT:
Yes, yes, I know, my love —

TODD:
We'll take the customers that we can get.

MRS. LOVETT:
High-born and low, my love.

TODD:
We'll not discriminate great from small.
No, we'll serve anyone —
Meaning anyone —

BOTH:
And to anyone
At all!

(*Music continues as the two of them brandish their "weapons." The scene blacks out.*)

The Prologue's front drop depicting in a honeycomb
the class system of mid-19th Century England

"The Worst Pies in London"
Mrs. Lovett (Angela Lansbury) and Sweeney Todd (Len Cariou)

"My Friends" Sweeney (Len Cariou)

468

Johanna (Sarah Rice) and Anthony (Victor Garber)

VAN WILLI

"Wait"
Mrs. Lovett (Angela Lansbury) and Sweeney (Len Cariou)

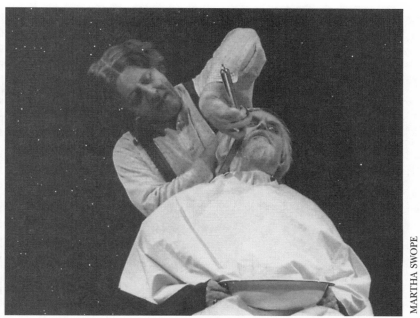

"Pretty Women"
Sweeney (Len Cariou) and Judge Turpin (Edmund Lyndeck)

"By the Sea"
Mrs. Lovett (Angela Lansbury)

"Not While I'm Around"
Tobias (Ken Jennings) and Mrs. Lovett (Angela Lansbury)

Sweeney has his revenge
Judge Turpin (Edmund Lyndeck) and Sweeney (Len Cariou)

VAN WILLIAMS

In the Final Sequence, Sweeney (Len Cariou) cradles the body of
the dead Beggar Woman (Merle Louise) as a now demented Tobias
(Ken Jennings) avenges Sweeney's victims

Bob Gunton as Sweeney Todd and Beth Fowler as Mrs. Lovett in the 1989 Circle-in-the-Square production

Sheila Hancock as Mrs. Lovett and Denis Quilley in the original London production

ACT II

Thanks to her increasing prosperity, MRS. LOVETT *has created a modest outdoor eating garden outside the pieshop,
consisting of a large wooden table with two benches, a few
bushes in pots, birds in cages. At rise, contented customers,
one of whom is drunk, are filling the garden, devouring
their pies, and drinking ale while* TOBIAS, *in a waiter's
apron, drums up trade along the sidewalk. Inside the
pieshop,* MRS. LOVETT, *in a "fancy" gown, a sign of her
upward mobility, doles out pies from the counter and col-
lects a few on a tray to bring into the garden subsequently.*
TODD *is pacing restlessly in the tonsorial parlor. The* BEG-
GAR WOMAN *hangs around throughout, hungry and omi-
nous.*

TOBIAS:
Ladies and gentlemen,
May I have your attention, perlease?
Are your nostrils aquiver and tingling as well
At that delicate, luscious ambrosial smell?
Yes they are, I can tell.
Well, ladies and gentlemen,
That aroma enriching the breeze
Is like nothing compared to its succulent source,
As the gourmets among you will tell you, of course.

Ladies and gentlemen,
You can't imagine the rapture in store —

(*Indicating the shop*)

Just inside of this door!

(*Beating his usual drum*)

There you'll sample
Mrs. Lovett's meat pies,
Savory and sweet pies,
As you'll see.
You who eat pies,
Mrs. Lovett's meat pies
Conjure up the treat pies
Used to be!

(TOBIAS *and customers sing, overlapping*)

1ST MAN:

Over here, boy, how about some ale?

2ND MAN:

Let me have another, laddie!

1ST WOMAN:

Tell me, are they flavorsome?

2ND WOMAN:

They are.

3RD WOMAN:

Isn't this delicious?

TOBIAS (*To* 2ND MAN):

Right away.

4TH MAN:

Could we have some service over here, boy?

4TH WOMAN:

Could we have some service, waiter?

3RD MAN:

Could we have some service?

2ND *and* 3RD WOMAN:
 Yes, they are.

1ST MAN:
 God, that's good!

2ND MAN:
 What about that pie, boy?

1ST WOMAN:
 Tell me, are they spicy?

2ND WOMAN:
 God, that's good!

5TH WOMAN:
 How much are you charging?

TOBIAS:
 Thruppence.

3RD WOMAN:
 Yes, what about the pie, boy?

4TH WOMAN:
 I never tasted anything so . . .

1ST *and* 5TH WOMAN:
 Thruppence?

5TH MAN:
 Thruppence for a meat pie?

1ST *and* 2ND MAN:
 Where's the ale I asked you for, boy?

TOBIAS:
 Ladies and gentlemen — !

MRS. LOVETT (*Ringing a bell to attract* TOBIAS*'s attention*)
 Toby!

 (*She starts into the garden with a tray of pies*)

TOBIAS:

Coming!

(*To a customer*)

'Scuse me . . .

MRS. LOVETT (*Indicating a beckoning customer*):

Ale there!

TOBIAS:

Right, mum!

(*He runs inside, picks up a jug of ale, whisks back out into the garden and starts filling tankards*)

MRS. LOVETT:

Quick, now!

CUSTOMERS (*Licking their fingers*):

God, that's good!

MRS. LOVETT (*A bundle of activity, serving pies, collecting money, giving orders, addressing each of the patrons individually and with equal insincerity*):

Nice to see you, dearie . . .

How have you been keeping? . . .

Cor, me bones is weary!

Toby — !

(*Indicating a customer*)

One for the gentleman . . .

Hear the birdies cheeping —

Helps to keep it cheery . . .

(*Spying the* BEGGAR WOMAN)

Toby!

Throw the old woman out!

CUSTOMERS:

God, that's good!

(TOBIAS *shoos the* BEGGAR WOMAN *away, but she soon comes back, sniffing*)

MRS. LOVETT (*To other customers, without breaking rhythm*):
  What's your pleasure, dearie? . . .
  No, we don't cut slices . . .
  Cor, me eyes is bleary! . . .
      (*As* TOBIAS *is about to pour for a plastered customer*)
  Toby!
  None for the gentleman! . . .
  I could up me prices —
  I'm a little leery . . .
  Business
  Couldn't be better, though —

CUSTOMERS:
  God, that's good!

MRS. LOVETT:
  Knock on wood.
                    (*She does*)

TODD (*Leaning out of window*):
  Psst!

MRS. LOVETT (*To a customer*):
  Excuse me . . .

TODD:
  Psst!

MRS. LOVETT (*To* TOBIAS):
  Dear, see to the customers.

TODD:
  Psst!

MRS. LOVETT (*Moving toward him*):
  Yes, what, love?
  Quick, though, the trade is brisk.

TODD:
  But it's six o'clock!

MRS. LOVETT:

    So it's six o'clock.

TODD:

    It was due to arrive
    At a quarter to five —

MRS. LOVETT:	TODD:
And it's probably already Down the block!	And it's six o'clock!
It'll be here, it'll be here! Have a beaker of beer	I've been waiting all day!
And stop worrying, dear. Now, now . . .	But it should have been here By now!

CUSTOMERS:

    More hot pies!

MRS. LOVETT (*Looking back, agitated at being pulled in two directions*):

Gawd.

        (*To* TODD, *moving back to the garden*)

Will you wait there,	TODD:
Coolly,	You'll come back
'Cos my customers truly	When it comes?
Are getting unruly.	

        (*Circulating again in the garden*)

And what's your pleasure, dearie?

           (*Spilling ale*)

Oops! I beg your pardon!
Just me hands is smeary —

        (*Spotting a would-be freeloader*)

Toby!
Run for the gentleman!

    (TOBIAS *catches him, collects the money;* MRS. LOVETT
    turns to another customer)

Don't you love a garden?
Always makes me teary .

(*Looking back at the freeloader*)
Must be one of them foreigners —

CUSTOMERS:
God, that's good that is delicious!
(*During the following a huge crate appears high on a crane and moves slowly downstage to the tonsorial parlor.* TODD *sees it*)

MRS. LOVETT:
What's my secret?
(*To a woman*)
Frankly, dear — forgive my candor —
Family secret,
All to do with herbs.
Things like being
Careful with your coriander,
That's what makes the gravy grander — !

CUSTOMERS:
More hot pies!
(MRS. LOVETT *hastens into the shop and loads the tray again*)
More hot!
More pies!

TODD (*Out the window*):
Psst!

MRS. LOVETT (*To a customer in the shop*):
Excuse me . . .

TODD:
Psst!

MRS. LOVETT (*To* TOBIAS):
Dear, see to the customers.

TODD:
Psst!

MRS. LOVETT:

Yes, what, love?

Quick, though, the trade is brisk.

TODD:

But it's here!

MRS. LOVETT:

It's where?

TODD:

Coming up the stair!

MRS. LOVETT:
(*Holding up the tray*)
I'll get rid of this lot
As they're still pretty hot   TODD:
And then I'll be there!   It's about to be opened
                                                Or don't you care?

No, I'll *be* there!
I will *be* there!   But we have to prepare!
But they'll never be sold
If I let 'em get cold —
(*During the following, the crate is lowered to the tonsorial parlor*)

MRS. LOVETT (*Without pausing for breath, smiling to a customer*):
Oh, and
Incidentally, dearie,
You know Mrs. Mooney.
Sales've been so dreary —
(*Spots the* BEGGAR WOMAN *again*)
Toby — !
(*To the same customer*)
Poor thing is penniless.
(*Indicating* BEGGAR WOMAN, *to* TOBIAS)
What about that loony?

(To the same customer, as TOBIAS *shoos the* BEGGAR WOMAN
away again)
Lookin' sort of beery —
Oh well, got her comeuppance —
　　　　(Hawklike, to a rising customer)
And that'll be thruppence — and

　　CUSTOMERS:
(Singing with mouths full)　　　　　　MRS. LOVETT:
God, that's good that is de have you　So she should.
Licious ever tasted smell such
Oh my God what more that's pies good!
　　*(*MRS. LOVETT *goes up to the tonsorial parlor, entering as*
　　TODD *opens the crate, revealing an elaborate barber chair)*

　　TODD *and* MRS. LOVETT *(Swooning with admiration)*:
Oooohhhh! Oooohhhh!
　　　　(The empty crate swings away on the crane)

　　　　TODD:
Is that a chair fit for a king,　　　MRS. LOVETT:
A wondrous neat　　　　　　　　It's gorgeous!
And most particular chair?　　　　It's gorgeous!
You tell me where
Is there a seat
Can half compare　　　　　　　It's perfect!
With this particular thing!　　　It's gorgeous!
I have a few
Minor adjustments　　　　　　You make your few
To make —　　　　　　　　　Minor adjustments.
They'll take
A moment.　　　　　　　　　You take your time,
I'll call you . . .　　　　　　I'll go see to the customers.

TODD *(Looking at the chair, as* MRS. LOVETT *goes back to the garden)*:
　　I have another friend . . .

483

TOBIAS:

(*To the customers*)
Is that a pie fit for a king,   MRS. LOVETT:
A wondrous sweet   It's gorgeous!
And most delectable thing?   It's gorgeous!
You see, ma'am, why
There is no meat   .
Pie can compete   It's perfect!
With this delectable   It's gorgeous!
Pie.

CUSTOMERS (*Simultaneously with above*):
Yum!
Yum!
Yum!

TOBIAS *and* MRS. LOVETT:
The crust all velvety and wavy,
That glaze, those crimps . . .
And then, the thick, succulent gravy . . .
One whiff, one glimpse . . .

CUSTOMERS (*Simultaneously with above*):
Yum! Yum!
Yum! Yum!
Yum! Yum!
Yum! Yum!

TODD:
And now to test
This best of barber chairs . . .

MRS. LOVETT:
So rich,   TOBIAS:
So thick   So tender
It makes you sick . . .   That you surrender . . .

CUSTOMERS (*Simultaneously with above*):
Yum!

484

Yum!
Yum! Yum!

TODD:
It's time . . .
It's time . . .
Psst!

MRS. LOVETT (*To the customers*):
Excuse me . . .

TODD (*From above*):
Psst!

MRS. LOVETT (*To* TOBIAS):
Dear, see to the customers.

TODD:
Psst!

MRS. LOVETT (*Moving toward him*):
Yes, what, love?

TODD:
Quick, now!

MRS. LOVETT:
Me heart's aflutter — !

TODD:
When I pound the floor,
It's a signal to show
That I'm ready to go,
When I pound the floor!

MRS. LOVETT:
When you pound the floor,
Yes, you told·me, I know,
You'll be ready to go
When you pound the floor —
Will you trust me?

I just want to be sure.
Will you trust me?
I'll be waiting below

When I'm certain that you're
In place —
For the whistle to blow . . .

TODD:

I'll pound three times.

(*He demonstrates on the frame of the window*)

Three times.

(*He does it again; she nods impatiently*)

And then you —

(*She knocks at the air two times*)

Three times —

(*She knocks heavily and wearily on the wall*)

If you —

(*She knocks again, rolling her eyes skyward*)

Exactly.

CUSTOMERS:

More hot pies!

MRS. LOVETT:

Gawd!

CUSTOMERS:

More hot!

MRS. LOVETT (*Over her shoulder to them*):

Right!

CUSTOMERS:

More pies!

TODD (*Seeing her attention waver*):

Psst!

CUSTOMERS:

More!

MRS. LOVETT:

Wait!

(*She runs into the bakehouse, which we see for the first time. Upstage are the large baking ovens. Downstage is a butcher's-block table, on which stands a bizarre meat-grind-*

ing machine. In the wall is the mouth of a chute leading down from the tonsorial parlor. Upstage is a trap door leading down to an invisible cellar. While music continues under, TODD *takes a stack of books tied together, puts it in the chair, then pounds three times on the floor.* MRS. LOVETT *responds by knocking three times on the mouth of the chute.* TODD *pulls a lever in the arm of the chair. The chair becomes a slide and the books disappear through a trap. Music. The books reappear from the hole in the bakehouse wall and plop on the floor. The chair resumes its normal position.* MRS. LOVETT *knocks three times excitedly on the chute;* TODD *responds by pounding on the floor three times)*

CUSTOMERS:
  More hot pies!
      (MRS. LOVETT *hurries out of the bakehouse)*
  More hot! More pies!
      (TODD *resumes tinkering happily with the chair)*
  More! Hot! Pies!

MRS. LOVETT *and* TOBIAS (*To the customers*):
  Eat them slow and
  Feel the crust, how thin I (she) rolled it!
  Eat them slow, 'cos
  Every one's a prize!
  Eat them slow, 'cos
  That's the lot and now we've sold it!
      (*She hangs up a "Sold Out" sign)*
  Come again tomorrow — !

MRS. LOVETT (*Spotting something along the street*):
  Hold it —

CUSTOMERS:
  More hot pies!

MRS. LOVETT:
  Bless my eyes — !

(For she sees the MAN WITH CAP, *from Act I, approaching the barber sign. He looks up and rings* TODD*'s bell — three times)*

Fresh supplies!

*(*TODD *leans out, sees the man, beckons him up; the man starts up the steps.* TODD *holds his razor. They both freeze.* MRS. LOVETT *takes down the "Sold Out" sign and turns back to the customers)*

MRS. LOVETT:	TOBIAS:
How about it, dearie?	Is that a pie
Be here in a twinkling!	Fit for a king,
Just confirms my theory —	A wondrous sweet
Toby — !	And most delectable
God watches over us.	Thing?
Didn't have an inkling . . .	You see, ma'am, why
Positively eerie . . .	There is no meat pie —

CUSTOMERS *(Simultaneously with above)*:

Yum!
Yum!
Yum!
Yum! Yum!
Yum!
Yum!

MRS. LOVETT *(Spotting the* BEGGAR WOMAN *again)*:

Toby!
Throw the old woman out!

(As TOBIAS *leads the* BEGGAR WOMAN *off again,* MRS. LOVETT *runs back to the pieshop)*

CUSTOMERS *(Starting with their mouths full, gradually swallowing and singing clearly)*:

God, that's good that is de have you
Licious ever tasted smell such
Oh my God what perfect more that's
Pies such flavor

(MRS. LOVETT *relaxes in the pieshop with a mug of ale*)
God, that's good!!!

(*The scene blacks out. The chimes of St. Dunstan's sound
softly. It is dawn.* ANTHONY *is searching the streets of
London for* JOHANNA)

ANTHONY (*Sings*):

I feel you, Johanna,
I feel you.
Do they think that walls can hide you?
Even now I'm at your window.
I am in the dark beside you,
Buried sweetly in your yellow hair,
Johanna . . .

(*As he continues the search, the light comes up on the tonsorial parlor.* TODD *is seated on the outside stairs, smoking
and enjoying the morning. During the following passage,
a customer arrives.* TODD *ushers him into the office and
into the chair, preparing him for a shave. Throughout the
song,* TODD *remains benign, wistful, dream-like. What he
sings is totally detached from the action, as is he. He sings
to the air*)

TODD:

And are you beautiful and pale,
With yellow hair, like her?
I'd want you beautiful and pale,
The way I've dreamed you were,
Johanna . . .

ANTHONY:

Johanna . . .

TODD:

And if you're beautiful, what then,
With yellow hair, like wheat?

I think we shall not meet again —
>(*He slashes the customer's throat*)

My little dove, my sweet
Johanna . . .

ANTHONY:

I'll steal you,
Johanna . . .

TODD:

Goodbye, Johanna.
You're gone, and yet you're mine.
I'm fine, Johanna,
I'm fine!
>(*He pulls the lever and the customer disappears down the chute*)

ANTHONY:

Johanna . . .
>(*Night falls. We see a wisp of smoke rise from the bakehouse chimney, a small trail gradually bellowing out into a great, noxious plume of black. As it thickens, we become aware of* MRS. LOVETT, *in a white nightdress, inside the bakehouse. The oven doors are open and cast a hot light. She is tossing "objects" into the oven. As the music continues under, a figure stumbles into view from the alleyway beside the chimney. It is the* BEGGAR WOMAN, *coughing and spitting and carrying a meager straw pallet, her bed*)

BEGGAR WOMAN (*In a rage, loudly, sings*):

Smoke! Smoke!
Sign of the devil! Sign of the devil!
City on fire!
>(*She tries to interest passers-by but, clearly revolted by her, they move away*)

Witch! Witch!
>(*Spits at the bakehouse*)

Smell it, sir! An evil smell!
Every night at the vespers bell —
Smoke that comes from the mouth of hell —
City on fire!

> (*The smoke trails away as dawn comes up*)

City on fire . . .
Mischief! Mischief!
Mischief . . .

> (*She shuffles off. It is now the next day.* ANTHONY *is searching through another part of London.* TODD *is upstairs and looking pleasantly down at the street. A second customer arrives and is shown into the shop and prepared, as before*)

TODD:

And if I never hear your voice,
My turtledove, my dear,
I still have reason to rejoice:
The way ahead is clear,
Johanna . . .

JOHANNA'S VOICE (*Heard only by* ANTHONY, *she becomes visible behind bars in a section of the madhouse, Fogg's Asylum, in which she is incarcerated*):

I'll marry Anthony Sunday . . .
Anthony Sunday . . .

ANTHONY:

I feel you . . .

TODD:

And in that darkness when I'm blind
With what I can't forget —

ANTHONY:

Johanna . . .

TODD:

It's always morning in my mind,

My little lamb, my pet,
Johanna . . .

JOHANNA'S VOICE:
I knew you'd come for me one day . . .
Come for me . . . one day . . .

TODD: ANTHONY:
You stay, Johanna —   Johanna . . .
(*As they both sing the second syllable of the name,* TODD
*slashes the second customer's throat so that his mouth
opens simultaneously with theirs*)

TODD:
The way I've dreamed you are.
                (*Dusk gathers;* TODD *looks up*)
Oh look, Johanna —
                (*He pulls the lever and the customer disappears*)
A star!

ANTHONY:
Buried sweetly in your yellow hair . . .

TODD (*Tossing the customer's hat down the chute*):
A shooting star!
                (*Night falls again. Smoke rises.* MRS. LOVETT *is again in
                the bakehouse. The* BEGGAR WOMAN *reappears, coughing
                fit to kill*)

BEGGAR WOMAN (*Pointing*):
There! There!
Somebody, somebody look up there!
                (*Passers-by continue to ignore her*)
Didn't I tell you? Smell that air!
City on fire!
Quick, sir! Run and tell!
Warn 'em all of the witch's spell!
There it is, there it is, the unholy smell!

Tell it to the Beadle and the police as well!
Tell 'em! Tell 'em!
Help!!! Fiend!!!
City on fire!!!

(*The smoke thins; dawn rises*)

City on fire . . .
Mischief . . . Mischief . . . Mischief . . .

(*She makes a feeble curse with her fingers at the bakehouse*)

Fiend . . .

(*Shrugs, turns pathetically to a passer-by*)

Alms . . . alms . . .

(*She shuffles off again. During the last section of the song which follows,* TODD *welcomes a third customer. He does not kill this one because a wife and child are waiting outside — the child has entered the room and sits on the chest watching* TODD. *By the end of the song* TODD *is again looking softly up at the sky*)

TODD (*Shaving the customer*):
And though I'll think of you, I guess,
Until the day I die,
I think I miss you less and less
As every day goes by,
Johanna . . .

ANTHONY:
Johanna . . .

JOHANNA'S VOICE:
With you beside me on Sunday,
Married on Sunday . . .

TODD (*Sadly*):
And you'd be beautiful and pale,
And look too much like her.
If only angels could prevail,
We'd be the way we were,
Johanna . . .

ANTHONY:

I feel you . . .
Johanna . . .

JOHANNA'S VOICE:

Married on Sunday . . .
Married on Sunday . . .

TODD (*Cheerfully, looking up at the sky*):

Wake up, Johanna!
Another bright red day!
                    (*Wistful smile*)

We learn, Johanna,
To say
Goodbye . . .
        (*Having completed the shave,* TODD *accepts money from
        the customer, who leaves with his family*)

ANTHONY (*Disappearing into the distance*):

I'll steal you . . .

> (*The scene fades and we see the barred door to Fogg's
> Asylum. From inside we hear a weird and frightening
> sound, the cries and gibbering of the inmates. After a
> moment, rising above the bizarre cacophony, we hear
> JOHANNA's voice from inside a window, singing a snatch
> of "Green Finch and Linnet Bird." A few moments later,
> she breaks off singing and the inmates quieten too as
> ANTHONY, dejected, enters. As he starts across the stage,
> once again we hear JOHANNA's voice, singing*)

ANTHONY (*Incredulous, overjoyed, stops in his tracks*): Johanna!
                (*Calling excitedly up at a window*)
Johanna! Johanna!
                (*A male passer-by enters*)
Oh sir, please tell me. What house is this?

PASSER-BY: That? That's Mr. Fogg's Private Asylum for the
Mentally Deranged.

ANTHONY: A madhouse!

PASSER-BY: I'd keep away from there if I were you.
  (*He exits. Once again we hear* JOHANNA*'s voice*)

ANTHONY: Johanna! Johanna!
  (*He starts beating wildly on the door*)
  Open! Open the door !
  (*The* BEADLE, *falsely amiable as ever, swaggers on, recognizes him*)

BEADLE: Now, now, friend, what's all this hollering and shouting?

ANTHONY: Oh, sir, there has been a monstrous perversion of justice. A young woman, as sane as you or I, has been incarcerated there.

BEADLE: Is that a fact? Now what is this young person's name?

ANTHONY: Johanna.

BEADLE: Johanna. That wouldn't by any chance be Judge Turpin's ward?

ANTHONY: He's the one. He's the devil incarnate who has done this to her.

BEADLE: You watch your tongue. That girl's as mad as the seven seas. I brought her here myself. So — hop it.

ANTHONY: You have no right to order me about.

BEADLE: No right, eh? You just hop it or I'm booking you for disturbing of the peace, assailing an officer —

ANTHONY: Is there no justice in this city? Are the officers of the law as vicious and corrupted as their masters? Johanna! Johanna!
  (*With a little what-can-you-do? shrug, the* BEADLE *blows a whistle. Two policemen hurry on. The* BEADLE *nods to*

ANTHONY. *The policemen jump on him but just before they subdue him, he breaks loose and runs away. The policemen start after him)*

BEADLE (*Calling after them*): After him! Get him! Bash him on the head if need be! That's the sort of scalawag that gets this neighborhood into disrepute.

(*As the scene dims we hear first, in the darkness, the shrieks and moans of the asylum inmates. Then loud and raucous, banishing them, we hear the sound of* MRS. LOVETT *singing, as lights come up on her back parlor)*

MRS. LOVETT (*Sitting at the harmonium*):
I am a lass who alas loves a lad
Who alas has a lass
In Canterbury.
'Tis a row dow diddle dow day,
'Tis a row dow diddle dow dee . . .
(*The parlor has been prettied up with new wallpaper and a second-hand harmonium.* TODD *is sitting on the love seat, cleaning his pipe.* MRS. LOVETT *is using the harmonium as a desk. She has a little cash book and is counting out shillings and pennies in piles)*
Nothing like a nice sit down, is there, dear, after a hard day's work?
(*Piling up coins*)
Four and thruppence . . . four and eleven pence . . .
(*Makes a note in the book and does some adding*)
That makes seven pounds nine shillings and four pence for this week. Not bad — and that don't include wot I had to pay out for my nice cheery wallpaper *or* the harmonium . . .
(*Patting it approvingly*)
And a real bargain it was, dear, it being only partly singed when the chapel burnt down.

(*Glancing at the unresponsive* TODD)
Mr. T., are you listening to me?

TODD: Of course.

MRS. LOVETT: Then what did I say, eh?

TODD (*Back in his reflections*): There *must* be a way to the Judge.

MRS. LOVETT (*Cross*): The bloody old Judge! Always harping on the bloody old Judge!
(*She massages his neck*)
We got a nice respectable business now, money coming in regular and — since we're careful to pick and choose — only strangers and such like wot won't be missed — who's going to catch on?
(*No response; she leans across and pecks him on the lips; sings*)
Ooh, Mr. Todd —
(*Kisses him again*)
I'm so happy —
(*Again*)
I could —
(*Again*)
Eat you up, I really could!
You know what I'd like to
Do, Mr. Todd?
(*Kisses him*)
What I dream —
(*Again*)
If the business stays as good,
Where I'd really like to go —
(*No response*)
In a year or so . . .
(*No response*)
Don't you want to know?

TODD (*Dully*): Of course.

MRS. LOVETT:

Do you really want to know?

TODD (*Feigned enthusiasm*): Yes, yes, I do, I do.
(*Music continues under*)

MRS. LOVETT (*Settling back, after a pause*): I've always had a
dream — ever since I was a skinny little slip of a thing and
my rich Aunt Nettie used to take me to the seaside August
Bank Holiday . . . the pier . . . making little castles in the
sand. I can still feel me toes wiggling around in the briny.
(*She sings*)
By the sea, Mr. Todd,
That's the life I covet;
By the sea, Mr. Todd,
Ooh, I know you'd love it!
You and me, Mr. T.,
We could be alone
In a house wot we'd almost own
Down by the sea . . .

TODD:

Anything you say . . .

MRS. LOVETT:

Wouldn't that be smashing?
(TODD *gives her a pained smile*)
With the sea at our gate,
We'll have kippered herring
Wot have swum to us straight
From the Straits of Bering.
Every night in the kip
When we're through our kippers,
I'll be there slippin' off your slippers
By the sea . . .
With the fishies splashing,

By the sea . . .
Wouldn't that be smashing?
Down by the sea —

TODD:

Anything you say,
Anything you say.

MRS. LOVETT:

I can see us waking,
The breakers breaking,
The seagulls squawking:
Hoo! Hoo!
　　(*She thinks she's being charming;* TODD *looks at her in terror*)
I do me baking,
Then I go walking
With you-hoo . . .

　　　　　　　　　　(*Waves*)
You-hoo . . .

I'll warm me bones
On the esplanade,
Have tea and scones
With me gay young blade,
Then I'll knit a sweater
While you write a letter,

　　　　　　　　　　(*Coyly*)
Unless we got better
To do-hoo . . .

TODD: Anything you say . . .

MRS. LOVETT:

Think how snug it'll be
Underneath our flannel
When it's just you and me
And the English Channel.
In our cozy retreat,

Kept all neat and tidy,
We'll have chums over every Friday
By the sea . . .

TODD:

Anything you say . . .

MRS. LOVETT:

Don't you love the weather
By the sea?
We'll grow old together
By the seaside,
Hoo! Hoo!
By the beautiful sea!

(She speaks, music under)

Oh, I can see us now — in our bathing dresses — you in a
nice rich navy — and me, stripes perhaps.

(Sings)

It'll be so quiet
That who'll come by it
Except a seagull?
Hoo! Hoo!
We shouldn't try it,
Though, till it's legal
For two-hoo!

But a seaside wedding
Could be devised,
Me rumpled bedding
Legitimized.
Me eyelids'll flutter,
I'll turn into butter,
The moment I mutter
"I do-hoo!"

(TODD *gives her a rather appalled glance*)

By the sea, in our nest,
We could share our kippers

With the odd paying guest
From the weekend trippers,
Have a nice sunny suite
For the guest to rest in —
Now and then, you could do the guest in —
By the sea.
Married nice and proper,
By the sea —
Bring along your chopper
To the seaside,

(*Two slashes*)

Hoo! Hoo!
By the beautiful sea!

(*Just before the end of the song, she plays a measure of "Here Comes the Bride" on the harmonium. After the song, she nuzzles up to* TODD *on the love seat*)

Come on, dear. Give us a kiss.

(*Kisses him*)

Ooh, that was lovely. Now, Mr. T., you do love me just a little bit, don't you?

TODD: Of course.

MRS. LOVETT: Then how about it? Of course, there'd have to be a little visit to St. Swithin's to legalize things. But that wouldn't be too painful, would it?

TODD (*Back with his obsession*): I'll make them pay for what they did to Lucy.

MRS. LOVETT (*Almost scolding*): Now, dear, you listen to me. It's high time you forgot all them morbid fancies. Your Lucy's gone, poor thing. It's your Nellie now. Here.

(*She takes a bon-bon from her purse*)

Have a nice bon-bon.

(*She kisses him over the bon-bon, has a thought*)

You know, it's seventeen years this Whitsun since my poor

501

Albert passed on. I don't see why I shouldn't be married in white, do you?

(*From the pieshop, upstage, we hear* ANTHONY *calling*)

ANTHONY (*Off*): Mr. Todd! Mr. Todd!

(*He comes running in*)

I've found her!

TODD (*Jumping up*): You have found Johanna?

ANTHONY: That monster of a Judge has had her locked away in a madhouse!

TODD: Where? Where?

ANTHONY: Where no one can reach her, at Mr. Fogg's Asylum. Oh, Mr. Todd, she's in there with those screeching, gibbering maniacs —

TODD: A madhouse! A madhouse!

(*Swinging around, feverishly excited, buzzing music under*)

Johanna is as good as rescued.

MRS. LOVETT (*Bewildered*): She is?

TODD: Where do you suppose all the wigmakers of London go to obtain their human hair?

MRS. LOVETT: Who knows, dear? The morgue, wouldn't be surprised.

TODD: Bedlam. They get their hair from the lunatics at Bedlam.

ANTHONY: Then you think — ?

TODD: Fogg's Asylum? Why not? For the right amount, they will sell you the hair off any madman's head —

MRS. LOVETT: And the scalp to go with it too, if requested. Excuse me, gentlemen, I'm out!

502

(Exits)

TODD *(Excitedly, to* ANTHONY*)*: We will write a letter to this Mr. Fogg offering the highest price for hair the exact shade of Johanna's — which I trust you know?

ANTHONY: Yellow.

TODD: Not exact enough. I must make you a credible wig-maker — and quickly.
(Sings)
There's tawny and there's golden saffron,
There's flaxen and there's blonde . . .
(Speaks)
Repeat that. Repeat that!

ANTHONY: Yes, Mr. Todd.

TODD: Well?

ANTHONY:

There's tawny and there's golden saffron,
There's flaxen and there's blonde . . .

TODD: Good.
(Sings)
There's coarse and fine,
There's straight and curly,   ANTHONY:
There's gray, there's white,   There's coarse and fine,
There's ash, there's pearly,   There's straight and curly,
There's corn-yellow   There's gray, there's white,
Buff and ochre and   There's ash, there's pearly,
Straw and apricot . . .   There's corn-yellow . . .

(They exit. As the lights dim, a quintet from the company appears and sings)

QUINTET *(Variously)*:
Sweeney'd waited too long before —

503

"Ah, but never again," he swore.
Fortune arrived. "Sweeney!" it sang.
Sweeney was ready, and Sweeney sprang.
Sweeney's problems went up in smoke,
All resolved with a single stroke.
Sweeney was sharp, Sweeney was burning,
Sweeney began the engines turning.
Sweeney's problems went up in smoke,
All resolved and completely solved
With a single stroke
By Sweeney!
Sweeney
Didn't wait,
Not Sweeney!
Set the bait,
Did Sweeney! Sweeney! Sweeney!
 (*During this,* TODD *appears on the staircase, accompanied
 by a strange figure; they enter the tonsorial parlor. We soon
 realize the figure is* ANTHONY, *disguised as as wigmaker*)

ANTHONY:
(*Finishing his catechism*)
With finer textures,
Ash looks fairer,   TODD:
Which makes it rare,   Good.
But flaxen's rarer —

                                No! No!
Yes, yes, I know —   The flaxen's cheaper . . .
Cheaper, not rarer . . .
            (*Music continues under*)

TODD: Here's money.
            (*Hands him purse*)
    And here's the pistol.
            (*Hands him a gun*)
    For kill if you must. Kill.

ANTHONY: I'll kill a dozen jailers if need be to set her free.

TODD: Then off with you, off. But, Anthony, listen to me once again. When you have rescued her, bring her back here. I shall guard her while you hire the chaise to Plymouth.

ANTHONY: We'll be with you before the evening's out,
(*Clasping both* TODD*'s hands*)
Mr. Todd. Oh, thank you — friend.
(*He hurries off.* TODD *goes to a little writing table, picks up a quill pen and starts to write. The quintet sings what he writes*)

QUINTET (*Variously, as* TODD *writes*):
Most Honorable Judge Turpin —
(TODD *pauses reflectively*)
Most Honorable —
(TODD *snorts derisively*)
I venture thus to write you this —
(*He resumes writing*)
I venture thus to write you this —
(*Thinks, choosing the word*)
Urgent note to warn you that the hot-blooded —
(*Thinks*)
Young —
(*Grunts with satisfaction*)
Sailor has abducted your ward Johanna —
(*Stares off sadly*)
Johanna — Johanna —
(*Resumes writing*)
From the institution where you —
(*Thinks*)
So wisely confined her but,
Hoping to earn your favor,
I have persuaded the boy to lodge her here tonight
At my tonsorial parlor —
(*Dips the pen*)
In Fleet Street.
If you want her again in your arms,

505

Hurry
After the night falls.
(*He starts to sign, then adds another phrase with a smile*)
She will be waiting.
(*Reads it over*)
Waiting . . .
(*Dips pen again, writing carefully*)
Your obedient humble servant,
Sweeney
(*A flourish of the pen*)
Todd.
(*Music continues under as* TODD *hurries across the stage to* JUDGE TURPIN'*s house, knocks on the door, which opens, and hands in the letter*)

TODD: Give this to Judge Turpin. It's urgent.

(*As he disappears, lights come up on the eating garden. It is early evening. The garden is deserted.* MRS. LOVETT *is sitting on the steps knitting a half-finished muffler. The bells of St. Dunstan's sound. After a beat,* TOBIAS *emerges from the shop with a "Sold Out" sign, puts it on the shop door, and goes to* MRS. LOVETT)

TOBIAS: I put the sold-out sign up, ma'am.

MRS. LOVETT: That's my boy.
(*Holding up the knitting*)
Look, dear! A lovely muffler and guess who it's for.

TOBIAS: Coo, ma'am. For me?

MRS. LOVETT: Wouldn't you like to know!

TOBIAS: Oh, you're so good to me, ma'am. Sometimes, when I think what it was like with Signor Pirelli — it seems like the Good Lord sent you for me.

MRS. LOVETT: It's just my warm heart, dear. Room enough there for all God's creatures.

506

TOBIAS (*Coming closer, hovering, very earnest*): You know, ma'am, there's nothing I wouldn't do for you. If there was a monster or an ogre or anything bad like that wot was after you, I'd rip it apart with my bare fists, I would.

MRS. LOVETT: What a sweet child it is.

TOBIAS: Or even if it was just a man . . .

MRS. LOVETT (*Somewhat uneasy*): A man, dear?

TOBIAS (*Exaggeratedly conspiratorial*): A man wot was bad and wot might be luring you all unbeknownst into his evil deeds, like.

MRS. LOVETT (*Even more wary*): What is this? What are you talking about?

TOBIAS (*Sings*):
Nothing's gonna harm you,
Not while I'm around.

MRS. LOVETT: Of course not, dear, and why should it?

TOBIAS:
Nothing's gonna harm you,
No, sir,
Not while I'm around.

MRS. LOVETT: What do you mean, "a man"?

TOBIAS:
Demons are prowling
Everywhere
Nowadays.

MRS. LOVETT (*Somewhat relieved, patting his head*): And so they are, dear.

TOBIAS:
I'll send 'em howling,

507

I don't care —
I got ways.

MRS. LOVETT: Of course you do . . . What a sweet, affection-
ate child it is.

TOBIAS:
No one's gonna hurt you,
No one's gonna dare.

MRS. LOVETT: I know what Toby deserves . . .

TOBIAS:
Others can desert you —
Not to worry —
Whistle, I'll be there.

MRS. LOVETT: Here, have a nice bon-bon.
(*Starts to reach for her purse, but* TOBIAS *stays her hand in adoration*)

TOBIAS:
Demons'll charm you
With a smile
For a while,
But in time
Nothing can harm you,
Not while I'm around.
(*Music continues*)

MRS. LOVETT: What is this foolishness? What're you talking
about?

TOBIAS: Little things wot I've been thinking and wondering
about . . . It's him, you see — Mr. Todd. Oh, I know you
fancy him, but men ain't like women, they ain't wot you
can trust, as I've lived and learned.
(*She looks at him uneasily*)
Not to worry, not to worry,

I may not be smart but I ain't dumb.
I can do it,
Put me to it,
Show me something I can overcome.
Not to worry, mum.

Being close and being clever
Ain't like being true.
I don't need to, I won't never
Hide a thing from you,
Like some.

(*Music continues under*)

MRS. LOVETT: Now Toby dear, haven't we had enough foolish chatter? Let's just sit nice and quiet for a bit. Here.
(*She pulls out the chatelaine purse, which is now immediately recognizable to the audience as* PIRELLI*'s money purse, and starts to fumble in it for a bon-bon*)

TOBIAS (*Suddenly excited, pointing*): That! That's Signor Pirelli's purse!

(MRS. LOVETT, *realizing her slip, quickly hides it*)

MRS. LOVETT (*Stalling for time*): What's that? What was that, dear?

TOBIAS: That proves it! What I've been thinking. That's his purse.

MRS. LOVETT (*Concealing what is now almost panic*): Silly boy! It's just a silly little something Mr. T. gave me for my birthday.

TOBIAS: Mr. Todd gave it to you! And how did he get it? How did he get it?

MRS. LOVETT: Bought it, dear. In the pawnshop, dear.
(*To distract him, she lifts the unfinished muffler on its needles*)

509

Come on now.
(*Sings*)

Nothing's gonna harm you,
Not while I'm around!
Nothing's gonna harm you, Toby,
Not while I'm around.

TOBIAS: You don't understand.
(*Sings*)

Two quid was in it,
Two or three —
(*Speaks, music continuing*)
The guvnor giving up his purse — with two quid?
(*Sings*)

Not for a minute!
Don't you see?
(*Speaks, music under*)
It was in Mr. Todd's parlor that the guvnor disappeared.

MRS. LOVETT (*With a weak laugh*): Boys and their fancies! What will we think of next! Here, dear. Sit here by your Aunt Nellie like a good boy and look at your lovely muffler. How warm it's going to keep you when the days draw in. And it's so becoming on you.

TOBIAS (*Sings*):
Demons'll charm you
With a smile
For a while,
But in time
Nothing's gonna harm you,
Not while I'm around!

MRS. LOVETT: You know, dear, it's the strangest thing you coming to chat with me right now of all moments because as I was sitting here with my needles, I was thinking: "What a good boy Toby is! So hard working, so obedient." And I thought . . . know how you've always fancied coming into the bakehouse with me to help bake the pies?

TOBIAS (*For the first time distracted*): Oh yes, ma'am. Indeed, ma'am. Yes.

MRS. LOVETT: Well, how about it?

TOBIAS: You mean it? I can help make 'em and bake 'em?
(MRS. LOVETT *kisses him again and, rising, starts drawing him back toward the pieshop*)

MRS. LOVETT: No time like the present, is there?
(*She leads him through the pieshop into the bakehouse*)

TOBIAS (*Looking around*): Coo, quite a stink, ain't there?

MRS. LOVETT (*Indicating the trap door*): Them steps go down to the old cellars and the whiffs come up, love. God knows what's down there — so moldy and dark. And there's always a couple of rats gone home to Jesus.
(*She leads him across to the ovens*)
Now the bake ovens is here.
(*She opens the oven doors. A red glow illuminates the stage*)

TOBIAS: They're big enough, ain't they?

MRS. LOVETT: Hardly big enough to bake all the pies we sell. Ten dozen at a time. Always be sure to close the doors properly, like this.
(*Closes doors. Draws him to the butcher's-block table*)
Now here's the grinder.
(*She turns its handle, indicating how it operates*)
You see, you pop meat in and you grind it and it comes out here.
(*Indicates the mouth of the grinder*)
And you know the secret that makes the pies so sweet and tender? Three times. You must put the meat through the grinder three times.

TOBIAS: Three times, eh?

MRS. LOVETT: That's my boy. Smoothly, smoothly. And as soon as a new batch of meat comes in, we'll put you to work.

(*She starts for the door back into the pieshop*)

TOBIAS (*Blissful*): Me making pies all on me own! Coo!
(*Noticing her leaving*)
Where are you going, ma'am?

MRS. LOVETT: Back in a moment, dear.
(*At the door she turns, blows him a kiss and then goes into the pieshop, slamming the door behind her and locking it, putting the key in her pocket.* TOBIAS, *too fascinated to realize he has been locked in, starts happily turning the handle of the grinder*)

TOBIAS: Smoothly does it, smoothly, smoothly . . .
(*As he grinds and* MRS. LOVETT *appears at the foot of the stairs to the tonsorial parlor, unseen by her the* BEADLE *enters the back parlor*)

BEADLE: Mrs. Lovett! Mrs. Lovett!

MRS. LOVETT (*Climbing the stairs, looking for* TODD): Mr. Todd! Mr. Todd!

BEADLE (*Notices the harmonium, sits down, and sings from a song book, accompanying himself*):
Sweet Polly Plunkett lay in the grass,
Turned her eyes heavenward, sighing,
"I am a lass who alas loves a lad
Who alas has a lass in Canterbury.
'Tis a row dow diddle dow day,
'Tis a row dow diddle dow dee . . ."

MRS. LOVETT (*Enters, clapping*): Oh, Beadle Bamford, I didn't know you were a music lover, too.

BEADLE (*Not rising*): Good afternoon, Mrs. Lovett. Fine instrument you've acquired.

MRS. LOVETT: Oh yes, it's my pride and joy.

BEADLE (*Sings, as she watches him uneasily*):
Sweet Polly Plunkett saw her life pass,
Flew down the city road, crying,
"I am a lass who alas loves a lad
Who alas has a lass loves another lad
Who once I had
In Canterbury.
'Tis a row dow diddle dow day,
'Tis a row dow diddle dow dee . . . "
> (*He speaks, leafing through the pages*)
Well, ma'am, I hope you have a few moments, for I'm here today on official business.

MRS. LOVETT: Official?

BEADLE: That's it, ma'am. You see, there's been complaints —

MRS. LOVETT: Complaints?

BEADLE: About the stink from your chimney. They say at night it's something foul. Health regulations being my duty, I'm afraid I'll have to ask you to let me take a look.

MRS. LOVETT (*Hiding extreme anxiety*): At the bakehouse?

BEADLE: That's right, ma'am.

MRS. LOVETT (*Improvising wildly*): But, it's locked and . . . and I don't have the key. It's Mr. Todd upstairs — he's got the key and he's not here right now.

BEADLE: When will he be back?

MRS. LOVETT: Couldn't say, I'm sure.

BEADLE (*Finds a particular song*): Ah, one of mother's favorites . . .
> (*Sings*)
If one bell rings in the Tower of Bray,

Ding dong, your true love will stay.
Ding dong, one bell today
In the Tower of Bray . . .
Ding dong!

TOBIAS (*Joining in from the bakehouse*):
One bell today in the Tower of Bray . . .
Ding dong!

BEADLE (*Stops playing*): What's that?

MRS. LOVETT: Oh, just my boy — the lad that helps me with the pies.

BEADLE: But surely he's in the bakehouse, isn't he?

MRS. LOVETT (*Almost beside herself*): Oh yes, yes, of course. But you see . . . he's — well, simple in the head. Last week he run off and we found him two days later down by the embankment half-starved, poor thing. So ever since then, we locks him in for his own security.

BEADLE: Then we'll have to wait for Mr. Todd, won't we?
(*Sings*)
But if two bells ring in the Tower of Bray,
Ding dong, ding dong, your true love will stray.
Ding dong —
(*Speaks*)
Since you're a fellow music lover, ma'am, why don't you raise your voice along with mine?

MRS. LOVETT: All right.

BEADLE (*Sings*):
If three bells ring in the Tower of Bray . . .
Ding dong!

MRS. LOVETT (*Another "inspiration"*): Oh yes, of course! Mr. Todd's gone down to Wapping. Won't be back for hours. And he'll be ever so sorry to miss you. Why, just the other day he was saying, "If only the Beadle would grace my tonsorial parlor I'd give him a most stylish haircut, the daintiest shave — all for nothing." So why don't you drop in some other time and take advantage of his offer?

BEADLE: Well, that's real friendly of him.
>> (*Immovable, he starts to sing another verse*)
If four bells ring in the Tower of —

MRS. LOVETT: Just how many bells are there?

BEADLE: Twelve.
>> (*Resumes singing*)
Ding dong!

MRS. LOVETT (*Resigned*):
Ding dong!

TOBIAS:
Ding dong!

BEADLE:
Ding dong!

BEADLE, MRS. LOVETT *and* TOBIAS:
Then lovers must pray! . . .
>> (*During this,* TODD *enters, reacts on seeing the* BEADLE)

MRS. LOVETT (*With a huge smile of relief*): Back already! Look who's here, Mr. T., on some foolish complaint about the bakehouse or something. He wants the key and I told him you had it. But . . .
>> (*Coquettishly, to the* BEADLE)
. . . there's no hurry, is there, sir? Why don't you run upstairs with Mr. Todd and let him fix you up nice and pretty — there'll be plenty of time for the bakehouse later.

BEADLE (*Considering*): Well . . . tell me, Mr. Todd, do you pomade the hair? I dearly love a pomaded head.

MRS. LOVETT: Pomade? Of course! And a nice facial rub with bay rum too. All for free!

BEADLE (*To* TODD): Well, sir, I take that very kindly.

TODD (*Bowing to the* BEADLE): I am, sir, entirely at your — disposal.
> (*The two men exit.* MRS. LOVETT *hesitates, then speaks*)

MRS. LOVETT: Let's hope he can do it quietly. But just to be on the safe side, I'll provide a little musical send-off.
> (*She goes to the harmonium, sits down on the stool and starts playing and singing a loud verse of "Polly Plunkett" which continues distantly during the following. In the bakehouse,* TOBIAS *stands by the grinding machine eating a pie. He feels something on his tongue, puts a finger in his mouth and pulls the something out, holding it up for inspection*)

TOBIAS: An 'air! Black as a rook. Now that ain't Mrs. Lovett's 'air. Oh, well, some old black cow probably.
> (*He continues to eat. He bites on something else, takes it out of his mouth, looks at it*)

Coo, bit of fingernail! Clumsy. Ugh!
> (*He drops the pie. Bored, he starts around the room, inspecting. He peers at an unidentifiable hole in the wall — the chute. He is baffled by it. As he does so, we hear a strange, shambling, shuffling sound as if a heavy object is falling inside the wall.* TOBIAS *spins around just as the bloody body of the* BEADLE *comes trundling out of the mouth of the chute.* TOBIAS *screams*)

No! Oh no!
> (*He dashes to the door, tries the handle; it is locked. He starts beating on it*)

Mrs. Lovett! Mrs. Lovett! Let me out! Let me out!
> (*Wildly he tries to break down the door. It is too solid for him. Whimpering, he stands paralyzed. Then he sees the open trap door leading to the cellar steps. He runs and dis-*

appears down them. In the parlor, MRS. LOVETT *continues to sing and play. After a suitable period, she stops*)

MRS. LOVETT:
. . . With a row dow diddle dow day.
(*As she gets up from the harmonium,* TODD *hurries in*)

TODD: It's done.

MRS. LOVETT: Not yet it isn't! The boy, he's guessed.

TODD: Guessed what?

MRS. LOVETT: About Pirelli. Since you weren't here, I locked him in the bakehouse. He's been yelling to wake the dead. We've got to look after him.

TODD (*Fiercely*): But the Judge is coming. I've arranged it.

MRS. LOVETT: You — worrying about the bloody Judge at a time like this!
(*Grabbing his arm and pulling him toward the door*)
Come on.

(*The scene blacks out. Members of the company appear and sing*)

COMPANY (*Variously*):
The engine roared, the motor hissed,
And who could see how the road would twist?
In Sweeney's ledger the entries matched:
A Beadle arrived, and a Beadle dispatched
To satisfy the hungry god
Of Sweeney Todd,

ALL:
The Demon Barber of Fleet . . .
Sweeney!
. . . Street.
Sweeney! Sweeney!

Sweeney! Sweeney! Sweeney!
Sweeney!
Sweeeeeneeeeey!

> (*And as they sing the name, they transform themselves into
> the inmates of Fogg's Asylum, which is now revealed: a
> huge stone wall and a heavy iron door. Behind the wall,
> the ragged inmates are crawling, lolling, capering, gig-
> gling, shrieking. In the center of them sits* JOHANNA, *her
> long yellow hair tumbling about her*)

INMATES (*Intoning, chattering, screaming*):
Sweeeeeeeeeeeeeeneeeeeeeeeeeeey . . .
Sweeneysweeneysweeneysweeney . . .

> (*These moans and humming noises continue under the
> following, occasionally interrupted by little mad birdlike
> outbursts of song.* MR. FOGG *enters with* ANTHONY *in his
> wigmaker's disguise. He carries a huge pair of scissors.
> Behind them is the asylum wall*)

FOGG: Just this way, sir.

ANTHONY: You do me honor, Mr. Fogg.

FOGG: I agree it would be to our mutual interest to come to
some arrangement in regard to my poor children's hair.

ANTHONY: Your — children?

FOGG: We are one happy family here, sir, and all my patients
are my children, to be corrected when they're naughty,
and rewarded with a sweetie when they're good. But to
our business.

> (*As they enter the inside of the asylum, lights come up
> behind the scrim wall revealing the shadows of the inmates.*
> MR. FOGG, *as in a shadow play, grabs one female by the
> hair, pulling her head up for* ANTHONY's *inspection*)

Here is a charming yellow, a little dull in tone perhaps,
but you can soon restore its natural gleam.

(*He drops the head, moves to a man and grabs his head up by the hair*)

Now here! A fine texture for a man and, as you must know, sir, there is always a discount on the hair of a male.

(ANTHONY *has been looking around and has spotted* JOHANNA)

ANTHONY: This one here has hair the shade I seek.

FOGG: Poor child. She needs so much correction. She sings all day and night and leaves the other inmates sleepless.

(*He goes to* JOHANNA *and tugs her, indignantly struggling, across the floor toward* ANTHONY, *by the hair*)

Come, child. Smile for the gentleman and you shall have a sweetie.

(*He brandishes the scissors*)

Now, where shall I cut?

JOHANNA (*Sees* ANTHONY): Anthony!

ANTHONY: Johanna!

FOGG: What is this? What is this?

ANTHONY (*Drawing his pistol*): Unhand her!

FOGG: Why you — !

(*Clutching the scissors, he moves resolutely toward* ANTHONY. ANTHONY *backs away a few steps, but* FOGG *keeps coming*)

ANTHONY: Stop, Mr. Fogg, or I'll fire.

FOGG: Fire, and I will stop.

ANTHONY: I cannot shoot.

(*Losing his nerve,* ANTHONY *drops the gun which* JOHANNA *catches in mid-air.* FOGG *moves toward* ANTHONY, *raising the scissors.* JOHANNA, *holding the gun with both hands, shoots* FOGG, *who falls. She drops the gun and together she and* ANTHONY *run out. Compelled by the ener-*

gy released by FOGG*'s death, the lunatics tear down the
wall and rush out of the asylum, spilling with euphoric
excitement onto the street*)

LUNATICS (*In three contrapuntal groups*):
City on fire!
Rats in the grass
And the lunatics yelling in the streets!
It's the end of the world! Yes!
City on fire!
Hunchbacks dancing!
Stirrings in the ground
And the whirring of giant wings!
Watch out!
Look!
Blotting out the moonlight,
Thick black rain falling on the
City on fire!
City on fire!
City on fire!
(*During this, police whistles sound.* ANTHONY *and* JOHAN-
NA *are still visible hurrying away,* ANTHONY *systematically
disposing of the wigmaker's costume, tossing the hat off
here, the cloak off there, etc. Throughout,* JOHANNA *is excit-
ed and chatty. At one point,* ANTHONY *stops briefly to
reconnoiter nervously*)

JOHANNA:
Will we be married on Sunday?
That's what you promised,
Married on Sunday!
                    (*Pensively*)
That was last August . . .
              (*He looks at her unbelievingly*)
Kiss me!
(*He drags her off as the lunatics reappear, this time in two
groups*)

520

LUNATICS:
    City on fire!
    Rats in the streets
    And the lunatics yelling at the moon!
    It's the end of the world! Yes!
    City on fire!
    Hunchbacks kissing!
    Stirrings in the graves
    And the screaming of giant winds!
    Watch out! Look!
    Crawling on the chimneys,
    Great black crows screeching at the
    City on fire!
    City on fire!
    City on fire!

(As they run off, lights come up on the bakehouse. TODD, holding a lantern, and MRS. LOVETT enter, looking around for TOBIAS)

MRS. LOVETT (Sings):
    Toby!
    Where are you, love?

TODD:
    Toby!
    Where are you, lad?

MRS. LOVETT:
    Nothing's gonna harm you . . .

TODD:
    Toby!

MRS. LOVETT:
    Not while I'm around . . .

TODD (Opening trap door, peering down):
    Toby!

MRS. LOVETT:
   Where are you hiding?
   Nothing's gonna harm you,
   Darling . . .

TODD:
   Nothing to be afraid of, boy . . .
               (*Closes the trap door, peers into the darkness*)

MRS. LOVETT:
   Not while I'm around.

TODD:
   Toby . . .

MRS. LOVETT (*She and* TODD *move upstage, where their voices
   echo*):
   Demons are prowling everywhere
   Nowadays . . .

TODD:
   Toby . . .
               (*They wander off as the lunatics run on*)

LUNATICS:
   City on fire!
   Rats in the streets
   And the lunatics yelling at the moon!
   It's the end of the world! Yes!
         (*Lights go down on them and come up on the* BEGGAR
         WOMAN, *peering off through the darkness as if at the
         pieshop*)

BEGGAR WOMAN:
   Beadle! . . . Beadle! . . .
   No good hiding, I saw you!
   Are you in there still,
   Beadle? . . . Beadle? . . .
   Get her, but watch it!

She's a wicked one, she'll deceive you
With her fancy gowns
And her fancy airs
And her —
                    (*Suddenly shrieking*)
Mischief! Mischief!
Devil's work!
                    (*Quietly calling again*)
Where are you, Beadle?
Beadle . . .

(*As she shuffles off toward the pieshop, lights dim on her and come up on the lunatics*)

LUNATICS:
City on fire!
Rats in the streets
And the lunatics yelling at the moon!
It's the end of the world! Good!
City on fire!
Hunchbacks kissing!
Stirrings in the graves
And the screaming of giant winds!
Watch out! Look!
Crawling on the chimneys,
Great black crows screeching at the
City on fire! . . .

(*Light comes up on the tonsorial parlor. It is empty for a moment, then* ANTHONY *and* JOHANNA, *who is now dressed in a sailor's uniform, enter; music under*)

ANTHONY: Mr. Todd?

JOHANNA: No one here. Where is this Mr. Todd?

ANTHONY: No matter. He'll be back in a moment, for I trust him as I trust my right arm. Wait for him here — I'll return with the coach in less than half an hour.

JOHANNA: But they are after us still. What if they trace us here? Oh, Anthony, please let me come with you.

ANTHONY: No, my darling, there is no safety for you on the street.

JOHANNA: But dressed in these sailor's clothes, who's to know it is I?

ANTHONY: No, the risk is too great.
>   (*As she turns away pouting, he sings*)
Ah, miss,
Look at me, look at me, miss, oh,
Look at me please, oh,
Favor me, favor me with your glance.
Ah, miss,
Soon we'll be, soon we'll be gone
And sailing the seas
And happily, happily wed
In France.
>   (*She looks at him and smiles*)

BOTH:
And we'll sail the world
And see its wonders
From the pearls of Spain
To the rubies of Tibet —

JOHANNA:	ANTHONY:
And then home.	And then come home to London.
Some day.	Some day.

>   (*They kiss*)

ANTHONY (*Starting out*): And I'll be back before those lips have time to lose that smile.
>   (*He rushes off. Music continues under. JOHANNA paces. She sees the barber chair, starts to move toward it. During*

this, the BEGGAR WOMAN *can be seen below approaching
the pieshop. A factory whistle blows.* JOHANNA *gasps, startled, then goes to the chair. She sits in it. Her hand moves
to inspect the lever, but before she touches it, the* BEGGAR
WOMAN *approaches, calling*)

BEGGAR WOMAN:
  Beadle! . . .
  Beadle!
  Where are you?
  Beadle, dear!
  Beadle!

JOHANNA (*Simultaneously, jumping up*): Someone calling the
  Beadle! I knew it!
    (JOHANNA *looks wildly around, sees the chest, runs to it
    and clambers in, closing the lid just as the* BEGGAR WOMAN
    comes shuffling on)

BEGGAR WOMAN (*Vacantly*):
  Beadle deedle deedle deedle deedle dumpling,
  Beadle dumpling, Be-deedle dumpling . . .
    (*Whimpers, growls lasciviously, dimly surveys the room.
    She sees the chest, feels it; screams and wails. She mimes
    opening a window, then clutches an imaginary baby to
    her; pats and rocks it, cradles it and smiles. Lullaby music
    begins underneath*)
  And why should you weep then, my jo, my jing?
  Ohh . . .
  Your father's at tea with the Swedish king.
  He'll bring you the moon on a silver string.
  Ohh . . .
  Ohh . . .

  Quickly to sleep then, my jo, my jing,
  He'll bring you a shoe and a wedding ring.
  Sing here again, home again,
  Come again spring.

He'll be coming soon now
To kiss you, my jo, my jing,
Bringing you the moon
And a shoe and a wedding ring.
He'll be coming here again,
Home again . . .
> (*Without warning, leaping in like a thunderbolt,* TODD *appears, the razor in his hand; music continues*)

TODD: You! What are you doing here?

BEGGAR WOMAN (*Clutching his arm*): Ah, evil is here, sir. The stink of evil — from below — from her!
> (*Calling*)

Beadle dear, Beadle!

TODD (*Looking anxiously out the window for the* JUDGE): Out of here, woman.

BEGGAR WOMAN (*Still clutching his arm*): She's the Devil's wife! Oh, beware her, sir. Beware of her. She with no pity . . . in her heart.

TODD: Out, I say!

BEGGAR WOMAN (*Peering dimly at him, sings*):
Hey, don't I know you, mister?
> (*On the street the* JUDGE *approaches the tonsorial parlor*)

TODD (*Seeing him*): The Judge. I have no time.
> (*He turns on the* BEGGAR WOMAN, *slits her throat, puts her in the chair and releases her down the chute. The* JUDGE *enters the room. Music continues under*)

JUDGE: Where is she? Where is the girl?

TODD: Below, your Honor. In the care of my neighbor, Mrs. Lovett. Thank heavens the sailor did not molest her. Thank heavens too, she has seen the error of her ways.

JUDGE: She has?

TODD: Oh yes, your lesson was well learned, sir. She speaks only of you, longing for forgiveness.

JUDGE: And she shall have it. She'll be here soon, you say?

TODD (*Sings*):
I think I hear her now.

JUDGE: Oh, excellent, my friend!

TODD:
Is that her dainty footstep on the stair?

JUDGE (*Listening*): I hear nothing.

TODD:
Yes, isn't that her shadow on the wall?

JUDGE: Where?

TODD (*Points*): There!
              (*The* JUDGE *looks, getting excited*)
Primping,
Making herself even prettier than usual —

JUDGE (*Sings*):
Even prettier . . .

TODD:
If possible.

JUDGE (*Blissful*):
Ohhhhhhh,
Pretty women!

TODD:
Pretty women, yes . . .

JUDGE (*Straightening his coat, patting his hair*): Quickly, sir, a splash of bay rum!

TODD (*Indicating the chair*): Sit, sir, sit.

JUDGE (*Settling into the chair, in lecherous rapture*):
Johanna, Johanna . . .
> (TODD *gets a towel, puts it carefully around him, moves to
> pick up a bottle of bay rum*)

TODD:
Pretty women . . .

JUDGE: Hurry, man!

TODD:
Pretty women
Are a wonder . . .

JUDGE: You're in a merry mood again today, barber.

TODD (*Joyfully*):
Pretty women!

JUDGE:
What we do for	TODD:
Pretty women!	Pretty women!

> (*During the following,* TODD *smooths bay rum on the*
> JUDGE's *face, reaching behind him for a razor*)

Blowing out their candles	Blowing out their candles
Or combing out their hair —	Or combing out their hair,
Then they leave —	
Even when they leave you	Even when they leave,
And vanish, they somehow	They still
Can still remain	Are there,
There with you there . . .	They're there . . .

> (*Music continues under*)

JUDGE: How seldom it is one meets a fellow spirit!

TODD (*Smiling down*): With fellow tastes — in women, at
least.

JUDGE: What? What's that?

TODD: The years no doubt have changed me, sir. But then, I

528

suppose, the face of a barber — the face of a prisoner in the dock — is not particularly memorable.

JUDGE (*With horrified realization*): Benjamin Barker!
(*The factory whistle blows; the* JUDGE *in terror tries to jump up but* TODD *slashes his throat, then pulls the lever and sends the body tumbling out of sight and down the chute. Music continues. For a long moment,* TODD *stands crouched forward by the chair, exhaling deeply. Then slowly he drops to his knees and even more slowly holds up the razor, gazing at it. He sings*)

TODD:
Rest now, my friend,
Rest now forever.
Sleep now the untroubled
Sleep of the angels . . .
          (*Suddenly remembering, speaks*)
The boy.
(*He starts down the stairs. He stops midway, remembering his razor*)
My razor!
(*He starts back up the steps just as* JOHANNA *has climbed out of the chest. She stands frozen*)
You! What are you doing here? Speak!

JOHANNA (*Deepening her voice*): Oh, dear. Er — excuse me, sir. I saw the barber's sign. So thinking to ask for a shave, I —

TODD: When? When did you come in?

JOHANNA: Oh, sir, I beg of you. Whatever I have seen, no man shall ever know. I swear it. Oh, sir, please, sir . . .

TODD: A shave, eh?
          (*He turns chair toward her*)
At your service.

JOHANNA: But, sir . . .

TODD: Whatever you may have seen, your cheeks are still as much in need of the razor as before. Sit, sir. Sit.

(TODD *sits* JOHANNA *in the chair. As he goes for the razor, simultaneously the factory whistle blows and* MRS. LOVETT *is heard screaming "Die! Die!" from the bakehouse below.* JOHANNA *jumps up and runs out,* TODD *lunges after her, misses her. She runs away.* TODD *pauses; another scream from the bakehouse sends him running down the stairs, and as he disappears into the pieshop, the company appears*)

COMPANY (*Sings*):
Lift your razor high, Sweeney!
Hear it singing, "Yes!"
Sink it in the rosy skin
Of righteousness!

(*Light comes up on the bakehouse.* MRS. LOVETT *is standing in horror by the mouth of the chute from which the* JUDGE, *still alive, clutches her skirt.* MRS. LOVETT *tries to tug the skirt away from the vise-like grip*)

MRS. LOVETT: Die! Die! God in heaven — die!

(*The* JUDGE'*s fingers relax their grip; he is dead. Panting,* MRS. LOVETT *backs away from him and for the first time notices the body of the* BEGGAR WOMAN. *She pauses*)

You! Can it be? How all the demons of Hell come to torment me!

(*Looks hastily over her shoulder*)

Quick! To the oven.

(*She starts to drag the* BEGGAR WOMAN *to the oven as* TODD *enters, runs to her*)

TODD: Why did you scream? Does the Judge still live?

MRS. LOVETT: He was clutching, holding on to my skirt, but now — he's finished.

(*Continues dragging* BEGGAR WOMAN *to oven*)

TODD: Leave them to me. Open the doors.
>	(*He starts to shove her toward the oven*)

MRS. LOVETT (*Clutching the* BEGGAR WOMAN*'s wrists*): No! Don't touch her!

TODD (*Pushing her to the oven doors and leaning down to pick up the* BEGGAR WOMAN): What is the matter with you? It's only some meddling old beggar —
>	(MRS. LOVETT *opens the oven doors and the light from the fire illuminates the* BEGGAR WOMAN*'s face. A chord of music as* TODD *realizes who she is*)
>	Oh no, Oh God . . . "Don't I know you?" she said . . .
>	(*Looks up*)
>	You knew she lived. From the first moment that I walked into your shop you knew my Lucy lived!

MRS. LOVETT: I was only thinking of you!

TODD (*Looking down again, sings*):
>	Lucy . . .

MRS. LOVETT: Your Lucy! A crazy hag picking bones and rotten spuds out of alley ashcans! Would you have wanted to know that was all that was left of her?

TODD (*Slowly looking up*): You lied to me.

MRS. LOVETT (*Sings*):
>	No, no, not lied at all.
>	No, I never lied.

TODD (*To the* BEGGAR WOMAN):
>	Lucy . . .

MRS. LOVETT:
>	Said she took the poison — she did —
>	Never said that she died —
>	Poor thing,
>	She lived —

TODD:

I've come home again . . .

MRS. LOVETT:

But it left her weak in the head,
All she did for months was just lie there in bed —

TODD:

Lucy . . .

MRS. LOVETT:

Should've been in hospital,
Wound up in Bedlam instead,
Poor thing!

TODD:

Oh, my God . . .

MRS. LOVETT:

Better you should think she was dead.
Yes, I lied 'cos I love you!

TODD:

Lucy . . .

MRS. LOVETT:

I'd be twice the wife she was!
I love you!

TODD:

What have I done? . . .

MRS. LOVETT:

Could that thing have cared for you
Like me?

(TODD *rises, soft and smiling;* MRS LOVETT *takes a step
away in panic. Waltz music starts*)

TODD:

Mrs. Lovett,

You're a bloody wonder,
Eminently practical and yet
Appropriate as always.
As you've said repeatedly,
There's little point in dwelling on the past.

MRS. LOVETT:	TODD:
Do you mean it?	No, come here, my love . . .
Everything I did I swear	
I thought	
Was only for the best,	Not a thing to fear,
Believe me!	My love . . .
Can we still be	What's dead
Married?	Is dead.

    (TODD *puts his arm around her waist; she starts to relax*
    in her babbling, and they sway to the waltz, her arms
    around his neck)

TODD:

  The history of the world, my pet —

MRS. LOVETT:

  Oh, Mr. Todd,
  Ooh, Mr. Todd,
  Leave it to me . . .

TODD:

  Is learn forgiveness and try to forget.

MRS. LOVETT:

  By the sea, Mr. Todd,
  We'll be comfy-cozy,
  By the sea, Mr. Todd,
  Where there's no one nosy . . .
        (*He waltzes her closer to the oven*)

TODD:

  And life is for the alive, my dear,

So let's keep living it — !

BOTH:

Just keep living it,
Really living it — !

(*He flings her into the oven. She screams. He slams the doors behind her. Black smoke belches forth. The music booms like an earthquake.* TODD, *gasping, sinks to his knees by the oven doors. Then he rises, moves back to the* BEGGAR WOMAN *and kneels, cradling her head in his arms*)

TODD (*Sings*):

There was a barber and his wife,
And she was beautiful.
A foolish barber and his wife,
She was his reason and his life.
And she was beautiful.
And she was virtuous.
And he was —

(*Shrugs*)

Naive.

(TOBIAS *emerges from the cellar, singing in an eerie voice. His hair has turned completely white*)

TOBIAS:

Pat-a-cake, pat-a-cake, baker man.
Bake me a cake —
No, no,
Bake me a pie —
To delight my eye,
And I will sigh
If the crust be high . . .

(*Sees* TODD, *speaks*)

Mr. Todd.

(*Notices the* BEGGAR WOMAN)

It's the old woman. Ya harmed her too, have ya? Ya shouldn't, ya know. Ya shouldn't harm nobody.

(*He bends to examine the body;* TODD, *suddenly aware of someone, pushes him violently aside. As* TOBIAS *staggers back and recovers his balance, he notices the razor on the floor, picks it up, plays with it*)

Razor! Razor! Cut, cut, cut cadougan, watch me grind my corn. Pat him and prick him and mark him with B, and put him in the oven for baby and me!

(*Cuts* TODD*'s throat.* TODD *dies across the body of* LUCY *as the factory whistle blows.* ANTHONY, JOHANNA *and* OFFI-CERS OF THE GUARD *come running on. Seeing the carnage, they all stop*)

You will pardon me, gentlemen, but you may not enter here. Oh no! Me mistress don't let no one enter here, for, you see, sirs, there's work to be done, so much work.

(*While they watch in horror, he moves to the grinding machine and slowly starts to turn the handle*)

Three times. That's the secret. Three times through for them to be tender and juicy. Three times through the grinder. Smoothly, smoothly . . .

(JOHANNA *gives a little cry.* ANTHONY *throws his arm around her. As the group stands watching, still in silence,* TOBIAS *continues to grind. Suddenly, the trap door slaps shut; the light brightens abruptly,* TOBIAS *steps back, looks up and sings . . .*)

Epilogue

TOBIAS:
Attend the tale of Sweeney Todd.
His skin was pale and his eye was odd.

JOHANNA *and* ANTHONY:
He shaved the faces of gentlemen
Who never thereafter were heard of again.

POLICEMEN:
He trod a path that few have trod,

POLICEMEN, JOHANNA *and* ANTHONY:
Did Sweeney Todd,

ALL:
The Demon Barber of Fleet Street.

BEGGAR WOMAN (*Rising*):
He kept a shop in London town,
Of fancy clients and good renown.

JUDGE (*Rising*):
And what if none of their souls were saved?
They went to their maker impeccably shaved

BEGGAR WOMAN, JUDGE *and* POLICEMEN:
By Sweeney,
By Sweeney Todd,

ALL:

The Demon Barber of Fleet Street.

PIRELLI *and* BEADLE (*Entering*):

Swing your razor wide, Sweeney!
Hold it to the skies!
Freely flows the blood of those
Who moralize!

(*The rest of the company enters*)

COMPANY:

His needs are few, his room is bare.
He hardly uses his fancy chair.
The more he bleeds, the more he lives.
He never forgets and he never forgives.
Perhaps today you gave a nod
To Sweeney Todd,
The Demon Barber of Fleet Street.

WOMEN:

Sweeney wishes the world away,
Sweeney's weeping for yesterday,
Hugging the blade, waiting the years,
Hearing the music that nobody hears.
Sweeney waits in the parlor hall,
Sweeney leans on the office wall.

MEN:

No one can help, nothing can hide you —
Isn't that Sweeney there beside you?

COMPANY:

Sweeney wishes the world away,
Sweeney's weeping for yesterday,
Is Sweeney!
There he is, it's Sweeney!
Sweeney! Sweeney!

(*Pointing around the theater*)

There! There! There! There!
There! There! There!
> (*Pointing to the grave*)

There!
> (TODD *and* MRS. LOVETT *rise from the grave*)

TODD *and* COMPANY:
Attend the tale of Sweeney Todd!
He served a dark and a hungry god!

TODD:
To seek revenge may lead to hell,

MRS. LOVETT:
But everyone does it, and seldom as well

TODD *and* MRS. LOVETT:
As Sweeney,

COMPANY:
As Sweeney Todd,
The Demon Barber of Fleet . . .
> (*They start to exit*)

. . . Street!
> (*The company exits.* TODD *and* MRS. LOVETT *are the last to leave. They look at each other, then exit in opposite directions,* MRS. LOVETT *into the wings,* TODD *upstage. He glares at us malevolently for a moment, then slams the iron door in our faces. Blackout*)

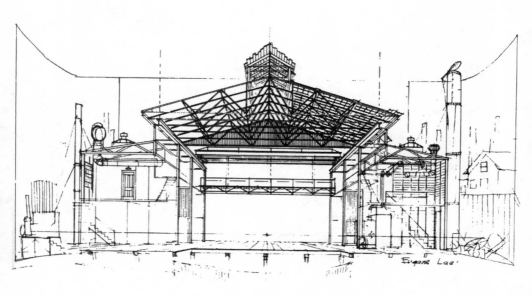

A perspective drawing of the set

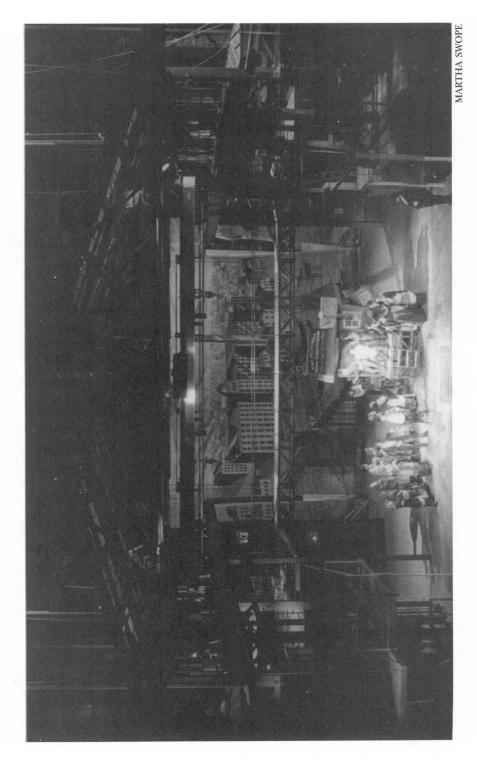

The set under construction at the Uris Theatre (*opposite page*) and the completed set (*below*)

SWEENEY TODD

FRANNE LEE

TOBIAS "1"

FRANNE LEE '78

MRS LOVETT #2

FRANNE LEE '78

MRS. LoveH #3   FRANIE LEE '78

JOHANNA

FRANNE LEE '76

MAJOR PRODUCTIONS

Sweeney Todd, the Demon Barber of Fleet Street was first presented by Richard Barr, Charles Woodward, Robert Fryer, Mary
Lea Johnson, Martin Richards, in association with Dean and
Judy Manos, at the Uris Theatre, New York City, on March
1, 1979, with the following cast:

(In order of appearance)

ANTHONY HOPE	Victor Garber
SWEENEY TODD	Len Cariou
BEGGAR WOMAN	Merle Louise
MRS. LOVETT	Angela Lansbury
JUDGE TURPIN	Edmund Lyndeck
THE BEADLE	Jack Eric Williams
JOHANNA	Sarah Rice
TOBIAS RAGG	Ken Jennings
PIRELLI	Joaquin Romaguera
JONAS FOGG	Robert Ousley

THE COMPANY: Duane Bodin, Walter Charles, Carole Doscher,
Nancy Eaton, Mary-Pat Green, Cris Groenendaal, Skip
Harris, Marthe Ihde, Betsy Joslyn, Nancy Killmer, Frank
Kopyc, Spain Logue, Craig Lucas, Pamela McLernon,
Duane Morris, Robert Ousley, Richard Warren Pugh,
Maggie Task. *Swings* — Heather B. Withers, Robert
Henderson.

Directed by Harold Prince
Dance and Movement by Larry Fuller
Production Designed by Eugene Lee
Costumes Designed by Franne Lee
Lighting Designed by Ken Billington
Orchestrations by Jonathan Tunick
Musical Direction by Paul Gemignani

The first section of *"The Contest"* (pages 61-62) and the scene in Judge Turpin's house, including the Judge's version of *"Johanna,"* (pages 68-72) were cut in previews for reasons of time.

Sweeney Todd, the Demon Barber of Fleet Street gave its first performance in New York City at the Uris Theatre, where it began previews on February 6, 1979, opened on March 1st and closed on June 29, 1980 after 557 performances and 19 previews.

AWARDS

New York Drama Critics Circle Award — Best Musical

Tony Awards: Best Musical, Best Book of a Musical (Hugh Wheeler), Best Music and Lyrics (Stephen Sondheim), Best Actor in a Musical (Len Cariou), Best Actress in a Musical (Angela Lansbury), Best Direction of a Musical (Harold Prince), Best Scenic Design (Eugene Lee), Best Costume Design (Franne Lee). Also received a Tony nomination for Best Lighting Design (Ken Billington).

Sweeney Todd, the Demon Barber of Fleet Street was first present-
ed in London by Robert Stigwood, in association with David
Land, and by arrangement with Richard Barr, Charles
Woodward, Robert Fryer, Mary Lea Johnson and Martin
Richards, at the Theatre Royal Drury Lane on July 2, 1980
for 157 performances, with the following cast:

SWEENEY TODD	Denis Quilley
MRS. LOVETT	Sheila Hancock
BEGGAR WOMAN	Dilys Watling
TOBIAS	Michael Staniforth
ANTHONY	Andrew C. Wadsworth
JOHANNA	Mandy More
JUDGE TURPIN	Austin Kent
BEADLE BAMFORD	David Wheldon-Williams
PIRELLI	John Aron
JONAS FOGG	Oz Clarke

THE COMPANY: Sylvia Beamish, Michael Bulman, Simon But-
teriss, Oz Clarke, Linda D'Arcy, Victoria Duncan,
Katherine Dyson, Mercia Glossop, Andrew Golder, Stuart
Haycock, Stephen Hill, Marie Jackson, Diane Mansfield,
Neil Michael, William Relton, Myra Sands, Suzanne
Sloan, Grant Smith, Rex Taylor Craig, David Urwin

Directed by Harold Prince
Dance and Movement by Larry Fuller
Production Designed by Eugene Lee
Costumes Designed by Franne Lee
Lighting Designed by Ken Billington
Orchestrations by Jonathan Tunick
Production Musical Director, Ray Cook

"Parlor Songs" was deleted and a new song, *"Beggar Woman's Lullaby"* (pages 167-168), was added.

AWARDS

London Standard Drama Award — Best Musical

Society of West End Theatre Awards: Best Musical and Best Actor in a Musical (Denis Quilley). Also received a nomination for Best Actress in a Musical (Sheila Hancock).

Sweeney Todd, the Demon Barber of Fleet Street was presented by the Houston Grand Opera (David Gockley, General Director, John DeMain, Music Director) at the Jones Hall for the Performing Arts, Houston, Texas, June 14-17 and 19-24, 1984 for 10 performances, with the following cast:

ANTHONY HOPE	Cris Groenendaal
SWEENEY TODD	Timothy Nolen
BEGGAR WOMAN	Adair Gockley
MRS. LOVETT	Joyce Castle
JUDGE TURPIN	Will Roy
THE BEADLE	Barry Busse
JOHANNA	Lee Merrill
TOBIAS RAGG	Steven Jacob
PIRELLI	Joseph Evans
JONAS FOGG	Rodney Stenborg

CHORUS: Robert Ard, Lezlie Cole, David Edlund, Lauren Edlund, Mary Jane Ely, Janey Hall, Patricia Hendrickson, Darlene Hitchman, Eileen Koyl, Scott Marshall, Ruth Porter, David Rumpy, Carl Saloga, Robert Sheets, James Sikorski, Margaret Stenborg, Rodney Stenborg, Diana Stoerzbach, James Tinkle, Graydon Vaught

SUPERNUMERARIES: Al Briscoe, Richard Engels, Walt Jaeschke, Bob Mitchell, Julie Stenborg, Mike Talcott, Charles Williams

Conductor, John DeMain
Directed by Harold Prince
Assistant to Mr. Prince, Arthur Masella
Production Designer, Eugene Lee
Costume Designer, Franne Lee
Lighting Designer, Ken Billington
Original Choreography, Larry Fuller

Original Choreography re-created by William Kirk
Sound Design, Jerry O'Brate
Chorus Preparation, Conoley Ballard
Musical Preparation, Stephen Sulich (*Principal Coach*) *and*
Craig Bohmler (*Assisting Coach*)
Technical Director, Drew Landmesser

Sweeney Todd, the Demon Barber of Fleet Street was first presented by the New York City Opera (Beverly Sills, General Director, Christopher Keene, Music Director) at the New York State Theatre, New York City, October 11-14 and November 14-18, 1984 for 13 performances, with the following cast:

(In order of appearance)

ANTHONY HOPE	Cris Groenendaal
SWEENEY TODD	Timothy Nolen
BEGGAR WOMAN	Adair Lewis
MRS. LOVETT	Rosalind Elias
JUDGE TURPIN	William Dansby
THE BEADLE	John Lankston
JOHANNA	Leigh Munro
TOBIAS RAGG	Paul Binotto
PIRELLI	Jerold Siena
JONAS FOGG	William Ledbetter

Conducted by Paul Gemignani
Directed by Harold Prince
Assistant to Mr. Prince, Arthur Masella
Scenery Designed by Eugene Lee
Costume Designed by Franne Lee
Lighting Designed by Ken Billington
Choreography by Larry Fuller

Sweeney Todd, the Demon Barber of Fleet Street was revived in London by the Half Moon Theatre, Mile End at the Half Moon Theatre, May 1, 1985 for 33 performances, with the following cast:

ANTHONY HOPE	Christopher Snell
SWEENEY TODD	Leon Greene
BEGGAR WOMAN	Ruth Mayo
MRS. LOVETT	Gillian Hanna
JUDGE TURPIN	Bernard Martin
BEADLE BAMFORD	Edward Clayton
JOHANNA	Eithne Hannigan
TOBIAS RAGG	Andrew Schofield
PIRELLI	John Aron
BIRD SELLER	Judith Street

Directed by Chris Bond
Production Designed by Elen Cairns
Costume Supervisor, Jayne Lambert
Lighting Designer, Jimmy Simmons
Musical Director, Graham Pike
Sound Designer, Tim Foster
Musical Arrangements, Rick Juckes

Sweeney Todd, the Demon Barber of Fleet Street was revived by Circle in the Square (Theodore Mann, Artistic Director, Paul Libin, Producing Director) at the Circle in the Square Theatre, New York City, on September 14, 1989, with the following cast:

JONAS FOGG	Tony Gilbert
POLICEMAN	David E. Mallard
BIRD SELLER	Ted Keegan
DORA	Sylvia Rhyne
MRS. MOONEY	Mary Phillips
ANTHONY HOPE	Jim Walton
SWEENEY TODD	Bob Gunton
BEGGAR WOMAN	SuEllen Estey
MRS. LOVETT	Beth Fowler
JUDGE TURPIN	David Barron
THE BEADLE	Michael McCarty
JOHANNA	Gretchen Kingsley
TOBIAS RAGG	Eddie Korbich
PIRELLI	Bill Nabel

Directed by Susan H. Schulman
Choreography by Michael Lichtefeld
Scenic Design by James Morgan
Costume Design by Beba Shamash
Lighting Design by Mary Jo Dondlinger
Musical Direction and Design by David Krane

This production was originally presented off-off-Broadway by the York Theatre Company (Janet Hayes Walker, Producing Director) at the Church of the Heavenly Rest, March 31-April 29, 1989 for 24 performances. Previews began at the Circle in the Square Theatre on August 5, 1989, and the show opened September 14th and closed February 25, 1990 after 189 performances and 46 previews.

Sweeney Todd, the Demon Barber of Fleet Street was presented on television by RKO/Nederlander and The Entertainment Channel on September 12, 1982, with the following cast:

ANTHONY HOPE	Cris Groenendaal
SWEENEY TODD	George Hearn
BEGGAR WOMAN	Sara Woods
MRS. LOVETT	Angela Lansbury
JUDGE TURPIN	Edmund Lyndeck
THE BEADLE	Calvin Remsberg
JOHANNA	Betsy Joslyn
TOBIAS RAGG	Ken Jennings
PIRELLI	Sal Mistretta
BIRD SELLER	Spain Logue
THE PASSERBY	Walter Charles
JONAS FOGG	Michael Kalinyen

THE COMPANY: Walter Charles, Roy Gioconda, Skip Harris, Michael Kalinyen, Spain Logue, Duane Morris, Patricia Parker, Meredith Rawlins, Stuart Redfield, Candace Rogers, Dee Etta Rowe, Carrie Solomon, Melanie Vaughan, Joseph Warner. *Swings*: Cheryl Mae Stewart, James Edward Justiss, William Kirk.

Executive Producers, Ellen M. Krass *and* Archer King
Produced by Bonnie Burns
Executive in Charge of Production, James Rich, Jr.
Directed for Television by Terry Hughes
Directed for the Stage by Harold Prince
Dance and Movement by Larry Fuller
Production Designed by Eugene Lee
Costumes Designed by Franne Lee

Lighting Designed for Television by Bill Klages
Orchestrations by Jonathan Tunick
Musical Conductor, Jim Coleman

The television production was taped at the Dorothy Chandler Pavilion, Los Angeles, where the touring company of *Sweeney Todd* was then performing. This production is available on video cassette: RKO 1002/Image 16008.

SELECTED DISCOGRAPHY

* <u>Original Broadway Cast Recording</u> (1979)
 RCA Records
  LP CBL2-3379 (S); 2 record set
  Cassette CBK2-3379; 2 tape set
  CD 3379-2-RC; 2 disc set
   (all of the above include the Judge's version of *"Johanna,"*
   which was cut from the original Broadway production)
  CD RCD1-5033 (highlights only)

A Stephen Sondheim Evening (1983)
 RCA Records
  LP CBL2–4745 (S); 2 record set
  Cassette CBK2–4745; 2 tape set
 Includes: *"Johanna"*—Cris Groenendaal

Evelyn Lear Sings Sondheim and Bernstein (1981)
 Mercury Records Golden Imports
  LP MR 75136
  Cassette MRI 75136
 Includes: *"Green Finch and Linnet Bird"*

A Stephen Sondheim Collection/Jackie Cain and Roy Kral (1982)
 Finesse Records
  LP FW 38324 (S)
  Cassette FWT 38324
 DRG Records (1990 reissue)
  Casette DSC 25102
  CD DSCD 25102
 Includes: *"Johanna"*—Roy Kral

A Little Sondheim Music/Los Angeles Vocal Arts Ensemble
(1984)
 Angel Records
  LP EMI DS-37347 (S)
  Cassette EMI 4DS-37347
 Includes: *"Prologue: The Ballad of Sweeney Todd"*—Ensemble; *"Green
   Finch and Linnet Bird"*—Delcina Stevenson; *"Pretty Women"*
   —Dale Morich, Michael Gallup; *"By the Sea"*—Janet
   Smith, Michael Gallup; *"Not While I'm Around"*—Paul
   Johnson, Janet Smith

* Winner of the Grammy Award for Best Original Cast Show Album

*The Broadway Album/*Barbra Streisand (1985)
Columbia Records
 LP OC 40092
 Cassette OCT 40092
 CD CK 40092
 Includes: *"Not While I'm Around," "Pretty Women"*

A Collector's Sondheim (1985)
RCA Records
 LP CRL4–5359 (S); 4 record set
 Cassette CRK4–5359; 4 tape set
 CD RCD3–5480; 3 disc set
 Includes: *"Pretty Women"*—Len Cariou, Edmund Lyndeck, Victor
   Garber; *"Epiphany"*—Len Cariou, Angela Lansbuy; *"A Little
   Priest"*—Angela Lansbury, Len Cariou (all three tracks from
   original Broadway cast recording); *"The Ballad of Sweeney
   Todd"* (disco version)—Gordon Grody (an edited version of
   the original disco release by His Majesty's Fish, featuring
   Gordon Grody, RCA Red Seals Disco—PD 11687 [33 1/3
   rpm single])

Sondheim (1985)
Book-of-the-Month Records
 LP 81–7515 (S); 3 record set
 Cassette 91–7516; 2 tape set
 CD 11–7517; 2 disc set
 Includes: *"The Worst Pies in London"*—Joyce Castle; *"A Little Priest"*
   —Joyce Castle, Timothy Nolen; *"Johanna"*—Chamber En-
   semble; *"Not While I'm Around"*—Steven Jacob

*Old Friends/*Geraldine Turner Sings the Songs of Stephen
Sondheim (1986)
Larrikin Records (Australia)
 LP LRF-169
 Cassette TC-LRF-169
   (This album was reissued by Silva Screen Records [London]
   under the title *The Stephen Sondheim Songbook*: LP Song 001,
   Cassette Song C001, CD Song CD001)
 Includes: *"Not While I'm Around"*

559

Cleo Sings Sondheim/Cleo Laine (1988)
  RCA Records
    LP 7702-1-RC
    Cassette 7702-4-RC
    CD 7702-2-RC
  Includes: *"Not While I'm Around"*

Julie Wilson Sings the Stephen Sondheim Songbook (1988)
  DRG Records
    LP SL 5206
    Cassette SLC 5206
    CD CDSL 5206
  Includes: *"Not While I'm Around"*

The Other Side of Sondheim/Jane Harvey (1988)
  Atlantic Records
    LP 81833-1
    Cassette 81833-4
    CD 81833-2
  Includes: *"Not While I'm Around," "Pretty Women"*

Symphonic Sondheim/Don Sebesky Conducts The London Symphony Orchestra (1990)
  WEA Records (London)
    LP 9031-72 119-1
    Cassette 9031-72 119-4
    CD 9031-72 119-2
  Includes: *"Sweeney Todd Suite," ("The Ballad of Sweeney Todd," "Johanna," "Pretty Women," "A Little Priest," "My Friends"*

Sondheim: A Celebration at Carnegie Hall (1992)
  RCA Victor
    CD 09026-61484-2; 2 CD set
  Includes: *"Johanna," "Pretty Women"*

SUNDAY
in the
PARK
with
GEORGE

Music and Lyrics by
STEPHEN SONDHEIM

Book by
JAMES LAPINE

Introduction by André Bishop

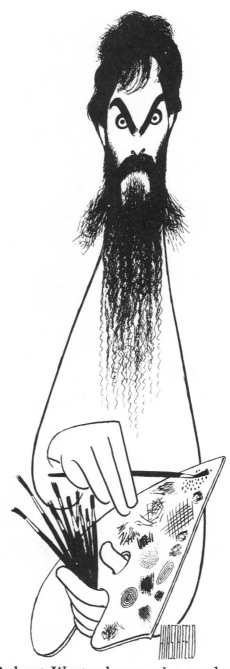

Robert Westenberg, who replaced
Mandy Patinkin in the role of George

INTRODUCTION

I did a great deal of reading about *Sunday in the Park with George* before I sat down to write this introduction. I discovered that masses of articles, interviews, and essays had been written about this landmark musical since its opening on Broadway in April of 1984. I realized that I had nothing especially new to say about the show—Sondheim's use of "chord clusters," Lapine's avoidance of Latin root words and contractions in an effort to simulate 19th Century French speech patterns, the trials and tribulations of getting the second act into shape and so on—all of these have been well documented.

I then did something you are about to do: I read the text. I was deeply moved. I found the sheer audacity of the *idea* of the show amazing. Imagine a musical in which the first act breathes dramatic life into one of the great works of late 19th Century painting. Then try to top Act One with a second act that takes place a hundred years later and deals satirically with the contemporary art world and then goes on to chronicle the sadness of a young artist who has lost his way in it.

Sunday in the Park with George is a very personal show and so it seems appropriate that this introduction be personal too. The show meant a great deal to its creators, indeed to all who worked on it. My presence in these pages can be explained because it was my theater, Playwrights Horizons, that commissioned the piece initially from James Lapine and then gave it its first home and its first production prior to the run on Broadway. My recollections of a hectic, exhilarating time are happy ones, although Playwrights Horizons had never produced a musical on such a large scale before. Enormous amounts of time and energy went into organizing ourselves to go into rehearsal for a piece that we knew very little about—there was a first act with a number of songs and a sketch of a second act. That was it.

People would say to me, "Why are you putting on such an elaborate production of something that is only half-written?" Indeed, though we called the event a "workshop" and believe me it was a *workshop*, we had to raise a great deal of money to do it and a lot of that money went into costumes and sets. It seems to me, as I look back, that we were always having benefits and that I was always lugging around color reproductions of *La Grande Jatte* to show to prospective donors! In any event, I believed that if you were doing a show about vision and creation and if the *event* was the recreation of a painting of people in a French park in 1884, you couldn't effectively "workshop" the visuals with women in rehearsal skirts, men in leotards, and a black velour surround. You had to do it full out or not at all.

One of the highlights of our production and of the show turned out to be the end of Act One when Seurat artfully arranges the various groups of squabbling Parisians into a perfect and harmonious picture. There was something about the scale of the final image that related beautifully to the dimensions of our small theater space. When everyone on stage sang the final three "Sundays," and the horn played, and the picture was complete and frozen, and the blank canvas that we used as a show curtain came in—well, it was a perfect blend for the ear and the eye. And most nights the audience (even some of the ancient ones who occasionally nodded off) would cheer and stomp and scream their approval. Though the show was infinitely better and more complete on Broadway, I always felt that the Act One finale worked best at Playwrights Horizons. It was literally and beautifully overpowering.

564

When we began performances in July of 1983, we had most of a first act ("Everybody Loves Louis," "Beautiful," and "Finishing the Hat" were added during our run) and hardly any Act Two. So we decided to only perform the first act—it was, after all, a fairly complete unit—and to add Act Two when the authors were ready. We hoped our loyal subscription audience would accept this in the spirit of a "work-in-progress," and they did. Part of the reason they did had to do with the speeches I felt I should give before each performance, explaining what we were up to in as inspiring a fashion as possible and then casually mentioning that Act Two wasn't quite ready and that we were sparing them great torment by not performing it that night. Actually, we only performed it three times!

People who know me know that I'll do anything to avoid having to speak in public, but such was my fate those muggy summer nights in 1983. When I look back on it, though, I wonder if I was able to get the audience on our side for no other reason than they felt sorry for me because I appeared to be so nervous. Ira Weitzman, our Musical Theater Program Director, was much more at ease when he had to "make the speech," and by the end of the run would stroll up to the apron of the stage, wearing shorts and a T-shirt, and sort of say, "Hi, folks, guess what? No Act Two tonight, but you're gonna *love* Act One!"

The best speech night and one of the great nights of my theater life was the night "Finishing the Hat" went into the show. Mandy Patinkin had learned the music but wanted to hold onto the printed lyrics. I explained in the speech that this night was something special because a new song was being added and that Seurat would, at one point, be holding some sheets of music. An audience loves being in on something for the first time. When Mandy picked up the music and sang the song—so carefully and lovingly—and the song turned out to be deeply personal, layered with meaning and metaphor, and beautifully spun out, we all felt that we had entered musical theater heaven. And we had. Even today I run into people who claim they saw the show the night "Finishing the Hat" went in and that it was a rare and special occasion.

Playwrights Horizons believes that opportunities create and sustain artists, and we felt that the best thing we could do for Sondheim and Lapine was to step back and give them a chance to discover their show. I wanted them to be free to do what they wanted without any kind of management pressure, without any kind of publicity or review, and most of all, without any kind of fear. I felt that they were onto something important, and I knew that the collaboration between the two men was new and at an early and delicate stage. Stephen Sondheim was working with a different partner for the first time in years, and he had never really worked in a non-profit situation in New York. Everyone at Playwrights Horizons wanted him to find us at our best and to work happily under a different system of creating shows than the traditional Broadway one.

Because I am writing this in June of 1990 when the National Endowment for the Arts in particular and non-profit arts subsidy in general are under attack, I want to note that the creative freedom that Sondheim and Lapine were given at my theater and the good advantage they took of it is directly due to funding dollars. If subsidy is taken away from theaters, especially those that deal with new, experimental, untried work, these theaters will fade away. And if this happens, there will be no venue for new work at all and any sort of new American theater will simply disappear. Artists will no longer have artistic homes away from the marketplace. What I'm trying to say is that had it not been for subsidy there would be no Playwrights Horizons and quite possibly no *Sunday in the Park with George*.

A month or so after the show closed at Playwrights Horizons, I flew to Chicago to go to the Art Institute where

Seurat's *A Sunday Afternoon on the Island of La Grande Jatte* hangs. I probably should have done this at the outset instead of at the end, because as I walked up the steps and got closer and closer to the treasured painting, I finally understood what it was the two authors were doing. In front of me, and massively so, was an extraordinary composition of shapes and colors and brushstrokes that reflected the work of a man obsessed with his art. Even to a jaded, late 20th Century New Yorker, who had seen countless reproductions of *La Grande Jatte* and had just done a show about it, the painting was startling and lovely and upsetting and inspiring. I stood and stared for hours, much as I imagine the authors did, until I felt I was both outside the painting and inside, and definitely part of it. There were many areas and people on the huge canvas that were not represented in the musical, and I wondered who they had been and why they were there. It must have been at this point of heightened curiosity and emotion that Lapine and Sondheim began their own search for a new form inspired by the legacy of an extraordinary artist from another century.

I am very proud of the part Playwrights Horizons played in the development of *Sunday in the Park with George.* I think the show represents what is best about the American musical theater, and it certainly came out of what is best about the non-profit theater.

André Bishop

Playwrights Horizons
June 1990

P.S. The two best and most detailed accounts of the partnership that created *Sunday in the Park with George* are to be found in the 2nd edition of Craig Zadan's *Sondheim and Co.* (Harper and Row) and Michiko Kakutani's article for *The New York Times,* reprinted in her book *The Poet at the Piano* (New York Times Books).

Bernadette Peters

Bernadette Peters and Mandy Patinkin

CAST OF CHARACTERS

ACT I

GEORGE, *an artist*
DOT, *his mistress*
OLD LADY
HER NURSE
JULES, *another artist*
YVONNE, *his wife*
LOUISE, *the daughter of Jules and Yvonne*
A BOATMAN
FRANZ, *servant to Jules and Yvonne*
FRIEDA, *cook for Jules and Yvonne, wife to Franz*
A SOLDIER
MR. *and* MRS., *an American couple*
LOUIS, *a baker*
A WOMAN *with baby carriage*
A MAN *with bicycle*
A LITTLE GIRL
CELESTE #1, *a shopgirl*
CELESTE #2, *another shopgirl*
A BOY *bathing in the river*
A YOUNG MAN *sitting on the bank*
A MAN *lying on the bank*

ACT II

GEORGE, *an artist*
MARIE, *his grandmother*
DENNIS, *a technician*
BOB GREENBERG, *the museum director*

NAOMI EISEN, *a composer*
HARRIET PAWLING, *a patron of the arts*
BILLY WEBSTER, *her friend*
A PHOTOGRAPHER
A MUSEUM ASSISTANT
CHARLES REDMOND, *a visiting curator*
ALEX, *an artist*
BETTY, *an artist*
LEE RANDOLPH, *the museum's publicist*
BLAIR DANIELS, *an art critic*
A WAITRESS
ELAINE, *George's former wife*

For Sarah Kernochan

"Sunday in the Park with George"
was originally produced on Broadway by
The Shubert Organization and Emmanuel Azenberg
By arrangement with
Playwrights Horizons

Playwrights Horizons, Inc., New York City,
Produced the original production of
"Sunday in the Park with George"
in 1983

MUSICAL NUMBERS

ACT I

"Sunday in the Park with George"	DOT
"No Life"	JULES, YVONNE
"Color and Light"	DOT, GEORGE
"Gossip"	CELESTE #1, CELESTE #2, BOATMAN, NURSE, OLD LADY, JULES, YVONNE
"The Day Off"	GEORGE, NURSE, FRANZ, FRIEDA, BOATMAN, SOLDIER, CELESTE #1, CELESTE #2, YVONNE, LOUISE, JULES, LOUIS
"Everybody Loves Louis"	DOT
"Finishing the Hat"	GEORGE
"We Do Not Belong Together"	DOT, GEORGE
"Beautiful"	OLD LADY, GEORGE
"Sunday"	COMPANY

ACT II

"It's Hot Up Here"	COMPANY
Chromolume #7	GEORGE, MARIE
"Putting It Together"	GEORGE, COMPANY
"Children and Art"	MARIE
"Lesson #8"	GEORGE
"Move On"	GEORGE, DOT
"Sunday"	COMPANY

573

Act I takes place on a series of Sundays from 1884 to 1886 and alternates between a park on an island in the Seine just outside Paris and George's studio.

Act II takes place in 1984 at an American art museum and on the island.

ACT I

A white stage. White floor, slightly raked and extended in perspective. Four white portals define the space. The proscenium arch continues across the bottom as well, creating a complete frame around the stage.

GEORGE *enters downstage. He is an artist. Tall, with a dark beard, wearing a soft felt hat with a very narrow brim crushed down at the neck, and a short jacket. He looks rather intense. He sits downstage on the apron at an easel with a large drawing pad and a box of chalk. He stares momentarily at the pad before turning to the audience.*

GEORGE: White. A blank page or canvas. The challenge: bring order to the whole.
> (*Arpeggiated chord. A tree flies in stage right*)
Through design.
> (*Four arpeggiated chords. The white portals fly out and the white ground cloth comes off, revealing a grassy-green expanse and portals depicting the park scene*)
Composition.
> (*Two arpeggiated chords. A tree tracks on from stage left*)
Balance.
> (*Two arpeggiated chords. Two trees descend*)
Light.
> (*Arpeggiated chord. The lighting bumps, giving the impression of an early morning sunrise on the island of La*

Grande Jatte — harsh shadows and streaming golden light through the trees)

And harmony.

(The music coalesces into a theme, "Sunday," as a cut-out of a couple rises at the back of the stage. GEORGE *begins to draw, then stops suddenly and goes to the wings and brings on a young woman,* DOT. *She wears a traditional 19th-century outfit: full-length dress with bustle, etc. When he gets her downstage right, he turns her profile, then returns downstage to his easel. He begins to draw. She turns to him. Music continues under. Annoyed)*

No. Now I want you to look out at the water.

DOT: I feel foolish.

GEORGE: Why?

DOT (*Indicating bustle*): I hate this thing.

GEORGE: Then why wear it?

DOT: Why wear it? Everyone is wearing them!

GEORGE (*Begins sketching*): Everyone . . .

DOT: You know they are.
                    (*She begins to move*)

GEORGE: Stand still, please.
                    (*Music stops*)

DOT (*Sighs*): I read they're even wearing them in America.

GEORGE: They are fighting Indians in America — and you cannot read.

DOT (*Defensive*): I can read . . . a little.
                    (*Pause*)
Why did we have to get up so early?

GEORGE: The light.

DOT: Oh.
> (GEORGE lets out a moan)
What's the matter?

GEORGE (Erasing feverishly): I hate this tree.
> (Arpeggio. A tree rises back into the fly space)

DOT (Hurt): I thought you were drawing me.

GEORGE (Muttering): I am. I am. Just stand still.
>(DOT is oblivious to the moved tree. Through the course of the scene the landscape can continue to change. At this point a sailboat begins to slide into view)

DOT: I wish we could go sailing. I wouldn't go this early in the day, though.

GEORGE: Could you drop your head a little, please.
> (She drops her head completely)
Dot!
> (She looks up, giggling)
If you wish to be a good model you must learn to concentrate. Hold the pose. Look out at the water.
> (She obliges)
Thank you.
> (OLD LADY enters)

OLD LADY: Where is that tree? (Pause) Nurse! NURSE!

DOT (Startled): My God!
> (Sees OLD LADY)
She is everywhere.
> (NURSE enters. She wears an enormous headdress)

OLD LADY: NURSE!

NURSE: What is it, Madame?

OLD LADY: The tree. The tree. Where is our tree?

NURSE: What tree?

OLD LADY: The tree we always sit near. Someone has moved it.

NURSE: No one has moved it, Madame. It is right over
there. Now come along —
> (NURSE *attempts to help the* OLD LADY *along*)

OLD LADY: Do not push me!

NURSE: I am not pushing. I am helping.

OLD LADY: You are pushing and I do not need any help.

NURSE (*Crossing the stage*): Yes, Madame.

OLD LADY: And this is not our tree!
> (*She continues her shuffle*)

NURSE: Yes, Madame.
> (*She helps* OLD LADY *sit in front of tree*)

DOT: I do not envy the nurse.

GEORGE (*Under his breath*): She can read . . .

DOT (*Retaliating*): They were talking about you at La
Coupole.

GEORGE: Oh.

DOT: Saying strange things . . .

GEORGE: They have so little to speak of, they must speak of
me?

DOT: Were you at the zoo, George?
> (*No response*)

Drawing the monkey cage?

GEORGE: Not the monkey cage.

DOT: They said they saw you.

GEORGE: The monkeys, Dot. Not the cage.

DOT (*Giggling*): It is true? Why draw monkeys?

OLD LADY: Nurse, what is that?

NURSE: What, Madame?

OLD LADY (*Points out front*): That! Off in the distance.

NURSE: They are making way for the exposition.

OLD LADY: What exposition?

NURSE: The International Exposition. They are going to build a tower.

OLD LADY: Another exposition . . .

NURSE: They say it is going to be the tallest structure in the world.

OLD LADY: More foreigners. I am sick of foreigners.

GEORGE: More boats.
>   (*An arpeggiated chord. A tugboat appears*)
More trees.
>   (*Two chords. More trees track on*)

DOT: George.
>   (*Chord*)
Why is it you always get to sit in the shade while I have to stand in the sun?
>   (*Chord. No response*)
George?
>   (*Still no response*)
Hello, George?
>   (*Chord*)
There is someone in this dress!
>   (*Twitches slightly, sings to herself*)
A trickle of sweat.
>   (*Twitch*)
The back of the —

>   (*Twitch*)

— head.
He always does this.
> (*Hiss*)

Now the foot is dead.
Sunday in the park with George.
One more Su —
> (*Twitch*)

The collar is damp,
Beginning to pinch.
The bustle's slipping —
> (*Hiss and twitch*)

I won't budge one inch.
> (*Undulating with some pleasure, mixed with tiny twitches of vexation*)

Who was at the zoo, George?
Who was at the zoo?
The monkeys and who, George?
The monkeys and who?

GEORGE: Don't move!

DOT (*Still*):

Artists are bizarre. Fixed. Cold.
That's you, George, you're bizarre. Fixed. Cold.
I like that in a man. Fixed. Cold.
God, it's hot out here.

Well, there are worse things
Than staring at the water on a Sunday.
There are worse things
Than staring at the water
As you're posing for a picture
Being painted by your lover
In the middle of the summer
On an island in the river on a Sunday.
> (GEORGE *races over to* DOT *and rearranges her a bit, as if*

she were an object, then returns to his easel and resumes sketching. DOT *hisses, twitching again)*
The petticoat's wet,
Which adds to the weight.
The sun is blinding.
> (*Closing her eyes*)

All right, concentrate . . .

GEORGE: Eyes open, please.

DOT:
Sunday in the park with George . . .

GEORGE: Look out at the water. Not at me.

DOT:
Sunday in the park with George . . .
Concentrate . . . concentrate . . .
> (*The dress opens and* DOT *walks out of it. The dress closes behind her, remaining upright;* GEORGE *continues sketching it as if she were still inside. During the following,* DOT *moves around the stage, continuing to undulate, taking representative poses as punctuation to the music, which is heavily rhythmic)*

Well, if you want bread
And respect
And attention,
Not to say connection,
Modelling's no profession.
> (*Does mock poses*)

If you want instead,
When you're dead,
Some more public
And more permanent
Expression
> (*Poses*)

Of affection,

581

(*Poses*)

You want a painter,
>   (*Brief, sharp poses throughout the following*)

Poet,

Sculptor, preferably:

Marble, granite, bronze.

Durable.

Something nice with swans

That's durable

Forever.

All it has to be is good.
>   (*Looking over* GEORGE*'s shoulder at his work, then at*
>   GEORGE)

And George, you're good.

You're really good.

George's stroke is tender,

George's touch is pure.
>   (*Sits or stands nearby and watches him intently*)

Your eyes, George.

I love your eyes, George.

I love your beard, George.

I love your size, George.

But most, George,

Of all,

But most of all,

I love your painting . . .
>   (*Looking up at the sun*)

I think I'm fainting . . .
>   (*The dress opens and she steps back into it, resumes pose,*
>   *gives a twitch and a wince, then sings sotto voce again*)

The tip of a stay.
>   (*Wince*)

Right under the tit.

No, don't give in, just
>   (*Shifts*)

Lift the arm a bit . . .

GEORGE: Don't lift the arm, please.

DOT:

Sunday in the park with George . . .

GEORGE: The bustle high, please.

DOT:

Not even a nod.
As if I were trees.
The ground could open,
He would still say "please."

Never know with you, George,
Who could know with you?
The others I knew, George.
Before we get through,
I'll get to you, too.

God, I am so hot!

Well, there are worse things
Than staring at the water on a Sunday.
There are worse things
Than staring at the water
As you're posing for a picture
After sleeping on the ferry
After getting up at seven
To come over to an island
In the middle of a river
Half an hour from the city
On a Sunday.
On a Sunday in the park with —

GEORGE (*The music stopping*): Don't move the mouth!!

DOT (*Holds absolutely still for a very long beat. As music resumes,
she pours all her extremely mixed emotions into one word*):

— George!
                              (*Speaks*)
I am getting tired. The sun is too strong today.

GEORGE: Almost finished.

DOT (*Sexy*): I'd rather be in the studio, George.

GEORGE (*Wryly*): I know.

OLD LADY (*Looking across the water*): They are out early today.

NURSE: It is Sunday, Madame.

OLD LADY: That is what I mean, Nurse! Young boys out swimming so early on a Sunday?

NURSE: Well, it is very warm.

OLD LADY: Hand me my parasol.

NURSE: I am, Madame.
   (NURSE *stands up and opens the parasol for the* OLD LADY.
   FRANZ, *a coachman, enters; stares at the two women for a
   moment, then moves downstage. He sees* GEORGE, *and
   affects a pose as he sits*)

DOT: Oh, no.

GEORGE: What?

DOT: Look. Look who is over there.

GEORGE: So?

DOT: When he is around, you know who is likely to follow.

GEORGE: You have moved your arm.

DOT: I think they are spying on you, George. I really do.

GEORGE: Are you going to hold your head still?
   (*The* NURSE *has wandered over in the vicinity of* FRANZ)

NURSE: You are here awfully early today.

FRANZ (*Speaks with a German accent*): *Ja.* So are you.

NURSE: And working on a Sunday.

FRANZ: *Ja* . . .

NURSE: It is a beautiful day.

FRANZ (*Sexy*): It is too hot.

NURSE: Do you think?

OLD LADY: Where is my fan!

NURSE: I have to go back.

OLD LADY: Nurse, my fan!

NURSE: You did not bring it today, Madame.

OLD LADY: Of course I brought it!

FRANZ: Perhaps we will see each other later.

NURSE: Perhaps . . .

OLD LADY: There it is. Over there.
>   (OLD LADY *picks up the fan*)

NURSE: That is my fan —

OLD LADY: Well, I can use it. Can I not? It was just lying there . . . What is all that commotion?
> (*Music. Laughter from off right. A wagon tracks on bearing a tableau vivant of Seurat's "Une Baignade Asnières"*)

FRANZ: Jungen! Nicht so laut! Ruhe, bitte!
> (*The following is heard simultaneously from the characters in the tableau*)

BOY: Yoo-hoo! Dumb and fat!

YOUNG MAN: Hey! Who you staring at?

MAN: Look at the lady with the rear!
>   (*The* YOUNG MAN *gives a loud Bronx cheer*)

BOY: Yoo-hoo — kinky beard!

YOUNG MAN: Kinky beard.

YOUNG MAN *and* BOY: Kinky beard!

> (GEORGE *gestures, as when an artist raises and extends his right arm to frame an image before him — all freeze. Silence. A frame comes in around them.* JULES *and* YVONNE, *a well-to-do middle-aged couple, stroll on and pause before the painting*)

JULES: Ahh . . .

YVONNE: Ooh . . .

JULES: Mmm . . .

YVONNE: Oh, dear.

JULES: Oh, my.

YVONNE: Oh, my dear.

JULES (*Sings*):
It has no presence.

YVONNE (*Sings*):
No passion.

JULES:
No life.

> (*They laugh*)

It's neither pastoral
Nor lyrical.

YVONNE (*Giggling*):
You don't suppose that it's satirical?

> (*They laugh heartily*)

JULES:
Just density
Without intensity —

YVONNE:
No life.
(*Speaks*)
Boys with their clothes off —

JULES (*Mocking*): *I* must paint a factory next!

YVONNE:
It's so mechanical.

JULES:
Methodical.

YVONNE:
It might be in some dreary
Socialistic periodical.

JULES (*Approvingly*): Good.

YVONNE:
So drab, so cold.

JULES:
And so controlled.

BOTH:
No life.

JULES: His touch is too deliberate, somehow.

YVONNE: The dog.
(*They shriek with laughter*)

JULES:
These things get hung —

YVONNE: Hmm.

JULES:
And then they're gone.

YVONNE: Ahhh . . .
Of course he's young —
(JULES *shoots her a look. Hastily*)

But getting on.

JULES: Oh . . .
All mind, no heart.
No life in his art.

YVONNE:
No life in his *life*—
(*JULES nods in approval*)

BOTH:
No—
(*They giggle and chortle*)

Life.
(*Arpeggio. The* BOYS *in the picture give a loud Bronx cheer. The wagon with the picture tracks off.* JULES *and* YVONNE *turn and slowly stroll upstage.*)

NURSE (*Seeing* JULES): There is that famous artist — what is his name . . .

OLD LADY: What *is* his name?

NURSE: I can never remember their names.
(*JULES tips his hat to the ladies. The couple continues towards* GEORGE)

JULES: George! Out very early today.
(*GEORGE nods as he continues sketching.* DOT *turns her back on them*)

GEORGE: Hello, Jules.

YVONNE: A lovely day . . .

JULES: I couldn't be out sketching today — it is too sunny!
(*YVONNE laughs*)

GEORGE: Have you seen the painting?

JULES: Yes. I was just going to say! Boys bathing — what a curious subject.

(YVONNE *stops him*)

We must speak.

YVONNE (*Sincere*): I loved the dog.
(*Beat*)

JULES: I *am* pleased there was an independent exhibition.

GEORGE: Yes . . .

JULES: We *must* speak. Really.
(*Beat*)

YVONNE: Enjoy the weather.

JULES: Good day.
(*As they exit,* YVONNE *stops* JULES *and points to* DOT)

YVONNE: That dress!
(*They laugh and exit*)

DOT: I hate them!

GEORGE: Jules is a fine painter.

DOT: I do not care. I hate them.
(JULES *and* YVONNE *return*)

JULES: Franz!

YVONNE: We are waiting!
(*They exit*)

FRANZ: *Ja*, Madame, Monsieur. At your service.
(FRANZ, *who has been hiding behind a tree, eyeing the* NURSE, *quickly dashes offstage after* JULES *and* YVONNE. GEORGE *closes his pad.* DOT *remains frozen*)

GEORGE: Thank you.
(*Beat*)

DOT (*Moving*): I began to do it.

GEORGE: What?

589

DOT: Concentrate. Like you said.

GEORGE (*Patronizing*): You did very well.

DOT: Did I really?

GEORGE (*Gathering his belongings*): Yes. I'll meet you back at the studio.

DOT (*Annoyed*): You are not coming?

GEORGE: Not now.
> (*Angry*, DOT *begins to exit*)
Dot. We'll go to the Follies tonight.
> (*She stops, looks at him, then walks off.* GEORGE *walks to the* NURSE *and* OLD LADY)
Bon jour.

NURSE: Bon jour, Monsieur.

GEORGE: Lovely morning, ladies.

NURSE: Yes.

GEORGE: I have my pad and crayons today.

NURSE: Oh, that would —

OLD LADY: Not today!

GEORGE (*Disappointed*): Why not today?

OLD LADY: Too warm.

GEORGE: It *is* warm, but it will not take long. You can go —

OLD LADY (*Continues to look out across the water*): Some other day, Monsieur.
> (*Beat*)

GEORGE (*Kneeling*): It's George, Mother.

OLD LADY (*As if it is to be a secret*): Sssh . . .

GEORGE (*Getting up*): Yes. I guess we will all be back.

(*He exits as lights fade to black*)

(GEORGE's *studio. Downstage,* DOT *[in a likeness of Seurat's "La Poudreuse"] is at her vanity, powdering her face. Steady, unhurried, persistent rhythmic figure underneath*)

DOT (*As she powders rhythmically*): George taught me all about concentration. "The art of being still," he said.
    (*Checks herself, then resumes powdering*)
I guess I did not learn it soon enough.
    (*Dips puff in powder*)
George likes to be alone.
    (*Resumes powdering*)
Sometimes he will work all night long painting. We fought about that. I need sleep. I love to dream.
    (*Upstage,* GEORGE *on a scaffold, behind a large canvas, which is a scrim, comes into view. He is painting. It is an in-progress version of the painting "A Sunday Afternoon on the Island of La Grande Jatte"*)
George doesn't need as much sleep as everyone else.
    (*Dips puff, starts powdering neck*)
And he never tells me his dreams. George has many secrets.
    (*Lights down on* DOT, *up on* GEORGE. *A number of brushes in his hand, he is covering a section of the canvas — the face of the woman in the foreground — with tiny specks of paint, in the same rhythm as* DOT's *powdering*)

GEORGE (*Pauses, checks*): Order.
    (*Dabs with another color, pauses, checks, dabs palette*)
Design.
    (*Dabs with another brush*)
Composition.
Tone.
Form.

Symmetry.
Balance.
> (*Sings*)

More red . . .
> (*Dabs with more intensity*)

And a little more red . . .
> (*Switches brushes*)

Blue blue blue blue
Blue blue blue blue
Even even . . .
> (*Switches quickly*)

Good . . .
> (*Humming*)

Bumbum bum bumbumbum
Bumbum bum . . .
> (*Paints silently for a moment*)

More red . . .
> (*Switches brushes again*)

More blue . . .
> (*Again*)

More beer . . .
> (*Takes a swig from a nearby bottle, always eyeing the canvas, puts the bottle down*)

More light!
> (*He dabs assiduously, delicately attacking the area he is painting*)

Color and light.
There's only color and light.
Yellow and white.
Just blue and yellow and white.
> (*Addressing the woman he is painting*)

Look at the air, Miss —
> (*Dabs at the space in front of her*)

See what I mean?
No, look over there, Miss —

(Dabs at her eye, pauses, checks it)

That's done with green . . .

(Swirling a brush in the orange cup)

Conjoined with orange . . .

(Lights down on GEORGE, *up on* DOT, *now powdering her breasts and armpits. Rhythmic figure persists underneath)*

DOT: Nothing seems to fit me right.

(Giggles)

The less I wear, the more comfortable I feel.

(Sings, checking herself)

More rouge . . .

(Puts puff down, gets rouge, starts applying it in small rhythmic circles, speaks)

George is very special. Maybe I'm just not special enough for him.

(Puts rouge down, picks up eyebrow tweezers, sings)

If my legs were longer.

(Plucks at her eyebrow)

If my bust was smaller.

(Plucks)

If my hands were graceful.

(Plucks)

If my waist was thinner.

(Checks herself)

If my hips were flatter.

(Plucks again)

If my voice was warm.

(Plucks)

If I could concentrate —

(Abruptly, her feet start to can-can under the table)

I'd be in the Follies.
I'd be in a cabaret.
Gentlemen in tall silk hats
And linen spats

Would wait with flowers.
I could make them wait for hours.
Giddy young aristocrats
With fancy flats
Who'd drink my health,
And I would be as
Hard as nails . . .
> (*Looks at her nails, reaches for the buffer*)

And they'd only want me more . . .
> (*Starts buffing nails rhythmically*)

If I was a Folly girl . . .
Nah, I wouldn't like it much.
Married men and stupid boys
And too much smoke and all that noise
And all that color and light . . .
> (*Lights up on* GEORGE, *talking to the woman in the painting. Rhythmic figure continues underneath*)

GEORGE: Aren't you proper today, Miss? Your parasol so properly cocked, your bustle so perfectly upright. No doubt your chin rests at just the proper angle from your chest.
> (*Addressing the figure of the man next to her*)

And you, Sir. Your hat so black. So black to you, perhaps. So red to me.

DOT (*Spraying herself with perfume*):
None of the others worked at night . . .

GEORGE: So composed for a Sunday.

DOT:
How do you work without the right
> (*Sprays*)

Bright
> (*Sprays*)

White
> (*Sprays*)

594

Light?
                              (*Sprays*)
How do you fathom George?

GEORGE (*Sings in a mutter, trancelike, as he paints*):
Red red red red
Red red orange
Red red orange
Orange pick up blue
Pick up red
Pick up orange
From the blue-green blue-green
Blue-green circle
On the violet diagonal
Di-ag-ag-ag-ag-ag-o-nal-nal
Yellow comma yellow comma
              (*Humming, massaging his numb wrist*)
Numnum num numnumnum
Numnum num . . .
              (*Sniffs, smelling* DOT*'s perfume*)
Blue blue blue blue
Blue still sitting
Red that perfume
Blue all night
Blue-green the window shut
Dut dut dut
Dot Dot sitting
Dot Dot waiting
Dot Dot getting fat fat fat
More yellow
Dot Dot waiting to go
Out out out but
No no no George
Finish the hat finish the hat
Have to finish the hat first
Hat hat hat hat

Hot hot hot it's hot in here . . .
> (*Whistles a bit, then joyfully*)

Sunday!
Color and light!

DOT (*Pinning up her hair*): But how George looks. He could
look forever.

GEORGE:
There's only color and light.

DOT: As if he sees you and he doesn't all at once.

GEORGE:
Purple and white . . .

DOT: What is he thinking when he looks like that?

GEORGE:
. . . And red and purple and white.

DOT: What does he see? Sometimes, not even blinking.

GEORGE (*To the young girls in the painting*):
Look at this glade, girls,
Your cool blue spot.

DOT: His eyes. So dark and shiny.

GEORGE:
No, stay in the shade, girls.
It's getting hot . . .

DOT: Some think cold and black.

GEORGE:
It's getting orange . . .

DOT (*Sings*):
But it's warm inside his eyes . . .

GEORGE (*Dabbing more intensely*):
Hotter . . .

DOT:

And it's soft inside his eyes . . .

(GEORGE *steps around the canvas to get paint or clean a brush. He glances at* DOT. *Their eyes meet for a second, then* DOT *turns back to her mirror*)

And he burns you with his eyes . . .

GEORGE: Look at her looking.

DOT:

And you're studied like the light.

GEORGE: Forever with that mirror. What does she see? The round face, the tiny pout, the soft mouth, the creamy skin . . .

DOT:

And you look inside the eyes.

GEORGE: The pink lips, the red cheeks . . .

DOT:

And you catch him here and there.

GEORGE: The wide eyes. Studying the round face, the tiny pout . . .

DOT:

But he's never really there.

GEORGE: Seeing all the parts and none of the whole.

DOT:

So you want him even more.

GEORGE (*Sings*):

But the way she catches light . . .

DOT:

And you drown inside his eyes . . .

GEORGE:

And the color of her hair . . .

DOT:	GEORGE:
I could look at him	I could look at her
Forever . . .	Forever . . .

(*A long beat. Music holds under, gradually fading*)

GEORGE (*At his work table*): It's going well . . .

DOT: Should I wear my red dress or blue?

GEORGE: Red.

(*Beat*)

DOT: Aren't you going to clean up?

GEORGE: Why?

DOT: The Follies, George!

(*Beat*)

GEORGE: I have to finish the hat.

(*He returns to his work.* DOT *slams down her brush and stares at the back of the canvas. She exits. Lights fade downstage as the rhythmic figure resumes. As he paints*)
Damn. The Follies. Will she yell or stay silent? Go without me or sulk in the corner? Will she be in the bed when the hat and the grass and the parasol have finally found their way? . . .

(*Sings*)

Too green . . .
Do I care? . . .
Too blue . . .
Yes . . .
Too soft . . .
What shall I do?

(*Thinks for a moment*)

Well . . .
Red.

(*Continues painting; music swells as he is consumed by light*)

(Afternoon. Another Sunday on the island. Downstage right GEORGE *sketches a* BOATMAN; *a cut-out of a black dog stands close by;* NURSE *and* OLD LADY *sit near their tree.* CELESTE #1 *and* CELESTE #2, *young shopgirls, sit on a bench stage left)*

BOATMAN: The water looks different on Sunday.

GEORGE: It is the same water you boat on all week.

BOATMAN (*Contentious*): It looks different from the park.

GEORGE: You prefer watching the boats to the people promenading?

BOATMAN (*Laughing*): People all dressed up in their Sunday-best pretending? Sunday is just another day.
  *(*DOT *and* LOUIS *enter arm in arm. They look out at the water)*
I wear what I always wear — then I don't have to worry.

GEORGE: Worry?

BOATMAN: They leave me alone dressed like this. No one comes near.
  (Music under)

CELESTE #1: Look who's over there.

CELESTE #2: Dot! Who is she with?

CELESTE #1: Looks like Louis the baker.

CELESTE #2: How did Dot get to be with Louis?

CELESTE #1: She knows how to make dough rise!
  (They laugh)

NURSE (*Noticing* DOT): There is that woman.

OLD LADY: Who is she with?

NURSE (*Squinting*): Looks like the baker.

OLD LADY: Moving up, I suppose.

NURSE: The artist is more handsome.
>   (DOT *and* LOUIS *exit*)

OLD LADY: You cannot eat paintings, my dear — not when there's bread in the oven.
>   (JULES, YVONNE, *and their child* LOUISE *appear. They stand to one side and strike a pose. Music continues under, slow and stately*)

JULES: They say he is working on an enormous canvas.

YVONNE: I heard somewhere he's painting little specks.

JULES: You heard it from me! A large canvas of specks. Really . . .

YVONNE: Look at him. Drawing a slovenly boatman.

JULES: I think he is trying to play with light.

YVONNE: What next?

JULES: A monkey cage, they say.
>   (*They laugh*)

BOATMAN: Sunday hypocrites. That's what they are. Muttering and murmuring about this one and that one. I'll take my old dog for company any day. A dog knows his place. Respects your privacy. Makes no demands.
>   (*To the dog*)

Right, Spot?

SPOT (GEORGE): Right.

CELESTE #1 (*Sings*):
They say that George has another woman.

CELESTE #2 (*Sings*):
I'm not surprised.

CELESTE #1:
They say that George only lives with tramps.

600

CELESTE #2:
 I'm not surprised.

CELESTE #1:
 They say he prowls through the streets
 In his top hat after midnight —

CELESTE #2:
 No!

CELESTE #1:
 — and stands there staring up at the lamps.

CELESTE #2:
 I'm not surprised.

BOTH:
 Artists are so crazy . . .

OLD LADY:
 Those girls are noisy.

NURSE: Yes, Madame.

OLD LADY (*Referring to* JULES):
 That man is famous.

NURSE: Yes, Madame.

OLD LADY (*Referring to* BOATMAN):
 That man is filthy.

NURSE: Your son seems to find him interesting.

OLD LADY:
 That man's deluded.
                    (NURSE *thinks, nods*)

THE CELESTES:
 Artists are so crazy.

OLD LADY *and* NURSE:
 Artists are so peculiar.

601

YVONNE: Monkeys!

BOATMAN:
Overprivileged women
Complaining,
Silly little simpering
Shopgirls,
Condescending artists
"Observing,"
"Perceiving" . . .
Well, screw them!

ALL:
Artists are so —

CELESTE #2:
Crazy.

CELESTE #1:
Secretive.

BOATMAN:
High and mighty.

NURSE:
Interesting.

OLD LADY:
Unfeeling.

BOATMAN: What do you do with those drawings, anyway?
(DOT *and* LOUIS *re-enter*)

DOT (*To* LOUIS): That's George.
(*All heads turn, first to* DOT, *then to* GEORGE)

JULES: There's a move on to include his work in the next group show.

YVONNE: Never!

JULES: I agree.

(*Pause*)

I agree.

(*They exit. Music stops*)

CELESTE #1: He draws anyone.

CELESTE #2: Old boatman!

CELESTE #1: Peculiar man.

CELESTE #2: Like his father, I said.

CELESTE #1: I said so first.

>(LOUIS *escorts* DOT *to a park bench stage left and exits. She sits with a small red lesson book in hand*)

DOT (*Very slowly, she reads aloud*): "Lesson number eight. Pro-nouns."

>(*Proudly, she repeats the word, looking towards* GEORGE)

Pronouns.

(*She reads*)

"What is a pronoun? A pronoun is the word used in the place of a noun. Do you recall what a noun is?"

(*Looks up*)

Certainly, I recall.

>(*She pauses, then quickly flips back in the book to the earlier lesson on nouns. She nods her head knowingly, then flips back to the present lesson. She reads*)

"Example: Charles has a book. Marie wants Charles' book."

(*To herself*)

Not Marie again . . .

(*Reads*)

"Marie wants *his* book. Fill in the blanks. Charles ran with Marie's ball. Charles ran with . . ."

(*She writes as she spells aloud*)

h–e–r ball.

(*To herself*)

Get the ball back, Marie.

603

(LOUISE *dashes in upstage*)

OLD LADY: Children should not go unattended.

NURSE: She is very young to be alone.

OLD LADY: I do not like what I see today, Nurse.

NURSE (*Confused*): What do you see?

OLD LADY: Lack of discipline.

NURSE: Oh.

OLD LADY: Not the right direction at all.

BOATMAN: Fools rowing. Call that recreation!

GEORGE: Almost finished.
> (LOUISE *has come up to pet the dog.* BOATMAN *turns on her in a fury*)

BOATMAN: Get away from that dog!
> (*All eyes turn to the* BOATMAN. LOUISE *screams and goes running offstage crying*)

GEORGE: That was hardly necessary!

BOATMAN: How do you know what's necessary? Who are you, with your fancy pad and crayons? You call that work? You smug goddam holier-than-thou shitty little men in your fancy clothes — born with pens and pencils, not pricks! You don't know . . .
> (BOATMAN *storms off.* GEORGE, *stunned, begins to draw the dog*)

CELESTE #1 (*To* GEORGE): Well, what are you going to do — now that you have no one to draw?

CELESTE #2: Sshh. Don't talk to him.

GEORGE: I am drawing this dog.

CELESTE #2: His dog!

CELESTE #1: Honestly . . .

GEORGE: I have already sketched you ladies.

CELESTE #1: What!

CELESTE #2: You have?
> (*The* CELESTES *approach* GEORGE)

CELESTE #1: I do not believe you.

CELESTE #2: When?
> (*During the above, the* OLD LADY *and* NURSE *have exited*)

GEORGE: A few Sundays ago.

CELESTE #1: But we never sat for you.

GEORGE: I studied you from afar.

CELESTE #2: No!

CELESTE #1: Where were you?

CELESTE #2: I want to see.

GEORGE: Some day you shall.

THE CELESTES: When?

GEORGE: Good day.
> (GEORGE *moves upstage*)

CELESTE #1: He did not so much as ask.

CELESTE #2: No respect for a person's privacy.

CELESTE #1: I would not sit for him anyway.

CELESTE #2: Probably that's why he did not ask.
> (*They exit*)

GEORGE (*From across the stage to* DOT): Good afternoon.

DOT (*Surprised*): Hello.

GEORGE: Lesson number eight?

DOT: Yes. Pronouns. My writing is improving. I even keep notes in the back of the book.

GEORGE: Good for you.

DOT: How is your painting coming along?

GEORGE: Slowly.

DOT: Are you getting more work done now that you have fewer distractions in the studio?

GEORGE (*Beat; he moves closer*): It has been quiet there.
    (LOUIS *bounds onstage with a pastry tin*)

LOUIS: Dot. I made your favorite —
    (*He stops when he sees* GEORGE)

GEORGE: Good day.
    (*He retreats across the stage.* DOT *watches him, then turns to* LOUIS)

LOUIS (*Opens the tin*): Creampuffs!
    (*The bench on which they are sitting tracks offstage as* DOT *continues to look at* GEORGE. GEORGE, *who has been staring at his sketch of* SPOT, *looks over and sees they have left. Music. He begins to lose himself in his work. Lights change, leaving the dog onstage.* GEORGE *sketches the dog*)

GEORGE (*Sings*):
If the head was smaller.
If the tail were longer.
If he faced the water.
If the paws were hidden.
If the neck was darker.
If the back was curved.
More like the parasol.

Bumbum bum bumbumbum
Bumbum bum . . .

606

More shade.
More tail.

More grass . . .
Would you like some more grass?
Mmmm . . .

SPOT (GEORGE) (*Barks*):
Ruff! Ruff!
Thanks, the week has been
                    (*Barks*)
Rough!
When you're stuck for life on a garbage scow —
                    (*Sniffs around*)
Only forty feet long from stern to prow,
And a crackpot in the bow — wow, rough!
                    (*Sniffs*)
The planks are rough
And the wind is rough
And the master's drunk and mean and —
                    (*Sniffs*)
Grrrruff! Gruff!
With the fish and scum
And planks and ballast,
                    (*Sniffs*)
The nose gets numb
And the paws get calloused.
And with splinters in your ass,
You look forward to the grass
On Sunday.
The day off.
                    (*Barks*)
Off! Off! Off!
Off!

The grass needs to be thicker. Perhaps a few weeds. With
some ants, if you would. I love fresh ants.

Roaming around on Sunday,
Poking among the roots and rocks.
Nose to the ground on Sunday,
Studying all the shoes and socks.
Everything's worth it Sunday,
The day off.

> (*Sniffs*)

Bits of pastry.

> (*Sniffs*)

Piece of chicken.

> (*Sniffs*)

Here's a handkerchief
That somebody was sick in.

> (*Sniffs*)

There's a thistle.

> (*Sniffs*)

That's a shallot.

> (*Sniffs*)

That's a dripping
From the loony with the palette.

> (*A cut-out of a pug dog,* FIFI, *appears*)

FIFI (GEORGE):
Yap! Yap!

> (*Pants*)

Yap!

> (*High voice*)

Out for the day on Sunday,
Off of my lady's lap at last.
Yapping away on Sunday
Helps you forget the week just past —

> (*Yelps*)

Yep! Yep!
Everything's worth it Sunday,
The day off.
Yep!

Stuck all week on a lady's lap,
Nothing to do but yawn and nap,
Can you blame me if I yap?

SPOT:
Nope.

FIFI: There's just so much attention a dog can take.
Being alone on Sunday,
Rolling around in mud and dirt —

SPOT:
Begging a bone on Sunday,
Settling for a spoiled dessert —

FIFI:
Everything's worth it

SPOT:
Sunday —

FIFI:
The day off.

SPOT (*Sniffs*):
Something fuzzy.

FIFI (*Sniffs*):
Something furry.

SPOT (*Sniffs*):
Something pink
That someone tore off in a hurry.

FIFI:
What's the muddle
In the middle?

SPOT:
That's the puddle
Where the poodle did the piddle.

(*Cut-out of* HORN PLAYER *rises from the stage. Two horn calls. Music continues under. Enter* FRANZ; FRIEDA, *his wife; the* CELESTES, *with fishing poles; and* NURSE)

GEORGE (*Sings*):
Taking the day on Sunday,
Now that the dreary week is dead.
Getting away on Sunday
Brightens the dreary week ahead.
Everyone's on display on Sunday —

ALL:
The day off!
(GEORGE *flips open a page of his sketchbook and starts to sketch the* NURSE *as she clucks at the ducks*)

GEORGE:
Bonnet flapping,
Bustle sliding,
Like a rocking horse that nobody's been riding.
There's a daisy —
And some clover —
And that interesting fellow looking over . . .

OLD LADY (*Offstage*): Nurse!

NURSE *and* GEORGE (*Sing*):
One day is much like any other,
Listening to her snap and drone.

NURSE:
Still, Sunday with someone's dotty mother
Is better than Sunday with your own.
Mothers may drone, mothers may whine —
Tending to his, though, is perfectly fine.
It pays for the nurse that is tending to mine
On Sunday,
My day off.
(*The* CELESTES, *fishing. Music continues under*)

CELESTE #2: This is just ridiculous.

CELESTE #1: Why shouldn't we fish?

CELESTE #2: No one will notice us anyway.
(SOLDIER *enters, attached to a life-size cut-out of another soldier, his* COMPANION)

CELESTE #1: Look.

CELESTE #2: Where?

CELESTE #1: Soldiers.

CELESTE #2: Alone.

CELESTE #1: What did I tell you?

CELESTE #2: They'll never talk to us if we fish. Why don't we —

CELESTE #1: It's a beautiful day for fishing.
(*She smiles in the direction of the* SOLDIERS)

SOLDIER (*Looking to his* COMPANION): What do you think?
(*Beat*)
I like the one in the light hat.
(LOUISE *enters, notices* FRIEDA *and* FRANZ, *and dashes over to them*)

LOUISE: Frieda, Frieda —

FRANZ: Oh, no.

FRIEDA (*Speaks with a German accent*): Not now, Louise.

LOUISE: I want to play.

FRANZ: Go away, Louise. We are not working today.

LOUISE: Let's go throw stones at the ducks.

FRIEDA: Louise! Do not throw stones at the ducks!

LOUISE: Why not?

FRANZ: You know why not, and you know this is our day off,

611

so go find your mother and throw some stones at her, why don't you.
>   (*He begins to choke* LOUISE; FRIEDA *releases his grip*)

FRIEDA: Franz!

LOUISE: I'm telling.

FRANZ: Good. Go!
>   (LOUISE *exits*)

FRIEDA: Franzel — relax.

FRANZ: *Ja* . . . relax.
>   (*He opens a bottle of wine.* GEORGE *flips a page and starts to sketch* FRANZ *and* FRIEDA)

GEORGE *and* FRIEDA (*Sing*):
>   Second bottle . . .

GEORGE *and* FRANZ (*As* FRANZ *looks off at* NURSE):
>   Ah, she looks for me . . .

FRIEDA:
>   He is bursting to go . . .

FRANZ:
>   Near the fountain . . .

FRIEDA:
>   I could let him . . .

FRANZ:
>   How to manage it — ?

FRIEDA:
>   No.
>   (*Speaks*)
>   You know, Franz — I believe that artist is drawing us.

FRANZ: Who?

FRIEDA: Monsieur's friend.

FRANZ (*Sees* GEORGE. *They pose*): Monsieur would never think
to draw us! We are only people he looks down upon.
(*Pause*)
I should have been an artist. I was never intended for work.

FRIEDA: Artists work, Franz. I believe they work very hard.

FRANZ: Work! . . . *We* work.
(*Sings*)
We serve their food,
We carve their meat,
We tend to their house,
We polish their
Silverware.

FRIEDA:
The food we serve
We also eat.

FRANZ:
For them we rush,
Wash and brush,
Wipe and wax —

FRIEDA:
Franz, relax.

FRANZ:
While he "creates,"
We scrape their plates
And dust their knickknacks,
Hundreds to the shelf.
Work is what you do for others,
Liebchen,
Art is what you do for yourself.
(JULES *enters, as if looking for someone. Notices* GEORGE
instead)

JULES: Working on Sunday again? You should give yourself a
day off.

613

GEORGE: Why?

JULES: You must need time to replenish — or does your well never run dry?
(*Laughs; notices* FRIEDA *and* FRANZ)
Drawing my servants? Certainly, George, you could find more colorful subjects.

GEORGE: Who should I be sketching?

JULES: How about that pretty friend of yours. Now why did I see her arm-in-arm with the baker today?
(GEORGE *looks up*)
She is a pretty subject.

GEORGE: Yes . . .

(BOATMAN *enters*)

JULES: Your life needs spice, George. Go to some parties. That is where you'll meet prospective buyers. Have some fun. The work is bound to reflect —

GEORGE: You don't like my work, do you?

JULES: I did once.

GEORGE: You find it too tight.

JULES: People are talking about your work. You have your admirers, but you —

GEORGE: I am using a different brushstroke.

JULES (*Getting angry*): Always changing! Why keep changing?

GEORGE: Because I do not paint for your approval.
(*Beat*)

JULES: And I suppose that is why I like you.
(*Begins to walk away*)
Good to see you, George.

(JULES *crosses as if to exit*)

GEORGE (*Calling after him*): Jules! I would like you to come to the studio some time. See the new work . . .

JULES: For my approval?

GEORGE: No! For your opinion.

JULES (*Considers the offer*): Very well.
(*He exits.* GEORGE *flips a page over and starts sketching the* BOATMAN)

GEORGE *and* BOATMAN (*Sing*):
You and me, pal,
We're the loonies.
Did you know that?
Bet you didn't know that.

BOATMAN:
'Cause we tell them the truth!

Who you drawing?
Who the hell you think you're drawing?
Me?
You don't know me!
Go on drawing,
Since you're drawing only what you want to see,
Anyway!
(*Points to his eyepatch*)
One eye, no illusion —
That you get with two:
(*Points to* GEORGE*'s eye*)
One for what is true.
(*Points to the other*)
One for what suits you.
Draw your wrong conclusion,
All you artists do.
I see what is true . . .

615

(*Music continues under*)
Sitting there, looking everyone up and down. Studying
every move like *you* see something different, like your
eyes know more —
(*Sings*)
You and me, pal,
We're society's fault.
(YVONNE, LOUISE, OLD LADY *enter.* GEORGE *packs up his
belongings*)

ALL (*Sing*):
Taking the day on Sunday
After another week is dead.

OLD LADY: Nurse!

ALL:
Getting away on Sunday
Brightens the dreary week ahead.

OLD LADY: Nurse!
(GEORGE *begins to exit, crossing paths with* DOT *and*
LOUIS, *who enter. He gives* DOT *a hasty tip-of-the-hat and
makes a speedy exit*)

ALL:
Leaving the city pressure
Behind you,
Off where the air is fresher,
Where green, blue,
Blind you —
(LOUIS *leaves* DOT *to offer some pastries to his friends in
the park. Throughout the song, he divides his time between*
DOT *and the others*)

DOT (*Looking offstage in the direction of* GEORGE*'s exit, sings*):
Hello, George . . .
Where did you go, George?
I know you're near, George.

616

I caught your eyes, George.
I want your ear, George.
I've a surprise, George . . .

Everybody loves Louis,
Louis' simple and kind.
Everybody loves Louis,
Louis' lovable.

FRANZ (*Greeting* LOUIS): Louis!

DOT:
Seems we never know, do we,
Who we're going to find?
                              (*Tenderly*)
And Louis the baker —
Is not what I had in mind.
But . . .

Louis' really an artist:
Louis' cakes are an art.
Louis isn't the smartest —
Louis' popular.
Everybody loves Louis:
Louis bakes from the heart . . .

The bread, George.
I mean the bread, George.
And then in bed, George . . .
I mean he kneads me —
I mean like dough, George . . .
Hello, George . . .

Louis' always so pleasant,
Louis' always so fair.
Louis makes you feel present,
Louis' generous.
That's the thing about Louis:

Louis always is "there."
Louis' thoughts are not hard to follow,
Louis' art is not hard to swallow.

Not that Louis' perfection —
That's what makes him ideal.
Hardly anything worth objection:
Louis drinks a bit,
Louis blinks a bit.
Louis makes a connection,
That's the thing that you feel . . .

We lose things.
And then we choose things.
And there are Louis's
And there are Georges —
Well, Louis's
And George.

But George has George
And I need —
Someone —
Louis — !
          (LOUIS *gives her a pastry and exits*)
Everybody loves Louis,
Him as well as his cakes.
Everybody loves Louis,
Me included, George.
Not afraid to be gooey,
Louis sells what he makes.
Everybody gets along with him.
That's the trouble, nothing's wrong with him.

Louis has to bake his way,
George can only bake his . . .
          (*Licks a pastry*)
Louis it is!

(She throws pastry away and exits. Enter an American southern couple, MR. and MRS., followed by GEORGE, who sketches them. They are overdressed, eating French pastries and studying the people in the park)

MR.: Paris looks nothin' like the paintings.

MRS.: I know.

MR. (*Looking about*): I don't see any passion, do you?

MRS.: None.

MR.: The French are so placid.

MRS.: I don't think they have much style, either.

MR.: What's all the carryin' on back home? Delicious pastries, though.

MRS.: Excellent.

MR.: Lookin' at those boats over there makes me think of our return voyage.

MRS.: I long to be back home.

MR.: You do?

MRS.: How soon could we leave?

MR.: You're that anxious to leave? But, Peaches, we just arrived!

MRS.: I know!

MR. (*Gives it a moment's thought*): I don't like it here either! We'll go right back to the hotel and I'll book passage for the end of the week. We'll go to the galleries this afternoon and then we'll be on our way home!

MRS.: I am so relieved.
(*As they exit*)
I *will* miss these pastries, though.

MR.: We'll take a baker with us, too.

MRS.: Wonderful!

(*They exit*)

CELESTE #1: You really should try using that pole.

CELESTE #2: It won't make any difference.

CELESTE #1 (*Starts yelping as if she had caught a fish*): Oh! Oh!

CELESTE #2: What is wrong?

CELESTE #1: Just sit there.

(*She carries on some more, looking in the direction of the* SOLDIER *and his* COMPANION, *who converse for a moment, then come over*)

SOLDIER: May we be of some service, Madame?

CELESTE #1: Mademoiselle.

CELESTE #2: She has a fish.

CELESTE #1: He knows.

SOLDIER: Allow me.

(SOLDIER *takes the pole from her and pulls in the line and hook. There is nothing on the end*)

CELESTE #1: Oh. It tugged so . . .

SOLDIER: There's no sign of a fish here.

CELESTE #1: Oh me. My name is Celeste. This is my friend.

CELESTE #2: Celeste.

(SOLDIER *fools with fishing pole*)

CELESTE #1: Do you have a name?

SOLDIER: I beg your pardon. Napoleon. Some people feel I should change it.

(*The* CELESTES *shake their heads no*)

CELESTE #2: And your friend?

SOLDIER: Yes. He is my friend.

CELESTE #1 (*Giggling, to* SOLDIER): He's very quiet.

SOLDIER: Yes. Actually he is. He lost his hearing during combat exercises.

CELESTE #1: What a shame.

SOLDIER: He can't speak, either.

CELESTE #2: Oh. How dreadful.

SOLDIER: We have become very close, though.

CELESTE #1 (*Nervous*): So I see.
(Music)

SOLDIER *and* GEORGE (*Sudden and loud, sing*):
Mademoiselles,
I and my friend,
We are but soldiers!
　(*Rumble from the* COMPANION*:* SOLDIER *raises hand to quiet him*)

SOLDIER:
Passing the time
In between wars
For weeks at an end.

CELESTE #1 (*Aside*):
Both of them are perfect.

CELESTE #2:
You can have the other.

CELESTE #1:
I don't want the other.

CELESTE #2:
I don't want the other either.

621

SOLDIER:
    And after a week
    Spent mostly indoors
    With nothing but soldiers,
    Ladies, I and my friend
    Trust we will not offend,
    Which we'd never intend,
    By suggesting we spend —

THE CELESTES (*Excited*):
    Oh, spend —

SOLDIER:
    — this magnificent Sunday —

THE CELESTES (*A bit deflated*):
    Oh, Sunday —

SOLDIER:
    — with you and your friend.
        (SOLDIER *offers his arm. Both* CELESTES *rush to take it;*
        CELESTE #1 *gets there first.* CELESTE #2 *tries to get in
        between the* SOLDIERS, *can't, and rather than join the* COM-
        PANION, *takes the arm of* CELESTE #1. *They all start to
        promenade*)

CELESTE #2 (*To* CELESTE #1):
    The one on the right's an awful bore . . .

CELESTE #1:
    He's been in a war.

SOLDIER (*To* COMPANION):
    We may get a meal and we might get more . . .
        (CELESTE #1 *shakes free of* CELESTE #2, *grabs the arm of the*
        SOLDIER, *freeing him from his* COMPANION)

CELESTE #1 *and* SOLDIER (*To themselves, as they exit*):
    It's certainly fine for Sunday . . .

It's certainly fine for Sunday . . .
>> (*Dejected,* CELESTE #2 *grabs the* COMPANION)

CELESTE #2 (*As she exits, carrying* COMPANION):
It's certainly fine for Sunday . . .
>> (GEORGE *is alone. He moves downstage as* FIFI *rises. He sits*)

GEORGE (*Leafing back through his sketches. Sings*):
Mademoiselles . . .
>> (*Flips a page*)

You and me, pal . . .
>> (*Flips*)

Second bottle . . .
Ah, she looks for me . . .
>> (*Flips*)

Bonnet flapping . . .
>> (*Flips*)

Yapping . . .
>> (*Flips*)

Ruff! . . .
Chicken . . .
Pastry . . .
>> (*Licks lip; looks offstage to where* DOT *has exited*)

Yes, she looks for me — good.
Let her look for me to tell me why she left me —
As I always knew she would.
I had thought she understood.
They have never understood.
And no reason that they should.
But if anybody could . . .

Finishing the hat,
How you have to finish the hat.
How you watch the rest of the world
From a window
While you finish the hat.

Mapping out a sky,
What you feel like, planning a sky,
What you feel when voices that come
Through the window
Go
Until they distance and die,
Until there's nothing but sky.

And how you're always turning back too late
From the grass or the stick
Or the dog or the light,
How the kind of woman willing to wait's
Not the kind that you want to find waiting
To return you to the night,
Dizzy from the height,
Coming from the hat,
Studying the hat,
Entering the world of the hat,
Reaching through the world of the hat
Like a window,
Back to this one from that.

Studying a face,
Stepping back to look at a face
Leaves a little space in the way like a window,
But to see —
It's the only way to see.

And when the woman that you wanted goes,
You can say to yourself, "Well, I give what I give."
But the woman who won't wait for you knows
That, however you live,
There's a part of you always standing by,
Mapping out the sky,
Finishing a hat . . .
Starting on a hat . . .
Finishing a hat . . .

(Showing sketch to FIFI)

Look, I made a hat . . .

Where there never was a hat . . .

(MR. *and* MRS. *enter stage right. They are lost. The* BOAT-
MAN *crosses near them and they stop him in his path)*

MR.: Excusez, Masseur. We are lost.

BOATMAN: Huh?

MRS.: Let me try, Daddy.

(Slowly and wildly gesticulating with her every word)

We are alien here. Unable to find passage off island.

BOATMAN *(Pointing to the water)*: Why don't you just walk into
the water until your lungs fill up and you die.

(BOATMAN *crosses away from them, laughing)*

MRS.: I detest these people.

MR. *(Spotting* LOUIS, *who has entered in search of* DOT): Isn't
that the baker?

MRS.: Why, yes it is!

(They cross to LOUIS. GEORGE *brings on the* HORN PLAYER
cut-out. OLD LADY *enters)*

OLD LADY: Where is that tree? Nurse? NURSE!

(Horn call. DOT *enters, and suddenly she and* GEORGE
*are still, staring at one another. Everyone onstage turns
slowly to them. People begin to sing fragments of songs.*
DOT *and* GEORGE *move closer to one another, circling each
other like gun duellers. The others close in around them
until* DOT *and* GEORGE *stop, opposite each other. Silence.*
DOT *takes her bustle and defiantly turns it around, creating a pregnant stance. There is an audible gasp from the
onlookers. Blackout)*

(Music. Lights slowly come up on GEORGE *in his studio,
painting.* DOT *enters and joins* GEORGE *behind the paint-*

ing. He continues painting as she watches. He stops for a moment when he sees her, then continues working)

DOT: You are almost finished.

GEORGE: If I do not change my mind again. And you?

DOT: Two more months.

GEORGE: You cannot change your mind.

DOT: Nor do I want to.
                    (*Beat*)
Is it going to be exhibited?

GEORGE: I am not sure. Jules is coming over to look at it. Any minute, in fact.

DOT: Oh, I hope you don't mind my coming.

GEORGE: What is it that you want, Dot?

DOT: George. I would like my painting.

GEORGE: Your painting?

DOT: The one of me powdering.

GEORGE: I did not know that it was yours.

DOT: You said once that I could have it.

GEORGE: In my sleep?

DOT: I want something to remember you by.

GEORGE: You don't have enough now?

DOT: I want the painting, too.
                    (GEORGE *stops painting*)

GEORGE: I understand you and Louis are getting married.

DOT: Yes.

GEORGE: He must love you very much to take you in that condition.

DOT: He does.

GEORGE: I didn't think you would go through with it. I did not think that was what you really wanted.

DOT: I don't think I can have what I really want. Louis is what I think I need.

GEORGE: Yes. Louis will take you to the Follies! Correct?

DOT: George, I didn't come here to argue.

(JULES *and* YVONNE *enter*)

JULES: George?

GEORGE: Back here, Jules.

DOT: I will go.

GEORGE: Don't leave! It will only be a minute —

JULES (*Crossing behind canvas to* GEORGE): There you are. I brought Yvonne along.

YVONNE: May I take a peek?

DOT: I will wait in the other room.

YVONNE (*Sees* DOT): I hope we are not interrupting you.
   (*She and* JULES *step back and study the painting.* GEORGE *looks at* DOT *as she exits to the front room*)

JULES: It is so large. How can you get any perspective? And this light . . .
   (GEORGE *pulls a lantern close to the canvas*)

GEORGE: Stand here.

YVONNE: Extraordinary! Excuse me.
   (YVONNE *exits into the other room.* DOT *is sitting at her vanity, which is now cleared of her belongings.* YVONNE *and* DOT *look at each other for a moment*)
Talk of painting bores me. It is hard to escape it when you are with an artist.

627

(Beat)

I do not know how you can walk up all those steps in your condition. I remember when I had Louise. I could never be on my feet for long periods of time. Certainly could never navigate steps.

DOT: Did someone carry you around?

YVONNE: Why are you so cool to me?

DOT: Maybe I don't like you.

YVONNE: Whatever have I done to make you feel that way?

DOT: "Whatever have I done . . . ?" Maybe it is the way you speak. What are you really doing here?

YVONNE: You know why we are here. So Jules can look at George's work.

DOT: I do not understand why George invites you. He knows you do not like his painting.

YVONNE: That is not entirely true. Jules has great respect for George. And he has encouraged him since they were in school.

DOT: That is not what I hear. Jules is jealous of George now.

YVONNE *(Beat)*: Well . . . jealousy is a form of flattery, is it not? I have been jealous of you on occasion.
(DOT *looks surprised*)
When I have seen George drawing you in the park. Jules has rarely sketched me.

DOT: You are his wife.

YVONNE *(Uncomfortable)*: Too flat. Too angular.

DOT: Modeling is hard work. You wouldn't like it anyway.

YVONNE: It is worth it, don't you think?

DOT: Sometimes . . .

YVONNE: Has your life changed much now that you are with the baker?

DOT: I suppose. He enjoys caring for me.

YVONNE: You are very lucky. Oh, I suppose Jules cares — but there are times when he just does not know Louise and I are there. George always seems so oblivious to everyone.
(*Lowers her voice*)
Jules says that is what is wrong with his painting. Too obsessive. You have to have a life! Don't you agree?
(DOT *nods*)

JULES: George . . . I do not know what to say. What *is* this?

GEORGE: What is the dominant color? The flower on the hat?

JULES: Is this a school exam, George?

GEORGE: What is that color?

JULES (*Bored*): Violet.
(GEORGE *takes him by the hand and moves him closer to the canvas*)

GEORGE: See? Red and blue. Your eye made the violet.

JULES: So?

GEORGE: So, your eye is perceiving both red and blue *and* violet. Only eleven colors — no black — divided, not mixed on the palette, mixed by the eye. Can't you see the shimmering?

JULES: George . . .

GEORGE: Science, Jules. Fixed laws for color, like music.

JULES: You are a painter, not a scientist! You cannot even see these faces!

GEORGE: I am not painting faces! I am —

JULES: George! I have touted your work in the past, and now

you are embarrassing me! People are talking —

GEORGE: Why should I paint like you or anybody else? I am trying to get through to something new. Something that is my own.

JULES: And I am trying to understand.

GEORGE: And I want you to understand. Look at the canvas, Jules. Really look at it.

JULES: George! Let us get to the point. You have invited me here because you want me to try to get this included in the next group show.

GEORGE (*Beat — embarrassed*): It will be finished soon. I want it to be seen.
(YVONNE, *who has been eavesdropping at the studio door, leans into the room*)

YVONNE: Jules, I am sorry to interrupt, but we really must be going. You know we have an engagement.

JULES: Yes.

YVONNE: Thank you, George.

JULES: Yes. Thank you.

GEORGE: Yes. Thank you for coming.

JULES: I will give the matter some thought.
(*They exit.* GEORGE *stands motionless for a moment staring at the canvas, then dives into his work, painting the girls*)

GEORGE: He does not like you. He does not understand or appreciate you. He can only see you as everyone else does. Afraid to take you apart and put you back together again for himself. But we will not let anyone deter us, will we?
(*Hums*)
Bumbum bum bumbumbum bumbum —

DOT (*Calling to him*): George!

(GEORGE, *embarrassed, crosses in front of canvas. He begins to speak.* DOT *tries to interrupt him*)

GEORGE:
Excuse me — speaking with
Jules about the painting — well,
I just picked up my brushes —
I do not believe he even looked
at the painting, though —

DOT:
You asked me to stay, George,
and then you forget that I am
even here. George!

DOT: I have something to tell you.

GEORGE: Yes. Now, about "your" painting —

DOT: I may be going away.

(*Beat*)

To America.

GEORGE: Alone.

DOT: Of course not! With Louis. He has work.

GEORGE: When?

DOT: After the baby arrives.

GEORGE: You will not like it there.

DOT: How do you know?

GEORGE (*Getting angry*): I have read about America. Why are you telling me this? First, you ask for a painting that is *not* yours — then you tell me this.

(*Beginning to return to the studio*)

I have work to do.

(*Chord; music continues under*)

DOT: Yes, George, run to your work. Hide behind your painting. I have come to tell you I am leaving because I thought you might *care* to know — foolish of me, because you care about nothing —

GEORGE: I care about many things —

DOT: Things — not people.

GEORGE: People, too. I cannot divide my feelings up as neatly as you, and I am not hiding behind my canvas — I am living in it.

DOT (*Sings*):
What you care for is yourself.

GEORGE: I care about this painting. *You* will be in this painting.

DOT:
I am something you can use.

GEORGE (*Sings*):
I had thought you understood.

DOT:
It's because I understand that I left,
That I am leaving.

GEORGE:
Then there's nothing I can say,
Is there?

DOT:
Yes, George, there is!

You could tell me not to go.
Say it to me,
Tell me not to go.
Tell me that you're hurt,
Tell me you're relieved,
Tell me that you're bored —
Anything, but don't assume I know.
Tell me what you feel!

GEORGE:
What I feel?
You know exactly how I feel.

632

Why do you insist
You must hear the words,
When you know I cannot give you words?
Not the ones you need.

There's nothing to say.
I cannot be what you want.

DOT:

What do *you* want, George?

GEORGE:

I needed you and you left.

DOT:

There was no room for me —

GEORGE (*Overriding her*):

You will not accept who I am.
I am what I do —
Which you knew,
Which you always knew,
Which I thought you were a part of!
                (*He goes behind the canvas*)

DOT:

No,
You are complete, George,
You are your own.
We do not belong together.
You are complete, George,
You are alone.
I am unfinished,
I am diminished
With or without you.

We do not belong together,
And we should have belonged together.
What made it so right together

Is what made it all wrong.

No one is you, George,
There we agree,
But others will do, George.
No one is you and
No one can be,
But no one is me, George,
No one is me.
We do not belong together.
And we'll never belong — !

You have a mission,
A mission to see.
Now I have one too, George.
And we should have belonged together.

I have to move on.

> (DOT *leaves.* GEORGE *stops painting and comes from around the canvas.   He is left standing alone onstage. The lights fade*)

> (*The set changes back to the park scene around him. When the change is complete, he moves downstage right with the* OLD LADY, *and begins to draw her.   They are alone, except for the cut-out of the* COMPANION, *which stands towards the rear of the stage.   There is a change of tone in both* GEORGE *and the* OLD LADY. *She has assumed a kind of loving attitude, soft and dreamlike.* GEORGE *is rather sullen in her presence*)

OLD LADY (*Staring across the water*): I remember when you were a little boy.   You would rise up early on a Sunday morning and go for a swim . . .

GEORGE: I do not know how to swim.

OLD LADY: The boys would come by the house to get you . . .

GEORGE: I have always been petrified of the water.

634

OLD LADY: And your father would walk you all to the banks of the Seine . . .

GEORGE: Father was never faithful to us.

OLD LADY: And he would give you boys careful instruction, telling you just how far to swim out . . .

GEORGE: And he certainly never instructed.

OLD LADY: And now, look across there — in the distance — all those beautiful trees cut down for a foolish tower.
(*Music under*)

GEORGE: I do not think there were ever trees there.

OLD LADY: How I loved the view from here . . .
(*Sings*)
Changing . . .

GEORGE: I am quite certain that was an open field . . .

OLD LADY:
It keeps changing.

GEORGE: I used to play there as a child.

OLD LADY:
I see towers
Where there were trees.

Going,
All the stillness,
The solitude,
Georgie.

Sundays,
Disappearing
All the time,
When things were beautiful . . .

GEORGE (*Sings*):
All things are beautiful,

Mother.
All trees, all towers,
Beautiful.
That tower —
Beautiful, Mother,
See?

(*Gestures*)

A perfect tree.

Pretty isn't beautiful, Mother,
Pretty is what changes.
What the eye arranges
Is what is beautiful.

OLD LADY:
Fading . . .

GEORGE:
I'm changing.
You're changing.

OLD LADY:
It keeps fading . . .

GEORGE:
I'll draw us now before we fade, Mother.

OLD LADY:
It keeps melting
Before our eyes.

GEORGE:
You watch
While I revise the world.

OLD LADY:
Changing,
As we sit here —
Quick, draw it all,
Georgie!

OLD LADY *and* GEORGE:
  Sundays —

OLD LADY:
  Disappearing,
  As we look —

GEORGE: Look! ... Look! ...

OLD LADY (*Not listening, fondly*):
  You make it beautiful.
                (*Music continues*)
  Oh, Georgie, how I long for the old view.
  (*Music stops. The* SOLDIER *and* CELESTE #2 *enter arm-in-arm and promenade*)

SOLDIER (*Noticing his* COMPANION): I am glad to be free of him.

CELESTE #2: Friends can be confining.

SOLDIER: He never understood my moods.

CELESTE #2: She only thought of herself.
  (MR. *and* MRS. *enter. He is carrying a big steamer trunk. She is carrying a number of famous paintings, framed, under her arm. They are followed by* DOT, *who is carrying her baby bundled in white, and* LOUIS)

SOLDIER:
It felt as if I had this
burden at my side.

MR.:
This damned island again!
I do not understand why we
are not goin' straight to
our boat.

CELESTE #2:
She never really cared
about me.

MRS.:
They wanted to come here
first.

SOLDIER:
We had very different
tastes.

637

<table>
</table>

CELESTE #2: She had no taste.	MR.: That much I figured out — but why? Didn't you ask them?
SOLDIER: She did seem rather pushy.	
CELESTE #2: Very! And he was so odd.	MRS.: I don't know.
SOLDIER: (*Angry*) HE IS NOT ODD!	(MR. *and* MRS. *are stopped by the* SOLDIER *'s line,* "*He is not odd*")

CELESTE #2: No. No, I didn't really mean odd . . .
> (*They exit.* LOUISE *runs onstage.* BOATMAN *rushes after her*)

BOATMAN (*Mutters as he chases after* LOUISE): . . . you better not let me get my hands on you, you little toad.
> (LOUISE *puts her hand over her eye and stiffens her leg in imitation of the* BOATMAN. *As he chases her offstage*)

Now stop that!

MR.: Are we ever going to get home?!
> (MR. *and* MRS. *exit.* DOT *crosses downstage to* GEORGE)

GEORGE (*Not looking up*): You are blocking my light.

DOT: Marie and I came to watch.

GEORGE (*Turning towards* DOT): Marie . . .
> (*Back to his sketch pad*)

You know I do not like anyone staring over my shoulder.

DOT: Yes, I know.
> (*She moves to another position*)

George, we are about to leave for America. I have come to ask for the painting of me powdering again. I would like to take it with me.

GEORGE (*He stops for a moment*): Oh? I have repainted it.
> (*He draws*)

DOT: What?

GEORGE: Another model.

DOT: You knew I wanted it.

GEORGE: Perhaps if you had remained still —

DOT: Perhaps if you would look up from your pad! What is wrong with you, George? Can you not even look at your own child?

GEORGE: She is not my child. Louis is her father.

DOT: Louis is not her father.

GEORGE: Louis is her father now. Louis will be a loving and attentive father. I cannot because I cannot look up from my pad.
> (*She stands speechless for a moment, then begins to walk away;* GEORGE *turns to her*)

Dot.
> (*She stops*)

I *am* sorry.
> (DOT *and* LOUIS *exit.* GEORGE *drawing* OLD LADY)

OLD LADY: I worry about you, George.

GEORGE: Could you turn slightly toward me, please.
> (*She does so*)

OLD LADY: No future in dreaming.

GEORGE: Drop the head a little, please.
> (*She does so.* CELESTE #1 *enters and goes to the* COMPANION)

OLD LADY: I worry about you and that woman, too.

GEORGE: I have another woman in my life now.

OLD LADY: They are all the same woman.

GEORGE (*Chuckles*): Variations on a theme.

OLD LADY: Ah, you always drifted as a child.

GEORGE (*Muttering*): Shadows are too heavy.

OLD LADY: You were always in some other place — seeing something no one else could see.

GEORGE: Softer light.
> (*Lights dim slowly*)

OLD LADY: We tried to get through to you, George. Really we did.
> (GEORGE *stops drawing. He looks at her. Looks at the page*)

GEORGE (*Laments*): Connect, George.
> (*Trails off*)

Connect . . .
> (FRIEDA *and* JULES *enter. They seem to be hiding*)

FRIEDA: Are you certain you wish to do this?

JULES (*Uncertain*): Of course. We just have to find a quiet spot. I've wanted to do it outside for a long time.

FRIEDA: Franz would kill you —

JULES (*Panics*): Is he in the park?

FRIEDA: I am not certain.

JULES: Oh. Well. Perhaps some other day would be better.

FRIEDA: Some other day? Always some other day. Perhaps you do not really wish to —

JULES (*Subservient*): I do. I do! I love tall grass.

FRIEDA: *Ja.* Tall grass. You wouldn't toy with my affections, would you?

JULES: No. No. Of course not.

FRIEDA: I see a quiet spot over there.

JULES (*Pointing where she did, nervous*): Over there. There are people in that grove —
> (FRIEDA *places his hand on her breast. They are interrupted by the entrance of* CELESTE #2 *and the* SOLDIER. FRIEDA, *then* JULES, *exits; as he leaves*)

Bon jour.

SOLDIER: Do you suppose there is a violation being perpetrated by that man?

CELESTE #2: What?

SOLDIER: There is something in the air today . . .

CELESTE #1 (*To the* COMPANION): Being alone is nothing new for me.

SOLDIER (*Noticing* CELESTE #1): Look who is watching us.

CELESTE #1: Sundays are such a bore. I'd almost rather be in the shop. Do you like your work? I hate mine!

CELESTE #2: I do not care if she never speaks to me again.

SOLDIER: She won't.
> (*Chord.* FRANZ *and the* NURSE *enter as if to rendezvous*)

YVONNE (*Entering*): FRANZ!
> (NURSE *exits.* YVONNE *goes to* FRANZ)

Franz, have you seen Louise?

FRANZ (*Angry*): *Nein*, Madame.

YVONNE: I thought Frieda was going to care for her today.

FRANZ: But it's Sunday.

YVONNE: What of it?

FRANZ: Our day off!

YVONNE: Oh. But I have just lost my little girl!

(FRANZ *shrugs his shoulders and begins looking for* LOUISE)

SOLDIER: Let's go say hello to Celeste.

YVONNE (*Calling*): Louise?

CELESTE #2 (*Indignant*): I do not wish to speak with her!

SOLDIER: Come. It will be fun!
(SOLDIER *takes* CELESTE #2 *toward* CELESTE #1. LOUISE *comes running in, breathless. She immediately goes to* YVONNE*'s side*)

YVONNE: Louise! Where have you been, young lady?!

LOUISE: With Frieda.

YVONNE (*To* FRANZ): There, you see.

FRANZ: Frieda?

LOUISE: And with Father.

YVONNE: Your father is in the studio.

LOUISE: No, he's not. He's with Frieda. I saw them.

FRANZ: Where?

LOUISE: Over there. Tonguing.
(FRANZ *exits. Music under, agitated*)

OLD LADY: Manners. Grace. Respect.

YVONNE (*Beginning to spank* LOUISE): How dare you, young lady!

LOUISE:	(SOLDIER *and* CELESTE #2
It's true. It's true!	*reach* CELESTE #1)
	CELESTE #1:
(JULES *enters, somewhat*	What do you want?
sheepishly)	
	SOLDIER:
	We've come for a visit.

YVONNE:
Where the hell have you
been? What are you doing
here?

CELESTE #1:
I don't want to say hello to
her. Cheap Christmas
wrapping.

JULES:
Darling, I came out here
looking for Louise.

CELESTE #2:
Cheap! Look who is talking.
You have the worst reputa-
tion of anyone in Paris.

LOUISE:
(*Crying*)
You came to tongue.

CELESTE #1:
At least I have a reputation.
You could not draw a fly
to flypaper!

(BOATMAN *enters and begins chasing* LOUISE *around the*
stage. MR. *and* MRS. *enter and are caught up in the frenzy.*
All hell breaks loose, everyone speaking at once, the stage
erupting into total chaos)

YVONNE:
How dare you, Jules!
(*She goes to him and begins*
striking him)

SOLDIER:
Ladies, you mustn't fight.

CELESTE #2:
I seem to be doing just fine.

JULES:
Nothing, I swear.

CELESTE #1:
Hah. With a diseased
soldier!

YVONNE:
Nothing. Look.
(FRANZ *drags in* FRIEDA)

SOLDIER:
Wait just a minute.

Have you been with my
husband?

FRIEDA:
Madame, he gave me no choice.

CELESTE #1:
Disgusting sores everywhere.

CELESTE #2:
Don't say that about him.

FRANZ:
What do you mean he gave you no choice?

SOLDIER:
Yes, don't say that —

JULES:
(*Letting go of* LOUISE, *who drifts off to the side*)
That is not so. Your wife lured me.

CELESTE #1:
I'll say whatever I like. You are both ungrateful, cheap, ugly, diseased, disgusting garbage . . .

FRIEDA:
Lured you! You all but forced me —

SOLDIER:
Listen here, lady, if in fact there is anything ladylike about you. You should be glad to take what you can get, any way you can get it and I —

JULES:
You are both fired!

FRANZ:
FIRED! You think we would continue to work in your house?

CELESTE #2:
You think you know everything. You are not so special, and far from as pretty as you think, and everyone that comes into the shop knows exactly what you are and what —

YVONNE:
Jules, you cannot change the subject. What were you doing?

(*Everyone has slowly fought their way to the middle of the stage, creating one big fight.* GEORGE *and the* OLD LADY *have been watching the chaos.* GEORGE *begins to cross stage to exit. Arpeggiated chord, as at the beginning of the play. Everybody suddenly freezes in place*)

OLD LADY: Remember, George.
>(*Another chord.* GEORGE *turns to the group*)

GEORGE: Order.
>(*Another chord. Everyone turns simultaneously to* GEORGE. *As chords continue under, he nods to them, and they each take up a position on stage*)

Design.
>(*Chord.* GEORGE *nods to* FRIEDA *and* FRANZ, *and they cross downstage right onto the apron. Chord.* GEORGE *nods to* MR. *and* MRS., *and they cross upstage*)

Tension.
>(*Chord.* GEORGE *nods to* CELESTE #1 *and* CELESTE #2, *and they cross downstage. Another chord.* JULES *and* YVONNE *cross upstage*)

Balance.
>(*Chord.* OLD LADY *crosses right as* DOT *and* LOUIS *cross center.* GEORGE *signals* LOUIS *away from* DOT. *Another chord.* SOLDIER *crosses upstage left;* LOUISE, *upstage right. Chord.* GEORGE *gestures to the* BOATMAN, *who crosses downstage right*)

Harmony.
>(*The music becomes calm, stately, triumphant.* GEORGE *turns front. The promenade begins. Throughout the song,* GEORGE *is moving about, setting trees, cut-outs, and figures — making a perfect picture*)

ALL (*Sing*):
Sunday,
By the blue
Purple yellow red water
On the green
Purple yellow red grass,

Let us pass
Through our perfect park,
Pausing on a Sunday
By the cool
Blue triangular water
On the soft
Green elliptical grass
As we pass
Through arrangements of shadows
Towards the verticals of trees
Forever . . .

                   (*The horn sounds*)

By the blue
Purple yellow red water
On the green
Orange violet mass
Of the grass
In our perfect park,

GEORGE (*To* DOT):

Made of flecks of light
And dark,
And parasols:
Bumbum bum bumbumbum
Bumbum bum . . .

ALL:

People strolling through the trees
Of a small suburban park
On an island in the river
On an ordinary Sunday . . .

    (*The horn sounds. Chimes. They all reach their positions*)
Sunday . . .

    (*The horn again. Everyone assumes the final pose of the painting.* GEORGE *comes out to the apron*)
Sunday . . .

(At the last moment, GEORGE *rushes back and removes* LOUISE*'s eyeglasses. He dashes back on to the apron and freezes the picture. Final chord. The completed canvas flies in. Very slow fade, as the image of the characters fades behind the painting with* GEORGE *in front. Blackout)*

George (Mandy Patinkin) and Dot (Bernadette Peters)

MARTHA SWOPE

GEORGE: "White. A blank page or canvas. The challenge: bring order to the whole." George (Mandy Patinkin)

"Sunday in the Park with George"
Dot (Bernadette Peters)

DOT: "I'd be in the Follies"   Dot (Bernadette Peters)

Seurat's "Jeune
Femme se
Poudrant"
("Woman
Powdering
Herself")

"Everybody Loves Louis" Louis (Cris Groenendaal) and Dot (Bernadette Peters)

Mr. and Mrs. (Kurt Knudson and Judith Moore)

651

Freida (Nancy Opel) and Franz (Brent Spiner); in background
Nurse (Judith Moore) Companion, Soldier (Robert Westenber

leste #1 (Melanie Vaughan), Celeste #2 (Mary D'Arcy),
d Jules (Charles Kimbrough)

"Putting It Together"
George (Mandy Patinkin), Elaine (Mary D'Arcy) and Mar

(Bernadette Peters), with a cut-out of George at far left

George (Mandy Patinkin) sketching the Boatman (William Parry); in background, Yvonne (Dana Ivey), Louise (Danielle Ferland, Jules (Charles Kimbrough), Nurse (Judith Moore), Old Lady (Barbara Bryne), Louis (Cris Groenendaal) and Dot (Bernadette Peters)

ACT II

Lights fade up slowly, and we see everyone in the tableau. There is a very long pause before we begin. The audience should feel the tension. Finally, music begins. One by one, they sing.

DOT:
It's hot up here.

YVONNE:
It's hot and it's monotonous.

LOUISE:
I want my glasses.

FRANZ:
This is not my good profile.

NURSE: Nobody can even *see* my profile.

CELESTE #1:
I hate this dress.

CELESTE #2:
The soldiers have forgotten us.

FRIEDA:
The boatman *schwitzes.*

JULES: I am completely out of proportion.

SOLDIER:

These helmets weigh a lot on us.

OLD LADY:

This tree is blocking my view.

LOUISE:

I can't see anything.

BOATMAN:

Why are they complaining?
It could have been raining.

DOT:

I hate these people.

ALL:

It's hot up here
A lot up here.
It's hot up here
Forever.

A lot of fun
It's not up here.
It's hot up here,
No matter what.

There's not a breath
Of air up here,
And they're up here
Forever.

It's not my fault
I got up here.
I'll rot up here,
I am so hot up here.

YVONNE (*To* LOUISE): Darling, don't clutch mother's hand
quite so tightly. Thank you.

CELESTE #1:

It's hot up here.

FRIEDA:

At least you have a parasol.

SOLDIER, NURSE, YVONNE, *and* LOUISE:

Well, look who's talking,
Sitting in the shade.

JULES (*To* DOT): I trust my cigar is not bothering you —
unfortunately, it never goes out.

(*She pays him no attention*)

You have excellent concentration.

SOLDIER (*To* COMPANION):

It's good to be together again.

CELESTE #2 (*To* CELESTE #1):

See, I told you they were odd.

CELESTE #1:

Don't slouch.

LOUISE:

He took my glasses!

YVONNE:

You've been eating something sticky.

NURSE:

I put on rouge today, too . . .

FRIEDA (*To* BOATMAN):

Don't you ever take a bath?

OLD LADY:

Nurse! Hand me my fan.

NURSE:

I can't.

FRANZ:
　At least the brat is with her mother.

LOUISE:
　I heard that!

JULES (*To* DOT):
　Do you like tall grass?

FRIEDA:
　Hah!

YVONNE:
　Jules!

BOATMAN:
　Bunch of animals . . .

DOT:
　I hate these people.

ALL:
　It's hot up here
　And strange up here,
　No change up here
　Forever.

　How still it is,
　How odd it is,
　And God, it is
　So hot!

SOLDIER: I like the one in the light hat.

DOT:
　Hello, George.
　I do not wish to be remembered
　Like this, George,
　With them, George.
　My hem, George:

Three inches off the ground
And then this monkey
And these people, George —

They'll argue till they fade
And whisper things and grunt.
But thank you for the shade,
And putting me in front.
Yes, thank you, George, for that . . .
And for the hat . . .

CELESTE #1:
It's hot up here.

YVONNE:
It's hot and it's monotonous.

LOUISE:
I want my glasses!

FRANZ:
This is not my good profile.

CELESTE #1:
I hate this dress.

(*Overlapping*)

CELESTE #2:
The soldiers have forgotten us.

CELESTE #1:
Don't slouch!

BOATMAN:
Animals . . .

JULES:
Are you sure you don't like tall grass?

NURSE:
I put on rouge today, too . . .

FRIEDA:
  Don't you ever take a bath?

SOLDIER:
  It's good to be together again.

OLD LADY:
  Nurse, hand me my fan.

DOT:
  It's hot up here.

YVONNE:
  It's hot and it's monotonous.

LOUISE:
  He took my glasses, I want my glasses!

FRANZ:
  This is not my good profile.

ALL:
  And furthermore,
  Finding you're
  Fading
  Is very degrading
  And God, I am so hot!

  Well, there are worse things than sweating
  By a river on a Sunday.
  There are worse things than sweating by a river

BOATMAN:
  When you're sweating in a picture
  That was painted by a genius

FRANZ:
  And you know that you're immortal

FRIEDA:
  And you'll always be remembered

NURSE:
Even if they never see you

OLD LADY:
And you're listening to drivel

SOLDIER:
And you're part of your companion

LOUISE:
And your glasses have been stolen

YVONNE:
And you're bored beyond endurance

LOUIS:
And the baby has no diapers

CELESTE #1 (*To* CELESTE #2):
And you're slouching

CELESTE #2:
I am not!

JULES:
And you are out of all proportion!

DOT:
And I hate these people!

ALL:
You never get
A breeze up here,
And she's (he's) up here
Forever.

You cannot run
Amok up here,
You're stuck up here
In this gavotte.

Perspectives don't

Make sense up here.
It's tense up here
Forever.

The outward show
Of bliss up here
Is disappear-
Ing dot by dot.
> (*Long pause. Music continues for a long moment*)

And it's hot!
> (*They shake themselves loose from the pose for a brief moment, but at the last beat of the music resume their positions.* GEORGE *enters downstage and stands on the apron in front of the tableau*)

GEORGE: A fascination with light. The bedroom where I slept as a child — it had a window. At night, the reflection of the light — that is, the light outside the window — created a shadow-show on my wall. So it was, lying in my bed, looking at the wall, I was able to make out shapes of night activity from the street. These images were not rich in detail, so my mind's eye filled in the shapes to bring them to life. Straying from the point. The point? Light and sleep. I didn't sleep. Well, of course I slept, but always when there was a choice, when I might fight the urge, I would lie awake, eyes fixed on the wall, sometimes until the bright sunlight of the morning washed the image away. Off and running. Off and running. First into the morning light. Last on the gas-lit streets. Energy that had no time for sleep. A mission to see, to record impressions. Seeing . . . recording . . . seeing the record, then feeling the experience. Connect the dots, George. Slowing to a screeching halt — in one week. Fighting to wake up. "Wake up, Georgie." I can still feel her cool hand on my warm cheek. Could darkness be an inviting place? Could sleep surpass off and running? No. Lying still, I can see the boys swimming in the Seine. I can see them all, on a sunny Sunday in the park.

(*He exits. During the following, the characters break from their poses when they speak. Accompanying their exits, pieces of scenery disappear; by the time the* BOATMAN *exits at the end of the sequence, the set is returned to its original white configuration*)

CELESTE #2: Thirty-one . . .

CELESTE #1: It is hard to believe.

CELESTE #2: Yes.

CELESTE #1: It seems like only yesterday we were posing for him.

CELESTE #2: We never posed for him!

CELESTE #1: Certainly we did! We are in a painting, aren't we?

CELESTE #2: It's not as if he asked us to sit!

CELESTE #1: If you had sat up —

SOLDIER: Will you two just keep QUIET!

(*He steps downstage. The* CELESTES *exit*)

I hardly knew the man. I would spend my Sundays here, and I would see him sketching, so I was surprised when he stopped showing up. Of course, I did not notice right away. But one day, I realized, something was different — like a flash of light, right through me, the way that man would stare at you when he sketched — I knew, he was no longer.

(SOLDIER *exits.* LOUISE *breaks away from her mother and dashes downstage*)

LOUISE: I am going to be a painter when I grow up!

BOATMAN: If you live.

(LOUISE *runs off*)

665

FRIEDA: Honestly!

BOATMAN: Keep your mouth shut!

FRIEDA: It is my mouth and I shall do as I please!

FRANZ: Quiet! George was a gentleman.

FRIEDA: Soft spoken.

FRANZ: And he was a far superior artist to Monsieur.

FRIEDA: George had beautiful eyes.

FRANZ: *Ja,* he — beautiful eyes?

FRIEDA: *Ja* . . . well . . . eyes that captured beauty.

FRANZ (*Suspicious*): *Ja* . . . he chose his subjects well.
> (*They exit*)

DOT: I was in Charleston when I heard. At first, I was surprised by the news. Almost relieved, in fact. Perhaps I knew this is how it would end — perhaps we both knew.
> (*She exits*)

OLD LADY: A parent wants to die first. But George was always off and running, and I was never able to keep up with him.

NURSE: No one knew he was ill until the very last days. I offered to care for him, but he would let no one near. Not even her.
> (OLD LADY *and* NURSE *exit*)

JULES (*Too sincere*): George had great promise as a painter. It really is a shame his career was ended so abruptly. He had an unusual flair for color and light, and his work was not as mechanical as some have suggested. I liked George. He was dedicated to his work — seldom did anything but work — and I am proud to have counted him among my friends.

666

YVONNE: George stopped me once in the park — it was the only time I had ever spoken to him outside the company of Jules. He stared at my jacket for an instant, then muttered something about beautiful colors and just walked on. I rather fancied George.

(JULES *looks at her*)

Well, most of the women did!

(JULES *and* YVONNE *exit*)

BOATMAN: They all wanted him and hated him at the same time. They wanted to be painted — splashed on some fancy salon wall. But they hated him, too. Hated him because he only spoke when he absolutely had to. Most of all, they hated him because they knew he would always be around.

(BOATMAN *exits. The stage is bare.*)

(*Lights change. Electronic music. It is 1984. We are in the auditorium of the museum where the painting now hangs. Enter* GEORGE. *He wheels in his grandmother,* MARIE *[played by* DOT*], who is ninety-eight and confined to a wheelchair.* DENNIS, GEORGE's *technical assistant, rolls on a control console and places it stage right. An immense white machine rolls on and comes to rest center stage. Our contemporary* GEORGE *is an inventor-sculptor, and this is his latest invention, Chromolume #7. The machine is postmodern in design and is dominated by a four-foot-in-diameter sphere at the top. It glows a range of cool colored light.* MARIE *sits on one side of the machine, and* GEORGE *stands at the console on the other. Behind them is a full-stage projection screen*)

GEORGE: Ladies and gentlemen, in 1983 I was commissioned by this museum to create an art piece commemorating Georges Seurat's painting "A Sunday Afternoon on the Island of La Grande Jatte." My latest Chromolume stands before you now, the seventh in a continuing series. Because I have a special association with this painting, the museum director, Robert Greenberg, suggested I assemble a short presentation to precede the activation of my latest invention. I have brought my grandmother along to give me a hand.

(*Introducing her*)

My grandmother, Marie.

(*What follows is a coordinated performance of music, text [read from index cards by* GEORGE *and* MARIE*], film projections of the images referred to, and light emissions from the machine. The first section is accompanied by film projections*)

MARIE: I was born in Paris, France, ninety-eight years ago. My grandson, George.

GEORGE: I was born in Lodi, New Jersey, thirty-two years ago.

MARIE: My mother was married to Louis, a baker. They left France when I was an infant to travel to Charleston, South Carolina.

GEORGE: Georges Seurat.

MARIE: Born: December 2, 1859.

GEORGE: It was through his mother that the future artist was introduced to the lower-class Parisian parks. Seurat received a classical training at the Beaux Arts.

MARIE: Like his father, he was not an easy man to know.

GEORGE: He lived in an age when science was gaining influence over Romantic principles.

MARIE: He worked very hard.

GEORGE: His first painting, at the age of twenty-four, "Bathing at Asnières," was rejected by the Salon, but was shown by the Group of Independent Artists.

MARIE: They hung it over the refreshment stand.
>
> (*Ad-libbing*)

Wasn't that awful?

GEORGE: On Ascension Day 1884, he began work on his second painting, "A Sunday Afternoon on the Island of La Grande Jatte." He was to work two years on this painting.

MARIE: He always knew where he was going before he picked up a paint brush.

GEORGE: He denied conventional perspective and conventional space.

MARIE: He was unconventional in his lifestyle as well.
>
> (*Ad-libbing again*)

So was I! You know I was a Florodora Girl for a short time — when I left Charleston and before I was married to my first husband —

GEORGE (*Interrupting her*): Marie. Marie!
>
> (*She looks over to him*)

The film is running.

MARIE: Excuse me.
>
> (*She reads*)

They hung it over the refreshment stand.

GEORGE: Marie!
>
> (*He reads*)

Having studied scientific findings on color, he developed a new style of painting. He found by painting tiny particles, color next to color, that at a certain distance the eye would fuse the specks optically, giving them greater intensity than any mixed pigments.

MARIE: He wanted to paint with colored lights.

GEORGE: Beams of colored light, he hoped.

MARIE: It was shown at the Eighth and last Impressionist Exhibition.

GEORGE: Monet, Renoir, and Sisley withdrew their submissions because of his painting.

MARIE: They placed it in a small room off to the side of the main hall, too dark for the painting to truly be seen.

GEORGE: The painting was ridiculed by most. But there were also a handful of believers in his work.

MARIE: He went on to paint six more major paintings before his sudden death at the age of thirty-one. He never sold a painting in his lifetime.

GEORGE: On this occasion, I present my latest Chromolume —

MARIE: — Number Seven —

GEORGE: — which pays homage to "La Grande Jatte" and to my grandmother, Marie. The score for this presentation has been composed by Naomi Eisen.
(NAOMI *enters, bows, and exits*)

MARIE (*She reads a stage direction by mistake*): George begins to activate the Chromolume machine as . . .

GEORGE: Don't read that part, Grandmother.

MARIE: Oh . . . don't read this . . .
(*Music begins to increase in volume and intensity. Strobe lights begin emitting from the machine along with side shafts of brilliant light. Colors begin to fill the stage and audience, creating a pointillist look. Just as the sphere begins to illuminate, producing various images from the painting, there is a sudden explosion of sparks and smoke. The lighting system flickers on and off until everything dies, including music. There is a moment of silence in the darkness*)

GEORGE (*Under his breath*): Shit.
>   (*Calling out*)
> Robert Greenberg?

GREENBERG (*From the back of the house*): Just a minute, George!
>   (*Some light returns to the smoke-filled stage*)

DENNIS (*Offstage*): It's the regulator, George.
>   (*Lights come up on* GEORGE, *who is looking inside the machine. He steps downstage toward the audience*)

GEORGE: My apologies, ladies and gentlemen. For precise synchronization of all the visual elements, I've installed a new state-of-the-art Japanese microcomputer which controls the voltage regulator. I think that the surge from the musical equipment has created an electrical short.
>   (*Beat*)
> Unfortunately, no electricity, no art. Give us a moment and we'll be able to bypass the regulator and be back in business.
>   (*After "no electricity, no art," GREENBERG has entered and stands to the side of the apron. DENNIS enters and joins GEORGE at the Chromolume*)

GREENBERG: I am very sorry, ladies and gentlemen. We seem to be having a little electrical difficulty.
>   (NAOMI *has entered and rushed to the machine*)

NAOMI: There's no juice!

GREENBERG: You must realize this is the first time we have had a collaboration like this at the museum and it has offered some extraordinary challenges to us here.
>   (NAOMI *and* DENNIS *exit arguing*)
> Now, I hope to see all of you at the reception and dinner which will follow the presentation. It's right down the hall in the main gallery, where the painting hangs. And we have a very special treat for you. As I am sure you have

noticed, in order to raise additional funds we have chosen to sell the air rights to the museum — and some of the twenty-seven flights of condominiums that stand above us now will be open for your inspection after dinner. You may even wish to become one of our permanent neighbors!

GEORGE: We're ready, Bob.

GREENBERG: Well . . . proceed. Proceed!
(*He exits*)

GEORGE (*Into his headset*): Dennis! Lights.
(*Lights dim and the presentation continues. Music gathers momentum. The Chromolume begins several seconds before the speaking resumes, with images from the painting projected on its sphere, illustrating the lecture*)

MARIE: When I was young, Mother loved telling me tales of her life in France, and of her work as an artist's model.

GEORGE: Her mother showed her this great painting and pointed to this woman and said that it was she.

MARIE: And she pointed to a couple in the back — they were holding an infant child — and she said that was me!

GEORGE: Shortly before my great-grandmother's death, she spoke of her association with the artist of this painting. She told Marie that Seurat was her real father.

MARIE: I was shocked!

GEORGE: My parents never believed this story. After all, there was no proof. I do not —

MARIE (*Produces a red book, unbeknownst to* GEORGE): My mother gave me this small red book.

GEORGE: Marie!

MARIE: Oh, George, I wanted to bring the book and show it.

(*To audience*)
In the back are notes about his great-grandfather, the artist.

GEORGE: Actually, this book is really just a grammar book in the handwriting of a child, and though there *are* notes in the back which mention a Georges — they could be referring to anyone.

MARIE: But they do not.

GEORGE: I do not know that there is any validity to this story.

MARIE: Of course there is validity!
(*To the audience*)
He has to have everything spelled out for him!

GEORGE: The facts are sketchy. The tales are many. I would like to invite you into *my* "Sunday: Island of Light." It will be on exhibition here in the upstairs gallery for three weeks.
(*Music crescendos, as laser beams burst over the audience. When they complete their course, the sphere begins to turn, sending out a blinding burst of light. The painting flies in*)

(*We are now in the gallery where the painting hangs and in front of which the reception is beginning.* HARRIET *and* BILLY *enter, closely followed by* REDMOND, GREENBERG, ALEX, BETTY, *and* NAOMI. *Cocktail music under*)

BILLY: Well, I can't say that *I* understand what that light machine has to do with this painting.

HARRIET: Darling, it's a theme and variation.

BILLY: Oh. Theme and variation.

GREENBERG (*To* REDMOND): Times change so quickly.

REDMOND: Lord knows.

GREENBERG: That's the challenge of our work. You never

673

know what movement is going to hit next. Which artist to embrace.

(*Rhumba music*)

NAOMI: I thought it went very well, except for that electrical screw-up. What did you guys think?

ALEX:		BETTY:
Terrible.		Terrific.

(*Short embarrassed pause*)

HARRIET (*Sings*):
I mean, I don't understand completely —

BILLY (*Sings*):
I'm not surprised.

HARRIET:
But he combines all these different trends.

BILLY:
I'm not surprised.

HARRIET:
You can't divide art today
Into categories neatly —

BILLY:
Oh.

HARRIET:
What matters is the means, not the ends.

BILLY:
I'm not surprised.

HARRIET *and* BILLY:
That is the state of the art, my dear,
That is the state of the art.

GREENBERG (*Sings*):
It's not enough knowing good from rotten —

REDMOND (*Sings*):
   You're telling me —

GREENBERG:
   When something new pops up every day.

REDMOND:
   You're telling me —

GREENBERG:
   It's only new, though, for now —

REDMOND:
   Nouveau.

GREENBERG:
   But yesterday's forgotten.

REDMOND (*Nods*):
   And tomorrow is already passé.

GREENBERG:
   There's no surprise.

REDMOND *and* GREENBERG:
   That is the state of the art, my friend,
   That is the state of the art.

BETTY (*Sings*):
   He's an original.

ALEX: Was.

NAOMI:
   I like the images.

ALEX: Some.

BETTY:
   Come on.
   You had your moment,
   Now it's George's turn —

ALEX (*Sings*):
 It's George's turn?
 I wasn't talking turns,
 I'm talking art.

BETTY (*To* NAOMI):
 Don't you think he's original?

NAOMI:
 Well, yes . . .

BETTY (*To* ALEX):
 You're talking crap.

ALEX (*Overlapping with* NAOMI):
 But is it really new?

NAOMI:
 Well, no . . .

ALEX (*To* BETTY):
 His own collaborator — !

BETTY (*Overlapping with* NAOMI):
 It's more than novelty.

NAOMI:
 Well, yes . . .

BETTY (*To* ALEX):
 It's just impersonal, but —

ALEX:
 It's all promotion, but then —

ALEX *and* BETTY (*To* NAOMI):
 That is the state of the art,
 Isn't it?

NAOMI (*Caught between them*):
 Well . . .

BILLY (*To* HARRIET):
   Art isn't easy —

HARRIET (*Nodding*):
   Even when you've amassed it —

BETTY:
   Fighting for prizes —

GREENBERG:
   No one can be an oracle.

REDMOND (*Nodding*):
   Art isn't easy.

ALEX:
   Suddenly —

                           (*Snaps fingers*)
   You're past it.

NAOMI:
   All compromises —

HARRIET (*To* BILLY):
   And then when it's allegorical — !

REDMOND *and* GREENBERG:
   Art isn't easy —

ALL:
   Any way you look at it.
      (*Chord, fanfare.* GEORGE *makes a grand entrance with*
      MARIE *and* ELAINE. *Applause from guests.* GEORGE *and*
      MARIE *move towards the painting. Lights come down on*
      GEORGE, *who sings*)

GEORGE:
   All right, George.
   As long as it's your night, George . . .
   You know what's in the room, George:

677

Another Chromolume, George.
It's time to get to work . . .
(*Music continues under*)

MARIE: George, look. All these lovely people in front of our painting.

GREENBERG (*Coming up to* GEORGE): George, I want you to meet one of our board members.
(*He steers* GEORGE *over to* BILLY *and* HARRIET)
This is Harriet Pawling.

HARRIET: What a pleasure. And this is my friend, Billy Webster.

BILLY: How do you do.

GREENBERG: Well, I'll just leave you three to chat.
(*He exits*)

BILLY: Harriet was so impressed by your presentation.

HARRIET: This is the third piece of yours I've seen. They are getting so large!

BILLY: What heading does your work fall under?

GEORGE: Most people think of it as sculpture.

BILLY: Sculpture . . .

GEORGE: Actually, I think of myself as an inventor as well as a sculptor.

BILLY: It's so unconventional for sculpture.
(*Lights down on* GEORGE)

GEORGE (*To audience and himself, sings*):
Say "cheese," George,
And put them at their ease, George.
You're up on the trapeze, George.
Machines don't grow on trees, George.

Start putting it together . . .

(*Lights up*)

HARRIET: I bet your great-grandfather would be very proud!
(*They are joined by* MARIE *and* ELAINE, *who have been nearby and overheard the conversation*)

MARIE: Yes. He would have loved this evening.

BILLY: How do you know?

MARIE: I just know. I'm like that.

HARRIET: Hi. I'm Harriet Pawling.

BILLY: Billy Webster.

MARIE: How do you do. This is Elaine — George's former wife.

ELAINE (*Embarrassed*): Hello.

MARIE: Elaine is such a darling, I will always think of her as my grand-daughter. I am so happy that these children have remained close. Isn't that nice?

BILLY: Yes. Harriet has just gone through a rather messy divorce —

HARRIET: Bill!

(*Awkward pause*)
What a fascinating family you have!

MARIE: Many people say that. George and I are going back to France next month to visit the island where the painting was made, and George is going to bring the Lomo-chrome.

(*Music*)

GEORGE: Chromolume. I've been invited by the government to do a presentation of the machine on the island.

MARIE: George has never been to France.

GEORGE (*Front, sings*):
Art isn't easy —
(*He raises a cut-out of himself in front of* BILLY *and* HARRI-
ET *and comes downstage*)
Even when you're hot.

BILLY (*To cut-out*): Are these inventions of yours one of a
kind?

GEORGE:
Advancing art is easy —
(*To* BILLY, *but front*)
Yes.
Financing it is not.

MARIE: They take a year to make.

GEORGE (*Front*):
A vision's just a vision
If it's only in your head.

MARIE: The minute he finishes one, he starts raising money
for the next.

GEORGE:
If no one gets to see it,
It's as good as dead.

MARIE: Work. Work. Work.

GEORGE:
It has to come to light!
(*Music continues under.* GEORGE *speaks as if to* BILLY *and*
HARRIET, *but away from them, and front*)
I put the names of my contributors on the side of each
machine.

ELAINE: Some very impressive people!

HARRIET: Well, we must speak further. My family has a foundation and we are always looking for new projects.

680

GEORGE (*Front, sings*):
  Bit by bit,
  Putting it together . . .

MARIE: Family — it's all you really have.

GEORGE:
  Piece by piece —
  Only way to make a work of art.
  Every moment makes a contribution,
  Every little detail plays a part.
  Having just the vision's no solution,
  Everything depends on execution:
  Putting it together —
  That's what counts.

HARRIET (*To cut-out*): Actually, the Board of the Foundation
  is meeting next week . . .

GEORGE:
  Ounce by ounce
  Putting it together . . .

HARRIET: You'll come to lunch.

GEORGE:
  Small amounts,
  Adding up to make a work of art.
  First of all, you need a good foundation,
  Otherwise it's risky from the start.
  Takes a little cocktail conversation,
  But without the proper preparation,
  Having just the vision's no solution,
  Everything depends on execution.

  The art of making art
  Is putting it together
  Bit by bit . . .
    (*The cut-out remains, as* BILLY *and* HARRIET *talk to it;*

681

GEORGE, *working away, is cornered by* CHARLES REDMOND.
Music continues under)

REDMOND: We have been hearing about you for some time. We haven't met. Charles Redmond. County Museum of Texas.

GEORGE: Nice to meet you.

REDMOND: Your work is just tremendous.

GEORGE: Thank you.

REDMOND: I don't mean to bring business up during a social occasion, but I wanted you to know we're in the process of giving out some very sizable commissions —

GREENBERG: You're not going to steal him away, are you?
(GEORGE *signals and another cut-out of himself slides in from the wings. He leaves his drink in its hand, then steps forward*)

GEORGE:
Link by link,
Making the connections . . .
Drink by drink,
Fixing and perfecting the design.
Adding just a dab of politician
(Always knowing where to draw the line),
Lining up the funds but in addition
Lining up a prominent commission,
Otherwise your perfect composition
Isn't going to get much exhibition.

Art isn't easy.
Every minor detail
Is a major decision.
Have to keep things in scale,
Have to hold to your vision —
            (*Pauses for a split second*)

682

Every time I start to feel defensive,
I remember lasers are expensive.
What's a little cocktail conversation
If it's going to get you your foundation,
Leading to a prominent commission
And an exhibition in addition?
(*The guests promenade briefly, working the room, then sing*)

ALL (*Except* MARIE):
Art isn't easy —

ALEX *and* BETTY:
Trying to make connections —

ALL:
Who understands it — ?

HARRIET *and* BILLY:
Difficult to evaluate —

ALL:
Art isn't easy —

GREENBERG *and* REDMOND:
Trying to form collections —

ALL:
Always in transit —

NAOMI (*To whoever will listen*):
And then when you have to collaborate — !

ALL:
Art isn't easy,
Any way you look at it . . .
(*Chord. Cocktail piano. During the above,* BLAIR DANIELS,
an art critic, has entered. GEORGE *is approached by* LEE
RANDOLPH *with* MARIE)

MARIE: George, you have to meet Mr. Randolph!

RANDOLPH: Hello! Lee Randolph. I handle the public relations for the museum.

GEORGE: How do you do.
> (NAOMI *joins them*)

NAOMI: There you are, George! Hi, Marie.
> (*To* RANDOLPH)

Naomi Eisen.

RANDOLPH: Delighted. You kids made quite a stir tonight.

NAOMI: You see, George — that electrical foul-up didn't hurt our reception.

RANDOLPH: There's a lot of opportunity for some nice press here.
> (GEORGE *gestures; a third cut-out of himself rises in front of* NAOMI *and* RANDOLPH. GEORGE *steps forward and sings*)

GEORGE:
Dot by dot,
Building up the image.
> (*Flash.* PHOTOGRAPHER *starts taking pictures of the cut-out*)

Shot by shot,
Keeping at a distance doesn't pay.
Still, if you remember your objective,
Not give all your privacy away —
> (*Flash. Beat; he glances at the first cut-out*)

A little bit of hype can be effective,
Long as you can keep it in perspective.
After all, without some recognition
No one's going to give you a commission,
Which will cause a crack in the foundation.
You'll have wasted all that conversation.
> (*Music stops suddenly as* DENNIS *comes over, disheveled and apologetic.* DENNIS *is something of a nerd*)

DENNIS: I am really sorry, George.

(*Cocktail music*)
I spoke with Naomi in great detail about how much electricity her synthesizer was going to use — I computed the exact voltage —

GEORGE: Dennis! It's okay.

DENNIS: The laser was beautiful, George.

GEORGE: It was, wasn't it? Now go get yourself a drink, Dennis. Mingle.

DENNIS: George. I have one more thing I wanted to talk to you about. I was going to wait — no, I'll wait —

GEORGE: What?

DENNIS: I'm quitting.
(*Music stops suddenly*)

GEORGE: Quitting?

DENNIS: I'm going back to NASA. There is just too much pressure in this line of work.

GEORGE: Dennis, don't make any rash decisions. Relax, sleep on it, and we'll talk about it tomorrow.

DENNIS: Okay, George.

GEORGE (*Front, sings, music under*):
Art isn't easy . . .
(ALEX *and* BETTY *approach*)

BETTY: Hey, it's the brains.

GEORGE:
Even if you're smart . . .

ALEX: Little technical screw-up tonight, Dennis?
(DENNIS exits)

GEORGE:
You think it's all together,

And something falls apart . . .
                    (*Music continues under*)

BETTY: I love the new machine, George.

GEORGE: Thanks. That means a lot to me.

ALEX: We saw you talking to Redmond from Texas.

GEORGE: Yeah.

BETTY: Did you get one of the commissions?

GEORGE: We talked about it. You guys?

ALEX: Her. My stuff is a little too inaccessible.

GEORGE: I love your work, Alex. I'll put in a good word for
   you.

ALEX (*Defensive*): He knows my work!

GEORGE (*Uncomfortable*): It's all politics, Alex. Maybe if you
   just lightened up once in a while.

BETTY (*Mollifying*): Texas would be fun!
   (GEORGE *beckons and a fourth cut-out slides in and heads
   toward* BETTY *and* ALEX)

GEORGE (*Front, sings*):
   Art isn't easy.
                    (*Gesturing towards* ALEX)
   Overnight you're a trend,
   You're the right combination —
   (*Behind him, cut-out #1 begins sinking slowly into the
   floor*)
   Then the trend's at an end,
   You're suddenly last year's sensation . . .
   (*Notices the cut-out, goes to raise it during the following*)
   So you should support the competition,
   Try to set aside your own ambition,
   Even while you jockey for position —

(Cut-out #4 has slid in too far, and BETTY *and* ALEX *have turned away;* GEORGE, *unflustered, spins it back around towards* BETTY *and* ALEX, *who resume talking to it)*
If you feel a sense of coalition,
Then you never really stand alone.
If you want your work to reach fruition,
What you need's a link with your tradition,
And of course a prominent commission,
　　(Cut-out #1 starts to sink again; GEORGE *hastens to fix it)*
Plus a little formal recognition,
So that you can go on exhibit —
　　　　　(Getting flustered)
So that your work can go on exhibition —
　　(Loud promenade, very brief, during which cut-out #1 starts to go again, but stops just as GEORGE *reaches it. As he does so,* BLAIR DANIELS *comes up to him. Chords under)*

BLAIR: There's the man of the hour.

GEORGE: Blair. Hello. I just read your piece on Neo-Expressionism —

BLAIR: Just what the world needs — another piece on Neo-Expressionism.

GEORGE: Well, I enjoyed it.
　　　　(Chords continue under, irregularly)

BLAIR: Good for you! Now, I had no idea you might be related to nineteenth-century France.

GEORGE: It's a cloudy ancestral line at best.

BLAIR: I'm dying to meet your grandmother. It was fun seeing the two of you onstage with your invention. It added a certain humanity to the proceedings.

GEORGE: Humanity?

BLAIR: George. Chromolume Number Seven?

687

GEORGE (*Sings to himself*):
  Be nice, George . . .
            (*Gestures for a cut-out; it doesn't rise*)

BLAIR: I was hoping it would be series of three — four at the most.

GEORGE:
  You have to pay a price, George . . .
            (*Gestures again; nothing*)

BLAIR: We have been there before, you know.

GEORGE: You never suffer from a shortage of opinions, do you, Blair?

BLAIR: You never minded my opinions when they were in your favor!

BLAIR:	GEORGE:
I have touted your work from the beginning, you know that. You were really on to something with these light machines — once. Now they're just becoming more and more about less and less.	They like to give Advice, George — (*Gestures offstage; nothing*) Don't think about it Twice, George . . . (*Gestures again; nothing*)

GEORGE: I disagree.
        (*Music.* BLAIR *turns briefly away from him, rummaging through her purse for a cigarette.* GEORGE *takes advantage of this to rush offstage and bring on cut-out #5, which he sets up in front of her during the following*)

BLAIR: Don't get me wrong. You're a talented guy. If you weren't, I wouldn't waste our time with my opinions. I think you are capable of far more. Not that you couldn't succeed by doing Chromolume after Chromolume — but there are new discoveries to be made, George.

    (*She holds up her cigarette and waits for a light from the cut-out*)

GEORGE (*Increasingly upset*):

Be new, George.

They tell you till they're blue, George:

You're new or else you're through, George,

And even if it's true, George —

You do what you can do . . .

    (*Wandering among cut-outs, checking them*)

Bit by bit,

Putting it together.

Piece by piece,

Working out the vision night and day.

All it takes is time and perseverance,

With a little luck along the way,

Putting in a personal appearance,

Gathering supporters and adherents . . .

    (*Music stops.* BLAIR, *getting impatient for her light, leaves the cut-out to join another group.* GEORGE *notices. Beat*)

HARRIET (*To* BILLY):

    . . . But he combines all these different trends . . .

    (*Beat. The cut-out with* HARRIET *and* BILLY *falters*)

GEORGE (*Moving to it smoothly as music resumes*):

Mapping out the right configuration,

             (*Adjusting it*)

Starting with a suitable foundation . . .

BETTY:

    . . . He's an original . . .

ALEX:

    . . . Was . . .

    (*During the following, all the cut-outs falter sporadically, causing* GEORGE *to move more and more rapidly among them*)

GEORGE:

    Lining up a prominent commission —
    And an exhibition in addition —
    Here a little dab of politician —
    There a little touch of publication —
    Till you have a balanced composition —
    Everything depends on preparation —
    Even if you do have the suspicion
    That it's taking all your concentration —

(Simultaneously, with GEORGE*)*

BETTY:

    I like those images.

ALEX:

    Some.

BETTY:

    They're just his personal response.

ALEX:

    To what?

BETTY:

    The painting!

ALEX:

    Bullshit. Anyway, the painting's overrated . . .

BETTY:

    Overrated? It's a masterpiece!

ALEX:

    A masterpiece? Historically important, maybe —

BETTY:

    Oh, now you're judging Seurat, are you?

ALEX:

    All it is is pleasant, just like George's work.

690

BETTY:
It's just your jealousy of George's work.

ALEX:
No nuance, no resonance, no relevance —

BETTY:
There's nuance and there's resonance, there's relevance —

ALEX:
There's not much point in arguing.
Besides, it's all promotion, but then —

BETTY:
There's not much point in arguing.
You say it's all promotion, but then —

GREENBERG:
It's only new, though, for now,
And yesterday's forgotten.
Today it's all a matter of promotion,
But then —

REDMOND:
Nouveau.
And yesterday's forgotten
And you can't tell good from rotten
And today it's all a matter of promotion,
But then —

HARRIET:
You can't divide art today.
Go with it!
What will they think of next?

BILLY:
I'm not surprised.
What will they think of next?

OTHERS:
Most art today
Is a matter of promotion, but then —

GEORGE:
The art of making art
Is putting it together —
Bit by bit —
Link by link —
Drink by drink —
Mink by mink —
And that
Is the state
Of the

ALL:
That is the state of the art —

And art isn't easy.

ALL:
Art!
>   (GEORGE *frames the successfully completed picture of the guests and cut-outs with his hands, as at the end of Act I. As soon as he exits, however, the cut-outs collapse and disappear.* MARIE *is over at the painting; She is joined by* HARRIET *and* BILLY)

GREENBERG: Ladies and gentlemen, dinner is served.
>   (*Most of the party exits*)

HARRIET (*To* MARIE): Excuse me, could you please tell me: what is that square form up there?

BLAIR (*Who has been standing nearby*): That is a baby carriage.

MARIE: Who told you that?!

BLAIR: I'm sorry to butt in. I'm Blair Daniels and I've been waiting for the opportunity to tell you how much I enjoyed seeing you on stage.

MARIE: Why, thank you. But, my dear, that is not a baby carriage. That is Louis' waffle stove.

BLAIR: Waffle stove? I've read all there is to read about this work, and there's never been any mention of a waffle stove!

MARIE (*Indicating red book*): I have a book, too. My mother's.

692

It is a family legacy, as is this painting. And my mother often spoke of Louis' waffle stove!

BLAIR: Louis. Yes, you mentioned him in your presentation.
(GEORGE *re-enters; stays off to one side*)

MARIE: Family. You know, it is all you really have.

BILLY: You said that before.

MARIE: I say it often.

HARRIET: Excuse us.
(HARRIET *and* BILLY *exit*)

MARIE: You know, Miss Daniels, there are only two worthwhile things to leave behind when you depart this world: children and art. Isn't that correct?

BLAIR: I never quite thought of it that way.
(ELAINE *joins them*)

MARIE: Do you know Elaine?

BLAIR: No. I don't believe we've met. Blair Daniels.

ELAINE: I've heard a lot about you.

BLAIR: Oh, yes.

MARIE: Elaine and George were married once. I was so excited. I thought *they* might have a child. George and I are the only ones left, I'm afraid.
(*Whispers*)
I want George to have a child — continue the line. You can understand that, can't you, Elaine?

ELAINE: Of course.

MARIE: Are you married, Miss Daniels?

BLAIR: Awfully nice to have met you.
(*She shakes* MARIE*'s hand and exits*)

MARIE: Elaine, fix my chair so I can see Mama.

(*She does.* ELAINE *crosses to* GEORGE)

ELAINE: George. I think Marie is a little too tired for the party. She seems to be slipping a bit.

GEORGE: I better take her back to the hotel.

ELAINE: I'll take her back. You stay.

GEORGE: Nah, it's a perfect excuse for me to leave early.

ELAINE: George. Don't be silly! You're the toast of the party. You should feel wonderful.

GEORGE (*Edgy*): Well, I don't feel wonderful.

ELAINE: Poor George. Well . . . tonight was a wonderful experience for Marie. I don't remember seeing her so happy. It was very good of you to include her.

GEORGE: She is something, isn't she?

ELAINE: Yes, she is . . .

(ELAINE *begins to leave;* GEORGE *stops her; they embrace. Then she exits. The preceding has been underscored with the chords from Act I.* MARIE *has been staring up at the painting*)

MARIE (*Sings*):
You would have like him,
Mama, you would.
Mama, he makes things —
Mama, they're good.
Just as you said from the start:
Children and art . . .
         (*Starts nodding off*)
Children and art . . .
         (*Awakens with a start*)
He should be happy —

694

Mama, he's blue.
What do I do?

You should have seen it,
It was a sight!
Mama, I mean it —
All color and light — !
I don't understand what it was,
But, Mama, the things that he does:
They twinkle and shimmer and buzz —
You would have liked them . . .
        (Losing her train of thought)
It . . .
Him . . .
        (Music continues, speaks)
Henry . . . Henry? . . . Henry . . .

GEORGE (*Coming over*): It's George, Grandmother.

MARIE: Of course it is. I thought you were your father for a
moment.
        (Indicating painting)
Did I tell you who that was?

GEORGE: Of course. That is your mother.

MARIE: That is correct.
        (Sings)
Isn't she beautiful?
There she is —
        (Pointing to different figures)
There she is, there she is, there she is —
Mama is everywhere,
He must have loved her so much . . .

GEORGE: Is she really in all those places, Marie?

MARIE:
This is our family —

This is the lot.
After I go, this is
All that you've got, honey —

GEORGE: Now, let's not have this discussion —

MARIE (*Before he can protest further*):
Wasn't she beautiful, though?

You would have liked her.
Mama did things
No one had done.
Mama was funny,
Mama was fun,
Mama spent money
When she had none.

Mama said, "Honey,
Mustn't be blue.
It's not so much do what you like
As it is that you like what you do."
Mama said, "Darling,
Don't make such a drama.
A little less thinking,
A little more feeling —"

GEORGE: Please don't start —

MARIE:
I'm just quoting Mama . . .
           (*Changing the subject, indicates* LOUISE)
The child is so sweet . . .
              (*Indicates the* CELESTES *at center*)
And the girls are so rapturous . . .
Isn't it lovely how artists can capture us?

GEORGE: Yes, it is, Marie.

MARIE:
You would have liked her —

696

Honey, I'm wrong.
You would have loved her.

Mama enjoyed things.
Mama was smart.
See how she shimmers —
I mean from the heart.
> (ELAINE *enters and stands off to the side*)

I know, honey, you don't agree.
> (*Indicates painting*)

But this is our family tree.
Just wait till we're there, and you'll see —
Listen to me . . .
> (*Drifting off*)

Mama was smart . . .
Listen to Mama . . .
Children and art . . .
Children and art . . .
> (*She falls asleep and* ELAINE *crosses to her and wheels her off. As they go:*)

Goodbye, Mama.
> (GEORGE *looks at the painting for a moment*)

GEORGE: Connect, George. Connect . . .
> (GEORGE *exits; the painting flies out*)

> (*The island is once again revealed, though barely recognizable as the trees have been replaced by high-rise buildings. The only tree still visible is the one in front of which the* OLD LADY *and* NURSE *sat.* DENNIS *kneels, studying his blueprints.* GEORGE *enters, camera in hand*)

GEORGE: Are you certain this is the best place for the Chromolume?

DENNIS: George, this is the largest clearing on La Grande Jatte.

GEORGE: Where's the still?

DENNIS: It has been built and should arrive tomorrow morning a few hours before the Chromolume. I wanted it here today, but they don't make deliveries on Sunday.

GEORGE: And fresh water for the cooling system?

DENNIS: We can draw it from the Seine. As for the electricity —

GEORGE: Did you see this tree?

DENNIS: No.

GEORGE: It could be the one in the painting.

DENNIS: Yes. It could.
(GEORGE *hands* DENNIS *the camera and goes to the tree.* DENNIS *takes a picture of him in front of it*)

GEORGE: At least something is recognizable . . . Now, about the electricity?

DENNIS: The wind generator's over there.

GEORGE: You have been efficient as always.

DENNIS: Thank you.

GEORGE: I will miss working with you, Dennis.

DENNIS: Well, I can recommend some very capable people to help you with the Texas commission.

GEORGE: I turned it down.

DENNIS: What?

GEORGE: Dennis, why are you quitting?

DENNIS: I told you, I want —

GEORGE: I know what you told me! Why are you really leaving?

DENNIS: George. I love the Chromolumes. But I've helped you build the last five, and now I want to do something different.

GEORGE: I wish you had told me that in the first place.

DENNIS: I'm sorry.

GEORGE: Why do you think I turned down the commission? I don't want to do the same thing over and over again either.

DENNIS: There are other things you could do.

GEORGE: I know that. I just want to do something I care about. (*Beat.* GEORGE *puts camera in pocket and pulls out* DOT*'s red book*)

DENNIS: I see you brought the red book.

GEORGE: Since Marie has died, I thought I would at least bring something of hers along.

DENNIS: Marie really wanted to make this trip.

GEORGE: I know.

DENNIS: I hope you don't mind, but I took a look at the book. It's very interesting.

GEORGE: It's just a grammar book, Dennis.

DENNIS (*Imploring*): Not that part. The notes in the back.
(GEORGE *leafs through it to the back*)
Well, we just have to wait for it to get dark. I'm not certain about the ambient light.

GEORGE: You go, Dennis. I'd like to be alone actually.

DENNIS: Are you sure?

GEORGE: Yeah. I'll see you back at the hotel.
(*He sits on the ground*)

DENNIS (*Begins to exit*): George. I look forward to seeing what you come up with next.

GEORGE (*Smiling*): You're not the only one, Dennis.

(DENNIS *exits. Music.* GEORGE *sings, leafing through the book, reading*)
"Charles has a book . . ."
                                    (*Turns a page*)
"Charles shows them his crayons . . ."
                              (*Turns back a few pages*)
"Marie has the ball of Charles . . ."
                (*Turns the book to read writing in the margin*)
"Good for Marie . . ."
              (*Smiles at the coincidence of the name, turns a page*)
"Charles misses his ball . . ."
                                    (*Looks up*)
George misses Marie . . .
George misses a lot . . .
George is alone.

George looks around.
He sees the park.
It is depressing.
George looks ahead.
George sees the dark.
George is afraid.
Where are the people
Out strolling on Sunday?

George looks within:
George is adrift.
George goes by guessing.
George looks behind:
He had a gift.
When did it fade?
You wanted people out
Strolling on Sunday —
Sorry, Marie . . .
                    (*Looks again at the name in the book*)
See George remember how George used to be,

Stretching his vision in every direction.
See George attempting to see a connection
When all he can see
Is maybe a tree —

          (*Humorously*)

The family tree —
Sorry, Marie . . .

George is afraid.
George sees the park.
George sees it dying.
George too may fade,
Leaving no mark,
Just passing through.
Just like the people
Out strolling on Sunday . . .

George looks around.
George is alone.
No use denying
George is aground.
George has outgrown
What he can do.
George would have liked to see
People out strolling on Sunday . . .

    (DOT *appears.* GEORGE *looks up and discovers her. He stands*)

DOT: I almost did not recognize you without your beard. You have my book.

GEORGE: Your book?

DOT: Yes.

GEORGE: It is a little difficult to understand.

DOT: Well, I was teaching myself. My writing got much better. I worked very hard. I made certain that Marie learned right away.

GEORGE (*Looks at the book*): Marie . . .

DOT: It is good to see you. Not that I ever forgot you, George. You gave me so much.

GEORGE: What did I give you?

DOT: Oh, many things. You taught me about concentration. At first I thought that meant just being still, but I was to understand it meant much more. You meant to tell me to be where I was — not some place in the past or future. I worried too much about tomorrow. I thought the world could be perfect. I was wrong.

GEORGE: What else?

DOT: Oh, enough about me. What about you? Are you working on something new?

GEORGE: No. I am not working on anything new.
　　　　　　　　　　(*Music begins*)

DOT: That is not like you, George.

GEORGE (*Sings*):
　I've nothing to say.

DOT: You have many things . . .

GEORGE:
　Well, nothing that's not been said.

DOT (*Sings*):
　Said by you, though, George . . .

GEORGE:
　I do not know where to go.

DOT:
　And nor did I.

GEORGE:
　I want to make things that count,

Things that will be new . . .

DOT (*Overlapping*):
  I did what I had to do:

GEORGE (*Overlapping*):
  What am I to do?

DOT:
  Move on.

  Stop worrying where you're going —
  Move on.
  If you can know where you're going,
  You've gone.
  Just keep moving on.

  I chose, and my world was shaken —
  So what?
  The choice may have been mistaken,
  The choosing was not.
  You have to move on.

  Look at what you want,
  Not at where you are,
  Not at what you'll be.
  Look at all the things you've done for me:
  Opened up my eyes,
  Taught me how to see,
  Notice every tree —

GEORGE:
  . . . Notice every tree . . .

DOT:
  Understand the light —

GEORGE:
  . . . Understand the light . . .

703

DOT:

Concentrate on now —

GEORGE:

I want to move on.
I want to explore the light.
I want to know how to get through,
Through to something new,
Something of my own —

GEORGE *and* DOT:

Move on.
Move on.

DOT:

Stop worrying if your vision
Is new.
Let others make that decision —
They usually do.
You keep moving on.

(*Simultaneously*)

DOT:	GEORGE
Look at what you've done,	(*Looking around*):
	. . . Something in the light,
Then at what you want,	Something in the sky,
Not at where you are,	In the grass,
What you'll be.	Up behind the trees . . .
Look at all the things	
You gave to me.	Things I hadn't looked at
Let me give to you	Till now:
Something in return.	Flower on your hat.
I would be so pleased . . .	And your smile.

GEORGE:

And the color of your hair.
And the way you catch the light . . .
And the care . . .

And the feeling . . .
And the life
Moving on . . .

DOT:
We've always belonged
Together!

GEORGE *and* DOT:
We will always belong
Together!

DOT:
Just keep moving on.

Anything you do,
Let it come from you.
Then it will be new.
Give us more to see . . .

(*Speaks*)

You never cared what anyone thought. That upset me at
the time because I wanted you to care what *I* thought.

GEORGE: I'm sure that I did.

DOT: I am sure that you did, too.

GEORGE: Dot.

(*He takes the book to her*)

Why did you write these words?

DOT: They are your words, George. The ones you muttered
so often when you worked.

GEORGE (*Reads slowly*):
"Order."

(*Chord.* OLD LADY *enters*)

OLD LADY: George. Is that you?

(GEORGE *turns to her. He looks back to* DOT, *who smiles,
then back to the* OLD LADY)

705

GEORGE: Yes.

OLD LADY: Tell me! Is this place as you expected it?

GEORGE: What?

OLD LADY: The park, of course.

GEORGE: Somewhat.

OLD LADY: Go on.

GEORGE: Well, the greens are a little darker. The sky a little greyer. Mud tones in the water.

OLD LADY (*Disappointed*): Well, yes, I suppose —

GEORGE: But the air is rich and full of light.

OLD LADY: Good.
>   (*Chord. As the* OLD LADY *leaves,* GEORGE *reads the next word:*)

GEORGE: "Design."
>   (*Music begins: "Sunday." The downstage right building begins to rise. The* CELESTES *appear and begin to cross the stage*)

"Tension."
>   (*Two buildings rise stage right and left. More characters from the painting appear and begin to promenade*)

"Composition."
>   (*Building rises*)

"Balance."
>   (*Buildings rise. The stage is filled by the characters from the painting*)

"Light."
>   (*The large building in the back rises*)

Dot. I cannot read this word.

DOT: "Harmony."

ALL
(*Sing*):

Sunday,
By the blue
Purple yellow red water
On the green
Purple yellow red grass,
As we pass
Through arrangements of
    shadows
Towards the verticals of trees
Forever
    (*All bow to* GEORGE)
By the blue
Purple yellow red water
On the green
Orange violet mass
Of the grass . . .

DOT:

In our perfect park . . .

GEORGE:

Made of flecks of light
And dark . . .

ALL (*Except* GEORGE *and* DOT):

And parasols . . .
People strolling through the trees
Of a small suburban park
On an island in the river
On an ordinary Sunday . . .
    (*The* COMPANY *has settled generally in the areas that they
    occupy in the painting*)
Sunday . . .

GEORGE
(*Reading again, struggling
    with the words*):

"So much love in his words
. . . forever with his colors
. . . how George looks . . .
he can look forever . . . what
does he see? . . . his eyes so
dark and shiny. . . so careful
. . . so exact. . . ."
    (DOT *takes* GEORGE *by the arm
    and turns him to the group*)

(All begin to leave very slowly, except DOT, *who remains downstage with* GEORGE)

Sunday . . .

*(*DOT *leaves* GEORGE, *crossing upstage into the park; she turns toward* GEORGE. *The white canvas drop descends)*

GEORGE *(Reading from the book)*: "White. A blank page or canvas. His favorite. So many possibilities . . . "

(He looks up and sees DOT *disappearing behind the white canvas. Lights fade to black)*

Set designs and sketches by Tony Straiges

Two Models of the Set

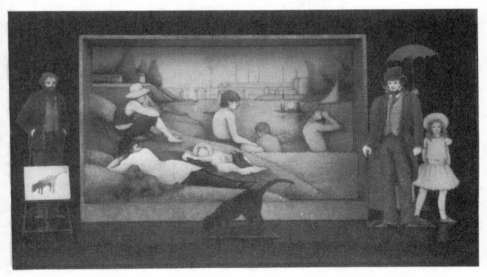

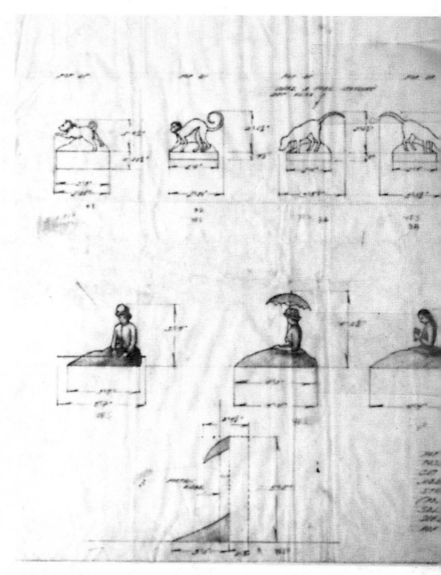

Blueprint for various of the onstage "pop-ups"
of characters and animals in the painting

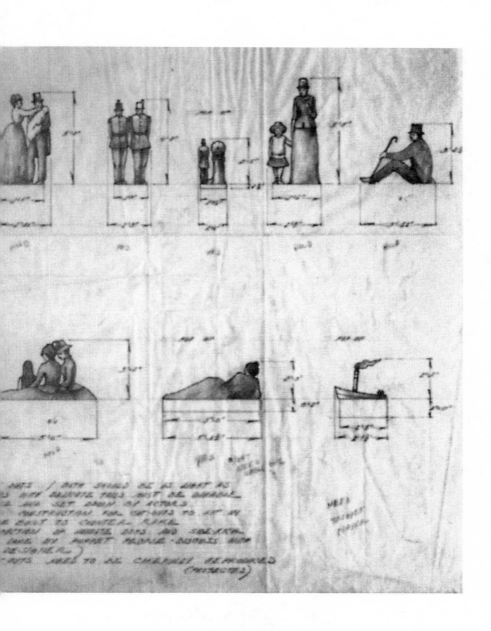

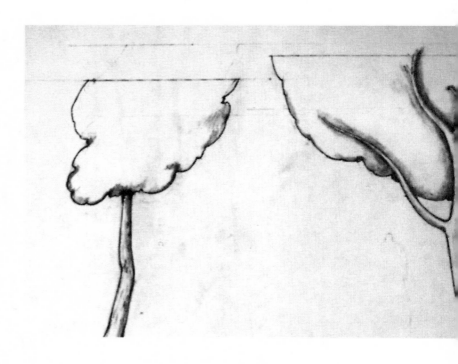

Sketches of scenic elements for Act I

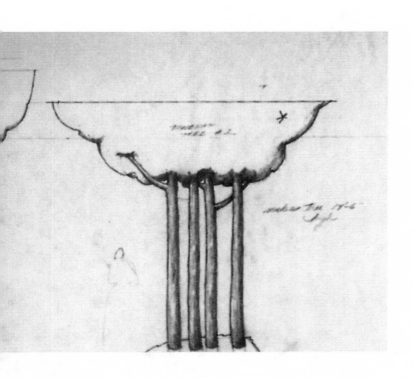

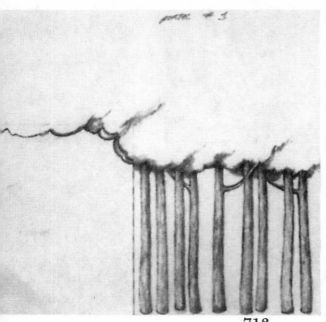

713

One of several working paintings
showing the painting in progress

714

1'-8"

4"

Costume sketches by Patricia Zipprodt

Dot

Costume for Dot's dress with bustle (*left*) and (*below*) the same dress with the bustle moved to the front to create her pregnant condition

Louis

Celeste #1

Companion and Soldier

ADDITIONAL LYRICS

with Commentary by Stephen Sondheim

"Yoo-Hoo!"

"Yoo-Hoo!" was sung in Scene I [at the place where the dialogue now starts on page 585].

(*Music. Laughter from stage right. A wagon tracks in. The sky backdrop lifts, revealing a large likeness of Seurat's "Une Baignade Asnières." The* BOY IN THE WATER *[foreground] and the* YOUNG MAN ON THE BANK *are real, as is the* PERVERT *[the man lying down]. The others are cut-outs in perspective. All direct a loud Bronx cheer at the island across the water. The* BOY *laughs, then turns to the others. He barks and yelps at the island, then laughs again. The* YOUNG MAN *echoes his laughter dull-wittedly*)

BOY (*Loudly, through cupped hands, sings*):
Yoo-hoo! Big and fat!
Who you think you're staring at?
　　　　　(*Stares exaggeratedly*)
In about a minute flat
We're all coming over to get you!
　　　(*He splashes water at the island. The* PERVERT *mutters something to the* BOY, *who nods delightedly and laughs*)
Yoo-hoo! Kinky beard!
Everybody knows you're weird!
　　　　　(YOUNG MAN *laughs while* PERVERT *mutters*)

PERVERT:
How'd you like your picture smeared?

BOY:
Yeah, how'd you like your picture smeared?

ALL:
We're coming right over to get you!
　　　(BOY *makes menacing noises while the* YOUNG MAN *laughs*)

721

BOY (*turning to his audience*): Watch this.
                    (*Flails as if drowning*)

PERVERT *and* YOUNG MAN:
   Nursie! Nursie!
   Help, he's drowning!
                    (*Drowning sounds*)
   Mercy! Nursie!

BOY:
   I'm not clowning!
                    (NURSE *and* DOT *are alarmed*)

PERVERT *and* YOUNG MAN:
   Can't you see he's drowning?
      (BOY *makes horrifying drowning sounds and disappears
      underwater, struggling; as the* NURSE *and* GEORGE *move,
      he suddenly pops up again*)

BOY:
   Na-Na-Na-Ni-Na-Na!
      (*Belches gigantically;* PERVERT *mutters to him; speaks*)
   Huh?
      (*The* PERVERT *mutters more fully, explaining.* YOUNG MAN
      laughs first, then the BOY, *nodding. He whistles sexily,
      sings*)
   Yoo-hoo! Lady, dear!
   Who are you hiding in the rear?

PERVERT:
   Would you like a volunteer?

YOUNG MAN:
   Why don't you come over here?
                    (*The* PERVERT *mutters*)

BOY:
   Feeling weary, dear?

BOY *and* PERVERT:

Don't you worry, dearie,

ALL:

We're
Coming right over — !

> (GEORGE *gestures; the* BOY, *the* YOUNG MAN *and the* PER-
> VERT *freeze into the familiar tableau as a frame comes in
> around them.* JULES *and* YVONNE *stroll on and examine
> the picture, laughing*)

"Soldiers and Girls" and "The One on the Left"

*"Soldiers and Girls" was replaced by "The One on the Left,"
which in turn was cut down to the fragment that now remains on
pages 621-623.*

"Soldiers and Girls"

SOLDIER (*Sudden and loud*):
Mademoiselles,
I and my friend
We are but soldiers —
> (*Listens to sidekick*)

Passing the time
In between wars,
However we may.

CELESTE #2:
Careful, he's peculiar.

CELESTE #1:
How is he peculiar?

CELESTE #2:
Soldiers are peculiar.

SOLDIER:
And after a week spent
Mostly indoors
With nothing but soldiers,
May we venture to say:
> (*Softening his ardor at a nudge from the other soldier*)

It's a glorious day.

CELESTE #2:
Wasn't that peculiar?

CELESTE #1:

No, it's not peculiar.

CELESTE #2:

Something is peculiar.
Shouldn't we be going?

CELESTE #1:

No, will you be quiet?

SOLDIER:

Sundays were made for soldiers and girls,
Don't you agree?
Sundays were made for medals
And ribbons arrayed with red sashes,
Buckles and braid,
And sabres —
And girls.

Sundays were meant for helmets and plumes,
Mademoiselles,
Meant for salutes
And epaulettes,
Glistening boots,
The heady perfumes
Of horses and grooms —
And beautiful girls!

(*Very loud*)

Mademoiselles!
I and my friend
Have a suggestion!

CELESTE #2:

Anyone can see that
That man is peculiar.

SOLDIER:

I and my friend

Wish to be friends
With you and your friend.

CELESTE #1:
See, he's very friendly.

CELESTE #2:
Yes, he's very friendly.
That's what is peculiar.

SOLDIER:
Only just now
I said to my friend
Of you and your friend,
"I suspect they are friends."

CELESTE #1:
Both of them are perfect.

CELESTE #2:
You can have the other.

CELESTE #1:
I don't want the other.

CELESTE #2:
I don't want the other either.

SOLDIER:
And, see, you are friends!

CELESTE #1 *and* #2:
What can be the harm in
Strolling in the park with
Soldiers even if they *are* peculiar?

SOLDIER:
And we shall be friends.

SOLDIER, CELESTE #1 *and* #2:
Sundays were made for soldiers and girls.

SOLDIER:
  Mademoiselles,
  Sundays were made for medals —
    (*Looks expectantly at* CELESTE #1, *who picks up her cue*)

CELESTE #1:
  And ribbons arrayed with red sashes —
                    (*Nudges* CELESTE #2)

CELESTE #2:
  Buckets and braid —

CELESTE #1 (*Whispers*): Buckles!

SOLDIER:
  And sabres —
    (*Looks at sidekick, who apparently conveys something;
    speaks*)
  Right!
                    (*Sings*)
  Sundays were made for banners and bells,
  Don't you agree?
  Made for whatever sparkles,
                    (*With meaning*)
  Whatever is fresh and sweet,
                    (CELESTES *giggle*)
  Everything casting colorful spells:
  For beaches and shells
                    (CELESTES *hum*)
  And scarlet lapels
                    (*Inhales*)
  And vigorous smells —
  And soldiers!
                    (*At a nudge from the sidekick*)
  And mademoiselles!

CELESTE #1 (*Aside*):
  Both of them are perfect.

CELESTE #2:
  You can have the other.

CELESTE #1:
  I don't want the other.

CELESTE #2:
  I don't want the other either.

SOLDIER:
  Mademoiselles,
  I and my friend,
  We are but soldiers —
    (*Rumble from his* COMPANION; SOLDIER *raises hand to
    quiet him*)
  Passing the time
  In between wars
  For weeks at an end.

CELESTE #2 (*Aside*):
  Shouldn't we be going?

CELESTE #1:
  No, will you be quiet?

CELESTE #2:
  Something is peculiar —

SOLDIER:
  And after a week
  Spent mostly indoors
  With nothing but soldiers,
  Ladies, I and my friend
  Trust we will not offend,
  Which we'd never intend,

728

By suggesting we spend —

BOTH CELESTES (*Excited*):
Oh, spend —

SOLDIER:
— This magnificent Sunday —

BOTH CELESTES (*A bit defeated*):
Oh, Sunday —

SOLDIER:
— With you and your friend.

CELESTE #2 (*Aside, to* CELESTE #1):
The one on the right seems quite attached.

CELESTE #1 (*Looking over, then back*):
As well as scratched.

SOLDIER (*Aside, to* COMPANION):
Admit it, old man, we're not badly matched.

ALL (*To themselves, shrugging*):
It's certainly fine for Sunday.

SOLDIER (*To* COMPANION):
The one on the left seems quite subdued.

CELESTE #2 (*As* CELESTE #1 *tries to elbow her over to the other side*):
I'm not in the mood.

CELESTE #1 (*To* CELESTE #2):
You're ruining things and we're being rude —

ALL (*Enthusiastically, to each other*):
It's certainly fine for Sunday!
> (*During the next section, as they all march around, both*
> CELESTES *fight for position*)

SOLDIER *and* CELESTE #1 (*Aside, to their partners*):
My only advice
Is don't think twice.

SOLDIER (*To* CELESTE #1):
Would you care for an ice?

BOTH CELESTES:
Oh, an ice would be nice!

CELESTE #2 (*To* CELESTE #1):
Will they buy us a drink?

SOLDIER (*To* COMPANION):
Are they virgins, you think?

ALL (*To each other*):
It's certainly fine for Sunday!

CELESTE #2 (*To* CELESTE #1, *referring to* COMPANION):
Is that a mustache
Or just a gash?

CELESTE #1 (*To* SOLDIER):
What a beautiful sash!

SOLDIER (*To* COMPANION):
Did you bring any cash?

CELESTE #1 (*To* CELESTE #2):
The buckles and braid —

CELESTE #2:
The gold brocade —

CELESTE #1:
The boots —

CELESTE #2:
The blade — !

SOLDIER:
Shall we head for the glade?

CELESTE #1 (*Excited, aside*):
Heading for the shadows — !

CELESTE #2 (*Also excited, but wary*):
Anything can happen —

CELESTE #1:
Wonder what they're planning.

CELESTE #2 (*Alarmed*):
What they're planning?

CELESTE #1:
What they're planning later on!

SOLDIER (*To* COMPANION):
The one on the right gave you a look —
Let's hope she can cook.

BOTH CELESTES (*Aside*):
Taking us to dinner —
Maybe to the Follies — !
Anyhow, it's certainly fine for Sunday!

CELESTE #1:
The one on the right is odd, it's true,
But what can we do?

SOLDIER (*To* COMPANION):
The one on the left —

CELESTE #1:
You're as odd as he —

SOLDIER:
— Has great esprit —

CELESTE #2:
I don't agree —

SOLDIER *and* CELESTE #1:
The one on the left is right for me —
    (*They switch positions so that* CELESTE #2 *has the* COMPANION)
So the one on the right is left for you.

731

MAJOR PRODUCTIONS

Sunday in the Park with George was first presented in a workshop production for 25 performances by Playwrights Horizons (André Bishop, Artistic Director; Paul Daniels, Managing Director; Ira Weitzman, Musical Theater Program Director), in association with the Herrick Theater Foundation, at Playwrights Horizons, New York City, July 6-July 31, 1983, with the following cast:

(*In order of appearance*)

ACT I

GEORGE, *an artist*	Mandy Patinkin
DOT, *his mistress*	Bernadette Peters
OLD LADY	Carmen Mathews
HER NURSE	Judith Moore
FRANZ, *a coachman*	Brent Spiner
BOY IN THE WATER	Bradley Kane
YOUNG MAN ON THE BANK	Kelsey Grammer
PERVERT	William Parry
LOUISE, *a little girl*	Danielle Ferland
JULES, *another artist*	Ralph Byers
CLARISSE, *his wife*	Christine Baranski
BOATMAN	William Parry
LOUIS, *a baker*	Kevin Marcum
CELESTE #1, *a shopgirl*	Melanie Vaughan
CELESTE #2, *another shopgirl*	Mary Elizabeth Mastrantonio
BETTE, *a cook*	Nancy Opel
SOLDIER	Kelsey Grammer
MR.	Kurt Knudson
MRS.	Judith Moore

ACT II

GEORGE, *a performance artist*	Mandy Patinkin
JED	Brent Spiner
DEE, *George's girlfriend*	Nancy Opel
ALEX	Kelsey Grammer
ANNETTE, *George's grandmother*	Bernadette Peters
NAOMI	Melanie Vaughan
ROBERT BLACKMUN, *the museum director*	Kurt Knudson
BILLIE GHERKIN, *a patroness of the arts*	Carmen Mathews
HARRIET PAWLING, *a patroness of the arts*	Judith Moore
WAITER	Ross Wassermann
CHARLES GREEN, *a museum curator*	William Parry
ALAN CASH, *museum benefactor*	Kevin Marcum
LINDA CASH, *his wife*	Mary Elizabeth Mastrantonio
BLAIR DANIELS, *an art critic*	Christine Baranski
WAITRESS	Johnna Murray

Directed by James Lapine
Set Design by Tony Straiges
Costume Design by Patricia Zipprodt *and* Ann Hould-Ward
Lighting Design by Richard Nelson
Sound Design by Scott Lehrer
Musical Director, Paul Gemignani

NOTE: It was only for the last three performances of the workshop production that the second act was presented.

MUSICAL NUMBERS

ACT I

"Sunday in the Park with George"	DOT
"Yoo-Hoo!"	BOY, YOUNG MAN, PERVERT
"No Life"	JULES, CLARISSE
"Color and Light"	DOT, GEORGE
"Gossip"	CELESTE #1, CELESTE #2, BOATMAN NURSE, OLD LADY, JULES, CLARISSE
"The Day Off"	GEORGE, SPOT, FIFI, NURSE, FRANZ, BETTE, BOATMAN, SOLDIER, CLARISSE, LOUISE, CELESTE #1, CELESTE #2
"Everybody Loves Louis"	DOT
"Soldiers and Girls"	SOLDIER, CELESTE #1, CELESTE #2
"Finishing the Hat"	GEORGE
"Beautiful"	OLD LADY, GEORGE
"Sunday"	COMPANY

ACT II

"It's Hot Up Here"	DOT, CLARISSE, LOUISE, FRANZ, NURSE, CELESTE #1, CELESTE #2, BETTE, JULES, SOLDIER, OLD LADY, BOATMAN
Performance Art Piece	GEORGE, JED, DEE, ALEX, ANNETTE, NAOMI
"Have to Keep Them Humming"	HARRIET, BILLIE, BLACKMUN, GREEN, NAOMI, ALEX, JED, LINDA, ALAN, GEORGE
"Sunday" (reprise)	COMPANY

Sunday in the Park with George was presented by The Shubert Organization and Emanuel Azenberg, by arrangement with Playwrights Horizons, at the Booth Theatre, New York City, on May 2, 1984, with the following cast:

(In order of appearance)

ACT I

GEORGE, *an artist*	Mandy Patinkin
DOT, *his mistress*	Bernadette Peters
AN OLD LADY	Barbara Bryne
HER NURSE	Judith Moore
FRANZ, *a servant*	Brent Spiner
A BOY *bathing in the river*	Danielle Ferland
A YOUNG MAN *sitting on the bank*	Nancy Opel
A MAN *lying on the bank*	Cris Groenendaal
JULES, *another artist*	Charles Kimbrough
YVONNE, *his wife*	Dana Ivey
A BOATMAN	William Parry
CELESTE #1	Melanie Vaughan
CELESTE #2	Mary D'Arcy
LOUISE, *the daughter of Jules and Yvonne*	Danielle Ferland
FRIEDA, *a cook*	Nancy Opel
LOUIS, *a baker*	Cris Groenendaal
A SOLDIER	Robert Westenberg
A MAN *with bicycle*	John Jellison
A LITTLE GIRL	Michele Rigan
A WOMAN *with baby carriage*	Sue Anne Gershenson
MR.	Kurt Knudson
MRS.	Judith Moore

ACT II

GEORGE, *an artist*	Mandy Patinkin
MARIE, *his grandmother*	Bernadette Peters
DENNIS, *a technician*	Brent Spiner
BOB GREENBERG, *the museum director*	Charles Kimbrough
NAOMI EISEN, *a composer*	Dana Ivey
HARRIET PAWLING, *a patron of the arts*	Judith Moore
BILLY WEBSTER, *her friend*	Cris Groenendaal
A PHOTOGRAPHER	Sue Anne Gershenson
A MUSEUM ASSISTANT	John Jellison
CHARLES REDMOND, *a visiting curator*	William Parry
ALEX, *an artist*	Robert Westenberg
BETTY, *an artist*	Nancy Opel
LEE RANDOLPH, *the museum's publicist*	Kurt Knudson
BLAIR DANIELS, *an art critic*	Barbara Bryne
A WAITRESS	Melanie Vaughan
ELAINE	Mary D'Arcy

Directed by James Lapine
Scenery by Tony Straiges
Costumes by Patricia Zipprodt *and* Ann Hould-Ward
Lighting Design by Richard Nelson
Special Effects by Bran Ferren
Movement by Randolyn Zinn
Sound by Tom Morse
Hair and Makeup by Lo Presto/Allen
Musical Direction by Paul Gemignani
Orchestrations by Michael Starobin

736

The following musical numbers were deleted prior to the May 2, 1984 opening: *"Yoo-Hoo!" "Soldiers and Girls," "Have to Keep Them Humming"*

Sunday in the Park with George gave its first performance in New York City at the Booth Theatre, where it began previews on April 2, 1984, opened on May 2nd and closed on October 12, 1985 after 604 performances and 35 previews.

AWARDS

Pulitzer Prize — Drama (1985)

New York Drama Critics Circle Award — Best Musical

Tony Awards: Best Scenic Design (Tony Straiges) and Best Lighting (Richard Nelson). Also received Tony nominations for Best Musical, Best Book of a Musical (James Lapine), Best Music and Lyrics (Stephen Sondheim), Best Direction of a Musical (James Lapine), Best Actor in a Musical (Mandy Patinkin), Best Actress in a Musical (Bernadette Peters), Best Featured Actress in a Musical (Dana Ivey), Best Costume Design (Patricia Zipprodt and Ann Hould-Ward).

Sunday in the Park with George was first presented in London by the Royal National Theatre in repertory at the Lyttelton Theatre on March 15, 1990 for a limited engagement of 117 performances, with the following cast:

(*In order of appearance*)

ACT I

GEORGE, *an artist*	Philip Quast
DOT, *his mistress*	Maria Friedman
AN OLD LADY	Sheila Ballantine
HER NURSE	Nuala Willis
FRANZ, *servant to Jules and Yvonne*	Michael O'Connor
BOY BATHER	Keir Charles or Samuel Woodward
SMALL BOY BATHERS	Christopher Line, Marc Bellamy or Marco Williamson, James Nyman
JULES, *another artist*	Gary Raymond
YVONNE, *his wife*	Nyree Dawn Porter
A BOATMAN	Michael Attwell
CELESTE #1	Megan Kelly
CELESTE #2	Clare Burt
LOUIS, *a baker*	Aneirin Huws
A SOLDIER	Nicolas Colicos
LOUISE, *daughter to Jules and Yvonne*	Naomi Kerbel or Ann Gosling
FRIEDA, *Jules and Yvonne's cook, wife to Franz*	Di Botcher
MAN PLAYING THE HORN	Barry Atkinson
DANCING GIRL	Antonio Boyd or Emily Sault
WOMAN LOOKING FOR A GLOVE	Ellen van Schuylenburch
MR. & MRS., *an American couple*	Matt Zimmerman and Vivienne Martin

ACT II

GEORGE, *an artist*	Philip Quast
MARIE, *his grandmother*	Maria Friedman
DENNIS, *a technician*	Michael O'Connor
BOB GREENBERG, *the museum director*	Gary Raymond
NAOMI EISEN, *a composer*	Nyree Dawn Porter
HARRIET PAWLING, *a patron of the arts*	Nuala Willis
BILLIE WEBSTER, *her friend*	Vivienne Martin
CHARLES REDMOND, *a visiting curator*	Matt Zimmerman
ALEX, *an artist*	Nicolas Colicos
BETTY, *an artist*	Clare Burt
LEE RANDOLPH, *the museum's publicist*	Michael Attwell
BLAIR DANIELS, *an art critic*	Sheila Ballantine
ELAINE, *George's former wife*	Di Botcher
CHROMOLUME PERFORMERS	Barry Atkinson, Aneirin Huws, Megan Kelly, Ellen van Schuylenburch
A WAITRESS	Buffy Davis
A PHOTOGRAPHER	Simon Fielder
GUESTS	Stephen Hanley, Erika Vincent

Directed by Steven Pimlott
Designed by Tom Cairns
Lighting by Wolfgang Gobbel
Orchestrations by Michael Starobin
Musical Direction by Jeremy Sams
Choreographer, Aletta Collins
Chromolume #7, Martin Duncan
Sound, Mike Clayton, Paul Groothius
Conductor, John Jansson

739

Sunday in the Park with George was presented by Michael Brandman and Emanuel Azenberg, in association with The Shubert Organization and American Playhouse, on cable television's "Broadway on Showtime" series on February 18, 1986, and subsequently on "American Playhouse" (PBS) on June 16, 1986, with the following cast:

GEORGE, *an artist*	Mandy Patinkin
DOT/MARIE	Bernadette Peters
JULES/BOB GREENBERG	Charles Kimbrough
OLD LADY/BLAIR DANIELS	Barbara Bryne
YVONNE/NAOMI EISEN	Dana Ivey
CELESTE #2/ELAINE	Mary D'Arcy
WOMAN/PHOTOGRAPHER	Sue Anne Gershenson
LOUIS/BILLY WEBSTER	Cris Groenendaal
MAN/PARTY GUEST	John Jellison
MR./PUBLICIST	Frank Kopyc
NURSE/MRS./HARRIET PAWLING	Judith Moore
FRIEDA/BETTY	Nancy Opel
BOATMAN/CHARLES REDMOND	William Parry
LOUISE	Natalie Polizzie
GIRL	Michele Rigan
FRANZ/DENNIS	Brent Spiner
CELESTE #1/WAITRESS	Melanie Vaughan
SOLDIER/ALEX	Robert Westenberg

Produced by Iris Merlis
Executive in Charge of Production, Greg Sills
Directed for Television by Terry Hughes
Directed for the Stage by James Lapine
Musical Director and Conductor, Paul Gemignani
Orchestrations by Michael Starobin

Scenery by Tony Straiges
Costumes by Patricia Zipprodt *and* An Hould-Ward
Lighting Design by Richard Nelson
Lighting Consultant, Bill Klages
Special Effects by Bran Ferren
Movement by Randolyn Zinn
Sound by Tom Morse

The television production was taped October 21-25, 1985 at the Booth Theatre shortly after the close of the Broadway production and with all but two members (Kurt Knudson and Danielle Ferland) of the original Broadway cast. This production is available on video cassette: Lorimar Home Video 370/Image Entertainment DG(S) ID5151.

SELECTED DISCOGRAPHY

* <u>Original Broadway Cast Recording</u> (1984)
    RCA Records
        LP HBC1-5042 (S)
        Cassette HBE1-51M2
        CD RCD1-5042

A Collector's Sondheim (1985)
    RCA Records
        LP CRL4-5359 (S); 4 record set
        Cassette CRK4-5359; 4 tape set
        CD RCD3-5480; disc set
    Includes: *"Children and Art"* Bernadette Peters, Mandy Patinkin; *"Move On"*—Bernadette Peters, Mandy Patinkin (both tracks from original Broadway cast recording)

Sondheim (1985)
    Book-of-the-Month Records
        LP 81-7515 (S); 3 record set
        Cassette 91-7516; 2 tape set
        CD 11-7517; 2 disc set
    Includes: *"Finishing the Hat"*—Cris Groenendaal

The Broadway Album/Barbra Streisand (1985)
    Columbia Records
        LP OC 40092
        Cassette OCT 40092
        CD CK 40092
    Includes:*"Putting It Together"* (with Sondheim's slightly revised lyric)

<u>Televised Video Recording</u> (1985)
    Karl-Lorimar Home Video   VHS 370
    Image   Laserdisc ID5151

Symphonic Sondheim/Don Sebesky Conducts The London Symphony Orchestra (1990)
    WEA Records (London)
        LP 9031-72 119-1
        Cassette 9031-72 1194
        CD 9031-72 119-2
    Includes: *"Finishing the Hat"*

Sondheim: A Celebration at Carnegie Hall (1992)
    RCA Victor
        CD 09026-61484-2; 2 CD set
    Includes: *"Sunday"*

* Winner of the Grammy Award for Best Original Cast Show Album

Larry Gelbart has written for radio, television, film and the stage. His radio credits include material for *Duffy's Tavern*, Jack Paar and Bob Hope, and for television he wrote for "The Bob Hope Show," "Caesar's Hour," "The Danny Kaye Show," for which he received a Peabody Award, and the Art Carney Specials, for which he received a Sylvania Award. He developed and co-produced with Gene Reynolds the television series *M*A*S*H*, which earned him an Emmy Award, Peabody Award, Humanitas Award and several Writers Guild of America Awards. His screenplays include *The Notorious Landlady* (1960), *The Wrong Box* (1966, co-authored with Burt Shevelove), *Oh, God!* (1977), for which he received the Writers Guild of America Award and Edgar Allen Poe Award and which received the Los Angeles and New York Film Critics Award and nominations for the Oscar and British Academy Award. For the stage he wrote the books for the musicals *The Conquering Hero* (1961), *A Funny Thing Happened on the Way to the Forum* (1962, in collaboration with Burt Shevelove) and *City of Angels* (1989), and his plays include *Jump* (1971), *Sly Fox* (1976, based on Ben Jonson's *Volpone*), *Mastergate* (1989) and *Power Failure* (1992). He received Tony Awards for *A Funny Thing Happened on the Way to the Forum* and *City of Angels*, and a second Edgar Allen Poe award for the latter. Mr. Gelbart is a member of the Dramatists Guild, the Writers Guild of America, West, the Writers Guild of Great Britain, ASCAP, and the Directors Guild. His autobiography, *Laughing Matters: On Writing M*A*S*H, Tootsie, Oh, God!, and a Few Other Funny Things*, was published in 1998.

Burt Shevelove made his Broadway debut as the director and co-author of the revue *Small Wonder* (1948). He co-authored with Larry Gelbart the book for *A Funny Thing Happened on the Way to the Forum* (1962), for which he received a Tony Award, directed the award-winning productions of *Hallelujah, Baby!* (1968) and *No, No, Nanette* (1971), for which he also restructured the long and involved book of the original 1925 production, adapted and directed William Gillette's play *Too Much Johnson* (1964) for off Broadway, wrote the book for and directed the musical *The Frogs*

(1974, adapted from the comedy by Aristophanes, with music and lyrics by Stephen Sondheim) and wrote and directed the musical *Happy New Year* (1980, adapted from Philip Barry's play *Holiday*). For the screen he co-authored with Larry Gelbart and co-produced *The Wrong Box* (1966), and for television he produced, directed and wrote hundreds of shows starring, among others, Jack Benny, Art Carney, Judy Garland, Frank Sinatra and Barbra Streisand, for which he received numerous awards, including Emmy, Sylvania and Christopher awards, and the Peabody Award for *Art Carney Meets Peter and the Wolf*. At the time of his death in 1982 Mr. Shevelove was preparing a musical version of *The Front Page*.

Stephen Sondheim wrote the music and lyrics for *A Funny Thing Happened on the Way to the Forum* (1962), *Anyone Can Whistle* (1964), *Company* (1970), *Follies* (1971), *A Little Night Music* (1973), *The Frogs* (1974), *Pacific Overtures* (1976), *Sweeney Todd, the Demon Barber of Fleet Street* (1979), *Merrily We Roll Along* (1981), *Sunday in the Park with George* (1984), *Into the Woods* (1986), *Assassins* (1990), *Passion* (1994) and *Saturday Night* (written in 1955, premiered in 1999), the lyrics for *West Side Story* (1957, music by Leonard Bernstein), and the music and lyrics for *Putting It Together*, a musical revue. He provided incidental music for the plays *The Girls of Summer* (1956), *Invitation to a March* (1961), *Twigs* (1971) and *Enclave* (1973). He wrote the music and the lyrics for the television production *Evening Primrose* (1966), composed the film scores for *Stavisky* (1974) and *Reds* (1981), wrote songs for the motion pictures *The Seven Percent Solution* (1976), *Dick Tracy* (1990) and *The Birdcage* (1996) and co-authored the film *The Last of Sheila* (1973). He won Tony Awards for his scores for *Company, Follies, A Little Night Music, Sweeney Todd* and *Into the Woods*, and all of these musicals won the New York Drama Critics Circle Award for Best Musical, as did *Pacific Overtures* and *Sunday in the Park with George*, the latter also receiving the Pulitzer prize in 1985. Mr. Sondheim is on the Council of the Dramatists Guild, having served as its president from 1973 to 1981, was elected to the American Academy and

Institute of Arts and Letters in 1983, received the London Evening Standard Award in 1988 for his contribution to the musical theater, and in 1988 was named the first Visiting Professor of Contemporary Theatre at Oxford University. *Stephen Sondheim: A Life*, his biography by Meryle Secrest, was published in 1998.

Hugh Wheeler was a novelist, playwright and screen writer. He wrote more than thirty mystery novels under the pseudonyms Z. Patrick and Patrick Quentin, and four of his novels were transformed into films: *Black Widow*, *Man in the Net*, *The Green-Eyed Monster* and *The Man with Two Wives.* For films he wrote the screenplays for *Travels with My Aunt*, *Something for Everyone*, *A Little Night Music* and *Nijinsky*. His plays include *Big Fish, Little Fish* (1961), *Look: We've Come Through* (1961) and *We Have Always Lived in the Castle* (1966, adapted from the Shirley Jackson novel), he co-authored with Joseph Stein the book for a new production of the 1919 musical *Irene* (1973), wrote the books for *A Little Night Music* (1973), a new production of *Candide* (1973), *Sweeney Todd, the Demon Barber of Fleet Street* (1979, based on a version of the play by Christopher Bond), and *Meet Me in St. Louis* (adapted from the 1949 M-G-M musical), contributed additional material for the musical *Pacific Overtures* (1976), and wrote a new adaptation of the Kurt Weill opera *Silverlake*, which was directed by Hal Prince at the New York Opera. He received Tony and Drama Desk Awards for *A Little Night Music*, *Candide* and *Sweeney Todd*. Prior to his death in 1987 Mr. Wheeler was working on two new musicals, *Bodo* and *Fu Manchu*, and a new adaptation of *The Merry Widow*.

Jonathan Tunick, long regarded as Broadway's re-eminent orchestrator, has contributed to the success of such landmark productions as *Sweeney Todd*, *Follies*, *A Little Night Music*, *Company*, *A Chorus Line*, *Into the Woods*, *Passion*, and the 1996 revival of *A Funny Thing Happened on the Way to the Forum*. He has also composed and conducted over thirty scores for motion pictures and television, including PBS's American Masters series and his Emmy-nominated scores for *Concealed Enemies* on PBS and NBC's *Tattinger's*. He is Music Director of the Opera Ensemble of New York, where he specializes in conducting classic light opera and musicals. He was the conductor of the CBS recording of Rodgers and Hammerstein's *South Pacific* with Kiri Te Kanawa and the London Symphony Orchestra. He has long been associated with Judy Collins as arranger-conductor, and has also performed in the same capacity with Barbra Streisand, Placido Domingo, Itzhak Perlman and Paul McCartney. He has received the Emmy and Drama Desk Awards, and for his work on the film version of *A Little Night Music*, the Academy Award. He was also awarded a Grammy as arranger-conductor of the RCA album *Cleo Sings Sondheim*. *The New Grove Dictionary of American Music* describes him as "A skillful technician, whose sympathetic understanding of orchestral instruments is often employed to heighten the dramatic effect of a work." Martin Gottfried, in *The Broadway Musical*, refers to him as "...the finest orchestrator in our theater's history." Mr. Tunick was the recipient of the first Tony Award for orchestration for his work on *Titanic* (1997).

Christopher Bond has spent the last 45 years acting, directing and writing for the stage and occasionally for television and radio. He lived and worked in Liverpool for 15 years, directing, writing and eventually becoming Artistic Director of both the Everyman and Playhouse Theatres there. He subsequently became Artistic Director of the Half Moon Theatre in London's East End from 1984 to 1989. He has worked extensively in Europe, Scandinavia, Israel and the United States as a director. He has written over 30 pieces for the Theatre including *Sweeney Todd, Downright Hooligan, Tarzan's Last Stand, Judge Jeffreys,* and new versions of *Dracula,* Wycherley's *The Country Wife,* Gay's *The Beggar's Opera* and Verdi's *Macbeth.*

James Lapine is a playwright and director who first became involved with the theater in the mid-seventies while working as a graphic designer at the Yale School of Drama, where he staged his interpretation of Gertrude Stein's *Photograph*. His plays include *Table Settings* and *Twelve Dreams,* and he wrote the books for the musicals *Sunday in the Park with George, Into the Woods* and *Passion*, all of which he also directed. He was the director of William Finn's award-winning musical *March of the Falsettos*, as well as the director and co-author of its sequel *Falsettoland* and Finn's most recent musical, *A New Brain*. He has directed productions of *Merrily We Roll Along* (at the La Jolla Playhouse, California), *A Midsummer Night's Dream*, *The Winter's Tale* (both for the New York Shakespeare Festival), *The Diary of Anne Frank*, and *A Golden Child*. In addition to the feature films *Impromptu* and *Life with Mikey*, he has directed a television adaptation of Anne Tyler's *Earthly Possessions*.

André Bishop is the Artistic Director of Theatre at the Lincoln Center for the Performing Arts. He is the former Artistic Director of Playwrights Horizons in New York City, a theater company devoted to the support and development of American playwrights, composers and lyricists and to the production of their work. Notable plays first produced there by Mr. Bishop include *Sister Mary Ignatius Explains it All For You* by Christopher Durang, *The Dining Room* by A. R. Gurney, *March of the Falsettos* by William Finn, among many others, and three Pulitzer Prize Winners— *Driving Miss Daisy* by Alfred Uhry, *The Heidi Chronicles* by Wendy Wasserstein, and, of course, *Sunday in the Park with George*.

THE LONGEST LINE

BROADWAY'S MOST SINGULAR SENSATION: A CHORUS LINE

BY GARY STEVENS AND ALAN GEORGE

Relive the glory of A Chorus Line from behind the scenes, as told by one hundred twenty five artists and professionals who made it happen — cast and management; costume, lighting and sound designers; musicians, carpenters, box office and crew; advertising execs and press agents.

Here is the final authoritative record and celebration of Broadway's "Most Singular Sensation." But it is also the most detailed, in-depth portrait of any musical in Broadway history.

More than 300 photos

Cloth ISBN: 1-55783-221-8 • Paper ISBN: 1-55783-363-X

A CHORUS LINE

THE BOOK OF THE MUSICAL

The Complete Book and Lyrics of the Longest Running Show in Broadway History

"*A Chorus Line* is purely and simply **MAGNIFICENT, CAPTURING THE VERY SOUL OF OUR MUSICAL THEATER.**"   Martin Gottfried

Photos from the original production

Cloth ISBN: 1-55783-131-9 • Paper ISBN: 1-55783-364-8

SPEAK WITH DISTINCTION
by Edith Skinner

"Speak With Distinction is the **most comprehensive and accessible speech book available** for teachers and students of speech."
>—Joan Washington, RSC, Royal Court
>& Royal National Theatre

"Edith Skinner's book is the **best book on speech I have ever encountered**. It was my primer in school and it is my reference book now. To the classical actor, or for that matter any actor who wishes to be understood, this method is a sure guide."
>—Kevin Kline

"Speak with Distinction is **the single most important work on the actor's craft** of stage speech. Edith Skinner's work must be an indispensable source book for all who aspire to act."
>—Earle Gister, Yale School of Drama

paper•ISBN 1-155783-047-9

THE MUSICAL

A LOOK AT THE AMERICAN MUSICAL THEATER
by Richard Kislan

New, Revised, Expanded Edition

Richard Kislan examines the history, the creators, and the vital components that make up a musical and demonstrates as never before how musicals are made.

From its beginnings in colonial America, the musical theater has matured into an impressive art and business, one that has brought millions the experience that director-choreographer Bob Fosse describes as when "everybody has a good time even in the crying scenes."

Kislan traces the musical's evolution through the colorful eras of minstrels, vaudeville, burlesque, revue, and comic opera up to the present day. You'll learn about the lives, techniques, and contributions of such great 20th-century composers and lyricists as Jerome Kern, Rodgers an d Hammerstein, Stephen Sondheim and others. Kislan explains all the basic principles, materials and techniques that go into the major elements of a musical production—the book, lyrics, score, dance and set design.

Richard Kislan's acclaimed study of America's musical theatre has been updated to bring it up to the cutting edge of today's musicals. A new section entitled: Recent Musical Theater: Issues and Problems includes chapters on **The British Invasion • Competition from the Electronic Media • Escalating Costs • The Power of the Critics • The Depletion of Creative Forces • Multiculturalism • The Decline of the Broadway Neighborhood* Stephen Sondheim** and his influence on the present day musical theater.

Paper • ISBN 1-55783-217-X

THE ACTOR AND THE TEXT
by Cicely Berry

As voice director of the Royal Shakespeare Company, Cicely Berry has worked with actors such as Jeremy Irons, Derek Jacobi, Jonathan Pryce, Sinead Cusack and Antony Sher. *The Actor and The Text* brings Ms. Berry's methods of applying vocal production skills within a text to the general public.

While this book focuses primarily on speaking Shakespeare, Ms. Berry also includes the speaking of some modern playwrights, such as Edward Bond.

As Ms. Berry describes her own volume in the introduction:

" … this book is not simply about making the voice sound more interesting. It is about getting inside the words we use …It is about making the language organic, so that the words act as a spur to the sound …"

paper•ISBN 1–155783–138–6

ON SINGING ONSTAGE

New, Completely Revised Edition
by David Craig

"David Craig **KNOWS MORE ABOUT SINGING IN THE MUSICAL THEATRE THAN ANYONE IN THIS COUNTRY**—which probably means the world. Time and time again his advice and training have resulted in actors moving from non-musical theatre into musicals with ease and expertise. **SHORT OF TAKING CLASSES, THIS BOOK IS A MUST."**

—Harold Prince

"STUDYING WITH DAVID CRAIG MEANS INFINITELY MORE THAN LEARNING HOW TO PERFORM A SONG. I find myself drawing upon this unique man's totally original techniques in all arenas of my work. If mediocrity ever enters his studio, it is never allowed to depart."

—Lee Remick

"David Craig, through his training has miraculously fused the art of acting and singing. **HE HAS PUT THE WINGS OF TALENT ON HIS STUDENTS."**

—Stella Adler

paper • ISBN: 1-55783-043-6

MONOLOGUE WORKSHOP
From Search to Discovery
in Audition and Performance
by Jack Poggi

To those for whom the monologue has always been synonymous with terror, *The Monologue Workshop* will prove an indispensable ally. Jack Poggi's new book answers the long-felt need among actors for top-notch guidance in finding, rehearsing and performing monologues. For those who find themselves groping for speech just hours before their "big break," this book is their guide to salvation.

The Monologue Workshop supplies the tools to discover new pieces before they become over-familiar, excavate older material that has been neglected, and adapt material from non-dramatic sources (novels, short stories, letters, diaries, autobiographies, even newspaper columns). There are also chapters on writing original monologues and creating solo performances in the style of Lily Tomlin and Eric Bogosian.

Besides the wealth of practical advice he offers, Poggi transforms the monologue experience from a terrifying ordeal into an exhilarating opportunity. Jack Poggi, as many working actors will attest, is the actor's partner in a process they had always thought was without one.

paper•ISBN 1-55783-031-2 • $12.95

MASTERGATE
&
POWER FAILURE
2 Political Satires for the stage
by Larry Gelbart

REVIEWS OF *MASTERGATE*:

"IF GEORGE ORWELL WERE A GAG WRITER, HE COULD HAVE WRITTEN *MASTERGATE*. Larry Gelbart's scathingly funny takeoff on the Iran-Contra hearings [is] a spiky cactus flower in the desert of American political theatre."
—Jack Kroll, NEWSWEEK

"Larry Gelbart has written what may be the MOST PENETRATING, AND IS SURELY THE FUNNIEST, exegesis of the Iran-Contra fiasco to date."
—Frank Rich, THE NEW YORK TIMES

REVIEWS OF *POWER FAILURE*:

"There is in his broad etching ALL THE ETHICAL OUTRAGE OF AN ARTHUR MILLER KVETCHING. AND, OH, SO MUCH MORE FUN!"
—Carolyn Clay, THE BOSTON PHOENIX

Larry Gelbart, the creator of M*A*S*H, is also the author of *SLY FOX, A FUNNY THING HAPPENED ON THE WAY TO THE FORUM* and *CITY OF ANGELS*.

paper • 1-55783-177-7

APPLAUSE

A LITTLE NIGHT MUSIC

Music and Lyrics by Stephen Sondheim, Book by Hugh Wheeler

"**Heady, civilized, sophisticated and enchanting**. Good God! An adult musical."
—Clive Barnes, The New York Times

Cloth ISBN: 1-55783-070-3 • Paper ISBN: 1-55783-069-X

A FUNNY THING HAPPENED ON THE WAY TO THE FORUM

Music & Lyrics by Stephen Sondheim, Book by Burt Shevelove & Larry Gelbart

"**A good, clean, dirty show! Bring back the belly laughs**"   —Time
"**It's funny, true nonsense! A merry good time!**" —Walter Kerr, Herald Tribune

Cloth ISBN: 1-55783-064-9 • Paper ISBN: 1-55783-063-0

SUNDAY IN THE PARK WITH GEORGE

Music and Lyrics by Stephen Sondheim, Book by James Lapine

"*Sunday* is itself a modernist creation, perhaps the first truly modernist work of musical theatre that Broadway has produced."
—Frank Rich, The New York Times

Cloth ISBN: 1-55783-068-1 • Paper ISBN: 1-55783-067-3

SWEENEY TODD

Music and Lyrics by Stephen Sondheim, Book by Hugh Wheeler

"**There is more artistic energy, creative personality, and plain excitement than in a dozen average musicals**."   —Richard Eder, The New York Times

Cloth ISBN: 1-55783-066-5 • Paper ISBN: 1-55783-065-7